Early Modern History: Society and Culture

General Editors: **Rab Houston**, Professor of Early Modern History, University of St Andrews, Scotland and **Edward Muir**, Professor of History, Northwestern University, Illinois

This series encompasses all aspects of early modern international history from 1400 to c.1800. The editors seek fresh and adventurous monographs, especially those with a comparative and theoretical approach, from both new and established scholars.

Titles include:

Robert C. Davis
CHRISTIAN SLAVES, MUSLIM MASTERS
White Slavery in the Mediterranean, the Barbary Coast, and Italy, 1500–1800

Rudolf Dekker
CHILDHOOD, MEMORY AND AUTOBIOGRAPHY IN HOLLAND
From the Golden Age to Romanticism

Steve Hindle
THE STATE AND SOCIAL CHANGE IN EARLY MODERN ENGLAND, 1550–1640

Craig M. Koslofsky
THE REFORMATION OF THE DEAD
Death and Ritual in Early Modern Germany, 1450–1700

A. Lynn Martin
ALCOHOL, SEX AND GENDER IN LATE MEDIEVAL AND EARLY MODERN EUROPE

Samantha A. Meigs
THE REFORMATIONS IN IRELAND
Tradition and Confessionalism, 1400–1690

Craig Muldrew
THE ECONOMY OF OBLIGATION
The Culture of Credit and Social Relations in Early Modern England

Niall Ó Ciosáin
PRINT AND POPULAR CULTURE IN IRELAND, 1750–1850

H. Eric R. Olsen
THE CALABRIAN CHARLATAN, 1598–1603
Messianic Nationalism in Early Modern Europe

Thomas Max Safley
MATHEUS MILLER'S MEMOIR
A Merchant's Life in the Seventeenth Century

Clodagh Tait
DEATH, BURIAL AND COMMEMORATION IN IRELAND, 1550–1650

Johan Verberckmoes
LAUGHTER, JESTBOOKS AND SOCIETY IN THE SPANISH NETHERLANDS

Claire Walker
GENDER AND POLITICS IN EARLY MODERN EUROPE
English Convents in France and the Low Countries

Johannes. C. Wolfart
RELIGION, GOVERNMENT AND POLITICAL CULTURE IN EARLY MODERN
GERMANY
LINDAU, 1520–1628

Early Modern History: Society and Culture
Series Standing Order ISBN 0–333–71194–7
(*outside North America only*)

You can receive future titles in this series as they are published by placing a standing order. Please contact your bookseller or, in case of difficulty, write to us at the address below with your name and address, the title of the series and the ISBN quoted above.

Customer Services Department, Macmillan Distribution Ltd, Houndmills, Basingstoke, Hampshire RG21 6XS, England

Christian Slaves, Muslim Masters

White Slavery in the Mediterranean, the Barbary Coast, and Italy, 1500–1800

Robert C. Davis
Professor of History
Ohio State University

First published 2003 by
PALGRAVE MACMILLAN
Houndmills, Basingstoke, Hampshire RG21 6XS and
175 Fifth Avenue, New York, N. Y. 10010
Companies and representatives throughout the world

PALGRAVE MACMILLAN is the global academic imprint of the Palgrave Macmillan division of St. Martin's Press, LLC and of Palgrave Macmillan Ltd. Macmillan® is a registered trademark in the United States, United Kingdom and other countries. Palgrave is a registered trademark in the European Union and other countries.

ISBN 0–333–71966–2

This book is printed on paper suitable for recycling and made from fully managed and sustained forest sources.

A catalogue record for this book is available from the British Library.

Library of Congress Cataloging-in-Publication Data

Davis, Robert C.
  Christian slaves, Muslim masters: white slavery in the Mediterranean, the
    Barbary Coast, and Italy, 1500–1800 / Robert C. Davis.
      p. cm. – (Early modern history)
  Includes bibliographical references and index.
  ISBN 0–333–71966–2
    1. Slave trade – Africa, North – History. 2. Slave trade – Italy – History. 3.
  Christians – Africa, North – History. 4. Christians – Italy – History. 5.
  Muslims – Commerce – Africa, North – History. 6. Muslims – Commerce –
  Italy – History. I.
  Title: White slavery in the Mediterranean, the Barbary Coast, and Italy,
  1500–1800. II.
  Title. III. Series.

  HT1342.D38 2003
  306.3'62'0945–dc21   2002192454

10   9   8   7   6   5   4   3   2   1
12 11 10 09 08 07 06 05 04 03

Printed and bound in Great Britain by
Antony Rowe Ltd, Chippenham and Eastbourne

Contents

List of Figures and Tables   vii

Some Currency Conversions   viii

Some Exemplary Prices   xi

Tables   xiv

Introduction and Acknowledgments   xxiv

Part I   White Slavery

1   How Many Slaves?   3

2   Slave Taking and Slave Breaking   27

Part II   Barbary

3   Slave Labor   69

4   Slaves' Life   103

Part III   Italy

5   The Home Front   139

6   Celebrating Slavery   175

Notes   194

Index   239

List of Figures and Tables

Figures

1. Slaves being disembarked in Algiers (from Pierre Dan, *Historie van Barbaryen en des zelfs Zee-Roovers*, Amersterdam, 1684) — 56
2. Slaves taken into the Badestan in Algiers (from Pierre Dan, *Historie van Barbaryen en des zelfs Zee-Roovers*, Amersterdam, 1684) — 60
3. Examining slaves in the Badestan (from Pierre Dan, *Historie van Barbaryen en des zelfs Zee-Roovers*, Amersterdam, 1684) — 61
4. Selling slaves (from Pierre Dan, *Historie van Barbaryen en des zelfs Zee-Roovers*, Amersterdam, 1684) — 65
5. Slaves digging lime or salt (from Pierre Dan, *Historie van Barbaryen en des zelfs Zee-Roovers*, Amersterdam, 1684) — 82
6. Slaves in chains (from Pierre Dan, *Historie van Barbaryen en des zelfs Zee-Roovers*, Amersterdam, 1684) — 109
7. Slave punishment (from Pierre Dan, *Histoire de la Barbarie et ses Corsaires*, Paris, 1649) — 130
8. Beating slaves (from Pierre Dan, *Histoire de la Barbarie et ses Corsaires* Paris, 1649) — 131
9. Procession of Freed Slaves (from Pierre Dan, *Historie van Barbaryen en des zelfs Zee-Roovers*, Amersterdam, 1684) — 180

Tables

1. Major Corsair Slave-taking Activity, 1516–1798 — xiv
2. Slave Counts in Algiers — xviii
3. Slave Counts for Tunis and Tripoli — xxi

Some Currency Conversions

Haëdo (1584)
Spanish 4 real piece = 40 Algerian aspers
Venetian sequin (zecchino) = 210 Algerian aspers

Saunders, pp. 3 and 10 (1585)
1 Venetian sequin = 7 English shillings
1 English pence = 2.5 Algerian aspers

Gonfalone, bu. 1139, fol. 363 (1587)
1 Roman scudo *d'oro in oro* = 3.7 Algerian dolas = 185 aspers

Coryate, p. 389 (1606)
1 Venetian sequin = $8\frac{3}{4}$ English shillings

Mascarenhas, pp. 75 and 168–9 (note 1) (1621)
1 Portugues réal = 0.025 Spanish réals
1 Algerian dola = a litle less than 2 Spanish réals
1 Algerian pataque = 10.25 Spanish reals

Rawlins, p. 256 (1622)
1 Algerian dobla = 1 English shilling
1 Algerian pataque = 5.14 dobla = 5s 2d English

Salvago, (French trans.) p. 478 (1624)
1 Venetian ducat = 50 Algerian aspers
(Italian trans.) p. 92
1 Venetian sequin = 1.5 talers

Napoli, bu. 10 (ca 1632)
1 Spanish piece of eight = 52 Tunisian aspers = ± 1 Venetian ducat

Knight, p. 11 (1637–40)
1 gold Turkish soltanie = 7 English shillings

Okeley (1639), p. 40
1 Spanish dobla = 1.1 English shillings

D'Aranda (1640).
p. 18 1 French réal = $\frac{1}{10}$ pataque
p. 48 1 Algerian "patacoon" = 2.83 French livres

Catalogo de' Schiavi Riscattati, p. 30 (1660)
1 Roman scudo = 1.18 Spanish pieces of eight
1 piece of eight = 0.85 scudo

Chastelet des Boys, p. 26 and note (1662)
1 Algerian asper = 4 French deniers = 1/3 sou

Correspondance des Beys de Tunis, p. 165 (1665)
1 Tunisian piastre forte = 175 Spanish pieces of eight
1 French livre = 7 3/4 Spanish pieces of eight = 9.1 Roman scudi

ASVat, Gonfalone, bu. 1144, fol. 275 (1676)
1 Spanish reale = $8\frac{1}{2}$ Roman giuli

ASVat, Gonfalone, bu. 1144, fol. 335 (1677)
1 Venetian sequin = 2.3 Roman scudi

ASVat, Gonfalone, bu. 1144, fol. 496 (1686)
1 Venetian sequin = 2.2 Roman scudi

ASVat, Gonfalone, bu. 8, fol. 264 (1704)
1 Venetian sequin = 1.9 Roman scudi

ASV, POLP, bu. 101 (1717)
1 Venetian ducat = 6 lire, 4 soldi of account

De La Motte, pp. 40 and 134 (1720)
1 heavy (Alexandria) dollar = 1 Seville piece of eight = 7/8 oz. silver
1 Seville dollar = 6 French livres/10 sols
1 Algerian Asper dollar = 4 livres/15 sols = 132 aspers

ASVat, Gonfalone, bu. 8, f. 398 (1721)
1 Roman scudo d'oro = 1 and 2/3 scudi of account

ASV, POLP, bu. 99 (1723)
1 Venetian sequin = 22 lire of account = 3.55 ducats

Laugier du Tassy, pp. 203–4 (1724)
1 Algerian pataque chica (pataca of aspers) = 232 aspers
1 paraque gorda (grossa) = 696 aspers
1 soltanine of Algiers = 1.04 Venetian sequins
1 Venetian sequin = 0.96 soltanine
1 Algerian saïme = 50 aspers

Propaganda Fide, Barbaria, bu. 5, fol. 216 (1728)
1 Spanish piece of eight = 1.85 Algerian piastre

1 Spanish dobla of gold = $5\frac{1}{4}$ – $5\frac{1}{2}$ Algerian piastre
1 "fresh minted" Venetian sequin = $3\frac{1}{3}$ Algerian piastre

Redemtiones Captivorum (1729–30)
1 Turkish piastra = 6 Roman giuli, 1 baiocco

Kingdon, p. 13 (1753)
1 pound sterling = 2 Venetian sequins
1 sequin = 10 shillings

ASV, POLP, bu. 98 (1764)
1 Venetian sequin = 3.55 Venetian ducats = 3.25 Algerian piastre
1 piastre = 1.1 Venetian ducats = 0.31 sequins

ASV, Provveditori sorpa Ospedali e Luoghi Pii (1764)
1 Algerian pataque grossa = 6 Roman baiocchi
1 Venetian sequin = 4.5 pataques

ASV, POLP, bu. 100 (1765)
1 Venetian ducat = 8 lire of account

ASV,POLP, bu. 102 (1767)
1 Venetian sequin = ±20 Roman paoli

Thédenat, p. 159 (1779)
1 Venetian sequin = $10\frac{1}{8}$ French livres

ASV, POLP, bu. 102 (1796)
1 Venetian sequin = 10 Algerian sequins

Some Exemplary Prices

ASVat, Gonfalone, bu. 1139, fol. 306 (1585)
Romans wished to spend no more than 150 scudi per slave

ASVat, Gonfalone, bu. 1139, fol. 361 (1585)
1 barrel of "country wine" in Rome cost 15 giuli = 1.5 ducats

ASVat, Gonfalone, bu 1139, fol. 363 (1587)
140 gold scudi = average ransom + taxes apiece for 80 slaves ransomed from Algiers

Mascarenhas, p. 74 (1621)
2–3 pataques per month bought a priest out of his required labor

Rawlins, p. 256 (1622)
sold at first purchase for 150 Algerian doblas = £7 10s English (these were "very easy rates" since he was lame)

ASV, POLP, bu. 98 (1628)
100 Venetian ducats = average ransom price of 250 slaves in Barbary

Davis, *Shipbuilders*, pp. 29–30 (1635–40)
salary of master carpenter in Venice = 5–7 ducats per day

D'Aranda, p. 9 (1640)
sold at first purchase for 200 "patacoons" = 566 French livres

ASN, SCRC, bu. 7, p. 10 (1651)
400–500 Neapolitan grossi = ransom demanded for a slave in Tunis

Francesco di S. Lorenzo, p. 10 (1654)
3 Spanish pieces of eight per month bought a slave out of has required labor

Mercedarian "Catalogo de' schiavi riscattati" (1660)
166 Roman scudi = average ransom apiece for 344 men, mostly Spanish slaves in Algiers
210 scudi = average ransom for 9 slave clerics in same expedition
250 scudi = average ransom for 17 non-noble female slaves

ASN, SCRC, bu. 7, p. 12 (1662)
300 Spanish pieces of eight = ransom demanded for slave sailor in Algiers

Correspondance des Beys de Tunis, p. 165 (1665)
French slaves cost 175 Spanish pieces of eight apiece

ASVat, Gonfalone, bu. 1144, fol. 108 (1666)
160 (later 100) Venetian sequins = ransom for fisherman's daughter in Dulcigno

Mercedarian Catalogo of mostly Spanish slaves ransomed in Algiers (1678)
1,948 Spanish silver reales = average total cost a piece to free 451 slaves, including ransom, taxes, transportation, quarantane, clothing, etc.

Galland, pp. 48–9 (1679)
Muslim surgeon charges 2 Algerian aspers to circumsize a boy

ASVat, Gonfalone, bu. 1139,
fol. 186 (1691)
200 Venetian sequins is "unproper and exorbitant" ransom for poor slave in Dulcigno
fol. 552 (1691)
93 Venetian sequins = average asking price in Dulcigno for 11 slaves

Propaganda fide, Barbaria bu. 3, fol. 64 (1692); prices for mass in Tunis:
$\frac{1}{2}$ piastra to attending priests
$\frac{1}{4}$ piastra each to the lay helpers
$1\frac{1}{2}$ piastre to the preacher
2 piastre to the singers
totaling 15–20 piastre per week

"Relazione delli schiavi cristiani" (1713)
537 Spanish pieces of eight = average ransom + taxes apiece to ransom 204 (mostly Spanish) soldiers and civilians, slaves in Algiers

ASV, Provveditori sorpa Ospedali e Luoghi Pii (1727)
263 Venetian ducats = average total ransom + taxes apiece to free 54 Venetian slaves in Constantinople

Propaganda fide, Barbaria, bu. 5, fol. 216 (1728)
350 Spanish pieces of eight called "extremely exorbitant" price to ransom female slave

"Redenzione di Venezia" (1730)
343 Venetian ducats = average ransom apiece of 24 Venetian men, slaves in Tripoli

ASV, Provveditori sorpa Ospedali e Luoghi Pii (1764)
313 Venetian sequins = average total cost apiece for all expenses to
ransom and bring home 91 Venetian slaves in Algiers

"Relazione del riscatto... dei schiavi siciliani" (1771)
278 Sicilian onze = average total cost apiece to free 81 Sicilian men and
women, slaves in Tunis

Tables

1 Major Corsair Slave-taking Activity, 1516–1798 (Mostly Italian) (number of captives taken: source)

1509: Spanish capture of Oran frees 15,000 Christian slaves (Foss, 86)
1510: Otranto (more than 100 villagers: Mafrici, 57)
1516: coast of Puglia ("many hundreds": Bono, 139)
1531: coast near Genoa (130: Calvini, 31)
1534: Cetara, near Amalfi (300: Mafrici, 78)
1535: Port Mahon in Minorca (6,000: Morgan, 282)
1535: On fleeing Tunis, Barbarosa left 7,000 slaves behind (Morgan, 283)
1543: Near San Remo, in Liguria (300: Borzacchiello, 9)
1544: Elba ("most of the inhabitants": Morgan, 292)
1544: Agropoli, below Salerno (100: Mafrici, 79)
1544: Ischia and Bay of Naples (7,000: Bono, 1454)
1546: Laigueglia, near Alassio (250: Borzacchiello, 9)
1551: Reggio Calabria (400: Morgan, 469)
1551: Goza, in Malta (6,300 out of 7,000: Morgan, 469)
1551: Augusta, in Sicily (400: Bono, 148)
1554: Vieste, in Calabria (6,000 slaves: Bono, 150)
1557: Recco, in Liguria (54: Borzacchiello, 9)
1558: Coast of Sorrento and Massa (1,493: Mafrici, 82)
1558: Cirella, in Calabria (76: Bono, 150)
1558: Spanish army defeated near Algiers (6,500: Morgan, 401)
1560: Spanish attack on Jerba fails (10,000: Morgan, 490)
1563: Coast near Genoa (270: Borzacchiello, 9)
1565: Raid on Lucchese coast (42: Lenci, 56)
1566: Granada (4,000: Braudel, vol. 1, 881)
1570–1606: 38 raids on Sicilian coast and shipping (Bonaffini, 52)
1574: Turkish capture of Tunis ("thousands": Morgan, 500)
1578: Quartu Sant'Elena, in Sardinia (200: Bono, 168)
1578: Portuguese defeated at Alcazarquivir (3,000)
1580: Policastro, in Calabria (200: Morgan, 566)
1582: Alicante (500), Oristano in Sardegna (700), Monticello in Corsica (400), Sori, near Genoa (130), near Barcelona (Morgan, 576–7)
1585: Canaries (300: Morgan, 588)
1587: Faringola, in Corsica (240: Morgan, 592)

1588: Calvi, near Genoa (100: Borzacchiello, 9)
1588: Coast of Lazio (150: Bono, 171)
1593–94: 28 ships taken by Tunis in 10 months (1,722: Ricard, 196)
1603–9: 466 English sailors captured by Algerians (Wolf, 184)
1605–32: Algerians take 600 ships (est. 7,200–12,000: Dan, 320)
1607: Algerians take 3 towns in Calabria (1,400: Gramaye/Purchas, 282)
1608: Algerians take 42 ships (860: Gramaye/Purchas, 282)
1609–16: 466 British ships taken (est. 5,600–9,300: Laird Clowes, 22)
1609–19: Algerians take 8,000 Christians/Spaniards (Gramaye/Purchas, 268)
1609: Algerians take 36 ships (632: Gramaye/Purchas, 282)
1610: Algerians take 23 ships (384: Gramaye/Purchas, 282)
1611: Algerians take 20 ships (464: Gramaye/Purchas, 282)
1612: Algerians attack Spain (3,804: Gramaye/Purchas, 282)
1613: Porto Santo in Canaries (700: Grammont, vol. 23, 138)
1613: Algerians take 16 ships just from Italy (230: Gramaye/Purchas, 282)
1613: Terseros, in Galicia (900: Grammont, vol. 23, 138)
1613–21: Algerians take 936 ships and boats (est. 11,000–19,000: Grammont, vol. 23, 138)
1614: Algerians take 35 ships (460: Gramaye/Purchas, 282)
1616: Algerians take 34 ships (767: Gramaye/Purchas, 282)
1617: Madeira (1,200: Dan, 312)
1617: 7 ships from British Grand Banks fishing fleet (Laird Clowes, 50)
1617: Algerians take 26 ships (1,763: Gramaye/Purchas, 282)
1618: Algerians take 19 ships & attack Lancerotta (1,468: Gramaye/Purchas, 282)
1619: San Marco near Palermo (400–500: Grammont, vol. 23, 138)
1620: Manfredonia, in Gargano (200: Mafrici, 65)
1623: Joint Tunisian/Algerian land/sea raid (623: Bachrouch, 140)
1624: Perasto, in Dalmatia (450: Salvago, 2)
1625: 27 English ships in ten days near Plymouth (est. 200: Laird Clowes, 23)
1627: Iceland (around 400: Helgason, 276; 800: Dan, 313)
1628–34: Algerians take ca. 80 French ships (1,331: Dan, 320)
1631: Baltimore, in Ireland (237: Dan, 313)
1636: Vico, in Calabria (700: *Gazette de France*)
1637: Ceriale (365) and Borghetto (140) near Genoa (Bono, 174)
1637: Colpe, in Spain (315: Knight, 9)
1637: French Bastion near Algiers captured ("At least 600": Morgan, 665)
1637: "Ocostra" (Ogliastro?), in Calabria (115: Knight, 19)

1639: Calabria and Sicily ("about a thousand": *Gazette de France*)
1641: Algerians capture packet "John Filmer" in Irish Sea (120 passengers: Playfair, 308)
1641–44: Algerians capture 1,700 Christian ships (5 English) (Playfair, 310–11)
1644: Rocca Imperiale, in Calabria (200: Bono)
1644: Mondragone, Squillace, Pouille, and Calabria (4,000: *Gazette de France*)
1645: Coast of Cornwall (240: Bono, 178)
1668–78: Tripolitans enslave 2,450 (Fontenay, 22)
1669–71: In 16 months, Tunis takes 510 French sailors as slaves (Bachrouch, 144)
1672–82: Algerians take 353 English ships (est. 4,200–7,000: de La Motte, 99)
1673: Torchiarolo, in Puglia (50: Mafrici, 66)
1675: Summer raids around Sardinia, Naples, Corsica, Sicily (Bono, 200)
1677–80: Algerians take 160 British ships in 40 months (est. 1,900–3,200: Morgan, v)
1677–85: Tripolitans take 75 ships (1,085: Pennell, 46)
1685–86: Algerians enslave 664 sailors in 18 months (Fontenay, 19)
1690: Tunisians take two French ships (270: Plantet, vol. 1, 434)
1711: Squinzano, in Puglia (44: Mafrici, 67)
1712–20: Algerians take 74 ships (1,668: de La Motte, 98)
1714–16: Raids near Lecce (80 total: Mafrici, 67)
1714–27: Algerians take 36 English merchant ships (393: de La Motte, 142–4)
1741: Tunisians conquer Tabarca (around 800: Valensi, 1282)
1771: Greek population of Tunis enslaved (200: CPF/SRC–7, fol. 509)
1785–93: Algerians take 13 American ships (130: Foss, 160–1)
1786–96: Tunisians take 776 Neapolitans and Sicilians (Valensi, 1277)
1794: Algerians capture Corsican coral fishing fleet (201: Foss, 136)
1798: Tunisians raid Isle San Pietro near Sardinia (900: Bono, 183)
1814: Tunisian raid on Crotone coast, Calabria (21: ASN, bu. 56)
1815: Isle of Sant'Antioco, Sardinia (150: Bono, 185)

References

ASN = Archivio di Stato di Napoli, Santa Casa per la Redentione dei Cattivi
CPF/SRC = Congregazione "De Propaganda Fide," "Scritture Riferte nei Congressi: Barbaria," vols. 1–7.
T a o u fik Bachrouch, "Rachet et libération des esclaves chrétiens à Tunis au XVIIe siècle," 121–62 in *Revue Tunisienne de Sciences Sociales* 11 (1975)

Giuseppe Bonaffini, *La Sicilia e i Barbareschi. Incursioni corsare e riscatto degli schiavi (1570–1606)* (Palermo, 1983).

Salvatore Bono, *I Corsari barbareschi* (Turin, 1964).

Antonio Borzacchiello, "Carità: Decumano Massimo," in *Corsari "turchi" e barbareschi: prigionieri, schiavi, riscatti: atti del 2. convegno di studi: Ceriale, 3 giugno 1989* (Ceriale, 1992).

Fernand Braudel, *The Mediterranean and the Mediterranean World in the Age of Philip II* 2 vols. (New York, 1972), vol. 2.

Nilo Calvini, "Opere sanremasche per la redenzione degli schiavi e cenni sull'attività del Magistrato di Genova e dei Trinitari di Torino," in *Corsari "turchi" e barbareschi: prigionieri, schiavi, riscatti: atti del 2. convegno di studi: Ceriale, 3 giugno 1989* (Ceriale, 1992).

Pierre Dan, *Histoire de la Barbarie et ses Corsaires* (Paris, 1649).

Michel Fontenay, "Le Maghreb barbaresque et l'esclavage méditerranéen aux XVIè–XVIIè siècles," 7–43 in *Les Cahiers de Tunisie*, 43 (1991).

John Foss, *Journal of Captivity* (Newport, n.d.).

Jean-Baptiste Gramaye, "Relations of the Christianitie of Africa, and especially of Barbarie, and Algier," 267–84 in *Purchas His Pilgrimes*, vol. 9 (Glasgow, 1905–7).

M. Guillerny, "Letter a M. de Peyresc (1623)," in H.–D. Grammont, ed., "Relations entre la France & la Régence d'Alger au XVIIe Siècle," in *Revue Africaine*, vol. 23 (1879), 135–51.

Bornsteinn Helgason, "Historical Narrative as Collective Therapy," pp. 275–89, *Scandinavean Journal of History* 22 (1977), pp. 275–6.

Francis Knight, *A Relation of Seaven Yeares Slaverie under the Turks of Argeire* (London, 1640)

W. Laird Clowes, *The Royal Navy. A History from the Earliest Times to the Present*, 5 vols. (London, 1897–98), vol. 2.

Philemon de La Motte, *Voyage pour la redemption des captifs aux royaumes d'Alger et de Tunis* (Paris, 1721), English trans. (by Joseph Morgan?) as *Several Voyages to Barbary* (London, 1736).

Marco Lenci, "Riscatti di Schiavi Cristiani dal Maghreb. La Compagnia della SS. Pietà di Lucca (Secoli XVII–XIX)," 53–80 in *Società e Storia*, 31 (1986).

Mirella Mafrici, *Mezzogiorno e pirateria nell'età moderna (secoli XVI–XVIII)* (Naples, 1995).

Joseph Morgan, *A Complete History of Algiers* (London, 1728–29; reprint: New York, 1970).

C. R. Pennell, ed. *Piracy and Diplomacy in Seventeenth-Century North Africa. The Journal of Thomas Baker, English Consul in Tripoli, 1677–1685* (London, 1989).

Eugene Plantet, ed. *Correspondance des Beys de Tunis et des Consuls de France avec la Cour, 1577–1830* (Paris, 1893).

Robert Playfair, "Épisodes de l'Histoire des Relations de La Grande-Bretagne avec les États Barbaresques avant la Conquête Française" pp. 305–19, 401–33 in *Revue africaine*, 22 (1878).

Robert Ricard, "Ibero-Africana: Le Père Jérome Gratien de la Mère de Dieu et sa Captivité a Tunis (1593–1595)," 190–200 in *Revue Africaine* 89 (1945).

Gio:Battista Salvago, *"Africa overo Barbarìa" Relazione al doge di Venezia sulle Reggenze di Algeri e di Tunisi del Dragomanno Gio.Batta Salvago (1625)*, A. Sacerdoti, ed. (Padua, 1937).

Lucette Valensi, "Esclaves chrétiens et esclaves noirs à Tunis au XVIIIe siècle,"
1267–85 in *Annales, Economies Societés Civilisation*, 22 (1967).
John B. Wolf, *The Barbary Coast: Algiers under the Turks, 1500–1830* (New York,
1979).

2 Slave Counts in Algiers

1578–81: 25,000 (Haëdo in Cresti, 159)
1585: 22,000 "mostly Italian, many from the Papal States" (Bono
[1955] 156)
1585: 25,000 recalculated by same redeemers (Bono [1955], 156)
1587: 20,000 (Lanfreducci and Bosio, 473)
1598: around 15,000 (Magini in Gramaye, 139)
1619: "more than 32,000" or "more than 35,000" (Gramaye, 138)
1619: "more than 50,000" (est. by clergy of Algiers, in Gramaye, 139)
1619: 120,000 Christian captives in "Argier, Tunes, Tripoli, Fesse"
(Gramaye/Purchas, 269)
1619: 2,000 slaves in Bagno del Rey (Gramaye/Purchas, 272)
1621–27: 20,000 (Braudel, vol. 1, 885)
1621: 18,000–20,000 (Guillerny)
1621: 8,000 Catholics (Mascarenhas, 74)
1625: 25,000 (Salvago, 86)
1631: "more than 20,000" (Serefin de Freytas, in Friedman, 617)
1634: 25,000 (Dan, 318)
1637: "fewer than 60,000" (Knight, 51)
1640: 30,000–40,000 "of all nations" (d'Aranda, 99)
1640: 40,000 (de Tamayo in Gramaye, 140)
1641: 3,000 British (State Papers)
1646: 650 British in Algiers, 100 in Algerian galleys (Playfair, 314–15)
1650: 8,000 (Bono, 220)
1656: 35,000 (Felipe Palermo in Friedman, 617)
1660: 35,000 (Davity in Cresti, 159)
1662: 12,000 (Auvry in Cresti, 159)
1664: "more than 40,000" (Du Val in Cresti, 159)
1669: 14,000–15,000, including 100 women, 300–400 children
(Mafrici, 98)
1675: 6,000–12,000 "Christians" (d'Arvieux, vol. 6, 225)
1678: 20,000–30,000 (De Fercourt in Cresti, 159)
1681: 5,000 "or a few more" (CPF/SOCG–1, fol. 503)
1682: 17,000 (Barbarella)
1683: 35,000–40,000 (Pétis de la Croix, 21)

1687: 10,000 (Bombard, vol. 2, 73)
1691: 36,000 "of all nationalities" (Plantet, 25 1)
1693: "more than 4,000" (CPF/SOCG–3, fol. 144)
1693–94: "more than 10,000" (CPF/SOCG–1, fol. 54)
1694: 2,000 Greeks, "almost all slaves" (CPF/SOCG–3, fol. 204)
1698: "2,800 Christiani" (CPF/SOCG–3, fol. 377)
1701: "more than 20,000 Christians" (CPF/SOCG–3, fol. 408)
1701: "not more than 3,000 Christians" (CPF/SOCG–3, fol. 414)
1719: 4,000 (Gueudeville in Cresti, 159)
1721: fewer than 5,000, "mostly schismatics and heretics" (CPF/SOCG–4, fol. 491)
1729: 9,000–10,000 (Fau in Cresti, 159)
1729: "more than 5,000" (Vander Aa in Cresti, 159)
1734: "more than 4,000" (CPF/SOCG–5, fol. 516)
1738: "around 2,000" (Shaw in Cresti, 159)
1749: 7,000 (Bombard, vol. 2, 429)
1749: 6,000–7,000 by "the most common opinion" (CPF/SOCG–6, fol. 210)
1763: 3,000 (CPF/SOCG–7, fol. 122)
1773: 2,000, presumably Catholics (CPF/SOCG–7, fol. 591)
1774: 1,900 Catholics (CPF/SOCG–7, fol. 653)
1779: 3,000 (Thédenat, 159)
1785: 1,800 Catholics, plus 100 Greek Orthodox (Bombard, vol. 2, 584)
1785: 315 French slaves ransomed from Algiers (Trinitarians)
1787: 2,000 (Venture de Paradis, 258)
1788: 800 (Von Rehbinder and Raynal in Cresti, 159)
1789: 500 (Venture de Paradis, 154)
1793: 1,200: 600 in each of two bagnos (Foss, 125)
1794: "about 500" enslaved Spanish deserters from Oran (Foss, 87)
1796: 700 (Alasia in Cresti, 159)
1801: 500 (Vicherat in Cresti, 159)
1805: 1,200 (Joussouy in Cresti, 159)
1816: 1,642 (Cresti/159)
1830: 122 (Cresti/159)

References

CPF/SRC = Congregazione "De Propaganda Fide," "Scritture Riferte nei Congressi: Barbaria," vols. 1–7.
Antonio Tedaldi Barbarella, Museo Correr, *Carte miscellanea, Provinenze diverse*, bu. 515, fol. 77, report dated 22 October 1682.

F. Bombard, ed. "Les Vicaires apostoliques de Tunis et d'Alger (1645–1827)," in *Revue Tunisienne*, 2 (1895), 73–76, 259–62, 429–32, 581–6.

Salvatore Bono, "La Missione dei Cappuccini ad Algeri per il riscatto degli schiavi cristiani del 1585," 149–63 in *Collectanea Franciscana* 25 (1955).

Salvatore Bono, *I Corsari barbareschi* (Turin, 1964).

Fernand Braudel, *The Mediterranean and the Mediterranean World in the Age of Philip II* 2 vols. (New York, 1972), vol. 2.

Stephen Clissold, *The Barbary Slaves* (Totowa, NJ, 1977).

Federico Cresti, "Quelques reflexions sur la population et la structure sociale d'Alger a la periode Turque (XVIe–XIXe siècles)," 151–64 in *Les Cahiers de Tunisie*, 34 (1986).

Pierre Dan, *Histoire de la Barbarie et ses Corsaires* (Paris, 1649).

Emanuel d'Aranda, *The History of Algiers and its Slavery* (London, 1666).

Laurent d'Arvieux, *Mémoires* (Paris, 1735), 6 vols.

Pétis de la Croix, "Description abrégée de la ville d'Alger," in M. Emerit, ed., "Un Mémoire sur Alger par Pétis de la Croix (1695)," 5–24 in *Annales de l'Institut d'Études orientales*, 11 (1953).

John Foss, *Journal of Captivity* (Newport, n.d.).

Ellen Friedman, "Christian Captives at 'Hard Labor' in Algiers, 16th–18th Centuries," 616–32 in *The International Journal of African Historical Studies*, 13 (1980).

Jean-Baptiste Gramaye, *Diarium rerum Argelae gestarum ab anno M.DC.XIX* (Cologne, 1623), republished in *Alger, XVIe–XVIIe siècle: Journal de Jean-Baptiste Gramaye, évêque d'Afrique*, Abd El Hadi Den Mansour, trans. & ed. (Paris, 1998).

Jean-Baptiste Gramaye, "Relations of the Christianitie of Africa, and especially of Barbarie, and Algier," 267–84 in *Purchas His Pilgrimes*, vol. 9 (Glasgow, 1905–7).

M. Guillerny, "Letter a M. de Peyresc (1623)," in H.-D. Grammont, ed., "Relations entre la France & la Régence d'Alger au XVIIe Siècle," in *Revue Africaine*, vol. 23 (1879), 135–51.

Francis Knight, *A Relation of Seaven Yeares Slaverie under the Turks of Argeire* (London, 1640).

François Lanfreducci, and Jean Othon Bosio. "Costa e Discorsi di Barbaria (1 Settembre 1587)," 421–80 in *Revue Africaine*, 66 (1925).

Mirella Mafrici, *Mezzogiorno e pirateria nell'età moderna (secoli XII–XVIII)* (Naples, 1995).

João Mascarenhas, *Récit de Captivité (1621–1626)*, Paul Teyssier, trans. and ed. (Paris, 1993).

Eugene Plantet, ed. *Correspondance des Beys de Tunis et des Consuls de France avec la Cour, 1577–1830* (Paris, 1893).

Gio:Battista Salvago, *"Africa overo Barbaria" Relazione al doge di Venezia sulle Reggenze di Algeri e di Tunisi del Dragomanno Gio.Batta Salvago (1625)*, A. Sacerdoti, ed. (Padua, 1937).

Emerit, Marcel, ed. "Les Aventures de Thédenat, Esclave et Ministre d'un Bey d'Afrique (XVIIIe Siècle)," 142–84 & 331–62 in *Revue Africaine* 92 (1948).

J. M. Venture de Paradis, "Alger au XVIIIᵉ siécle," E. Fagnan, ed. in *Revue Africaine*, 40 (1896), 33–78 & 256–77.

3 Slave Counts for Tunis and *Tripoli*

1535: 22,000 (Morgan, 308)
1553: 450 Christians (HCRT)
1564: 4,025 Christians (HCRT)
1572: 2,200 Christians (HCRT)
1584: 700 Christians (HCRT)
1613: 240 Christians (HCRT)
1625: "fewer than 10,000" (Salvago, 86)
1625: 400–500 (Salvago, 86)
1634: 7,000 (Dan, 319)
1634: 400–500 (Dan, 319)
1635: 500 Christians (HCRT)
1649: 650 Christians (HCRT)
1651: 6,000 (Bombard, 388)
1654: 8,000 (Francesco di S. Lorenzo, 12)
1658: "1,000 and more Christians" (CPF/SORCG, Tri, fol. 88)
1659: "2,500 Christians" (CPF/SORCG, Tri, fol. 90)
ca. 1660: 10,000–12,000 (Valensi, 1277)
1660: 1,150 Christians (HCRT)
1664: "4,000 Christian slaves" (CPF/SORCG, Tun, fol. 65)
1665: 1,500 (CPF/SORCG, Tri, fol. 95)
1667: "at least 3,000... of the Latin rite" (CPF/SORCG, Tun, fol. 124)
1669: 1,370 (CPF/SRC–1, fol. 166)
1670: 5,000–6,000 "souls" (CPF/SOCG–1, fol. 176)
1670: "2,000 Christians divided in four bagnos" (CPF/SOCG–1, fol. 184)
1671: 1,559 (Bono, 220)
1672: 1,658 Christians (HCRT)
1674: 2,000 Christians (HCRT)
1675: 2,130 Christians (HCRT)
1676: 1,275 Christians (HCRT)
1679: 700 of "our people" plus 1,000 "schismatic Greeks" (CPF/SOCG–1, fol 457)
1680: 2,000 "Christians" and "300 schismatics & heretics" (CPF/SOCG–1, fol. 478)
1681: 2,200 slaves in Tunis and ports (CPF/SOCG–1, fol. 583)
1681: "a few more than 1,000" (CPF/SOCG–1, fol. 455)
1686: 1,500–2,000 (Mafrici, 99)
1686: 7,000–8,000 (Mafrici, 97)
1689: "Barely 500" (CPF/SOCG–2, fol. 378)
1691: 270 (Mafrici, 99)

1704: 194 (Mafrici, 99)
1721: 5,000 Catholics (CPF/SOCG–4, fol. 491)
1722: "around 3,000 from the various nations" (CPF/SOCG–4, fol. 485)
1752: 1,400 (Poiron, 17)
1765: 30 Catholics (CPF/SOCG–7, fol. 274)
1766: 25 Catholics (CPF/SOCG–7, fol. 299)
1767: 30 Catholics (CPF/SOCG–7, fol. 364)
1767: 267 Catholics and "a few schismatic Greeks" (CPF/SOCG–7, fol. 281)
1772: 483 Catholics (CPF/SOCG–7, fol. 560)
1773: 320 Catholics and 280 Greeks (CPF/SOCG–7, fol. 585)
1774: 240 Catholics (CPF/SOCG–7, fol. 653)
1780: 2,000 (Valensi, 1276)
1790: "more than 200 Neapolitan slaves, not counting Sicilians" (ASN/SCRC, bu. 56)
1797: at least 1,500 (Valensi, 1278)
1810: more than 2,000 (MacGill, 77)

References

ASN = Archivio di Stato di Napoli, Santa Casa per la Redentione dei Cattivi
CPF/SRC = Congregazione "De Propaganda Fide," "Scritture Riferte nei Congressi: Barbaria," vols. 1–7.
CPF/SOCG = Congregazione "De Propaganda Fide," "Scritture originali riferite nelle Congregazioni generali," vols. 253 (Tripoli = "Tri") and 254 (Tunis = "Tun").
HCRT = Anon., "Histoire chronologique du royaume de Tripoly de Barbarie" (1685), in the Bibliothèque Nationale de France, Paris, 12199–12200, fol. 61^v.
F. Bombard, ed. "Les Vicaires apostoliques de Tunis et d'Alger (1645–1827)," in *Revue Tunisienne*, 2 (1895), 73–6, 259–62, 429–32, 581–6.
Salvatore Bono, *I Corsari barbareschi* (Turin, 1964).
Pierre Dan, *Histoire de la Barbarie et ses Corsaires* (Paris, 1649).
Thomas MacGill, *Account of Tunis* (London, 1811).
Mirella Mafrici, *Mezzogiorno e pirateria nell'età moderna (secoli XVI–XVIII)* (Naples, 1995).
Joseph Morgan, *A Complete History of Algiers* (London, 1728–29; reprint: New York, 1970).
M. Poiron, *Mémoires concernans l'état présent du Royaume de Tunis*, J. Serres, ed. (Paris, 1925).
Robert Ricard, "Ibero-Africana: Le Père Jérome Gratien de la Mère de Dieu et sa Captivité a Tunis (1593–1595)," 190–200 in *Revue Africaine* 89 (1945).
Gio:Battista Salvago, *"Africa overo Barbarìa" Relazione al doge di Venezia sulle Reggenze di Algeri e di Tunisi del Dragomanno Gio.Batta Salvago (1625)*, A. Sacerdoti, ed. (Padua, 1937).

Francesco di S. Lorenzo, *Breve relatione, del calamitoso stato, crudeltà, e bestiali attioni, con le quali son trattati da' barbari li cristiani fatti schiavi, e tutto quello, ch'è passato nel viaggio della redentione de' fedeli di Christo nella città di Tunisi l'anno 1653* (Roma, 1654).

Lucette Valensi, "Esclaves chrétiens et esclaves noirs à Tunis au XVIIIe siècle," 1267–85 in *Annales, Economies Societés Civilisation*, 22 (1967).

J. M. Venture de Paradis, "Alger au XVIIIe siécle," E. Fagnan, ed. in *Revue Africaine*, 40 (1896), 33–78 and 256–77.

Introduction and Acknowledgments

> In twenty years of wearisome work as a missionary in Aleppo, Baghdad, Grand Cairo, and Suez on the Red Sea, I have seen the infinite miseries of the poor Christians oppressed by the barbarian cruelty of Mohammedans.
>
> (Padre Biaggio di Turena: 1670s)[1]

This book has come out of my desire to rethink the story of European enslavement in the early modern Mediterranean world – to place, as much as possible, this always rather neglected, even derided, form of slavery in the larger context of slave studies world-wide. I have been particularly interested in casting white slavery in the Maghreb in the terms that have been developed by historians and sociologists to cope with the much vaster and politically fraught topic of trans-Atlantic slavery – the bondage of black Africans to white Europeans or Americans that has become for many scholars the archetype and model of all slave studies. In part, I chose to do so because the topics and approaches that have grown up around American slavery provide such fertile conceptual ground for application to the Barbary Coast, where slavery is a hardly unknown, but still strangely neglected field in intellectual (as opposed to narrative) terms. In the course of my study of the so-called Barbary regencies and of the Italians who were caught up in the Islamic slavery practiced there, I was also increasingly impressed by other reasons that make these two arenas of bondage – black/American and white/African – an especially appropriate intellectual and historical pairing.

I have been struck that slavery both in the Mediterranean and across the Atlantic arose and flourished – if such a term can be used – at almost exactly the same time: one might even say for the same reason. Of course, slavery had been practiced since the earliest histories in both places, its roots going deep into both the classical cultures of Egypt, Greece, and Rome, as well as the Amerindian empires in Mexico and Central America. Yet it was only at the beginning of the modern age that slavery in each of these regions took a leap in quality and quantity, until both became institutions of large scale and high efficiency.

The cause, at least in part, can be traced to the events of 1492. In August of that year Christopher Columbus set sail to find the New World for Europe, and in so doing put in motion all the mechanisms of conquest and extractive exploitation that would eventually give rise to the sprawling system of plantation slavery in both American continents. Less than two months earlier, however, the final Spanish conquest of Granada had also set the stage for what would be the mirror image of this American institution. By expelling the Moors from southern Spain, Ferdinand and Isabella created an implacable enemy for their resurgent kingdom, one that would find a new home very near by, in Morocco, Algiers, and eventually along the entire Maghreb. The newly reinvigorated Islamic societies they helped to create there soon set out, consciously and passionately, to square accounts with Christendom, building galleys, attacking European merchant shipping, raiding coastal communities, and taking slaves.

This is the simple version, of course: other forces have to be factored in to explain fully the strength, extent, and sheer tenacity of this pernicious institution in either arena. Yet even in such simple terms, one element does stand out: slavery in the Americas differed at its inception from that in the Maghreb by being above all a matter of business, as opposed to passion. Black slaves were hauled to the Americas to wring profit from lands that could not be otherwise exploited, at least not for the cash crops that the markets in Lisbon, London, and Amsterdam clamored to buy. The slave traffickers and plantation owners may have experienced contempt, pity, or disgust for their human chattel, but they bought and sold them primarily for the work they could do, and it made no more sense to despise these slaves than it did to look down on oxen or horses. Such a failure of basic humanity is still felt centuries later in all the nations that were caught up in the shameful spiral – the more so because it was a misery fueled by greed, more than any ideology or cause. In Barbary, those who hunted and traded slaves certainly hoped to make a profit, but in their traffic in Christians there was also always an element of revenge, almost of *jihad* – for the wrongs of 1492, for the centuries of crusading violence that had preceded them, and for the ongoing religious struggle between Christian and Muslim that has continued to roil the Mediterranean world well into modern times.

It may have been this spur of vengeance, as opposed to the bland workings of the marketplace, that made the Islamic slavers so much more aggressive and initially (one might say) successful in their work than their Christian counterparts. By all indications, as this study attempts to show, Mediterranean slaving out-produced the trans-Atlantic trade during the sixteenth and into the seventeenth century, and this is only in terms of the Barbary Coast – without taking into account Muslim slaving activities in the Levant and eastern Europe, nor the counter-enslavement that some Christian states were practicing at the same time on their Islamic foes. In the long run, however, market imperatives would give American slavery and the trans-Atlantic trade more staying power than the Maghrebian version, which was ultimately less concerned with profiting from the labor of slaves than in using them to secure the status of their individual masters or to power large-scale building programs for the states that owned them. It was at just about the time when Mediterranean slaving began to falter – around the mid-1600s – that the trans-Atlantic trade really took off: a second surge of this poisonous wave that brought American slavery to a peak in the later 1700s.

It has been thirty years since Eugene Genovese published *Roll, Jordan, Roll*, presenting a striking portrait of American slave culture as seen from the inside, as it was lived. Genovese's is just one of the many scholarly works of the last generation that have made it all but unthinkable to assert, or even to imply, that slavery in the Americas provided its victims with the sort of paternalistic care and ultimately civilizing influence that its antebellum supporters once claimed for it – and that certain schools of American historical thought kept alive until well into the twentieth century. Interestingly, over this same generation scholarship on Barbary Coast slavery has been tending in just the opposite direction, with the flows and eddies of post-colonial and post-modern thought much more inclined at least implicitly to treat slaves there as pre-imperialists and their masters as proto-nationalists. Some have suggested that for white Europeans enslavement in the Maghreb was no more cruel or brutal than prison or even ordinary working life in much of Europe; others have chosen to emphasize instances of Muslim masters' kind treatment of their bondsmen. History is, often as not, our present politics projected onto the past, and the ways in which the intellectual tide has flowed in different directions over these two sorts of slavery may well say more about our own times than about the world of 300 years ago. Yet even two or three centuries ago, many Europeans apparently agreed with the French cleric Philemon de La Motte that "As for the Slaves at *Algiers*, they are not indeed so unhappy;" and with the French traveler Laugier de Tassy's claim that no white slaves in the Maghreb really "suffer[ed] those dismal Miseries which Monks, and other designing Persons, who have experienced this Servitude, would make the World believe."[2]

Such assertions may have fitted in well with the anti-clericalism and newfound enthusiasm for things Oriental that marked those Enlightened times – even as attempts today to cast white slave narratives as strings of literary tropes several removes from experience or to endow the slaves themselves with an Imperial Gaze may well satisfy many academic tempers of our times. Nevertheless, slave studies in the Americas have done much to remind us – and why should we need reminding? – that enslavement, whatever its mitigating circumstances or literary possibilities, still means the loss of freedom of action, the denial of personhood, and at some level a constant climate of coercive violence. De La Motte recognized this, even as he was asserting that the slaves' life in Barbary was "not indeed so unhappy," for he went on to conclude: "But still they are Slaves; always hated on account of their Religion [and] incessantly over-burdened with Labor." We may wish to appreciate the Turkish and Moorish cultures that shaped the Barbary regencies – indeed, we should – but not to deny the basic humanity, the perceptions, or the experiences of the slaves themselves, many of whom certainly suffered, just as many also died. It was in good part for this reason that I have chosen the epigraph to this Introduction, which includes the phrase "Barbarian Cruelty" – not, perhaps, the most acceptable of phrases for this new millennium, but one very much in line with how the victims of corsair slaving saw the relationship between their captors and themselves two centuries ago. Indeed, several books from those days carried those words for their title, and the term recurs in narratives in many languages.[3]

Slaves are slaves, after all, and within the structuring relationship of bondage are to be found many of the same features anywhere in the world where there is or has been slavery. It is, in fact, precisely because studies in American and trans-Atlantic slaving have paid such attention to the actual experience of enslavement – to its material aspects, to the physical and emotional bond between master and slave, and to its cultural expressions – that this branch of the field can prove so useful a model. Certainly it has given me the framework to apply and the questions to ask about bondage as it was found and lived in Barbary.

It has also helped me to structure this book in a way that I hope lends some insight into what turns out to be a very broad topic indeed. The text that follows is in three parts, each with its own geographic, but also intellectual scope. Beginning with "White Slavery," there are two chapters that explore the size and the nature of the phenomenon: How many slaves were there? How were they procured? How were they enslaved, both physically and mentally? In "Barbary," the second part, are two chapters dedicated to what slaves did and how they survived – those that did, at least – in Algiers, Tunis, and Tripoli, the three cities that form both the heart of Barbary and the core of this study. The final third of the book, "Italy," takes the story back to my own field of specialization, primarily to ask how one society responded, economically and culturally, to the depredations of corsair slaving, whose continuous and corrosive effects it had to withstand for well over three centuries.

Faced with a topic of such breadth, each of these parts and consequently the book itself necessarily suffers from inevitable constraints of space, sources, and scope. Mediterranean slavery was by no means limited to the Barbary regencies or even to the Muslim world. The independent kingdom of Morocco to the west and the populous Levant, from Cairo to Constantinople, had enormous slaving cultures; likewise, the Christian states of Spain, France, Tuscany, and Malta were all active in enslaving Muslims – and sometimes Protestants. I must admit that I have chosen Barbary out of all these slaving cultures in good part just because the region is so fascinating. The regencies were unique semi-states like no others of their time: neither completely independent of Turkish control, as was Morocco, nor anywhere near as closely bound to Ottoman power, as were points further east, Algiers, Tunis, and Tripoli could and largely did pursue their own course of self-enrichment. As Sir William Monson once described them:

> The Inhabitants consist principally of desperate *Rogues* and *Renegadoes*, who live by Rapine, Theft and Spoil, having renounced GOD and all Virtue, and become Reprobates to all the *Christian* World.... [They] are a Sort of Outlaws, or Miscreants, who live in Enmity with all the World, acknowledging the *Grand Turk* in some Measure for their Sovereign, but no farther than they please themselves.[4]

Reprobates ... Outlaws ... Miscreants: Who could not be fascinated by such a cast? At the same time, I have also found and followed an especially rich vein of source materials to Barbary. Algiers in particular figured highly in the white slave narratives which were so copiously produced between the sixteenth and eighteenth centuries. Of still more consequence for the work here have been the records of the Catholic missionizing arm, the Congregation *De Propaganda Fide*, which are archived by region, with one especially rich trove labeled "Barbaria."[5]

I have also had to limit my exploration of corsair slaving's impact largely to Italy, if only because that is my own area of expertise and past experience. With such a variety among the Christian states that were touched by this phenomenon – Catholic and Protestant, monarchies and republics, urban and agrarian – I could never claim that Italy or indeed any other single area in Europe could stand as representative of the many responses made to the enslavement threat. For a student of Mediterranean slaving, Italy does have the advantage of providing much of this variety in miniature, however, an advantage compounded by the presence in Rome of the Catholic Church, along with the headquarters of its various missionary and redemptive organs. The peninsula was also, along with the Mediterranean coast of Spain, arguably the area of Christianity hardest hit by the corsair slavers, from the days of Fra Lippo Lippi (who was carried off to Tunis) until well into the nineteenth century. A great deal of this long story has been preserved in the many local archives available for consultation throughout the peninsula – some of religious background, some confraternal, and many others produced by the various Italian states themselves.

The Italian material I draw on here can in many ways speak only to the Italian situation, and I have tried to use it to explore the real and specific effects that three centuries of corsair depredations had on Italian society and culture: on the evolution of state and church bureaucracies, on shifts in populations and economies, and on the transformation of social and religious thought – all in response to the threat from Barbary. Nevertheless, I have also sought to approach and present Italy in ways that will shed light on a pan-Mediterranean situation, and certainly what I have found there about the impact of corsair slaving – the depopulation, redemptive practices, and what I have come to call the celebration of slavery – can all be extrapolated to other Christian states, especially Spain or France.

Such states have not been without their champions in the story of the corsairs and white slavery: Spain and France have attracted a good deal of study in this context, at least since the time of Braudel. Britain, Germany, and the Low Countries have gained somewhat less, though one hopes that more attention will be directed in the future towards what seem to be rich sources in their state archives on Algerian and Salé raiding in these northern waters. For Italy, I have been particularly fortunate in having at hand the vast amount of published research on corsair slaving that has been produced by Professor Salvatore Bono and his many students, research that has not only sought to place the whole of the Italian situation in the greater, Mediterranean context, but that has also produced a number of case studies on specific Italian cities or city states and their activities in ransoming or self-defense.

For a scholar like myself, who was not able to visit all the archives of the many centers of slave redemption in Italy, the work of these historians – who have provided both synthetic studies and generous collections of transcribed documents – has been invaluable. I would especially like to thank Professor Bono for the personal encouragement he gave me in my research.

What research I was able to do from one end of Italy to the other, I could carry out only because of the generosity of a number of societies and funding organizations. First among these was the American Academy in Rome, which granted me almost a year of residency in Rome, in 1996–97; research fellowships in this same period from the Fulbright Foundation and the Gladys Krieble Delmas Foundation helped me extend my research at that time to Livorno and Venice; a subsequent College of Humanities grant from the Ohio State University later allowed me to include Naples as well. My thanks also to the Folger Library and the John Simon Guggenheim Foundation, whose generous support gave me the free time to write up the results of my research in 1999–2001.

Everywhere I went in Italy I received the kind support of friends, scholars, archivists, and librarians, without whose assistance and advice this project would have been impossible. In particular, though, I would like to thank Claudio Bernabei, Michela Dal Borgo, Roberto De Mattei, Annì Governale, Padre Juan Pujana, and Roberto Rusconi. Of the many colleagues here in America who helped me with their ideas and suggestions, I am especially indebted to David Brion Davis, Don Davis, Robert Forster, Ed Muir, Gilian Weiss, and Steve Whitman, all of whom kindly read early chapter drafts and generously offered me their comments. My particular thanks to Beth Lindsmith, who worked through the manuscript and never spared it her editing pen; and, finally, my thanks to my wife Cindy, who has put up with and encouraged me in this project for the whole ten years it has lasted.

Part I
White Slavery

1
How Many Slaves?

January the 16th. day, in the year before nominated [1631]; I arrived in [Algiers,] that Citie fatall to all *Christians*, and the *butchery* of *mankind* ... my condolation is for the losse of many Christians, taken from their parents and countries, of all sorts and sexes. Some in Infancy, both by Land and by Sea, being forced to abuses (most incorrigible flagitions) not onely so, but bereft of Christian Religion, and means of grace and repentence. How many thousands of the *Nazarian* nations have beene and are continually lost by that monster, what rationall creature can be ignorant of?[1]

The question that Francis Knight asked here – "How many thousands?" – was no doubt a heartfelt one: he himself had been enslaved in Algiers and on the Algerian galleys for seven years and had seen his share of suffering. It also provides a good indication that, for the sailors and merchants of his day, enslavement was not something that white Europeans did to other peoples, to black Africans in particular. Even the English, though remote from Barbary and themselves already among the more aggressive slave runners in the 1630s, were enslaved by Muslim corsairs operating out of Tunis, Algiers, and Morocco, and in numbers that were not inconsiderable. During these years, when the English share of the Atlantic slave trade still averaged barely 1,000 Africans annually, the Algerian and Salé rovers may have been enslaving almost as many British subjects every year from the scores of ships they were taking: by 1640, upwards of 3,000 British were enslaved in Algiers alone (and another 1,500 or so in Tunis), "undergoing divers and most insufferable oppressions."[2] Throughout the first half of the seventeenth century, while the Barbary corsairs ranged freely around

3

the Mediterranean, these pirates also sailed by the dozen up the Channel and even into the Thames estuary, plundering local shipping and coastal towns, such that, as the minutes of Parliament put it, "The fishermen are afraid to put to sea, and we are forced to keep continual watches on all our coasts."[3] Though the raids on the British Isles themselves may have dropped off by the later 1600s, the capture of British ships continued. The Algerians were said to have taken no fewer than 353 British ships between 1672 and 1682 – which would mean they were still picking up between 290 and 430 new British slaves every year.[4]

However much they may have preyed on the British, the Barbary corsairs were far more of a threat to those closer to their home shores: Flemish, French, Spanish, Portuguese, and Italians were all hauled off into slavery at a much greater rate throughout the sixteenth and seventeenth centuries. Yet it is striking that we have only the vaguest idea of the overall magnitude of the slave traffic in white Europeans, the more so because it was taking place at the same time as the Atlantic slave trade at which so much serious scholarship has been directed. Indeed, well over a generation ago, Philip Curtin recognized that having a reliable reckoning of how many Africans were enslaved was an essential foundation for the entire field of slave studies in the Americas. With his *The Atlantic Slave Trade: a Census*, Curtin laid out the initial calculations that have contextualized debate on the topic ever since and have provided the basis for subsequent detailing of precisely which and how many Africans were taken on the Middle Passage.[5] By contrast, although it has been over fifty years since Fernand Braudel first highlighted the place of piracy and the slave trade in the sixteenth-century Mediterranean social economy, there has still been no broad, analogous census of Mediterranean slaving.[6] Instead, scholars have generally restricted themselves to deep, focused studies, often based on single runs of archival sources. In consequence they have often detailed only a particular slave type, nationality, condition, or time frame, rather than the entire trade.[7] Such case studies have been vital for illuminating the dynamics of Mediterranean slavery, but they have contributed only tangentially to our understanding of the true extent and global impact of this phenomenon. Indeed, by approaching it in this piecemeal fashion, they have contributed to an already widespread conviction that Barbary slaving was nothing like the massive and systematic Atlantic phenomenon, as detailed by Curtin, Paul Lovejoy, and many others, but was rather a somewhat peripheral sideline of the business of corsair piracy – something that happened to at most a few scores of thousands of unfortunate individuals from various Christian nations during the three centuries between 1500 and 1800.[8]

It may be the supposition that Mediterranean-based slaving was a minor activity that explains why so few scholars have even speculated about how to estimate the extent of the traffic. Braudel as much as anyone may have helped to downplay the long-term economic and social relevance of Mediterranean slavery, even as he was drawing attention to it. Evidently unable to decide between the two options that he himself advanced – that the Mediterranean was "a sea teeming with pirates who dealt savage blows" and that "the wicked role played by Moslem pirates in general and the Barbary corsairs in particular has been much exaggerated" – the master of the *Annales* sought to prune down the phenomenon to its core aspect, ship-on-ship piracy, as conducted by the corsairs of Algiers between 1560 and 1620. Coming up with what even he allowed were some "extremely hypothetical estimates" of corsair predation, Braudel concluded that "these figures are not spectacular," a position taken by many students of the Mediterranean who have followed him.[9] Some recent scholars have moreover sought to minimize the impact of Barbary slaving in another way, by observing that the depredations Muslim corsairs inflicted on the Christian world, whatever they were, were more than matched by their Christian counterparts, who operated out of Malta, Livorno, and even Portsmouth, and were as likely to prey on neutral Europeans as on Barbary shipping.[10] Others have taken the position that the Europeans carried off to Barbary and the Levant were not slaves at all, but rather prisoners of war, who could expect to regain their freedom through ransom or exchange after a short confinement as captives.[11]

While both arguments have a certain validity, neither, as this study will attempt to show, succeeds in comprehending the extent of white slaving activities in this era or the impact it had on Europeans at the time. Suffice it to say, for the moment at least, that, although most modern scholarship has tended to minimize the scope of corsair piracy, those Europeans who lived during these centuries took the threat to their freedom and lives a good deal more seriously. Diplomatic reports, popular broadsheets, and simple word of mouth circulated throughout Europe, telling and retelling of Christians taken by the hundreds and thousands on the high seas or during coastal sorties, and hauled off in chains to a living death of hard labor in Morocco, Algiers, Tunis, or Tripoli. One could (as some have) dismiss all this as "corsair hysteria" which gripped much of Europe during these centuries, a general panic fueled by a combination of fear and fantasy. Nevertheless, it is not difficult to turn up some hard figures that back up this sense of general disquiet. The corsairs captured Christian ships in enormous numbers, for example, and this was a matter of sufficient importance to merchants and insurers to generate much suggestive data. One reads in a variety of contemporary sources, for example, that between November 1593 and August 1594, the Tunisian corsairs brought in around 28 prizes with 1,722 captives; that between 1628 and 1634 the Algerians captured 80 merchant vessels from the French alone (taking 986 captives in the process), while between 1628 and 1641 they took 131 "ships and barks" from the English, totalling 2,555 "of his Majesty's subjects;" that the rovers of Tripoli, although running one of the smaller slaving operations, succeeded in bringing in 75 Christian ships with 1,085 captives between 1677 and 1685.[12]

Such accounts are, by their nature, hugely incomplete: for the most part we have no prize or slave registers in the cities of Barbary, beyond sporadic consular records.[13] Other accounts list the number of ships taken in a specific period, but omit a count of the captives. Yet these too are suggestive of some very large numbers: Britain's Royal Navy admitted losing 466 English and Scottish ships to Algerian corsairs between 1606 and 1609; the Trinitarian father Pierre Dan claimed that these same rovers seized 936 vessels from France, Holland, Germany, England, and Spain between 1613 and 1621; while John Morgan wrote, "I have by me a List, printed in London in 1682," that inventoried 160 "Ships and Vessels belonging to Subjects of these [British] Realms," which the Algerians had taken or destroyed between July 1677 and October 1680.[14]

If even as few as ten men were captured with each vessel (the average rate appears to be 8–12, with many crews escaping in small boats), the corsairs were enslaving tens of thousands of men at sea. Their slave raids on land could prove even more productive, however, or at least more spectacular (see Table 1, p. xiv). Some of their coastal slaving expeditions entered into legend among those living on the north Mediterranean shores, as almost annual events of terror and pillage: the 7,000 captives that the Algerians took in the Bay of Naples in 1544, for example; the 6,000 snapped up when they sacked Vieste in Calabria in 1554; the 4,000 men, women, and children seized in Granada in 1566 (after which they said it was "raining Christians in Algiers"). The take shrank somewhat in the seventeenth century, in part because the Imperial Turkish fleet was no longer participating, but also because many coastal dwellers had simply packed up and fled. Still, the Barbary rovers kept coming ashore, sometimes by the thousands, in raids like those that captured 1,200 men and women in Madeira in 1617; almost 400 in Iceland in 1627; and 700 in Calabria in 1636, another 1,000 there in 1639, and yet another 4,000 in 1644; in 1640, dispatches to London told how "those roguish Turkish pirates" had snatched 60 men, women, and children from the Cornish coast, near Penzance; in the spring of 1641, Algerian pirates seized the packet *John Filmer* just hours after it had set off from Youghal, in Ireland, on its way to England, enslaving the 120 passengers on board and "putting all the men in irons."[15]

Impressive as these expeditions may have been – and they were the events most likely to go into the records – it is safe to assume that for each spectacular attack there were dozens, perhaps hundreds, of much smaller sorties, played out by a dozen corsairs in a tartan or felucca against a handful of poor fishermen caught too far out at sea or a couple of village women snapped up while working in the fields.[16] Thomas Baker, Britain's consul in Tripoli in the 1680s, called such activities "Christian stealing," which gives a good impression of the level on which many of these cut-rate corsairs operated, especially by the later 1600s.[17] Such minor thuggery may not have made the diplomatic reports, yet it was these small as much as the great predations "which doe much offend the Christians, in taking their ships, Tartanes, and Satties, and other small vessels, making all the Christians that they take slaves."[18] Relentless and almost unstoppable, petty piracy probably cost Christendom more in slaves and booty over the long run than all the spectacular coups taken together. Braudel, characteristically, summed up this balance of attrition neatly and evocatively:

> Besides the great predators, lesser scavengers prowled the seas.... These were humble men with humble ambitions: to capture a fisherman perhaps or rob a granary, kidnap a few harvesters.... Such minor carnivores did not always inflict the least damage, nor amass the smallest fortunes in the end.[19]

While the Dutch diplomat Thomas Hees was negotiating a treaty with the Pasha of Algiers in the winter of 1685–86, he noted just this sort of a steady trickle of prizes in his diary: Portuguese caravels, Dutch fluyts, Genoese and English brigs – eleven vessels with over 300 fresh slaves all captured and brought in over just four weeks, during what was the corsairing off-season.[20] The Sicilian archives also provide good evidence about these small-scale land raids: the hundreds of ransom requests sent to Palermo by Sicilian slaves and their relatives indicate that the island was attacked at least 136 times between 1570 and 1606, sometimes in sorties that penetrated 10 or even 20 miles inland. Yet only two or three of these raids seemed important enough at the time to merit a mention in contemporary chronicles of the island's history; the rest come to light at all only because they figured in the private tragedy recounted by some unlucky petitioner seeking ransom.[21] Moreover, in the little stories these slaves told, they often alluded to others taken with them – like the day laborer, seized from a monastery near Bari in 1678, "along with eighteen other persons;" or the worker taken that same year near Otranto together with five others. These anonymous fellow fishermen or villagers, who never appeared in the official records beyond these fleeting references, ended up uncounted among the many victims of corsair slaving.[22]

For those who had to deal with the Barbary regencies, these states seemed to be the "flail of the Christian world ... the terror of Europe ... the pinnacle of cruelty in all its forms and the asylum of impiety." Charges like these may strike the modern reader as no more than rhetorical flourishes and to an extent, of course, they were, but some observers backed up their claims with equally serious figures.[23] Emanuel d'Aranda, a Flemish gentleman-soldier who was enslaved in Algiers in the 1640s, called that city the place "where the miseries of Slavery have consum'd the lives of six hundred thousand Christians, since the year 1536, at which time *Cheredin Barberossa* brought it under his own power."[24] And if Algiers was generally the most active, it was by no means the only city in the Maghreb that flourished on the business of enslaving Europeans: towns from Salé to Tripoli, the whole length of Barbary, all took their share in the trade, leading d'Aranda's contemporary, Pierre Dan, to conclude that, for the years 1530 to 1640, "it would not be stretching the truth to say that they have put a million [Christians] in chains."[25]

Even when compared to the atrocities of the Atlantic slave trade, which shipped some 10–12 million black Africans as slaves to the Americas over four centuries, these claims about what a hundred years of Mediterranean slaving accomplished do not dwindle into insignificance. Nor is this to deny or trivialize the well-documented Christian enslavement of Moors and Turks which was going on at the same time. Certainly, the Spanish, Tuscans, and Maltese were all eager participants in the enslavement of their Muslim foes, largely to work them as galley slaves. Among Christian states, however, the practice was never as pervasive or as massive as in Barbary and died out sooner, as most European nations switched from galleys to sail and from slaves to convicts in those galleys they did retain.[26] There were in any case far fewer Islamic merchant ships on which to prey in the western Mediterranean, and, among Europeans, only the Spanish ever seem to have tried mounting slave raids into Muslim territories. Despite some attempts to label the two forms of Mediterranean slavery as pernicious mirror images, most students of the period still have to agree that, at least after 1571, corsair slaving was "a prevalently Muslim phenomenon."[27]

Nevertheless, if Dan and d'Aranda were right, and Barbary corsair slaving was indeed significant, it may be necessary to rethink our present-day understanding of what slavery itself meant to sixteenth- and seventeenth-century Europeans. Not only does enslavement turn out to have been a very real possibility for anyone who traveled or lived in the Mediterranean, but it was also likely to be religion or ethnicity, not race, that determined who would capture and enslave whom. The problem, of course, is, how much faith can be placed in such estimates? Neither Dan nor d'Aranda supplied much rationale for his figures, and there is little documentation that directly supports them – certainly nothing like the sustained runs of shipping records and censuses that have been available to Curtin and those who followed him. North African sources on corsair slaving activities turn out to be very thin – "cruelly deficient" and "almost nonexistent for the period before 1736," according to two modern-day scholars – while those in Europe are scattered widely in national and local archives or various religious orders and confraternities.[28] What material there is turns out to be more anecdotal than serial by nature and, although often highly suggestive, these sources by no means allow one to total with any hope of accuracy all those enslaved by the Barbary corsairs, in piratical attacks of all sorts and sizes.

Nevertheless, the problem can still be tackled, though more obliquely. Many Europeans besides Dan and d'Aranda offered estimates for Mediterranean slave populations for the period between the late sixteenth and the early nineteenth centuries, though they mostly did so for specific Barbary Coast cities rather than for the entire Maghreb. Such counts are fairly numerous (there are over 50 complete and dozens of partial estimates for Algiers alone), even if many were arrived at in such mysterious ways as to be of rather uncertain value (see Table 2, p. xviii). The record they provide also has its gaps: the estimates for Tunis and Tripoli are somewhat patchier than those for Algiers – about 25 for each city during these centuries – while for many smaller port and inland towns, there may be only one or two counts for the whole period (see Table 3, p. xxi).[29] A further problem is that between 1500 and 1578 there are essentially no slave figures at all. This is not such a problem for Tunis and Tripoli, which were variably under European control for much of that time, but a significant loss for Algiers, whose corsairs carried out some spectacular slave raids between 1518 and 1560, under the leadership of Kheir-ed-din Barbarossa and Turgut Re'is. Often these plundering campaigns were in reality full-scale naval expeditions, resulting in pitched battles that might bring home thousands of captives at a time, taken from Christian fleets and from the coasts of Valencia and Granada, the Balearics, Campania, Calabria, and Sicily. So many prisoners flooded into the slave market of Algiers on occasion that, as the saying had it, one could "swap a Christian for an onion."[30]

In any case, even those estimates we do possess have been treated with suspicion by many present-day historians. Such scholars have tended to dismiss the larger, rounder slave counts, like many of those from Algiers and Tunis, as the guesswork of untrained, Eurocentric dilettantes.[31] Certainly the figures can offer some wild variations: we find in just one six-year period, between 1681 and 1687, slave population counts for Algiers that vary from 5,000 ("or a few more") to 17,000, 30,000–40,000, and then back down to 10,000.[32] Norman Bennett has expressed doubts about figures made by the slaves themselves, as perhaps reflecting the "natural exaggeration of men who had been deprived of their freedom," but suspicion has especially fallen on estimates provided by the Trinitarians and Mercedarians.[33] These priests of the redemptive orders, who were so important in ransoming Christian slaves in Barbary, were accused even in their heyday of "spread[ing] about a thousand Fables, in order to enhance the *Merit* of those services they do the Public, in passing over to *Barbary* to redeem Captives."[34] There is no doubt some truth to the misgiving – occasionally voiced even by some of those same orders – that these ransoming fathers had a vested interest in exaggerating their slave counts, as a means of instilling a sense of urgency in and thus opening the purses of their pious contributors.[35]

It should, however, be remembered that not all of those who tallied up slave populations in Barbary had a reason to exaggerate: far from it. Estimates survive that by their very nature needed to be as reliable as possible: they were provided by resident consuls or the merchant agents who were periodically commissioned by their home state to find out just how many of their fellow citizens were being held as slaves in a given city. This might be carried out as a preliminary step for a peace treaty or for a state ransoming venture, and to get such information, the French and the English relied on their consuls. Most of the small Italian states, on the other hand – the Sicilians, for example, the Venetians, or the Papacy – had to entrust the task to their own magistracies or quasi-governmental confraternities, which might commission a merchant on the spot. These estimates – in effect government reports, which were more or less official in nature – were usually restricted to a specific nationality in a particular town.[36] Occasionally, however, the agents might offer a more sweeping view of both the individual Barbary regencies and all the slaves there. François Lanfreducci and Jean Othon Bosio produced such a survey for the knights of Malta in 1587, as did the dragoman and merchant Gianbattista Salvago for Venice in 1625; another Venetian, the ex-slave, Antonio Tedaldi Barbarella, submitted a shorter but also detailed report to the Venetian Senate in 1682, breaking down his total slave count by nationality.[37] Such estimates are unfortunately not as common as those from missionary and redemptive fathers or the ex-slaves, but what matters most is that they are not significantly out of line with them either, differing by 10–20 percent at most. In this regard, although the government reports are too patchy to provide a complete survey of slave populations, they do give greater credibility to the much more numerous efforts of the religious and secular "non-professionals."[38]

One should not in any case underestimate how very difficult it must have been to make an accurate slave count in Barbary during the sixteenth and seventeenth centuries, especially when dealing with the many slaves who belonged to private masters. Even modern-day census takers would find it challenging to come up with precise tallies of these thousands of individuals, many of whom lacked any form of written identification or even a last name; thousands were moreover regularly hired out to work in other towns or sold to other masters – like the eighteenth-century Venetian shipbuilder (one of many such on a ransoming list) who was said to have been "taken by the Tripolitans, sold to the Tunisians, then to the Algerians."[39] Others were routinely sent by their masters to labor in one of the many small farm plots that surrounded the city, thus keeping them out of sight of contemporary observers. The only way to count them seemed to be to calculate how many of the plots – known by the slaves as *masseries* or *giardini*, called *fahs* by the Algerians – there were and then multiply by what appeared to be the appropriate number of slaves per plot. Jean-Baptiste Gramaye claimed to have done as well as anyone at this, saying he had taken a look "at the account books of the Pasha," thus allowing him to come up with a precise total of 14,698 of such *masseries* others, from the time of Diego de Haëdo in the 1580s into the early 1700s, reported that the plots numbered between 10,000 and 18,000.[40]

Once he had arrived at such a number, however, an estimator could be completely at sea when it came to choosing his multiplying factor, which was in fact anyone's guess. As the missionary Giovanni di S. Bonaventura put it, in somewhat contorted form: "in each *Giardino* there are two or four or even six Christians, or at least one."[41] Counts reached by this approach, which the historian Michel Fontenay has rather dryly termed *passablement impressionniste*, were both impressively large and hopelessly vague: the implication was that there were anywhere between 20,000 and 60,000 slaves engaged in just this one type of labor, a result that seems to have struck most of those who used this method as more suggestive than concrete.[42]

If the estimators found slaves belonging to private individuals hard to count, they were on somewhat safer ground when it came to dealing with those known as "public slaves" in the Barbary regencies. These were the chattels of the state, for the most part owned by either the local ruler or the governing council, called the *divan.* Typically, they worked as galley slaves or in construction gangs in the city. At the end of each day these men were locked up in one of the local *bagni* (or bagnos) – the "baths," as the barracks-like slave prisons were known. Each morning they were tallied by their keeper, known as the guardian bagno, so that they could be accounted for and allocated to work sites in town or to the departing galleys.[43] Since, at least by 1700, each bagno also had a Catholic chapel, the priests who served there might also produce a count of those men who had taken Easter communion. When would-be estimators had access to lists like these, they could produce fairly secure counts of these public slaves at one moment in time. In consequence, there are some relatively hard figures available. We find, for instance, that 4,000 Christians were held in the sixteen bagnos of Tunis in 1664; that in 1696, "the Christians in the four *bagni* [of Algiers] do not exceed in all the number of 1600;" that twenty years later there were "upwards of 2,000" slaves kept in the Bagno Beyliç alone in that city, and so on.[44] The counts could also be constructed more specifically, depending on the interests of the observer (or his readers). The French consuls in Tunis and Algiers, for example, were as assiduous in reporting the number of Frenchmen held in the bagnos there as were Rome's missionaries in sending back tallies of practicing Catholics.[45] The specificity of these counts has sometimes caused problems for modern-day scholars, who have not always recognized that the missionaries who sent back counts of those they called "Christian slaves" might in fact have been referring only to "Catholic slaves." Their estimates, which have been taken as complete slave counts, were only partial tallies of those in the bagnos, leaving out an often not inconsiderable population of "schismatics and heretics" – that is, Orthodox and Protestant slaves – producing a much lower count as a result.[46]

For contemporary estimators, the figures for the bagnos seem to have formed the core of many a global slave count. Dan, for one, underscored that of his estimated 25,000 Christian captives in Algiers, "more than two or three thousand are ordinarily locked up in the Bagnes, or Prisons of the City," but there are many other examples. The slave priest Jerónimo Gracián, for instance, calculated in the early 1590s there were 1,600 Christian slaves in Tunis, of whom around 600 were held in the bagnos. Likewise Father Niccolò da Sciò, prefect of the missionary church in Tripoli, noted in 1701 that when masses were sung in the chapels of the local bagnos, the 500 slaves held there were joined by "three hundred and more [slaves] of private owners."[47]

On the other hand, slave counts in the bagnos had to be made with care, simply because the number of these "public slaves" could fluctuate sharply, from year to year or even month to month.[48] Disease and redemptions, as we shall see, could cause significant, short-term reductions, but numbers in the bagnos could also fall or rise abruptly when the galleys set out or returned from the *corso*, bringing with them their thousands of slave oarsmen.[49] By the same token, though probably more confusing to the estimators, large blocs of slaves forever came and went with arriving or departing viceroys or other imperial officers, who customarily traveled with considerable servile retinues. It was also difficult to keep track of all the various *deys*, pashas, and corsair captains (*re'is*) who regularly moved slaves from city to city, as they gave, sold, or rented whole squads of captives to one another.[50]

Keeping these caveats in mind, it is possible to assemble from these various estimates a general overview that both compares the slave populations of the various Barbary regencies and charts how they changed over time. In Algiers, for example, counts fluctuated from 20,000 to 40,000 Christian slaves between 1580 and 1680; thus it would be reasonable, if not somewhat conservative, to set a running average for the city at 25,000.[51] After the 1680s, though, we find a fairly sharp drop: reports coming from Algiers for the most part told of many fewer slaves in the city, usually between 2,000 and 10,000. Contemporaries pointed to both diplomatic and structural causes. Some noted that more determined reprisals by Europe's great powers had persuaded the Barbary pashas to think twice about giving their *re'is* free reign to plunder and take slaves. Others observed that these were also the years when a general move in the Mediterranean from rowed galleys to sailing vessels was reducing much of the demand for galley slaves, thus decreasing corsair incentives to hunt specifically for new *galleotti*.[52] Yet there still remained considerable profit to be made in slaving for the sake of ransom, such that both the corsairs and the pashas stubbornly resisted European efforts to suppress their slave-taking activities altogether.[53] Although some reports had the slave population in Algiers as low as 500 by the 1790s, the numbers escalated again during the Napoleonic Wars, when the general disorders in the Mediterranean and the advent of American ships on the scene made slaving attractive and profitable once more. Only with the reestablishment of European peace, backed by a strong British naval presence in the Mediterranean, did corsair slaving collapse, so that when the French captured Algiers in 1830, they found only 122 slaves in the bagno.[54]

Slave demographics elsewhere in the Maghreb followed a similar pattern, although always on a smaller scale, since no town in Barbary had invested quite as much in slaving as Algiers.[55] Much more populous overall, seventeenth-century Tunis typically had only around a quarter to a third as many slaves as Algiers, perhaps not so much a sign that the Tunisian corsairs felt any great aversion to slaving in itself – they regularly pillaged the coasts and shipping of southern Italy, Sicily, and Sardinia for captives – but rather that there was less need for slave labor in Tunis, which had little industry and only moderate agricultural activity.[56] Other Barbary Coast ports, generally poor and underpopulated, were in an altogether different league.[57] Tripoli, the largest and a particular adversary of the Venetians, was never reported to have had more than 2,500 Christian slaves; 1,500 seems more typical during the seventeenth century. A handful of slaves might typically also be found in many of the provincial ports subject to these regency capitals, usually for work about the port or in shipbuilding. "Eight or ten" turn up in the Tripolitan port of Susa, 200 or 300 in the Tunisian towns of Porto Farina and Biserte; a score or fewer in the Algerian port of Bône and in Constantine, and so on.[58]

Although all these slave counts fluctuated in the short term, there are enough and they are consistent enough over the long run to produce a workable total for the slave populations in Barbary for the century 1580–1680 – "Th e Time I take to be," John Morgan later commented, "when those Corsairs were in their *Zenith*."[59] Even when keeping to the lower estimates – as scholars have customarily done when dealing with slavery in the Maghreb – the averages soon add up: around 27,000 in Algiers and its dependencies, 6,000 in Tunis, and perhaps 2,000 in Tripoli and the smaller centers combined. The resulting 35,000 is very near the figure that Pierre Dan came up with in 1634:

> As to the slaves of both sexes that are in Barbary today, there are a quantity of them from all the Christian nations, such as France, Italy, Spain, England, Germany, Flanders, Holland, Greece, Hungary, Poland, Slovania, Russia, and so forth. The number of these poor captives reaches about thirty-six thousand, according to the enumeration that I have carried out on the spot and to the records that have been furnished and sent to me by the Christian Consuls who live in the Corsair Cities.[60]

The figure of 35,000 that we have arrived at here can be taken as an averaged-out white slave count for Barbary, roughly how many captives were held at any given time between 1580 and 1680. It does not, however, say anything (or little) about the total number of slaves taken by the corsairs over this period. To accomplish this, given the lack of any comprehensive registers of captives, it is necessary to turn the question around and work in terms of what might be called the demand side of the Mediterranean slave traffic. Since, despite regional fluctuations, the average Christian slave population in the Barbary regencies seems to have stayed fairly close to 35,000 during this century, one can ask how many slaves the corsairs would have needed to capture to maintain this number. It is possible to approach the problem this way because of an important aspect of white slavery in Barbary, one that sharply distinguished it from its black African counterpart in the Americas: slaves in the Maghreb were at least 90 percent men and were rigorously denied access to local or slave women.[61] It can therefore be assumed that they were incapable of reproducing themselves, and as such, whatever attrition their numbers may have suffered would have necessarily had to have been made up through new captures.[62] By going over the various factors that produced population decline among these slaves and estimating the extent of their impact, we can hope to arrive at a figure for compensatory captures, one which, if necessarily derivative, is still likely to be more informative and complete than any attempted direct tally of captured slaves.

A given slave population might decline in any number of ways, but the most obvious was that slaves died. This the slaves in Barbary did for the same depressing reasons as did slaves in the New World or anywhere else: from abuse, disease, overwork, lack of food, and despair. As a Neapolitan captive wrote home from Tunis: "we are mistreated, beaten with sticks, starved, and called faithless dogs, [such] that I would willingly die and God alone knows what will happen."[63] The mass of "public slaves," the workhorses of the regency cities, were treated with particular brutality and neglect. During their time ashore they were herded together every evening into the often overcrowded and filthy bagnos and given only moldy black bread "that the dogs themselves would not eat," together with whatever they could scrounge or steal; on occasion they would even have to pay for their drinking water.[64] Their work ashore typically consisted of laboring on large-scale public works, in particular, quarrying and dragging boulders to repair the city walls or the harbor mole (which, in Algiers, was constantly falling apart). When rowing the galleys at sea, half-naked and exposed to the sun, they were not infrequently left so desperately short of drinking water that they drank sea water or died on their benches; never allowed to lie down to sleep, many of them had fallen into "continuall extasies" before their voyage was over.[65]

So-called private slaves might be much better treated, even coddled in their masters' household.[66] A few lived very well indeed, even running businesses and owning slaves of their own, but more typically a private slave was either put to work on his master's *masserie* or set to selling water about town, required to turn over to his master a certain sum every week, on pain of being beaten.[67] Just as ill-fed, poorly clothed, and roughly treated as any galley slave, many of these men too died in captivity. Michel Fontenay has shown that the 2,450 Christian slaves brought into Tripoli between 1668 and 1678 suffered what he has termed a "normal" mortality rate of around 20 percent per year.[68]

Clearly, though, what was "normal" could vary hugely depending on circumstances. Slaves who had been sailors or fishermen were typically used to hard physical labor and short rations, and their survival rate seems to have been higher: of the 989 French seamen brought to Algiers between 1628 and 1634, 119, or 12 percent, died.[69] On the other hand, slaves taken in corsair raids on coastal villages in Italy or Spain were often the weaker members of society: women with children or the aged, who had not managed to outrun the plunderers. They died at a higher rate: of the 450 or so villagers taken in a raid on the

Venetian outpost of Perasto in 1624, around a third had perished within a year.[70] Still less able to withstand the rigors of life and hard labor in North Africa were those seized and brought to Barbary from the North: the nearly 400 Icelanders captured in an Algerian raid of 1627 were reduced to only 70 survivors eight years later; of around 237 Irish captives taken in a raid of 1631, only two or three were ever ransomed and returned home.[71]

Nevertheless, considering that the great majority of those enslaved by the corsairs were reasonably hearty and able to adapt to both the hard work and climate in Barbary, it might still be reasonable to assume a "normal" death rate among slaves of 15 percent rather than Fontenay's 20 percent. Higher rates may well have prevailed among newcomers, still reeling from what Fontenay called "the effect of psychological shock," but once slaves had settled in, many proved to be surprisingly resilient.[72] Particularly hardy in this regard were those enslaved when the Tunisians seized Tabarca in 1741: the Tabarcans (families for the most part of Genoese background who had settled on the island for the coral fishing) had numbered 900 or so at the time of their capture and were down to 635 three years later, equal to an average loss of barely 10 percent per year, with over a third of these deaths occurring in the first six months of slavery. Since many Tabarcan families were left intact within the captured community, their natural reproduction eventually brought this population decline to a halt at about this point and even produced a slight rebound.[73]

Even those who otherwise adjusted to the mistreatment and meager rations that typified the lot of Barbary slaves were never safe from the Coast's most notorious killer – the plague. Fontenay's mortality figures for Tripoli indicate that twice as many slaves died in the plague outbreak that struck the city in 1675 as in the rest of the decade; if he had counted these deaths from plague among his "normal" deaths, the mortality rate among Christians in Tripoli between 1668 and 1678 would have risen from 20 percent to an alarming 46 percent. The plague was so common in North Africa in these years that it is, in fact, difficult to place it outside the normal demographics of Barbary Coast slavery. There were at least 21 significant occurrences in one or more of the major cities of the Maghreb in the seventeenth century and twelve more in the eighteenth. Algiers itself was afflicted at least twice a decade between 1647 and 1699, and by all indications the disease swept freely and with numbing regularity along the whole North African coast.[74] It was not the least impeded by local authorities who, according to bitter (and often soon-to-be-dead) Christian observers, "did not avail themselves of either precaution or prevention, and they deal with those [who arrive] suspected or infected with the plague as they do with those who are healthy ..."[75] Some Europeans believed that the Muslims in general thought that any attempt to avoid the plague through quarantine was pointless resistance to the Will of God. True or not, the cities of North Africa were especially hard hit by the disease.[76] Even in the more moderate outbreaks, some 10 percent of a city's population would perish, while a so-called "Great Plague," known as the *Konia*, might easily carry off a third of a town's inhabitants: 30,000–50,000 died in Algiers in 1620–21, 1654–57, 1665, 1691, and 1740–42; an estimated 30,000 in Tunis in 1622, 1644, and 1787–88.[77]

Malnourished and overcrowded as they generally were, coming from lands where both the disease itself and acquired immunity to it were becoming increasingly rare, Christian slaves died at the same or greater rate than the free population. In 1663, the head of the Christian mission in Tunis wrote that, having buried "a good six hundred plague-ridden Christians with [my] own hands," he himself contracted the disease but managed to recover his health "against every hope"; in 1676, the padre resident in Tunis asked for more priests to care for the sick, "who every Day are dying like Flies"; in 1691, the head of mission of Algiers reported that eight months of plague had killed 40,000 Turks and Moors in the city, as well as "a little more than a thousand of my Christian sons."[78] Rarely would the disease run its course – through the galleys, the bagnos, and the *masseries* outside the city – without killing 20–30 percent of the local slave population. When plague broke out in Algiers' overcrowded slave pens in 1662, some said that it carried off 10,000 (others claimed 20,000) of the city's 30,000 captives; in 1699, it cut the already reduced slave count in that city by a further quarter; in 1675, half the 750 slaves in Tripoli died, about the same proportion that had perished there during the plague of 1584.[79] Averaged out, the plagues that struck the cities along the Barbary Coast around twice a decade in the seventeenth century would have conservatively added at least 2 percent per year to a posited "normal" slave death rate of 15 percent. Although plague was rarer in Barbary during the eighteenth century, its effect on those unlucky enough to be enslaved there when it did strike remained devastating. Of the 130 American seamen enslaved by the Algerians between 1785 and 1793, for example, 36 (28 percent) died in captivity there, almost all of them during outbreaks of "that fatal and tremendous disorder" in 1788 and 1793.[80]

At around 17 percent, death was the greatest if by no means the only form of attrition in slave populations. Some slaves escaped – by stealing a boat, stowing away on board a friendly European merchant ship, or (with much more difficulty) evading local Berber tribesmen and fleeing overland.[81] Some scholars have claimed that escapes were easy and common, but there seems little beyond anecdotes to back up such assertions and certainly no reports from missionaries or consuls that even as many as 1 percent (that is, 300) of the slaves in Algiers ever managed to flee in a single year.[82] Norman Bennett was probably closer to the truth when he claimed that "such action affected a very limited number of captives, and most were doomed to live in the hope of a distant ransom."[83]

Any individual slave's hope of being ransomed may have been as distant as Bennett claimed, but ransoming did play a significant part in reducing slave populations overall. It was also probably the best documented form of such attrition, since both the European states that began to mount "general redemptions" as early as the 1530s and the ransoming orders of the Trinitarians and the Mercedarians, which often acted on their behalf, routinely printed lists of the slaves they bought out and brought back. Sometimes these might run to a thousand or more men, women, and children, all of them delineated by name and age, often with their occupation and point of origin as well; some lists also featured clerical and military captives.[84] The Spanish were especially good at such large-scale undertakings, perhaps having learned the business through prisoner-of-war exchanges during the 1500s. Their efforts were in any case buoyed by enthusiastic state support and donations raised throughout Iberia and Latin America, allowing the Spanish Trinitarians alone to carry out no fewer than 72 redemptions in 77 years during the 1600s, liberating 15,573 slaves in the process, or an average of 220 slaves per trip.[85]

Such efforts certainly had an impact on slave populations. Indeed, by the end of the seventeenth century Rome's vicar in Algiers noted that one reason there were only 2,800 slaves left in the city was that "some [slaves] are being ransomed every day, and the recent charity [that is, the redemption] has taken away many of them."[86] Still, even with all their combined efforts (and sometimes competition), there is no sign that the Trinitarians and the Mercedarians, on the average, year-in year-out, redeemed more than around 600 slaves annually – barely 2 percent of those enslaved during the boom years of white slaving in Barbary, from 1580 to 1680. Moreover, other European powers – England, Holland, and such Italian states as Rome and Venice – generally chose, for reasons of religion or politics, not to avail themselves of the ransom-ing expertise of the Trinitarians and Mercedarians. Without the redemp-tive fathers' negotiating skills, their agents could easily be hoodwinked or cheated by Muslim slave owners, often returning with only a few of the captives they had come to ransom, and sometimes having paid much more than they had intended.[87] Faced with such embarrassments, these Protestant and minor Catholic states might ignore or avoid the whole difficult and expensive business for as long as possible, some-times letting decades elapse between ransoming expeditions and leaving many slaves to lament, as a group of Piedmontese did in 1786, that they had been "completely abandoned by their government."[88] Although the ransoming activities on behalf of the dozen or more states besides Spain and France whose subjects were enslaved in Barbary have not yet been studied extensively, the available evidence – redemption lists, references to redemptions in narrative sources, and so forth – makes it plain that these nations were only minor contributors to slave attrition through ransoming, generally adding not more than a few hundred annually to the number brought back by the redemptive orders.[89]

Some modern scholars have concluded that these ransoming efforts were far more effective than that: Jean Dams, for one, estimates that the Trinitarians ransomed more than 100,000 captives, though not all in Barbary.[90] Examining Mercedarian redemption lists from the 1660s and 1670s, Claude Larquié concluded that the great majority of the slaves mentioned were ransomed to freedom in under five years; he has taken this as a sign of the effectiveness of the redemptive orders, at least when it came to freeing Spanish slaves.[91] Such an interpretation, as we shall see, is open to question; for the moment, it is enough to keep in mind what might seem the otherwise obvious point that these redemption lists do indeed provide only the names of those slaves who were actually ransomed. Such men and women no doubt were the most readily identifiable among slaves – those in particular who had been requested (and partially paid for) by their families or home towns; not surprisingly, their time in slavery was often destined to be fairly short. Those many slaves who died in their first year of captivity, on the other hand, like those thousands who fell into the admittedly very wide cracks of the redemption effort – sold into the sultan's Imperial Fleet, for example, or traded to new masters in the Levant – not sur-prisingly fail to appear on any redemption list, quite simply because they never were ransomed, or at least not until decades later.[92] The identification, tracking down, and eventual ransoming of slaves certainly improved over the course of the eighteenth century, even as the Muslim slave owners themselves, becoming increasingly interested in investing in human chattel for the sake of ransom rather than labor, sought to encourage the redemptive orders in their efforts. Until that time, however, it seems to have been far more likely that slaves in Barbary would perish before they could be freed – which is just what some 3,000 "poor seamen captive in Algiers" reminded the British government, in a petition they sent to Parliament in 1640.[93]

At best, it seems that ransoming efforts and escapes taken together would not have added more than another 3–4 percent to the 17 percent attrition rate caused by the death of slaves in Barbary. On top of this, however, must also (and finally) be added those slaves who reduced the captive population because they had renounced their Christianity and embraced Islam. The numbers of these so-called renegades were considerable: Dan estimated that there were 9,500 in Algiers alone (about an eighth of the free population), and a total of around 14,000 in all of Barbary – something on the order of two-fifths of the number of slaves he calculated there in the 1630s.[94] It was a truism among virtually all those who wrote of European captivity in Barbary that many slaves were forced to convert, if not by the direct demand of their masters, then by their inability to withstand the harshness of their treatment or the despair of their situation. As the 3,000 British seamen who petitioned Parliament from Algiers in 1640 put it:

> withal suffering much hunger, with many blows on our bare bodies with which their cruelty many (not being able to undergo) have been forced to turn to their Mahomotest sect and devilish paganism.[95]

Such was often the excuse offered by many a slave who had renounced his religion and then, one way or another, managed to get out of Barbary. It should be noted, however, that most of those who converted remained slaves, at least for a time after their conversion: "freed from the Oar, tho' not from his Patron's Service," as Morgan put it, since a renegade generally escaped only such truly onerous slave tasks as rowing in the galleys or working at heavy construction.[96] Of course, it was precisely for this sort of work that replacements had to be found, if the slave societies in Barbary were to keep going, since every slave that converted to Islam was one less available to drive the ships that brought in new captives.

The extent to which these renegades might have reduced the captive population in Barbary is not easily calculated, however, given that some (probably significant) percentage of these apostates had never been slaves at all, but had come to Barbary voluntarily, looking for a new life and taking up a new religion along the way. The history of the Maghreb is full of such characters, sometimes whole shiploads of them coming to North Africa together to seek their fortunes. They were disaffected soldiers or sailors, peasants oppressed by feudal lords, or perhaps merchants looking for advantage.[97] Even so, the majority of renegades had probably started out as slaves at some point, especially in the sixteenth and early seventeenth centuries, before enough missionaries were on hand to dissuade mass abjurings that could sweep through newly captured groups such as soldiers (the Spanish were especially known for this) or peasants taken in land raids.[98] Even after the missionaries had shown up in force, the trend continued: between 1609 and 1619, for example, of 8,000 slaves taken by the Algerians, 1,925 adults and around 300 children, or about 28 percent, had "turned Turk;" Dan reported that 149 (16 percent) of the 986 French captives brought to Algiers between 1628 and 1634 went renegade; in 1687, the apostolic vicar Michel Montmasson claimed that, of the 10,000 slaves then in Algiers, 14 percent had "made themselves muslims in despair."[99]

Despite the alarmist claims from gloomy clerics like Father Alfonso Dominici that fully half the Christian slaves were converting, it is unlikely that apostasy caused anything like that sort of attrition among the slave populations in Barbary.[100] The Muslim masters themselves were usually opposed to opportunistic conversions: for certain categories of slaves, it is true, owners might be quite willing – even insistent – to allow a conversion, but they were well aware that this greatly reduced a slave's resale value.[101] Moreover, the missionaries did apparently dissuade many from abjuring, and by the later 1600s they evidently kept the overall move to Islam – after the first rush of conversions among newly captured slaves – down to a fairly low, if steady erosion of the captive population. This may have been a loss lamented by the mission fathers as "a knife in the heart," but it is still doubtful that such abjurings depleted slave ranks by much more than 1,000 each year – at most perhaps 4 percent for all of Barbary.[102] In terms of percentages, this would fit fairly well with the claim of the Portuguese Friar Jaono dos Sanctos, that annually in Algiers in the 1620s, "above nine hundred become Mahumetan apostates besides about fifty boys yearly circumcised against their wills."[103] Something like 1,000 new apostates for all of Barbary during the century 1580–1680 would in any case have been necessary to keep renegade populations constantly replenished, replacing those who died every year.[104]

Putting all these forms of slave decline together yields a combined attrition rate of 24–25 percent: that portion of the slave population in Barbary that would have had to be replaced each year if levels were to remain as stable as they apparently were, between 1580 and 1680. Such a rate, given the average captive population of around 35,000 during these years, would translate into roughly 8,500 new slaves needed annually – a figure that, over the course of the century, falls a little short of Dan's "million slaves they have put in chains," but not by much. Indeed, if we consider the entire 250 years over which corsair slaving was a significant factor in the Mediterranean, the total number of slaves soon exceeds a million. Thus, for the following century, 1680–1780, assuming that attrition rates remained about the same even as slave populations in Barbary shrank to about a fifth of their former size, corsairs would have needed to take another 175,000 captives to maintain the dwindling Christian slave presence in the regencies.[105] For the sixteenth century the situation is more complex, since both Tunis and Tripoli were under European control for much of the fifty years before 1580. Still, the Algerian corsairs appear to have amply made up for the absence of their brethren. From 1530, when Kheir-ed-din Barbarossa solidified his power there, until the culminating decade of 1560–70, which Braudel termed "the first brilliant age of Algiers," the city's *ra'is* plundered the coasts of Italy and Spain almost unopposed, repeatedly filling their galleys almost to the foundering point with Christian captives.[106] Diego de Haëdo estimated that there were 25,000 slaves in Algiers in 1579, and, considering how many slaves were pouring into the city in the decades before that, such a figure is very likely a valid minimum for much of the half-century 1530–80. Assuming that the attrition rate among slaves in the sixteenth century was no lower than in the seventeenth (deaths by plague may have been less, but in recompense there were a number of large-scale abjurations among captive Christians) the Algerian *ra'is* probably brought in as many as 300,000 European slaves in these fifty years.[107]

The result, then, is that between 1530 and 1780 there were almost certainly a million and quite possibly as many as a million and a quarter white, European Christians enslaved by the Muslims of the Barbary Coast. Such an estimate is only as good as the figures on which it is based, of course, and it could never be claimed that those collected and examined here would measure up to the much more formidable shipping tallies available for calculating the volume of the Atlantic slave trade. But setting a number – or in any case a range – on the Barbary Coast trade at least makes it possible to put this particular arena of slaving activity into the more general historiographical debate on the nature and extent of slave trafficking, a debate that, as Paul Lovejoy has commented, is "far from a quibble over numbers."[108]

In fact, even a tentative slave count in Barbary inevitably begs a host of new questions. To begin with, the estimates arrived at here make it clear that for most of the first two centuries of the modern era, nearly as many Europeans were taken forcibly to Barbary and worked or sold as slaves as were West Africans hauled off to labor on plantations in the Americas. In the sixteenth century especially, during which time the Atlantic slave runners still averaged only around 3,200 Africans annually, the corsairs of Algiers – and later Tunis and Tripoli – were regularly snatching that many or more white captives on a single raiding voyage to Sicily, the Balearics, or Valencia.[109] Hardest hit in these escalating raids were the sailors, merchants, and coastal villagers of Italy and Greece and of Mediterranean Spain and France. Testimony abounds of the near-paralysis of commercial shipping and the desolation of many coastal lands, which was so severe in some areas that the corsairs themselves scarcely bothered to raid there:

> Everyone ... could see with their own eyes the desolation of the Spanish, French, and Italian coasts, thanks to the pertinacious infestation of these pirates: the wretched beaches, the abandoned islands, the shacks [reduced to] ashes, the fishermen in flight, and the vessels of the Barbarian rovers loitering about on the sea.[110]

Since these attacks were for the most part limited to merchant shipping and the fairly narrow coastal zones of states that were, comparatively speaking, both wealthy and populous, the economic and social damage they caused might strike some as having been little more than visual and fleeting. Certainly their cumulative devastation fell far short of that produced by the slaving wars that were even then beginning to ravage the interior of West Africa; nor did they provoke anything like the net population decline that would later afflict the African states.[111] When the political will existed, the Spanish and French monarchies, as well as many of the smaller Italian states, could afford to give their citizens at least some protection and bring back some of them from slavery. Clearly those African kingdoms caught up in the Atlantic slave trade had no analogous opportunities to send ransoming parties –

much less punitive expeditions – to the Americas in order to free their people.[112] Yet just what such continual efforts cost the Europeans – in terms of personal wealth, but also in such public expenditures as charitable spending, coastal fortifications, and naval squadrons – is still surprisingly unclear. Even for the most robust economies of the era, such regular outlays and losses could not have been lightly borne: Pierre Dan estimated that between 1605 and 1634 the Algerians took over 600 ships, worth "more than twenty million [livres];" the 80 French merchant ships they captured between 1628 and 1635 were valued at 4,752,000 livres; likewise, ransoming 1,006 slaves from Algiers in 1768 cost the French Trinitarians 3,500,000 livres.[113] What paying out such sums over the course of several centuries meant to the states involved – in terms of lost investment capital, frustrated development projects, or abandoned human settlements – has yet to be fully explored.[114]

On the African side of the Mediterranean the slave trade also left profound traces, even if not as marked as that produced by the Atlantic slave trade in the Americas and primarily in racial and cultural terms. Even though the breeding activities of male slaves were tightly, even ferociously controlled, the many female European captives who were taken sexually by their masters and the thousands of immigrant renegades all brought a great deal of European blood into local gene pools. Moreover, others of European origin long enjoyed prominence in these outlaw societies, especially in Algiers. The 20,000 or more janissaries who formed the core of Turkish power in that city were by definition all born of Balkan parents; their bastard children from slave or Moorish women – the *couloglis* – were so numerous as to constitute their own social caste in many of the regencies. There was also an elite and highly influential stratum of renegades throughout the century between 1580 to 1680, again particularly in Algiers. Lists of the corsairing *ra'is* from this period make it clear that more than half of these pirate captains were of European origin, men who came to hold considerable economic sway in cities that were dependent on piracy for their well-being.[115] Their wealth and power made many of them dominant figures in the local culture; the slipshod (though often ferocious) Islam they practiced and the bastardized *lingua franca* they spoke to their fellow citizens had an enduring impact on the unique creole communities that developed and flourished for several centuries in the Maghreb.

By the late 1700s visitors were noting how "the inhabitants of Algiers have a rather white complexion," an observation that more recent scholars have confirmed.[116] Once an almost equal amalgam of

European slaves, janissaries, renegades, Moors, Berbers, and Jews, Algiers might indeed be offered as the region's best example of a creole society in the 1600s and 1700s. Yet after flourishing for centuries, this complex dynamic eventually failed, submerged by the advent of colonialism and then independence, evaporating before the steady inflow of surrounding, indigenous cultures and peoples arriving from the hinterland.[117]

Three centuries of a slave culture thus appear to have left only faint traces on the Barbary ports. Today, what remains of their mixed-race societies is an amalgam of Moorish, Berber, and sub-Saharan peoples, but little recalls the many thousands of Europeans – Latins, Germans, English, Flemish, Irish, Greeks, Albanians, and Slavs – who spent decades and often ended their lives in these towns. There is nothing like the tangible genetic presence of black Africans in the Americas, nor the cultural and racial heritage of the Chinese who were once brought to the American west coast as contract laborers, nor of Indians who spread throughout the British Empire. Nor have these slaves left behind much in the way of physical remnants: except in Morocco, one searches in vain for the markets where these slaves were once sold and for the prisons in which they were incarcerated. Indeed, what scant cultural contribution European slaves might have made to these societies was obliterated, first by a century of (predominantly French) colonial presence, then by nearly fifty years of self-rule throughout the Maghreb. All that remains are the products of slave labor: the palaces, fortifications, streets, and harbor works they built, "vilely compelled to drag wagons, carry most immense cannon, very heavy stones, and other similar burdens under which some, for the great effort, often died."[118] Yet even these monuments to Barbary's special world of opulence and cruelty have for the most part been torn down or buried by more recent expansions and improvements. The Other Slavery, in other words, has also become the invisible slavery: an institution that, having survived for over three centuries to a greater or lesser degree, has now vanished, almost without a trace.

2
Slave Taking and Slave Breaking

> 11th March 1683: The Mayorkeen [Majorcan] Renegado that went to Sea ... the 24th of January being off the West end of Candy [Crete] mett with the *Three Kings of Marseilles* homeward bound from Scanderoon [Iskanderun] mounted with Twelve Guns and manned with 46 men Passengers included, kept her company two dayes and at night, Laid her aboard and entred her ... and without any further resistance carryed her (For the Captain wth all his company (three excepted) manfully defended themselves in the hold as deep as they could creep) and this afternoone conducted her into this Port. It proves y[e] richest Prize that was ever brought into this Place by a single ship, being really worth Dollers 120,000.[1]

In the journal he kept between 1679 and 1685, during his term as English consul in Tripoli, Thomas Baker noted the principal ship traffic in and out of the city. This included the usual run of merchant shipping from the European states, come to trade with special passport and license from the Tripolitan pasha; he also recorded at least some of the various local vessels, departing and returning from this middling-sized Libyan port.[2] It was no secret that most of these latter were setting off "in corso," their corsair crews, as Baker bluntly put it, "going out a theeving" – hunting the seas and coastlines between Tripoli, Ionian Italy, and the Greek Islands for any Christian prize too small or ill-defended to protect itself. Opportunists on the lookout for all sorts of portable and saleable loot, the Libyans, like all the Barbary corsairs, were especially dedicated to the business of what contemporary observers called "man taking," or "Christian stealing," so much so, that Baker once tartly remarked that "To steale Christians ... [is] their Lawfull Vocation."[3]

In Baker's time, slave taking in the Mediterranean was indeed something of a "Lawfull Vocation." Throughout the previous century, it had been pursued on a massive scale by both Christians and Muslims – a central feature of the long, imperial struggle between the Hapsburgs and Ottomans, for whom the taking of slave prisoners on the battlefield was the traditional bounty due to the victors in their armed, interfaith conflicts. Clashes on land or at sea between the Turks and their allies or surrogates and the Christian forces of Spain, Italy, and Portugal regularly brought thousands of captives to the slave markets of Fez, Algiers, Constantinople, Malta, Livorno, Lisbon, and Marseilles. On the Turkish side, enslaving Christians had been elevated to something approaching state policy, especially between the 1530s and 1570s, when first Kheir-ed-din Barbarossa and then Dragut Re'is were appointed by the sultan in Constantinople as both his principal viceroys in Barbary and admirals of his fleet. Virtually every year for four decades, these pirate princes led enormous flotillas against European shipping and the coastal lands of Spain, Tyrrhenian Italy, and the major Mediterranean islands, bent on crushing Christian resistance to the western expansion of the Turks. At times, the combined forces of corsairs and Turks totaled 10,000 or more soldiers and janissaries in over 100 galleys, and the sheer size of the fleets they commanded meant they could attack at will throughout the western Mediterranean, blockading such major ports as Genoa and Naples with impunity, threatening Rome, and sacking dozens of middle-sized coastal cities in Spain and Italy. Although both Barbarossa and Dragut spent much of their time at sea in military campaigns against Christian naval and land forces, they were never averse to snapping up enemy merchant ships or ravaging poorly defended coastal areas in an endless pursuit of plunder and, in particular, of slaves.[4]

As the Hapsburg–Ottoman conflict wound down in the years following Lepanto, and the Turks began to restrict their war fleet's activities largely to the Levant, the pashas who ruled in Algiers and Tunis as the sultan's viceroys continued to raid Christian shipping and settlements throughout the western Mediterranean, in the name of the Ottoman Empire and at the head of their own cities' fleets. Like Barbarossa and Dragut, even if on a necessarily smaller scale, these minor marauders also carried out grand slaving sweeps along the coasts of Spain and Italy. Hassan Pasha's summer campaign of 1582 was perhaps typical of these almost annual raids. Hassan, a renegade also called "the Venetian," pasha of Algiers, and commander of 22 galleys and galleots with at least 1,500 janissaries and soldiers, seems to have envied the recent successes of one of his best corsairs, Morat Re'is, who had recently returned with 500 captives seized from the Spanish coast near Alicante. To demonstrate his own prowess as a slave raider, Hassan Pasha directed his fleet first towards Sardinia, where his men penetrated 40 miles inland and carried off 700 villagers. Buoyed up by such a good beginning, Hassan's company then raided in a long arc across the north-western Mediterranean, beginning with the Corsican town of Monticello (400 slaves); proceeding to Sori, on the Genoese coast (130 slaves); and finally taking the village of Pineda, not far from Barcelona (50 slaves). Quite likely, Hassan would have continued his "Christian stealing" down the Spanish coast, except that he had already signed a profitable contract to ship some 2,000 Moriscos from Spain to a new life in Barbary. As a result, the Algerians cut their expedition short, and with their galleys packed with over 3,300 passengers and slaves, headed back to Algiers, pausing only to snap up an occasional merchant ship along the way.[5]

By the first decades of the seventeenth century, such state-directed slaving expeditions had become less frequent: as far as the sultan's viceroys in Barbary were concerned, it may have seemed more comfortable to remain in Algiers or Tunis and enjoy the eighth share of the prizes and slaves brought in by their *re'is*, as one of their rights of office. Less a state enterprise, corsair slaving transformed itself yet again while continuing on a smaller scale, as the fleets shrank in size, from a dozen or more down to just a few galleys at a time. Yet by all accounts the impact of these freebooters on Christian shipping and settlements may not have declined all that much, if only because a new generation of *re'is* began going out more often than before – sometimes "three or four Voyages in a Year" – and adopting new tactics and technologies to make their single ships or small squadrons more effective in dealing with the slowly improving Christian defenses.[6]

Operating under very little control but with the tacit protection of their local pashas – and, at another remove, with the benign and neglectful tolerance of the sultans in Constantinople – the Barbary corsairs carried on their looting and slaving as a peculiar and especially virulent form of corporate private enterprise. Fernand Braudel may indeed have been somewhat precipitous in ending what he termed "the second brilliant age of Algiers" in 1620, since that city's piratical activities flourished at least into the 1660s. Writing almost a century later, the British historian of Algiers Joseph Morgan singled out the year 1641 as the peak of the city's activities: "This," he observed, "I take to be the Time when those Corsairs were in their *Zenith*."

Morgan's insight now seems perceptive, one that looked beyond the decline of Turkish power and large-scale Ottoman-sponsored piracy to recognize the enduring significance of this combination of private initiative and state oversight during much of the 1600s.[7]

Their mixing of slave taking and more general brigandage distinguished the Barbary corsairs from the Portuguese, Spanish, English, and Dutch slavers who were developing the Atlantic slave traffic from sub-Saharan Africa to the Americas at about the same time. The Atlantic slavers specialized in running and selling slaves, but rarely involved themselves in other sorts of commerce (except as subsidiary to their slave dealing) or in the messy and potentially dangerous work of capturing their own stock to ship on the Middle Passage. That grim business was left to the warring African states eager to sell black captives taken in battles or raids to a succession of African or Arab middlemen. The white slavers were content to pay for these fresh captives from the interior in cash or kind to be brought to the coastal barracoons, to await collection.[8] In this sense, the Atlantic slave running was true trade. European slavers initiated exchange at both ends of what would become known as the Middle Passage, meeting the market requirements for labor in plantations located far across the Atlantic by projecting demand deep into the African interior. Operating as the independent link between these two poles of trade, they themselves were free to concentrate on and develop the transit traffic itself: this they did with a chilling, almost industrial efficiency that would eventually make possible the transshipment of millions of captives from one continent to another, while also developing new sources of slaves ever further inland.[9]

The Barbary corsairs, by contrast, never achieved or apparently even aimed at such diversified linkages of supply or distribution. Instead, they took on the entire process of slaving themselves, from capturing to shipping and selling. Not quite trade, this corsair *Christian stealing* was more fundamentally extractive by nature, a kind of Islamic gold rush aimed at the poorly defended shores and shipping of the Christian world, its targets provided first by the peculiar climate of imperial conflict and *jihad* that predominated in the Mediterranean basin throughout the sixteenth century, and then by the much more open-ended imperatives of individual free enterprise (or free booting) on into the seventeenth.[10] Never really requiring a complex organization to accomplish its ends, Barbary slaving, compared to the Atlantic trade, remained at heart a pre-modern enterprise, not much more elaborate in structure than the simple *commenda* that had typified

Mediterranean maritime commerce in the Middle Ages. Unlike the medieval *commenda*, however, where just two or three partners might buy shares in a voyage, with one – the captain – often contributing his navigational expertise in lieu of start-up capital, arrangements in Barbary were much more diffused and, in a sense, more democratic. Since they sailed with the intention of plunder, corsairs had no need to find any initial capital to buy trade goods for their voyages. Instead, those *re'is* who wished to go out *al corso* had only to round up enough investors, or *armadores* (*taifa*, in Turkish), to outfit their ships, fill them with provisions, and provide sufficient galley slaves. When trade was good in the Mediterranean and prizes were known to be plentiful, it was never hard to attract a crew: there were plenty of men willing to sign on without any wages at all. Instead, crews enrolled for a fixed share of any loot: "upon the precarious Foundation," as Morgan put it, "of *No Purchase, No Pay.*"[11]

These were, then, enterprises of pure speculation, where everyone – from the *armadores* to the *re'is*, the soldiers, their officers, the crew, and even the galley slaves themselves (if they could indeed be said to have signed on) – was allotted a set number of shares, appropriate to his rank or (in the case of the *armadores*) proportionate to the amount he had put up, of any prizes that might be taken. The polity of Algiers itself, in the person of the pasha, received an eighth of the take, as well as "the naked Shells" – the stripped, captured vessels. The remainder was split equally between those who owned the ship, which effectively meant the *armadores*, and those who sailed it, with the *re'is* counted as one of the *armadores*. Of the crews' portion, three shares each went to the captain (*aga*) and first lieutenant (*bash-sota-re'is*) of the soldiers, the clerk, chief gunner, and steward; two shares went to the under-lieutenants, gunners and helmsmen; one share went to the soldiers. The slaves themselves might receive between $1\frac{1}{2}$ and three shares between them, though their masters usually took a share of this allotment – de la Motte said a third – as "compensation" for their wear-and-tear.[12]

A successful voyage that brought back ships, goods, and slaves could make all parties wealthy, perhaps fabulously so – even the slaves might make enough to buy their freedom, assuming their master (who was often the *re'is* himself) had left them anything. Ambitious young corsairs, from the poorest of backgrounds, could start by investing nothing more than their own labor or buying just a small share of a galley, and work their way up to eventual fame and riches: such was the story, most famously, of Dragut Re'is himself, but also of many other great corsairing captains.[13] But the system of underwriting this corsairing activity was necessarily precarious, for it offered little if any financial protection for an undertaking whose possible returns were matched only by the risks involved. As Morgan put it: "this Cruising-Trade of theirs [is] a perfect *Lottery* ... and has brought as many to Beggary and Ruin, as it has others to immense Opulency." Many investors – "Merchants and Shop-Keepers who never used the Sea in their whole Lives, but ventured Part of their Substance in that *Lottery*" – ended up like William Okeley's master, who had tried to make himself a modest living by investing in the *corso* but eventually went bankrupt when "the last Ship he had put to Sea broke his back."[14]

The difficulty was that, even though the Mediterranean was wealthy and well populated with people for the stealing, independent corsairing typical of the seventeenth century demanded a great deal of skill and luck.[15] Baker's journal offers figures on the Tripolitan corsairs that amply bear out the possibilities and the risks involved: whereas five of the 120 ships he counted as returning from the *corso* between 1679 and 1685 brought in fabulous prizes worth $100,000 or more with dozens of slaves apiece, another 19, or around 16 percent, came back "without a rag of purchase," even though some of them had been at sea for upwards of six months. Baker himself took special note of one Mustafa Caddi, a *re'is* who seems to have been especially unlucky when it came to prizes:

> having already made Twelve Voyages as a man of War, this day [he] adventured on a thirteenth, and doubtless to ye same good end, never as yet having to value himselfe on ye Least Prize taken by him, I would to God Algier afforded noe better Sailors nor Souldiers![16]

If one wished to explain the ferocity and tenacity with which the Barbary corsairs so famously pursued their Christian victims, it is well worthwhile to start here, with the financial situation in which so many found themselves. Not only were many of them perpetually on the brink of ruin, but all were fully aware of the fabulous wealth that their more fortunate brethren had won. To many of the *re'is*, every risk and effort might have seemed both possible and worthwhile, if that was the way to build the reputation as a pirate and slaver necessary to attract the capital to outfit their ship. The crew and soldiers aboard these galleys, many of whom were janissaries enjoying regular pay from Istanbul, were far less exposed to the vagaries of the corsairing trade than their entrepreneurial captain, who, regardless of his successes or failures at sea, was still "obliged to find [his crew] the same Portion of

Biscuit, or rather Rusk, Vinegar and Oil, as he does the Rowers and other Slaves." He also had to procure galley slaves. This may have come easily enough for those few *re'is* who operated on a grand scale, with their own stable of captives, but not for those who had to hire each oarsman from a slave dealer, at the rate, in Morgan's time, of "twelve Gold Ducats *per* Voyage, Prize or no Prize." Those who had no ready cash up front for their rowers were obliged to borrow, often from professional moneylenders and at ruinous rates of interest, if they were ever to get their ships to sea at all.[17]

Once at sea, the *re'is* sought their slaves in two principal arenas. In addition to those relatively few unlucky European travelers who fell into Muslim hands when their vessels were wrecked on the North African coast, the great majority of Christians taken into slavery in Barbary were either seized when corsairs captured the ship on which they were traveling or were snatched during slaving raids, mostly on the Mediterranean islands or the coasts of Spain, Italy, or Greece.[18] Comparatively speaking, it would seem that more slaves were taken from ships than from the land, but it is difficult to calculate how many more. One can at least make a rough inference about which form of slave taking was more frequent from such sources as Baker's journal, which noted 30 occasions in seven years when slaves were brought to Tripoli together with the ships on which they had been captured, as compared to six occasions when Christians had been taken in coastal raids. Gramaye recorded a very similar ratio for the six months that he was in Algiers in 1619: five corsairs brought in loads of slaves they had taken in land attacks, compared to 25 who had picked up their captives from prizes taken at sea.

Such evidence, scanty as it is, may be a sign that most Barbary corsairs preferred to try their luck at sea, even against fairly large and sometimes well-armed merchant ships, instead of bringing their galleys to shore and disembarking their men, with all the risks that this might expose them to from counterattacks by both land and sea. On the other hand, when it came to slaving as opposed to the piracy of goods, coastal raids tended to produce much bigger hauls than attacks on shipping. Thus it turns out that such raids could pay off out of all proportion to their frequency: the five land raids that Gramaye recorded were responsible for upwards of two-thirds of all the slaves he counted coming into Algiers during his six months there; less relatively productive, those six raids noted by Baker still bagged a significant percentage of the total captives delivered to Tripoli, especially considering that over half the ships brought back as prizes had no slaves aboard them at all – their crews usually having abandoned their vessel at the last moment to avoid capture.[19]

Though less frequent, these land raids may thus have accounted for the majority of slaves taken to Barbary, especially during the century or so prior to 1640, when the coasts of Spain and Italy were still relatively populated and coastal defenses fairly weak. Despite this importance as a means of procuring new slaves, much less is known about the entire process of coastal raiding than about sea-going slaving. Much of this has to do with sources. Barbary coast slave scholarship, much more than that of African-American slavery, has always relied heavily on narratives written by the slaves themselves, especially in light of the gaps that exist in such documentation as shipping records or the accounts of local observers.[20] Such accounts have the drawback, however, of almost invariably coming from captives taken at sea, most of them of noble, clerical, administrative, or at the very least, military backgrounds, able to reflect on their experience in slavery and write about it. There also survive a few accounts of enslavement written by professional sailors, providing something of the point-of-view of these workers. What is totally lacking, however, are descriptive narratives from the sorts of men and women who were typically taken in coastal raids: peasants, fishermen, or rural laborers, or others who made their living near the sea.[21] It is indeed fortunate that the voices of this largely illiterate class of captives come through at all, in the form of letters home they managed to have written on their behalf.

What little can be gleaned about the raids – from a scattering of chronicles, government reports, and some firsthand accounts by slaves who took part in such attacks – can still throw light on the distinguishing characteristics of these Barbary slavers. Although their Christian counterparts only rarely mounted slaving raids on the Muslim territories of North Africa, for the Barbary corsairs this was a well-established means of slave taking from at least the early sixteenth century.[22] Between the 1530s and 1570s, in conducting their massive raids on Christian lands, the great corsairing viceroys Barbarossa and Dragut developed the techniques that were appropriate for the overwhelming military force at their disposal. They knew how to capitalize on the mobility offered them by the sea, such that, by rapidly shifting their fleets, they could appear seemingly out of nowhere, along thousands of miles of coastline, and disembark enough men and weaponry to smash through all but the stoutest defenses of a local garrison. If the territory looked rich, they might choose a protected spot to set themselves up and simply move in. For several weeks they could so dominate the surrounding lands that "by imagination they Reigned Kings," free to run their galleys up on land and "*make Tent* ... that is, draw Sails over their Heads to shade themselves," setting out to slaughter stray cattle, cut firewood, and begin "dressing pillow [i.e., pilaf, or couscous], a chief dish and pleasing to their pallats."[23] Barbarossa and Dragut knew that local defenses – usually neighborhood militias poorly supported by a handful of cavalry – would not put up much of a fight against several thousand heavily armed corsairs. In any case, at least during these first decades of the struggle, all serious Christian forces in Italy were far away in the capital or provincial centers, comfortable in their barracks or arsenal. Held under the timid and often corrupt control of court-appointed commanders, who preferred to pass the time "Trumpeting, Gaming and Banqueting in the Ports of *Christendom*," they were typically slow to move out of their barracks and pursue a foe that was both frustratingly elusive and exceptionally ruthless.[24]

Unable to cope with the corsair onslaughts, which could return to the same stretch of coast almost annually, local authorities might simply order the general evacuation of threatened areas. Such was especially the case in Italy, where fragmented power and a distant, vice-regal rule over much of the peninsula left many areas with no other defense. This was the decision taken by the provincial governor in July and August 1566, when an army of 6,000 Turks and corsairs sailed up the Adriatic and disembarked at Francavilla. In one way, the move was a success: thanks to the order, probably thousands of Italians escaped enslavement. The cost, however, was high. The corsairs found themselves in possession of an immense stretch of coast, which they had gained without encountering the slightest resistance. Unimpeded, the Turks had all the time they needed to work their way inland and south as far as Serracapriola, over 60 miles down the coast, enjoying their pick of the loot from over 500 square miles of abandoned towns and villages.[25]

Indeed, the very success of these large-scale raids typically came to mean that sooner or later, when the corsairs returned to pillage again, they would find long stretches of coastland abandoned and virtually uninhabited. Already by the 1580s, Haëdo could assert, "Thus it is, as you know, that they have ravaged and ruined Sardinia, Corsica, Sicily, Calabria, the coasts of Naples, Rome and Genoa, the Balearics, and all the coasts of Spain."[26] After suffering the initial attacks that carried off so many inhabitants, many coastal villages apparently never recovered at all but entered a long period of demographic decline, continuing to lose population even during the lulls between raids. With her studies

of selected towns and settlements along the coasts of the Kingdom of
Naples, Mirella Mafrici has given some substance to claims made by
contemporary observers of the extensive depopulation brought about
by these slaving raids. Towns like San Lucido, in western Calabria, and
Vieste and Manfredonia, on the Gargano, all suffered a demographic
collapse of between 40 and 80 percent, with the declines in every case
beginning with a corsair raid.[27] Although Mafrici's findings cannot
explain the villagers' motives for abandoning their homeland, one can
well imagine how little appeal there must have been in continuing to
eke out a life that had always been impoverished but was becoming
increasingly dangerous as well – especially with the booming baroque
capitals of Rome, Naples, or Palermo acting as powerful magnets for
poor emigrants from the hinterland.

The negative demographic impact of these raids may have been
enhanced by the comparatively large number of local women the corsairs took. Overall, relatively few Christian females ended up enslaved
in Barbary – some estimates place their proportion as low as 5 percent
among the generality of European slaves there.[28] Such female slaves as
there were, though, were almost all taken in land raids, partly since
women made up only a minuscule proportion of the passengers or
crews captured on merchant ships, and partly because, according to
some calculations, around three-eighths of all those captured on land
were female.[29] Women in the harems and households of Barbary
appear to have been about eight to ten times more likely to have come
from coastal villages than from captured shipping. It is not clear
whether the corsairs actively sought them out in response to the
market demand in Barbary for harem or domestic slaves, or whether
women – as a rule slower than men and often burdened with their children – were simply easier to catch. One can, at least, posit that when
the raiders carried off a large percentage of the females of reproductive
age, it became especially hard for communities that were already in
demographic crisis to recover from their progressive decline in population.

When coastal residents fled their village homes, they tended to make
for a nearby provincial center along the coast, if they did not head for
the capital itself. Unfortunately, their presence in such towns, even
when they were fairly well defended, could make the place too attractive for the corsairs to pass up. More than one middle-sized town,
swollen with refugees, was unable to withstand a frontal assault by
several hundred corsairs, and the *re'is*, who might otherwise have had
to seek slaves a few dozen at a time along the beaches and up into the

hills, could find a thousand or more captives all conveniently gathered in one place for the taking.[30] The townspeople themselves, knowing that a great influx of fleeing villagers meant that they, along with their greater wealth, would very likely be the corsairs' next target, often fell into a complete panic that could only have made their predators' job easier. In 1623, the mere rumor that raiders had landed at Sperlonga supposedly had residents of the much larger and "well-armed" Gaeta, 10 miles away, "fleeing for the hills as fast as they could," pausing only to hide what they could of value:

> They buried in the dung heaps here and there
> Their jewels, riches, gold and silver;
> Only to convince the Turks that they had left nothing
> They even threw their own beds into the wells.[31]

By the mid-seventeenth century, however, as raiding parties diminished in size and coastal defenses stiffened, attacks on population centers such as Gaeta, Manfredonia, and Vieste in Calabria became rarer. Likewise, the *re'is* began to find that frontal assaults on coastal territories and deep sorties inland were too risky with only a few hundred men, and they generally abandoned such tactics in favor of less ambitious raids using more devious methods. When middle-sized towns took to building protective walls and towers, the corsairs began to focus on weaker prey: isolated dwellings, monasteries, or sometimes even single individuals.[32] With many areas in Italy and Spain increasingly protected by naval patrols and cavalry units that could be mobilized in just a few hours, fewer of the *re'is* "landed boldly", or ran their galleys on the beach "at mid-day or according to their whim" so their men could disembark to collect fuel and water and pillage the surrounding countryside at their leisure.[33] Instead, corsairs took to keeping their main galleys and galleots just over the horizon or behind a convenient off-shore island, allowing them to assess potential targets in advance.[34] They might send in one or more fishing boats, previously captured with just this sort of eventuality in mind, to cruise close to the village they intended to attack. They might also disguise the rigging, markers, and banners of their own galleys to make them look like Christian vessels – easy enough to do, if the ships had been taken as prizes in the first place; to make sure that none of the slave oarsmen spoke out and gave the game away, all the rowers were gagged with "a morsel of cork that they carry for this purpose, hung about their necks like a reliquary sack."[35]

When these corsairs came ashore, it was usually in the early hours of the morning, their own galleys and smaller boats often interspersed with the returning fishing fleet. If the raiders were particularly interested in slave taking, they aimed at getting as close to their victims as possible before anyone could raise the alarm. To do so, they would "remove the ropes from the [church] bells, so they could not be sounded," and did their best not to be spotted by guards in the local watchtower, hundreds of which had been built along the coasts of Christian states during the hottest period of the Hapsburg–Ottoman conflict.[36] There were well over 500 towers guarding the southern half of Italy and the major Italian islands: on Sicily alone there were 137, an average of one every 5–6 miles. Although many were equipped with cannon, no state had the resources to protect all its beaches with direct fire. The primary purpose of the structures was instead for signaling, to "make lightes at the topp of theire tours," as Thomas Dallam reported on Sicily in 1600, "to shew unto other watche toures how many ships they saw that weare not their frends." Passing the word rapidly along the coast, it was then theoretically possible to mobilize the only defense that corsairs on shore seemed to have feared – the local cavalry.[37] For this reason the raiders made a point of destroying the towers whenever they could; their efforts, combined with the inevitable neglect that such structures suffered during periodic lulls, meant that the network was often too dilapidated to function well.[38]

To get round what defenses they might face, corsairs relied on inside information, in particular intelligence provided by renegades or galley slaves who had come from the target area. Both Christians and ex-Christians seem to have been willing to provide information about the secret approaches to their native villages in exchange for their freedom, even if it meant effectively condemning their former neighbors and even their own families to slavery. "What is most to be lamented," as Francis Knight observed, "[is] how voluntary Christians are to discover the greatest secrets though to the ruine of their own countries."[39] Recently captured slaves might deliver up their home towns out of fear of being tortured or in response to corsair blandishments offering them their freedom or even – should they convert – a couple of slaves of their own.[40] Others who had already been with the galleys for years offered up their villages as a last hope for gaining their freedom; they might rationalize their treachery by claiming that their relatives had in any case been slow or completely negligent in ransoming them. The *re'is* obviously prized such information, even to the point of completely rethinking their earlier strategy to take advantage of it. When it came to using their treacherous captives to lead the raid, however, they apparently never trusted them enough to let them set off in the dark without chains and a close guard.[41]

Although corsairs came ashore looking for loot of any sort, most of the villages they attacked had little in the way of removable wealth beyond the actual humans who lived there. As a rule, the raiders could expect to receive ten ducats from their *armadores* for every captive they managed to drag on board their ship, and if things went according to plan, they might be able to seize their victims "peaceful and still naked in their beds," unable to either flee or put up a fight.[42]

This experience of the corsairs dropping down on the unwary and spiriting them away certainly left its mark on the victims themselves: it has been neatly preserved in the modern-day Sicilian expression, *pigliato dai turchi*, or "taken by the Turks," to mean caught by surprise, perhaps while muddled by sleep or distracted by worry.[43] But even if the word got out early, and someone began to ring the bells, the resulting panic could also work to the corsairs' advantage. Villagers generally responded to such alarms with a headlong flight inland, stopping neither to dress nor pick up valuables, but instead racing as fast as possible to those grottos, culverts, and hiding places in the nearby hills that only they knew of:

> Blessed was he who could flee his bed,
> That there was no other safety or shelter
> Than to run away leaving all his goods....
> The mother abandoned her own child,
> The husband his wife, the son his father,
> Never asking advice from anyone,
> But, by back roads, indirect and little-known,
> Everyone tried to flee the danger.[44]

If they felt bold enough, the corsairs might well set off in hot pursuit; besides, venturing further inland might also net them some additional inhabitants from the interior, who might be snatched up completely unaware that a raid was in progress. The archives are filled with the unhappy tales of men and women, taken singly or in twos or threes while they were keeping watch over their sheep, pruning vines, harvesting, gleaning, or out looking for nuts.[45] Although they ran a considerable risk of being cut off by cavalry coming along the coast, it was not uncommon for small squads of a few dozen corsairs to penetrate 5 or even 10 miles along local roads or stream valleys; sometimes they managed to sack defenseless villages that were "tens of kilometers" inland.[46] In his short letter of 1678, the rural laborer Carlo de Mellis, from the town of Tursi in Basilicata, told just such a story: how he and many other men and women working on the Jesuit-owned farm at Policoro, several miles from shore, were surprised as they slept, "an hour before daybreak, [when] the Turks came into the said farm."[47]

Beyond grabbing as much loot, human or otherwise, as they could lay their hands on, corsairs might also make a point of laying waste the villages and countryside they came across. Destroying important settlements, besieging and demolishing towers, burning food stores to deny them to the enemy: these were the normal practices of invading armies and very much a central activity of the full-scale naval invasions of the sort that Barbarossa and Dragut carried out on the Italian and Spanish coasts in the mid-sixteenth century. Thus, in 1541, when they took the fortified town of Fondi, 5 miles inland in Lazio, they not only killed over 100 inhabitants, but also destroyed or damaged the castle tower and over 1,000 houses. When they seized the island of Ischia in 1544, "they enslaved almost all those who lived in the country and burned the larger villages, especially Forìo."[48]

Such systematic attacks continued long after their military value had declined or vanished, however. Sometimes the raiders' motives for what they did can be guessed at, sometimes they were ambiguous at best. The corsairs typically hauled off the church bells from the villages they sacked, for example – in part because bronze was valuable and the looting of bells was the prerogative of invading armies everywhere, but perhaps also because, as William Davies suggested, they "abhore the ringing of Bels, being contrary to their Prophets command," and sought to silence them whenever they could.[49] Much less practical, or even symbolic, a purpose can be detected in the behavior of the corsairs observed by Francis Knight, who was himself a galley slave on one such raid:

> The bold Turke landed on the maine [in Calabria], and set fire their houses, burnt fisher boates, passage boates, horses, and travellers provisions, without feare, baryed all the Coasts, killing beeves, and other Cattle, and setting whole fields of corne on fire and committing many other outrages, to the great damage of the country; insomuch, as it was disliked by some Turkes themselves.[50]

Knight ventured no opinion why "some Turkes" found such behavior improper, though it may have been more because it meant wasting time and energy rather than for any humanitarian impulses. Actually, once the alarm had been sounded and the villagers were in panic, such actions could make good sense in another way, for increasing the chaos and confusion by burning buildings, firing guns, and wrecking over as wide an area as possible could only have helped the corsairs set on snatching freshly awakened locals as they blundered through the flames and darkness. Yet it also seems that raiders might use their destructive violence to wreak more symbolic damage, particularly against local churches and Christian shrines – "spitting upon, and otherwise reviling Images, stabbing pictures, or the like." In his epic in *ottava rima*, "Il sacco e rovina di Sperlonga," Curthio Mattei offers a poetic account of the desecration that the corsairs might carry out on a village church:

> And just think of the strange and horrible damage
> Done by these cursed people
> That the altar of the High and Sovereign Lord
> Should be profaned so unjustly
> And ... the outrage done to God, the offense and the damage
> The crucifixes and the images of the saints,
> Of God, of the Madonna and the Holy Sacrament
> Were mocked and pierced through with arrows
> And in a moment thrown to the ground,
> Thrown down were the altars and on the ground
> The images were skewered to the floor with daggers
> The whole place mocked and profaned
> And then, these tyrants, they set it on fire.

Desecrating shrines was a standard feature of the millennial struggle between Christians and Muslims across the Mediterranean, a custom of ritual spoilage that went well beyond stealing any holy artefacts of value. Morgan, among others, deduced that the Barbary raiders were especially prone to these acts of desecration as their expression of rage and frustration when their intended victims had managed to flee, but there are also signs that such destruction was carried out after successful raids as well, possibly as the corsairs' symbolic and public announcement of the invasive superiority of Islam.[51] Mattei claimed that the corsairs even

> Dug up the bones from the tombs
> Of these poor and wretched dead

To burn them and drag them outside the walls
To make to God and to us the gravest of insults
Oh, the judgement of God!
The bones of our dead are not secure underground
That dozens of years after death
They could still be the prey of these impious Tyrants!

Such transgressive rampages, brusquely violating all spiritual norms, could certainly have their practical aim in further enhancing the widely held reputation that the corsairs came straight from Hell and were Satan's personal agents in the tormenting of Christians and Christian society. (To this day, some southern Italians maintain that the prejudice against black cats in their part of the country comes from the old belief that these were corsairs' cats – their familiars, actually – left behind, either accidentally or as spies, when the raiders sailed away.) Very likely local villagers experienced the laying waste of their local church and its shrines as a direct (and successful) attack on what many considered their first line of defense against these devilish predators – religion. In the face of the relative impotence of civic authorities, many had little recourse but to pray to their protective saints and especially to the Virgin, who was often evoked as a defender against both heathen attacks and enslavement, by lay Catholics and by the ransoming fathers who served them.[52] At the same time, these displays could carry clear and specific messages of revenge. Although nominally separated by the breadth of the Mediterranean, the two sides, Muslim and Christian, apparently often knew enough about each other, and the targets they were attacking, that many of these raids looked beyond simple looting to more complex acts of betrayal or revenge, often meted out in a form of rough, ritual justice. Thus did the renegade known as Ochali (whom Morgan praised as one of history's "very few Examples of a Man's making so remarkable a Figure in the World, from Beginnings so very mean and abject") come back to his native village of Licastelli in Calabria, intent both on destroying the property of the provincial nobles who had tormented him in his youth and on rewarding those of his relatives who chose to convert and join him in Algiers. Others might mount a destructive attack to even a score with an especially hated Christian leader who lived or held property in the area, possibly in revenge for his own earlier mistreatment of his Muslim foes.[53]

As the story of Ochali indicates, much of this destruction, religious or otherwise, appears to have been carried out by Christian renegades, in particular those who had come from the target area itself. Morgan dismissively considered this sort of extreme behavior an expression of the "mock Zeal" that these turncoats displayed to convince their fellow Muslims that they were as serious in their hatred of Christians as any born Turk: "Not that," he observed, "the Generality of the *Turks* have one Jot the better Opinion of them on those Scores."[54] Other contemporaries, by contrast, saw something darker in how willingly these turncoats "Pilated the Turke to the place where they were borne, and beene instruments in the captivating of their owne fathers and mothers and all their Lineage, taking their part of the price for which their Parents were sold in the Market." The rage that such renegades vented on their birthplace suggests that rancorous vendetta was on their minds – against the local lord, the clerical and lay establishment, peasant society in general, and perhaps even their own families. Indeed, the peculiar dynamic of symbolic and physical destruction in such raids was often rooted in a community's uneasy relationship with such renegades, coming back home to square accounts for real or imagined wrongs of rejection, abandonment, or persecution.[55]

Even taking time out to pillage, vandalize, and chase locals far into the surrounding hills, the corsairs still did their best to clear the scene, hustle their captives on board the galleys, and row back out to sea as soon as possible – sometimes even before the day had fully begun. "They grabbed young women and children," recalled one Sicilian villager, "they snatched goods and money, and in a flash, back aboard their galleys, they set their course and vanished."[56] After a day or two lurking over the horizon or down the coast, however, the raiders would also customarily return to the area they had just pillaged, hoisting a white flag or some other sign to indicate that those villagers who had escaped might safely come on board to negotiate for the ransom of their captured relatives. Here the essentially extractive nature of Mediterranean slaving reveals itself, for even if these newly captured slaves might go for deeply discounted prices compared to what they could fetch in the slave markets of Algiers or Tunis, the corsairs still found it easier to convert them to cash immediately rather than risk them dying or overloading the galleys on the way back to Barbary. Although some of the *re'is* might indeed proffer their captives "with sincerity and correctness," it is clear that for the most part this ritual offer of resale was designed primarily to give those coming aboard a terrifying glimpse of the certain fate that awaited their enslaved relations if they failed to come up with the ransoms demanded.[57] This was particularly effective when the captives were children or youths, who might be brought before their parents in the custody of a fearsome and leering Moor, to leave no doubt what awaited them in slavery, perhaps even before they arrived in Barbary.[58] Just as frightening for many parents, however, was the spiritual fate of their younger children, who, it was commonly believed, would be forced to abjure their Christianity and convert to Islam.

As a rule, relatives were given 24 hours – or sometimes just until sundown – to come up with the ransom. Even though the corsairs might only demand a quarter or a fifth of what the same slave would later cost to be ransomed out of Barbary, it was still almost impossible for many of these peasants and fishermen to raise such sums at short notice – or indeed any notice, since many of them lived their lives largely without cash, getting by on barter and subsistence. Unable to borrow from their equally cash-poor neighbors, the only possible relief for many – if indeed that is the right term – was to turn to petty specu-lators. These outsiders were often on the scene soon after a raid, willing to advance the necessary 50 or 60 ducats in exchange for the deeds to whatever property – a house, a farm plot, a fishing boat – the victims or their relatives might be able to put forward.[59] Even this might not be easy, considering how difficult it could be for such people to show title in only a few hours, without going to a notary or judge in the nearest provincial center. Once the deal was complete, victims could then find themselves safely back home but very likely restored to families com-pletely impoverished by this brief experience with enslavement, reduced perhaps from a precarious freeholder status to that of impecu-nious and dependent laborers, possibly even toiling on the same prop-erty they had once owned. Such corsair raids thus worked their negative results into the long-term social fabric of the villages they despoiled. Not only did they take away many local men and women permanently, they also rearranged the property relationships within the community, causing long-term damage to the self-sufficient peas-antry that was so important to the economic health of the coasts.[60]

The corsairs' time ashore was not only spent in looting. Since the *re'is* normally provisioned their galleys with just a few days' drinking water, to keep them as light and swift as possible, it was also necessary to refill their casks: otherwise, as occasionally happened, both the slave rowers and their masters risked dying from thirst.[61] Some of their favorite spots have become part of the local toponymy in southern Italy – Acqua dei Corsari, a short way east of Palermo, for example, or the Fosso dei Saraceni, outside Ortona, in the Abruzzi.[62] Eventually, however, the corsairs wound up both their negotiations and their provisioning and set off with whatever slaves they still retained – probably the great majority – who had not been able to come up with the necessary ransom. Taking advantage of their mobility on the sea, the *re'is* could switch their hunting grounds – from Italy to the islands or to Greece – in a matter of a few days or weeks. Unlike those who had taken any fair-sized Christian ship, corsairs who concentrated on coastal settlements did not customarily return directly to port after a successful raid, but might continue at sea for weeks, dangerously overloaded with human cargo, before returning to their home port.[63]

Over the course of the seventeenth century Muslim slaving raids against Christian lands became less frequent, or at least less massive, even if they continued to be a fact of life for much of southern Italy into the early nineteenth century. Corsairs who tried to mount such snatch-and-grab attacks found themselves faced with a stiffening Christian resistance that better coordinated land and sea forces, and overly bold pirates who tried large-scale landings could find themselves trapped between the shore and the sea, blockaded in an unsafe harbor by a quickly responding Christian counterattack – as happened to Mohammed Ali, whose galleys were surrounded and eventually destroyed in the port of Valone (modern-day Vlorë, in Albania) by the Venetians in 1638.[64]

The gradual abandonment of such slave raids made the occasional sorties that were carried off all the more spectacular by contrast. Thus, all of Rome was convulsed in the spring of 1727 by the news that a Tunisian *fusta*, guided by a Neapolitan renegade "skilled and knowledgeable about that place," had successfully attacked the nearby seaside village of San Felice Circeo, in Lazio, carrying off 29 captives, of whom 21 were women or girls. Fourteen years later, the *bey* of Tunis struck the trading island of Tabarca, under the nominal control of Genoa, enslaving all 700 of its residents and setting off an international crisis in the process. In 1798, the Tunisians finished off the century with a raid on the little island of San Pietro, off southern Sardinia, spiriting away upwards of 900 captives. Taking advantage of the disorders of the Napoleonic Wars, they continued their raids on the Italian mainland and the great islands almost annually, snatching no fewer than 150 slaves from the Sardinian island of Sant'Antioco in the year of peace, 1815.[65]

For most corsairs operating after 1700, however, merchant vessels remained the preferred target. The sheer volume of Mediterranean shipping was an irresistible lure to the freebooters, and, as Braudel has observed, the piracy that flourished between Gibraltar and the Levant can be taken as a sign of the region's economic vitality as much as of its political disorder.[66] Merchant ships also usually made much easier prey than land targets, in part simply because it was too difficult to coordinate so much commercial traffic. Ship masters found it difficult or impractical to remain together in convoy and were often unwilling to watch out for each other, with the result that the corsairs were constantly coming across single, ill-protected vessels on the open sea. With the advantage of their oared galleys, the corsairs could pounce on ships that were becalmed in the unpredictable Mediterranean waters; with their swift, lanteen-rigged *fuste* and *xebecs* they could hope to outrun all but the smallest and lightest of merchantmen. As we have seen, many Christian crews (and their masters) preferred to abandon ship rather than risk capture and enslavement, but those who were willing to put up a serious fight could cause the attackers serious problems, sending more than a few corsair galleys back into port empty handed and seriously mauled by their supposed victims.[67]

As a result, the *re'is* did their best to take other ships through trickery whenever possible, using a number of ruses that would allow them to get close enough to attack and board their intended victim before it could either flee or mount a serious defense. Typically, the *re'is* carried on board the flags and banners of every imaginable seafaring power, ready to run aloft whichever one might allow them to get near enough to an unsuspecting prey to take her by surprise. To increase the deception, they also might dress a few of their own renegades in European clothing, "*alla Cristianesca*," and have them call out ambiguous messages or questions that would allow them to get within boarding range.[68] By the eighteenth century, when each of the regencies and the Moroccans had signed treaties of non-interference with at least some of the European powers, the corsairs also became adept in the subtle art of disguising themselves as each other, pretending to come from one of the cities with which their intended victims were meant to be at peace.[69]

According to their victims, the *re'is* were willing to attack virtually any Christian vessel they came across, if it looked weak enough to capture. In fact, they were only supposed to take on the avowed enemies of their respective regency, which in turn was meant to be acting under the protection and in the interests of its Ottoman overlord. All corsairing activities were thus theoretically directed against the ships of those nations at war with the Turks, which in practice meant above all the Spanish, along with all other dominions of the Hapsburg dynasty, who were in armed conflict with the Turks throughout most of the early modern era. Although the battleground between these two empires stretched from the Azores to India and from Vienna to Oman, the center of their contention during the sixteenth and much of the seventeenth centuries was Spain's Mediterranean coast, Italy – with its Hapsburg dominions of Naples and Milan – and the great islands of Sicily, Sardinia, and the Balearics. From the point of view of the *re'is,* virtually any ship from these states was fair game – they called it "a good prize" – as was any ship from Spanish Flanders, and (between 1581 and 1640, when their Crown was united with Spain) any Portuguese vessel.[70] Another perpetual foe, although a target only for the most aggressive corsairs, were the war galleys of the Knights of Malta, busy carrying on their own *jihad* against Islam anywhere in the Mediterranean. Also acceptable as targets were the fleets and merchant shipping of the smaller Mediterranean powers, on the occasions when they were at war with the Ottomans or just simply allied with the Hapsburgs: in Italy this meant Venice, Genoa, Florence, and the States of the Church. Even France, which generally maintained friendship treaties with the regencies and especially Algiers, could find its shipping under occasional attack.[71]

The issue was often more confused than that, however. Even when one of these lesser states was officially at peace with the Turks, their vessels might still be seized by the corsairs. According to the laws of the sea – at least as the *re'is* interpreted them – a merchant ship, even one from a neutral nation, that fired on a corsair galley gave the *re'is* the right to reply in kind, and even take her by force. Some corsairs extended this principle of implicit hostility to a merchant ship merely refusing an "inspection" and attempting to flee. Ever inventive, some of the *re'is* became adept at provoking neutral ships into firing on them, even using the ploy of disguising themselves in reverse, as it were – as corsairs from one of the regencies that was at war with the neutral power in question. Once the corsairs managed to board a Christian vessel, all the advantages went to the attackers. If a ship from any neutral state – including the French, Dutch, and English – was found to be carrying any Spanish or Spanish-Italian merchandise or passengers, or that of any other enemy, it could be impounded and taken back to Barbary.[72] Since goods on board were often poorly labeled, an ambitious corsair captain could always turn up enough questionable merchandise to justify taking almost any vessel he boarded as a prize to Algiers or Tunis. If that (and all else) failed, it was always possible for the corsairs to come aboard in apparent friendship and then have one of their renegades accuse a passenger of being of an enemy nation – a Spaniard, for example, as happened to the French cleric Jean-Baptiste Gramaye, although he protested,

> that I did not know a single word of that language, [at which] they whipped me with blows of a rope to the head, swearing that they would teach it to me well. Then, hearing me speak French and seeming to willingly believe that I had nothing in common with Spain, they insisted that I was a Jew.[73]

Once ships were brought into Barbary as prizes, it was often difficult for their home state to keep their merchandise from melting away and their crews from vanishing into slavery. Protecting these men and goods should have been one of the primary responsibilities of each power's resident consul, but the various European powers – with the notable exception of the French in Algiers – waited until well into the seventeenth century to open consulates in the principal regencies. Instead, most states continued to cling to the fiction that lodging protests with the sultan in Constantinople would get their impounded ships returned and their crews released. As a result, with no one to turn up and keep an eye out when newly captured slaves were being unloaded, it was easy for seamen and passengers from supposedly friendly states to be sold in the market along with those who were fair game for the slavers. Even after the French had their consul on the spot in Algiers, there was still the fear that the corsairs would sail "either to Tripoli or to some other place not associated with the French," and sell their captives there.[74]

Thomas Baker's journal provides some idea of how slaves fitted economically into the loot that Muslim corsairs took from ships. Most striking in his lists of prizes brought back to Tripoli between 1679 and 1685 is, as already noted, how few of these captured vessels had any slaves at all: of the 71 ships taken in these six years, only 30, or about two-fifths, came in with captives; from the remainder the crews and passengers had all fled in small boats, once it was obvious that they could not outsail the corsairs. Deserting one's ship seems to have been a common enough reaction to pirate attack in the Mediterranean, an act Baker at least seems to have considered the only rational thing to do. Noting that a good many prizes were brought in unmanned because "all the Christians had ye witt to escape in their Boat," Baker apparently agreed with the crews that there was little point in staying to fight and risk death or a lifetime of slavery simply to protect the investment of owners who remained safe back home in London, Amsterdam, or Marseilles.

Those prizes that were brought into Tripoli with captives, according to Baker's journal, carried an average of around 30 saleable slaves per ship, a total of 900 men and women in these six years. Baker also recorded estimates for the value of the ships and cargoes captured, as well as recording the rough averages for what the captives would fetch in the local slave market – 200 or 300 dollars, varying from one year to the next, "Christians taken one with another," as he put it. As a result, some generalizations can be ventured about the place of slave taking in corsair piracy. Even in this small sample, one interesting point emerges: masters and crewmen turn out to have been less likely to abandon ships with more precious cargoes. Thus, the 30 ships taken with their crews had an aggregate estimated value of around $690,000 according to Baker, or around $23,000 apiece; the remaining 41 ships, all of whose crews had fled, were said to be worth a total of only $350,000, or barely $8,500 per prize.[75] Seen in this light, the captives represented a fairly small portion of the overall value of the profit the corsairs could realize from a prize and its cargo – somewhat between a fifth and a quarter, or about $6,500 worth of slaves per prize. Such a figure is considerably skewed, however, by five very lucrative prizes taken during Baker's tenure – the kind of merchant vessels, loaded down with cash or bullion, as well as "bales of silk ... fine Spanish wool ... cochineal and other rich goods," that were every corsair's dream.[76] When these few fat hauls are factored out of the list, the remaining 25 ships – variably laden "wth corne ... oyle and wine ... tymber ... beanes ... cordovans ... cotton ... potashes ... Venice Looking Glasses ... Corral ... Milstones ... Acorne-shells ... Rice &c[a]," were together worth a mere $160,000, or $6,400 per prize. If one were to focus only on these more modest but also more typical prizes, a context is created in which the value of potential slaves becomes more evident, since the crews taken with their ships would in such cases have greatly increased the corsairs' chance of turning a profit: the 665 captives taken on these vessels were worth, in Baker's estimation, around $150,000, or very nearly as much as the prizes themselves.[77]

Although single ships rarely yielded as many slaves as did land raids, the individual captives themselves could be of much greater potential value than coastal peasants and fisherfolk. The twenty or so sailors who were normally taken on middling sized Dutch, English, or French ships were, at the very least, healthy enough to last several years in the Barbary galleys. Moreover, some nations had made the ransoming of their subject seamen a matter of state policy, something that was no doubt well known among the*re'is* and an important factor in making such captives especially attractive to the slave dealers in Barbary.[78] Much more valuable were the ships' carpenters, sail masters, bosuns, or other skilled seamen, two or three of whom typically sailed on any merchantman. They could be sent directly to the shipyards in Algiers or Porto Farina, where they were so prized that few had any chance of ever getting away; instead, as Giovanni Salvago reported to Venice in 1624, they would be "forced and compelled to work at making seaworthy the [corsairing] *bertoni* and at making *galeotte* and*bergantini*; they are held at high prices, on a thousand thalers or a thousand scudi each, and some Masters will not let theirs go for any money."[79]

A ship's officers were also valuable, in part because they might fetch higher ransoms from the vessel's owners, but also because, in a more immediate sense, they could be coerced with threats or torture into revealing both what valuables might be hidden about the ship and – probably more important – disclosing what they knew of the wealth or status of the passengers. Chastelet des Boys noted that the master on his ship, Jacques Denyan of Olone, was not easily intimidated by the corsairs and refused to admit anything, even after they had "placed [him] face down on the deck, in a position to be cruelly beaten on the soles of his feet." Denyan's resistance was worth little in the long run, however, because the corsairs promptly turned to other crewmen. They soon found that the bosun was the sort who began "trembling at the first interrogations, and without waiting for further more pressing [questions]," came out with a "pusillanimous confession," not only revealing where the passengers and crew had stashed their silver about the ship, but also blurting out that before the voyage he had seen one of the passengers while still on shore, "dressed in cloth of silver and scarlet brocade." The corsairs promptly turned their attentions to that unhappy captive.[80]

It was the passengers in particular who made the real difference between slave taking from ships and from land. Whereas the great majority of those plucked in coastal raids were simple fishermen and sailors worth more as slave labor than for any ransom they could bring in, passengers could prove fantastically profitable for the *re'is* who were lucky enough to capture those of rank, personal wealth, or connections back home. As a result, although the corsairs were the self-proclaimed and dogged enemies of everything Christian, they also turned out to have quite a discriminating eye when it came to assessing the nuances of hierarchy and status that so dominated the baroque European society on which they preyed. Christian merchants were valued not only for their family ties, but also for those they enjoyed with their trading firm, either one of which might be willing to pay for their release. Better yet were European Jews, for they could be made to appeal to their families and to their Jewish community and as a result could usually be counted on for a large ransom. Nobles of any rank were desirable, but still better were bishops and other senior clerics, since it was understood that the papacy was often quite generous when it came to freeing its top churchmen from the degradations of slavery.

Keenly aware of the corsairs' interest in their status and their wealth, most passengers did their best to hide both when they saw that their ship was about to be boarded. It would indeed seem that prudent travelers made a point of confiding nothing about themselves to the captain or their fellow passengers, in case someone on board, in an attempt to curry favor or avoid a beating, might identify them to their captors as a person of wealth and consequence in Christian society. As a result, Mediterranean voyages must have been rather stand-offish affairs, with no one willing to reveal much of anything about himself, for the risks one ran for displaying too much pomp and affluence were often made painfully obvious when the corsairs came on board.[81]

Passengers' attempts to disguise themselves were one of the tropes of the Barbary enslavement narrative genre, lending a comic opera atmosphere to these otherwise frantic last moments before enslavement. Knowing full well that should the corsairs find any obvious signs of wealth aboard they would not rest until they had tracked down the owners, passengers

> Threw the better part of their silver money, flashy dress suits, gilded swords, embroidered belts, boots, letters, and other indicators of wealth and quality helter-skelter into the sea, either ... [in] apprehension of being seen by the enemy as possessing such goods or out of a desire to disguise themselves, to avoid the demands of a huge ransom.[82]

As the corsairs drew near, bishops hastily dressed themselves as simple priests, nobles and wealthy merchants grabbed sailors' smocks or sought to disguise themselves as poor soldiers-of-fortune; everyone tried to be ready with a name to call himself that might reveal as little about his origins as possible.[83] Men and women who were accustomed to authority and ease at home tried desperately to pass themselves off as humble and uneducated workers – a difficult task that was made still more arduous by their clumsy efforts to hide about themselves a few coins or jewels.

Such pathetic stratagems, though they may have been attempted by some of Europe's best educated and most sophisticated elites, still had much in common with the ploys of newly taken slaves anywhere in the world, trying in any way possible to divert the attention and greed of their captors and blend in with their fellow victims. It was a passive, mimetic resistance with which the corsairs were quite familiar, however, and breaking these new slaves of such attempts at disobedience was one of their first tasks. Custom among the Barbary rovers dictated that, when capturing a ship that had offered any form of resistance, the first corsair who came on board had his choice of any one of the passengers to take as his own slave. As a result, the mass of soldiers among the raiders, whose blood was up in any case from battle and greed, tended to rush pell-mell aboard every prize they took, grabbing both goods and humans with violence and abandon:

> shouting, wandering about, searching here and there on the bridge, in the waist, and at the bottom of the hold: with blows of axes they broke open the trunks.... gorging themselves with booty, smashing into the stores, breaking the seals [on merchandise], and making an inventory all at the same time.[84]

For the first half hour or so, any passenger or crewman who moved too slowly or got in the corsairs' way could well be beaten bloody or even hacked to pieces, a risk that convinced Louis Marott it was best to climb the mast and conceal himself aloft "until their fury was over."[85] This initial turmoil and the fright it produced were only the first of a series of torments that either in effect or by design tended to break the new captives' sense of individuality and willingness to put up resistance. One gets the impression that many of the passengers lacked the psychological resilience to deal with the unexpected, but perhaps it was just because they had heard too many stories from "some knowledgeable adventurers of the sea ... and other experienced sailors" about what fate awaited them. As Chastelet des Boys described the state of mind of the passengers on his ship, even before their captors had boarded them:

> Unable to cure [ourselves] of a certain lethargic melancholy, we were incapable of giving or receiving advice: our imaginations were left stupefied by fear, to the point of persuading ourselves that, in boarding, these brutally martial people would sacrifice every one of us on the edge of their scimitars.[86]

To further this mood of fatalistic passivity, the corsairs set about freely abusing and humiliating their new slaves in ways that undermined their sense of self-worth. Claiming that they wanted to make sure no one was concealing cash or jewels inside his clothing or insisting that some among the passengers were (circumcised) Jews in disguise, the corsairs might force male slaves to strip naked, encouraging them along with a volley of punches and lashings with a knotted rope. It was a ploy often used on African captives by the European slavers, who might use the excuse of hygiene but achieved a similar, demoralizing effect. White captives of stature, like Jean-Baptiste Gramaye – arch-deacon, canon, professor, and apostolic protonotary – who were used to a certain respect back in Christian society, could be quickly reduced "to a piteous state" even by this simple abuse and thereafter offered no further psychological resistance to their corsair captors.[87]

Others might have it much worse, however. One of the passengers, possibly because he was thought to know something of his shipmates, might be singled out and tortured systematically in front of the others, to force him to reveal both his true identity and, whenever possible, that of his fellow passengers. The preferred method was to give him 100 or more blows with a stick – as Morgan put it, "in such Cases ... the *bastinado* begins to stir about upon the Posteriors of such as are suspected" – but canings were also inflicted on the victims' stomach, the soles of their feet, or on their lower back "almost enough to break the kidneys." Gramaye was especially horrified when a Portuguese merchant was picked to play this role of involuntary informer – not only at having to watch a fellow passenger thrashed almost to the point of unconsciousness, but also at the man's consequent willingness to swear in writing both that Gramaye himself was a bishop in disguise and that one of Gramaye's servants was a Knight of Malta.[88]

Finally, when there was nothing more to be gleaned from the new slaves, the corsairs would be on their way. If the *re'is* intended to continue his freebooting, he might decide to put some of his new prisoners straight to work at the oars. Some unfortunates were thus thrown from their accustomed lives of ease to excruciatingly hard labor and short rations in the space of just a few hours: Jan Struys wrote how, within minutes of his capture, "they put me in a Galley, stript off my Robes, shaved my head, and set me to an Oar, which was work enough for six of us to tug at."[89] More typically, however, captives would be chained together and hustled down to a storage room or hold below deck – Gramaye called the one where he was kept a *cubiculo obscuro* – where they were "chayned together in heaps, and thrust up like

Herrings in the bottome of the ship, to be kept for the Butherie or Market," often to the point where it was difficult for everyone to sit or lie down at once. For security's sake, captives were kept below for the rest of the voyage, and Foss wrote of the new slaves having to "creep in, upon our hands and knees," into a lockup, where they found it impossible to sleep for "such quantities [of] ... vermin, such as lice, bugs and fleas." Elliot recalled how "We lay in this miserable Condition about forty days, oppressed as with many Inconveniences, so especially I remember with the stench and nastiness of our Lodging."[90]

Whether put to the oar or locked below decks, it seems that many captives never survived the trip to port, dying from the shock of their capture and sudden reversal of their fortunes, perhaps, or from the beatings, insufficient food and water, and unsanitary conditions that were suddenly their lot. Just how many came to this end and what their proportion was of the total is unknown, since their bodies were "thrown into the sea without the slightest regard."[91] One can only presume that a captive's chance of survival was linked to the time it took to get them back to port, and this could vary considerably. Some narrators reported being taken directly to Algiers or Tunis in brief voyages that lasted no more than a week or two; others, who had been unfortunate enough to have been taken at the beginning of the corsairs' run or who, like William Okeley or Nicholas Roberts, had been captured in the Atlantic, could expect a trip of several excruciating months, sometimes with stops along the way to sell slaves or acquire new ones.[92] In this regard, the corsair slavers resembled their European counterparts, said to spend weeks sailing along the African coast, "from barracoon to barracoon until a quota was reached." As one slave from Gaeta recounted:

> We were made slaves on Monday evening and we took a great deal of time to arrive in Algiers, with a great deal of suffering, from hunger in particular and from other things, and we were forty days in a town called Bugia with the very bad weather, and God knows in what fashion we made do to keep ourselves from dying.[93]

The *re'is* brought their new booty – ships, loot, and human cargo – back home with a great deal of fanfare and as much pomp as they could muster: "With all their banners, their bells, their short trumpets, their artillery salvos," wrote Mascarenhas, "to celebrate a festival that, for us captives, could have only been sad, painful, and unfortunate."

Beyond gaining them immediate public honor, their displays also served to spread the news throughout the city about what they had taken, a matter of considerable interest for those who dealt in slaves and pirated goods, and especially those who had invested in a given captain's voyage. As Morgan noted:

> One may readily know when a Corsair has taken a Prize, since, if the Weather will permit, he always brings her in-tow, and approaches, firing every now and then A Gun, till he enters the Port: And sometimes, for Joy, he continues firing the whole Day long. One may, likewise, know at a Distance what Nation the Prize is of, by her Colours, which he commonly brings in flying at the Bolt-sprit-Top. If it is a very rich Prize indeed, he spares no Powder, but fires perpetually, even before he can be seen or heard from *Algiers*[94]

Some slaves reported being paraded through town, "led foorth in triumph ... with infinite scoffings" in a procession that effectively proclaimed their shame and social death. Since the arrival of new slaves was a sign of prosperity and an occasion of civic pride for all the townsfolk, the resident Turks, Moors, Jews, and renegades all turned out to cheer and taunt the newcomers. Local children especially followed the slaves as they shuffled along, loudly humiliating them and sometimes threw refuse at them.[95] Foss described the experience as it was in Algiers in 1793, fairly late in the annals of Barbary enslavement:

> [W]e were rowed on shore, and landed amidst the shouts and huzzas of thousands of malicious barbarians.... [A]s we passed through the streets, our ears were stunned with shouts, clapping of hands and other acclamations of joy from the inhabitants; thanking God for their great success and victories over so many Christian dogs and unbelievers.[96]

Even before they were subjected to this humiliation, some captives might be put to work directly, since someone had to take on the laborious task of dismantling their ship – unloading its cargo and hauling the ballast, hawsers, sails, and oars off to storage under lock and key, in conformity with local laws meant to make it difficult if not impossible for anyone stealing a vessel in a bid for freedom.[97] Such men were certainly treated as slaves by the *re'is* who had captured them and set to hard labor under the whips of the galley's bosun or the masters of the port. Yet these prisoners were in reality masterless slaves, belonging to

Slaves being disembarked in Algiers (from Pierre Dan, *Historie van Barbaryen en des zelfs Zee-Roovers*, Amersterdam, 1684)

so many disparate individuals – the *armadores,* corsair officers and men, the admiral of the city, and the local pasha himself, all of whom could claim a share of them – that they might as well have belonged to no one at all.[98] It might take some time for slaves to get out of this liminal state: those who arrived during the month of Ramadan, for instance, typically had to wait until it was over before they could move on to the next stage of their bondage. Others might find that the local slave dealers liked to wait until a significant number of captives had been brought in – perhaps as many as thirty or forty – before taking the whole group together as a lot.[99]

While still in this ambiguous state slaves might be sent to the palace of one of the wealthy slave dealers or government officials (in Algiers, they were often the same man), and there they were given little to do beyond waiting, worrying, and perhaps helping out with light chores. To an extent, this can be seen as similar to the "seasoning" to the new environment that black Africans brought to North America were sometimes allowed – a breaking-in period during which new captives might adjust to the climate and their newly servile status. To help this process along, it was "the custom of this country" in Barbary, very much as in parts of the Americas, to give the newcomers a chance to mingle with some of the older, or at least seasoned slaves, men experienced in local ways and practices and, one presumes, trusted by their masters. These veterans came to offer advice and services to the new slaves, sometimes lending them money as well, evidently at the behest of their owners, to make recent arrivals less prone to panic or depression.[100] Knowing from their own experience what particularly worried new captives, they trafficked in information, or at least gossip, about the world of enslavement, providing counseling about how to behave in this unfamiliar world of bondage and subservience – when, for example, one should kiss the hem of the robe of one's master.[101] They provided for many newcomers a first introduction to *lingua franca*, the pidgin of slaves and masters in the Mediterranean. They also advised on the best kinds of owners a slave could hope for and some even offered to help arrange that a slave be purchased by one of the better sorts of master.[102] Helpful though these slaves might be, some observers and ex-slaves warned against being too open with them when they came around whispering information and advice during this nervous period of idle captivity. Though perhaps offering helpful advice, they were also in all probability working for the slave buyers, who were said to pay them for any information they could glean from the newcomers "relating to their Birth and Circumstances, what Prospect there is of their being soon ransomed, and what their Parents or Relations are able to give" – anything that might help the dealers later when demanding a higher sale price or ransom.[103]

It was customary in all the Barbary regencies that the ruling pasha of the city had his pick of a certain percentage of the booty brought into his port by corsairs.[104] This claim, known as the ruler's *penjic,* extended to captives, and in most places, most of the time, the pasha could claim one prisoner in eight as his own (some observers maintained it was one in ten, seven, or even one in five). Some said that, in addition, the ruler could choose "one of the important personages" among the group of captives, though d'Aranda, among others, maintained that such an individual counted against the one in eight and might even represent the pasha's total share.[105] His interest with such individuals lay in their potential for bringing him a good ransom, and some claimed that this extended to "Women of any Rank, whom [he] never fails to take to his Share."[106]

Certainly for the more ordinary sort of slaves the pasha was one owner to be avoided. His first choice was generally men for the fleet. If he picked skilled seamen – "the Commanders or Masters, the Surgeons, the Carpenters, &c" – he sent them to the harbor or the public arsenal. Though the labors demanded of these men might not be too exhausting and their rations reasonable, their desirability for keeping the pasha's fleet in good order meant that many of them would never be given the opportunity of release; most could expect to stay until they managed to escape or died. The other men picked by the pasha were generally destined for his galleys, and they would soon disappear into the mass of captives held in one of the public bagnos – the *Bagno Beyliç* or the *Bagno del Rè*, where hundreds were held when not out on the *corso*. These unfortunates, who served under the ruler's various underlings or under the *re'is* to whom he hired them out, had a much harder time capturing the attention or the good opinion of their owner than those chosen by a private master. As such they had little chance of getting better treatment or even having a ransom set. Worse still, when the pasha, as representative of the sultan in Algiers, Tunis, or Tripoli, finished his tour of duty and returned to the Levant, it was customary that he took his slaves with him – to work them in the galleys in his next assignment or

> to sell [them] in Alexandria, Constantinople or Cairo and everywhere else, with the result that one can never more get the word out about the place of one's detention ... [and] the recovery of liberty becomes almost impossible.[107]

The fate awaiting those chosen by the pasha was thus by no means an enviable one, a reality that some rulers, depending on their mood at the time, might choose to underscore. John Foss reported that, having made his choice, the pasha of Algiers, his new owner, greeted him and his fellow slaves with the encouraging words, "Now I have got you, you Christian dogs: you shall eat stones!"[108] Despite such unpromising beginnings, the selection process itself was usually a fairly civilized affair. The captives were made to line up in rows, sometimes shaven-headed but generally in the same clothes in which they had been taken, with "heads and feet bare," as the ruler strolled among them and

> had long and confidential conferences (without making a secret of it) with the many Jews and Turks ["serving as experts to the pasha when he makes his choice"], who, never ceasing to consider us very carefully, one after the other, seemed to be giving him advice.[109]

Slaves selected at this point, together with some others preemptively picked by other state agents, were then sent to the public bagnos, where in most cases "a Ring of Iron was fastened on one of their Ancles ... to let it be known they are *Beliç* Slaves."[110] They were then taken to a barber to be "forceablie and most violentlie shaven, head and beard," if they had not already been shaved while still on their way into port. One can discern in such treatment, besides the obvious need to give new slaves their own, distinctive look, a desire to further the process of breaking and demoralizing, now that they were indeed bonded to a master. As such, it resembled the first stages of boot camp for new soldiers, though in fact the experience in Barbary was if anything still more traumatic, since in the sixteenth and seventeenth centuries a great deal more of a man's identity was wrapped up in his hair and beard. It was indeed a saying among the locals in Barbary that a superior and active man, one who was "too cunning to be imposed upon," was "a Man with a Beard;" thus, those who were reduced to hairlessness were not complete men. Slaves clearly accepted this association of shaved heads with newcomer status, since once they had established themselves, many captives seemed determined never to have their hair cut again, letting it (and themselves) get to the point where they looked like (and indeed were) lice-ridden, ragged derelicts, with beards "[that] hang down to their Waste, which gives them a frightful Appearance."[111]

After a few other preemptive selections were made, by various public groups and organizations that had a claim on the booty, the remaining captives were taken to the slave market, known in Algiers and Tripoli as the *badestan* and in Tunis (to this day) as the *Souq el Berka*.[112] The experience of being haggled over in the market, "like they sell the

Slaves taken into the Badestan in Algiers (from Pierre Dan, *Historie van Barbaryen en des zelfs Zee-Roovers*, Amersterdam, 1684)

animals," was the key rite of passage into slavery, and it figures, more or less prominently, in virtually every captivity narrative. "Here begins our Tragedy," wrote d'Aranda, and it was certainly unnerving for many to be demeaned in such a casual fashion by dealers in human flesh. When the necessary thirty or forty slaves had been assembled to initiate a sale, they were led to the market, where they were given to the charge of slave brokers, whom d'Arvieux called *délats*, or informers, and de la Motte referred to as *"Dilaleen*, or Auctioneers."[113] George Elliot, sold in the Moroccan city of Salé, reported that he "had a great *Black* who was appointed to sell me," while d'Aranda was met by

> a certain old man with a staff in his hand [who] took me by the arm, and led me several times about the Market-place, and those who were desirous to buy me, ask'd me my Country, name, and profession.[114]

In the course of these turns about the market, slave dealers tried "with some good words" to cajole from each captive as much personal

Examining slaves in the Badestan (from Pierre Dan, *Historie van Barbaryen en des zelfs Zee-Roovers*, Amersterdam, 1684)

information as they could. Slaves were advised by the old hands to answer the questions of these *maquignons* or horse traders, as they were known, but to give away as little as possible in the process, "without directly rebuffing their inquiries." Such evasiveness tended to restrict buyers to what they could learn from the slaves' physique, but they were specialists in the trade in humans – "a good many of them do not do any other sort of commerce" – and, like any dealers in animals, excelled in what they could learn by sight and touch alone.[115] According to Dan, slaves could be stripped naked at this point, "as seems good to [the dealers], without any shame." Their primary need was to determine whether a slave was worth buying primarily for resale – in particular for ransoming – or whether he (or she) might be more profitably employed as a laborer, artisan, or for domestic or (sometimes) sexual purposes. D'Aranda noted how the price would vary (downward), "when the value is set accourding to the body, and not according to the ransom that may be gotten."[116] It was fairly easy to detect those who were born into the laboring classes, since their hands, above all, would have been made "hard and brawny by working."[117]

As with slave dealers anywhere, these *maquignons* were unwilling to buy a man whose physical infirmities might restrict his ability to work

– "for according to age and strength they are prized" – and with this in mind "they make [the slaves] walk, jump and leap about with blows of a stick, in order to recognize thereby that they do not have any gout." They also examined slaves' teeth, not, as horse dealers did, to discover their age, but to see if they would be able to successfully gnaw the tough ship's biscuit and dried beef eaten in the galleys. In the same way, considerable attention was given to slaves' arms and legs, to make sure they were not lame – presumably some captives were not above faking this – since "anything Analogical to *Spavin* or *Ring-bone* ... will bring down the Market wonderfully."[118]

A serious problem for the *maquignons* was how to arrive at some idea of the age of those for sale, since as Okeley notes, "they that sell them, did *not breed them*, and therefore they know nothing, more or less of that." Buyers might ask the slaves themselves, but obviously could not always expect a truthful response, or indeed any at all. Age was an important issue when it came to figuring how hard a male slave might be able to labor and whether a female was worth buying as a possible consort for the harem. Solid and reliable indicators of age are notoriously hard to come by with human chattel, however, forcing many *maquignons* to rely on their experience as dealers: "They go by general conjectures from the Beard, Face, or Hair, but a *good set of Teeth* will make one *ten Years Younger*, and a *broken one* ten Years *older than the Truth*."[119]

Always on the lookout for signs of wealth or connections that many slaves were at pains to conceal, dealers carefully checked their haircuts, to see "if they are of good family," and the palms of their hands "to judge the delicacy of the skin." There was also a belief among dealers (at least according to Dan) that the true nature of a prospective purchase could be told from reading his palm, making the hands a doubly important point of inspection.[120] Above all, d'Arvieux claimed, they examined the captives' earlobes, to see if these had been pierced, "from which they infer that they are people of quality and distinguished from common folk, since as infants they had worn ear-bobs."[121]

When it came to a ransom, a slave's origins also played an important role, for, as already noted, some states were more willing or able to redeem their citizens than others. To this end, renegades who spoke a variety of languages moved among those being offered for sale, to make sure that the slaves' claims about where they were born accorded with the language they spoke. D'Arvieux reported that in the mid-1600s "the French are ordinarily those who sell at the cheapest price," both because they tended to be among the poorest captives and because "Owners feared that the King [of France] would take them back through some Treaty, and they would be obliged to give them up [only] for the purchase price." Worse, however, were the Spanish, who sometimes took a low market evaluation as a personal insult,

> preferring to live longer as a Slave and even die as such than to lower [the price] a little. They say proudly that they are Gentlemen, that they are rich, and that their relatives are grand Señors who will not suffer them to be Slaves [but] will rather send considerable sums for their ransom. It is said that a Spaniard, upon hearing that he was to be sold for one hundred piastres, demanded all puffed up with rage to the one who had purchased him whether he took him for a donkey, that he should value a man of his fashion at such a price.[122]

Playing as it does on some fondly held stereotypes, this tale would have struck contemporary (and some modern) readers as quite amusing, which was obviously d'Arvieux's intention. Yet it could not have been altogether easy for even the most timid Europeans to have placidly endured not only the examinations to which they were subjected, but also the haggling, much as practiced by animal dealers everywhere, in which the potential buyer was obliged to denigrate the product just as much as the seller was to praise it. Even if the slaves barely understood what was being said about them, they could have been in little doubt about its general import, from the gestures of the dealers and perhaps from their experience in buying and selling animals back home. William Okeley offered a nice verbal pastiche of the experience, to drive home how the Algerians sold Christians "in their markets like horses: for according to age and strength they are prized":

> *Oh*, says the Seller, *mark what a back he has, what a breadth he bears between the shoulders! What a Chest! How strong set! How fitted on the nonce for Burdens! He'le do but e'ne too much work. Pish*, says the Buyer. *He looks like a Pillard, like a very Meacock at his Provender, and one that seems to be surfeited.*[123]

For those slaves whose marketability lay in their skills rather than their workability or their birth, the problem was more difficult, for the former were easier to hide and the incentive to do so was, if anything, even greater. A wealthy captive could, in time, find the necessary funds to pay all but the most exaggerated ransom, but many talented artisans soon discovered that their masters were "not inclined to sell them back at any price." In light of most captives' refusal to reveal such information about themselves, many *maquignons* had to take a chance and buy on speculation.[124] It appears, in fact, that after an unsuccessful first purchase many a slave found himself back in the *badestan*, sometimes more than once, as his unhappy master sought to offload him. It was at this point that buyers and sellers swapped (and often exaggerated in the process) any knowledge of a slave's skills or abilities that may have been gleaned over the previous weeks and months – either from what he may have inadvertently disclosed to the city's ubiquitous informers, or simply from their having kept a close eye on him as he moved about the city, doing his tasks.[125]

The show at the *badestan* ended when the *délat* took the slaves one at a time by the arm and paraded each "three or four times about the Market, crying *Arrache, Arrache*, that is, *Who offers most?*" As Laugier de Tassy observed, "Persons of all Nations are permitted to bid, and the Auction is carried on until there are no more Bidders. Then the Clerk of the Sale books the Price."[126]

Yet, despite all the apparent energy that went into the ritual of slave dealing in the *badestan* or the *berka*, it was generally not in the public market where the business was concluded. Indeed, in Algiers this phase was often referred to as merely "the first sale," about which de La Motte further observed, "Nor does this first Offer rise very high, because the ultimate Sale passes in the *Dey's* Court-yard and Presense."[127] The whole point of the first sale was to establish the price for each slave that would be paid to those responsible for capturing him – the *re'is*, the *armadores*, and others of the corsairing crew. To underscore this intent, sometimes the price their captors hoped to get from each slave was written on his or her bare breast, to provide a benchmark.[128] It was understood, however, that "all who are really disposed to purchase" would then go to the palace a day or so later to conclude the deal. The pasha and his agents at this point had the right to purchase any slave for the first bid, which was generally quite low. After the pasha had made his selections, the real bidding began, often resulting in a final sale price that was twice the first price. Traders generally kept their *badestan* bids low, knowing that nothing would be settled until this second bid, a practice that has made it annoyingly difficult to establish any firm sense of the costs – and thus the profits – involved in the Barbary slave trade.

Finally, after all the slaves for sale had been thoroughly inspected again, they were offered, one at a time, to the bidders, who called out their offers as the uncomprehending merchandise was led by, until at

Selling slaves (from Pierre Dan, *Historie van Barbaryen en des zelfs Zee-Roovers*, Amersterdam, 1684)

last "the bargain was concluded" with a sale to the highest bidder. "These purchases are always made with ready Money," observed Laugier de Tassy, and the difference between each slave's first and second sale price was claimed by the *beliç*, or public fisc, as its profit from the trade. Then the slaves were handed over to their new masters, who in the manner of slave owners everywhere took possession of their new chattel and set them "to such Work as is most comfortable to the Slave's Abilities, or his own Conveniency."[129]

Part II
Barbary

3
Slave Labor

> Certainly there is no worse moment in life than that where a captive waits to discover what master will have him, since a man cannot know a greater misfortune, nor, for the punishment of his sins, a grander misery than that of being a slave, but if his bad luck leads him to be the slave of a malicious master, he can expect nothing good of his future and must consider himself the most unhappy of men: there is no worse hell in this life.[1]

So wrote the Portuguese merchant João Mascarenhas, recording his thoughts while waiting to discover his own fate, and there is little question that this transaction, so freighted with sheer chance, could make a tremendous difference in every slave's life. Mascarenhas' immediate concern was with the temperament of his future master, and he was indeed right to worry: as chattel of whomsoever chose to buy him, he would be utterly without rights or a will of his own, his very life forfeit to the whim of his new owner, who "could resell him, overload him with work, imprison him, beat him, mutilate him, kill him, without anyone interfering."[2] There was no countervailing force to protect the slave from his master's violence: no local anti-cruelty laws, no benign public opinion, and rarely any effective pressure from foreign states. As William Okeley observed, "If a Patron shall *kill his Slave*, for ought I could perceive, he suffers no more for it, than if he should *kill his Horse*."[3] The few, rather openended verses in the Koran that counseled patience and justice in treating slaves, were, as most observers agreed even at the time, probably less important in shielding a slave from his owner's whim than the simple self-interest which prevents anyone from destroying his own valuable property.[4] Some slaves indeed believed that it was only the greed of their masters, who coupled current exploitation with the hope of future, greater gain through eventual resale, that kept them alive at all. William Okeley, writing of his experience in 1639, perceived the situation with slave owners in blunt and mercenary terms:

> Their *Cruelty* is great, but their *Covetousness* exceeds their *Cruelty*; could they make as much of us *Dead*, as they make *alive*, that so both the *Interests* of *Cruelty*, and of *Covetousness* might be *secured and reconciled*, we are well assured which way it should have gone with us. But it must be a good deal of *Tallow and Fat* that will answer *two or three Dollars a Moneth*.[5]

Much of how a slave would fare – as Mascarenhas and other newly arrived captives were quite aware – depended on the purpose for which he was purchased. As Henri-David Grammont would observe two centuries later, all new captives, upon arrival, "were separated into two quite distinct classes: the slaves of ransom and the slaves of work." Which class a slave fell into depended largely on the individual himself, according to Grammont: those who made it clear to prospective buyers that they had enough wealth and connections at home to buy themselves out of captivity were purchased by speculators hoping for a good return on their investment.[6] Such buyers, according to contemporary observers, were for the most part "Moors" or "Tagarins" (past Islamic residents of Iberia who had been expelled or fled from Spain) and "European" renegades. They were said to see their slaves as an investment, and indeed, slave ownership of this sort, as Taoufik Bachrouch recently noted, should be viewed "as a form of capital acquisition analogous to [that of] money, *rentes*, or the 'change in Christendom'."[7]

Ali Pegelin (or Bitchnin or Picheny or Pichellin, depending on the author), one of the great slave-holders in mid-seventeenth-century Algiers, was thus only stating the obvious when he commented, "I have bought my Slaves to make some advantage by them."[8] From what little is known of the initial selling price of slaves in the *badestan*, that hoped-for advantage was to make around 10–12 percent per slave per year.[9] If investors like Pegelin were not to lose money on their principal, it was necessary that their slaves bring in some sort of income during the long wait until their ransom was paid. Masters therefore usually tried to find their slaves work that would generate cash without damaging them too much physically. Their logic of operation was spelled out in 1789, by the French diplomat Venture de Paradis:

> those who buy slaves for speculation rent them out at the rate of an Algerian half-sequin per lunar month. By this method, the slave gives a return on the money that he has cost, and his master waits for the moment to extract a good ransom from him.[10]

Those purchasers who were said to "only buy slaves to serve them, not for the traffick" were for the most part Turks or janissaries, the so-called Levantine (that is, Greek or Orthodox) renegades, and sometimes the agents of the local governing council, commonly known as the *divan*. Such buyers were not necessarily immune to the temptations of a good ransom, rather they were not especially hopeful that the lower-class slaves they mostly dealt in would ever be able to raise the cash. Seeking to profit from the labor of their slaves rather than from an eventual ransom, these owners set their chattel to a broader range of tasks than did those who purchased for resale. The labors of this class of slaves turn out to have been much more varied than what was generally demanded of black Africans freshly arrived in the Americas. There, the principal need, especially in the seventeenth and eighteenth centuries, was for plantation workers to produce commercial crops – sugar, rice, cotton, and tobacco. Yet despite the variety of their work, the tasks white slaves were set to tended to fall into one or another category of labor – and indeed whole sectors of the economy – that the slave-holding traditions of Barbary had over the centuries come to define through custom and usage as "the tasks that free men were no longer willing to do."[11]

Some of the slaves ended up with relatively easy posts, usually in household service. This seems to have been the lot of virtually all female slaves not taken by their buyers specifically as concubines: d'Aranda wrote that his own master, Ali Pegelin, had "twenty Women-slaves, Christians, who waited on his wife;" he wrote of another who was "an excellent Needle-woman," working in the household of a wealthy Turkish woman.[12] Some male slaves, too, were pressed into relatively light duties as lackeys and servants. While dining at the villa of Mehmed Chelebi (also known as Dom Philippe), outside Tunis, the French emissary Laurent d'Arvieux was served by "a troop of Slaves, very appropriately dressed;" he then had the pleasure of "a concert of harps, violins, guitars, imperials, cistres, angeliques, on which the slaves of Dom Philippe played some Italian and Spanish tunes perfectly well."[13] One may assume that, in their daily lives, such privileged slaves passed their time much like their free counterparts in the great households of baroque Europe. Some of them found opportunities to profit from their master's business, which might increase their ease but not their freedom, since few owners seem to have willingly ransomed such agreeable chattel as long as they could afford to hold on to them.[14]

Over the course of the seventeenth century, as the emissaries from various Christian nations and from Rome began to establish themselves in consulates or missions in the regency capitals, new positions opened up for slaves, as the hired household servants of these free Europeans. By paying their owners for the services of these slaves – at the cost of "their Victuals and Clothing, and a current Piastre *per* Moon," according to Laugier de Tassy – such outsiders were creating a demand for slave-servants which in a very real sense supported the enslavement of their fellow Christians.[15] If they had an excuse to offer, it would have been that at least such unfortunates would probably receive better treatment from them than from their actual masters. It would also seem that before too long this captive (as it were) market for servants was sufficiently part of the social landscape in the Barbary regencies that those whose budgets would not allow such an indulgence felt they had cause to complain. Thus, friar Girolamo da Sassari, apostolic vicar in Tunis in the 1660s, wrote to his superiors:

> So many are the labors that he [Girolamo] endures in serving the poor Christian [slaves] that quite often he returns to his dwelling tired from the work and often weak from hunger, desirous of some comfort, [but] not finding even water to drink nor food to restore his flesh, and all this caused by the lack of a person to serve him. And though it is true that [by] taking a Christian from some Bagno he could get by, anyway past experience does not allow him to, since more than [the fact] that when the galleys go out he would have to send [the slave] back to his Bagno, it is also necessary to pay [the slave's] Master two *piastre* a month, which are 24 a year, a sum that [Girolamo] would not even know how to get, and, in paying [for] the servant, there would not remain anything for him to live on.[16]

Of the more mundane tasks that household slaves might be called on to do, the Trinitarian father Pierre Dan provided a detailed list. He did not distinguish between the work of male and female slaves, perhaps because he had information only on men's work or perhaps because some of the positions were interchangeable. Some of these duties were not that dissimilar to a paid servant's chores in Europe: get the water at dawn to clean out the house toilets, fetch hot bread every morning, wash down the house and courtyard tiles once a week, wash and bleach the sheets, whitewash the walls of the house twice a month, mind the children of the household.[17] Chastelet des Boys described his own (relatively brief) interlude as one of the house slaves of a renegade's widow in almost idyllic words:

> We lived on rather good terms, without [her] begrudging us more or less work; my ordinary task was nothing more than to fetch water from the neighboring fountain to clean up and make suitable the residence, and the rest of the day [I had to] carry around in my arms a young child of two or three years.[18]

Fetching water and nursing an infant were not, perhaps, the most honorable duties for a slave who had come from a privileged background in Europe, but such chores were fairly light and probably allowed for a good deal of free time during which one could either loaf around or seek ways of earning extra income. Certainly household work was far easier than the tasks to which most slaves were apparently assigned – in quarrying, construction, logging, farming, and, of course, rowing in the galleys.[19]

It was the galleys that came to epitomize slavery for white Europeans in Barbary, much as cutting cane did among Africans laboring in the Americas. As the Portuguese slave João Mascarenhas put it, "According to the captives in Algiers, if one has not been a *galeotto*, he could not say that he has been a slave. And this is quite true." Not only was it among the most widely shared of slave experiences in North Africa, but it was also one of the most grueling. "Alas!" as Father Dan lamented,

> It is a pity without compare to see the poor Christian captives, forced by great, crippling blows and by sticks to play the oars.... Of all the evils that the poor captives are forced to endure, the worst without doubt is that which they suffer in the galleys of the Turks and Barbarians.[20]

The majority of slaves were swept up into galley service because they had no other talents or virtues to save them. The men – no record of any female galley slave has yet turned up – who ended up in the galleys were those who showed no particular skills or obvious signs of wealth or rank when originally put up for sale. Generally they had been peasants taken in shore raids, fishermen, ordinary soldiers, or common sailors – first-class ratings and petty officers would be drafted as crewmen, rather than rowers. But buyers, whether the pasha and his agents at the palace or slave dealers at the *badestan*, were also looking for special qualities in potential *galeotti* as they strolled among the ranks of fresh captives. To discover those most suited for the job, purchasers had slaves jump about "to test the elasticity of their limbs;" they also made prospective purchases form a fist to test their grip, and checked the men's teeth to make sure that they could chew the tough biscuit that would be their almost exclusive diet while at sea. Those deemed most fit for the work could obviously fetch a higher price, but being judged aged or frail did not necessarily mean a slave would escape galley service: some auctions ended with the unbought old and infirm sold off by the job lot to the slave dealers. These agents could always hope to find one of the *re'is* who was poor and desperate enough to pay a knock-down price even for expendable chattel such as these. If not, they might mix them in with a batch of healthier slaves and, chaining them together, march them all off, either to the holding pens or directly to the ships waiting in the harbor.[21]

Gentlemen might be sent to the galleys as well, though probably by accident. Purchasers interested in buying slaves for their ransom value were always on the lookout for "persons of quality" and tended to hold them back from the galleys, lest they lose this valuable property at sea, where mortality was high. Still, elites were sometimes put to the oar, perhaps because they had simply been too clever in concealing their rank from their new owners. This may have been the fate of both João Mascarenhas and Louis Marott; just as likely, their masters may have sought to teach them a lesson or to convince them to put more pressure on any wealthy relations they might have back home. The fact that a few of them did end up in the galleys has in any case been a boon – for posterity, if not for themselves – since much of what we know about this particularly grueling slave experience comes from the writings of these literate few.[22]

Galley slavery was extremely widespread in the early modern Mediterranean, drawing its victims not only from the ranks of the enslaved, but also from convicts, prisoners-of-war, and not a few paid workers.[23] By the mid-sixteenth century, both the Christian powers and the Turkish empire were capable of mustering huge fleets of hundreds of galleys and galleots, each requiring between 150 and 300 oarsmen. It was a labor force that probably reached its maximum around the time of the battle of Lepanto, in 1571, when an estimated 80,000 rowers were sent into action against each other – most of them slaves, and not just on the Muslim side: in the galleys of Spain, France, Malta, and some Italian states one could find thousands of Moors, Turks, Catholic convicts, and not a few Protestants condemned to the oars.[24] Still, by the later 1600s, galley slavery can be considered primarily an Islamic rather than a Christian institution, in part because the Barbary corsairs were more successful in capturing slaves, but also because the Christian powers were quicker to convert to fully-rigged sailing ships that could cruise the Mediterranean without recourse to oarsmen.[25]

In the Barbary regencies, the peak of corsairing activity – and thus the peak of demand for galley slaves – came between the late 1580s and the 1640s, a period in which the *re'is* of Algiers, Tunis, and Tripoli, with their 50–60 galleys, would have required 10,000–15,000 slave rowers to man the fleets.[26] It was only towards the end of the seventeenth century, as corsairs themselves finally made the change from oared galleys to sail, that the need for slave muscle finally slackened. The various sloops, feluccas, frigates, and men-of-war they built thereafter, like the various Christian vessels they captured, needed only a dozen or so slave sailors, and although slave oarsmen do feature in some eighteenth-century accounts, these were generally for ceremonial purposes, a motley handful kept on to row the state galley on festive occasions.[27]

Life as a corsair galley slave has been called "a real, living hell for those poor wretches," and even attempts by recent scholars to play down the experience by claiming that conditions on these galleys were "at least consistent with the standards of the age" to be found on Christian ships cannot dismiss one of the most brutal forms of slave labor ever devised.[28] Depending on the size of their galley, slaves were assigned three, four, or five to an oar, although even the smaller ships generally required four men to manage the big stern oars.[29] Oarsmen were chained by their wrists to the oar itself and also by their ankles, which were attached to a chain that ran the length of each bench and was bolted to the ship's ribbing.[30] This left them with extremely restricted movement: "We were then also vilely manackled," complained Thomas Saunders, "in such sort, that we could not put our handes the length of a foote asunder the one from the other, and every night they searched our chaines three times, to see if they were fast reaucted." The only motion possible seems to have been along the bench itself. When the ship was idle, slaves who needed to relieve themselves could make their way to the opening at the hull side of their bench, known as the *borda*, dragging their part of the chain and presumably climbing over their sleeping companions – "The only liberty that is given us in the Galley," recalled Louis Marott, "is to go to this place when we have occasion."[31] This, however, many slaves were apparently too exhausted or dispirited to do and often ended up simply fouling themselves where they sat. The resulting stench, as many observers agreed, was beyond belief, but besides the fumes in which they labored, the shackled *galeotti* were also tormented by rats, fleas, bedbugs, and other parasites.[32]

For their clothing, oarsmen could generally expect only "a short linnen paire of breeches to cover their privities;" they were issued no shirts to shield their naked backs from the rain or the sun, so that, according to Knight, "their flesh is burned off their backes." Rations on board were meager, although just how much each *galeotto* could expect seems to have varied from ship to ship, perhaps improving somewhat over time. The slave friar Diego Haëdo wrote in the 1580s that every day on board the oarsmen were allotted "no more than a bit of bread crumbs, two or three pieces of dirty and often rotten biscuit ... a little diluted vinegar;" Mascarenhas spoke in the 1620s of "two handfuls of black biscuit a day, nothing more." By 1700, however, things seem to have improved, and Joseph Morgan wrote that, along with their "scarce-sufficient Quantity of Rusk," the *galeotti* might also receive an occasional "Mess of Gruel of their coarsest *Burgol*," along with the usual vinegar-water mix, "with a few Spots of Oil swimming thereon."[33] Ellen Friedman has recently asserted that such rations were much the same as those provided for renegade and Muslim sailors or soldiers on the same galleys, and this may well have been true: the continual concern of every *re'is* was to keep his vessel as light and nimble as possible, often at the expense of sufficient stores of food, water, or clothing.[34] Nevertheless, if a captain expected to attract sufficient corsairs aboard to do his proper work, he had to make some concessions to the free men, in terms of rations and the occasional right to pillage food ashore. In any case, it must be kept in mind that, unlike the slaves, the free seamen and soldiers on a galley were able – and, indeed, expected – to bring supplies of their own, to supplement such meager fare.[35]

It does not appear to have been their poor rations or even the work itself that troubled the slaves as much as sleep deprivation. With no room to lie down – the benches to which they were chained were only a foot or so wide ("four hand-spans," according to Mascarenhas) – they had to find what sleep they could while seated: "five slaves sitting at an angle ... without being able to turn around," "their pillow the banke up right, and that dubble, not having so much roome as to stretch their legges."[36] If their *re'is* demanded it, the oarsmen had to row even while they ate their meager meals, and in the normal course of propelling the ship, they were lucky if they got even a brief respite in which to sleep: "an houre in twelve, and that at night," was Knight's experience, "when the one halfe Roaes and the other slumbers." Indeed, Knight blamed exhaustion and the sheer want of sleep for driving many *galeotti* into what he called "continuall extasies," none of which was helped by the direct sun beating on their naked backs and a thirst that often became so extreme that some oarsmen resorted to drinking sea water.[37]

These were the normal conditions of work on a galley. There were also extraordinary occasions when the slaves were pushed even further beyond these relatively commonplace travails. Situations of hot pursuit or flight, for example, could require the *galeotti* to row flat out "for whole Days and Nights successively." Morgan could recall instances when, "for many and many a League upon a Stretch, the miserable Tuggers have been urged forward, unintermittingly ... till several of the Wretches burst their Gall, and expired."[38] To urge them on, to "force the poor slaves to draw on all the force of their bodies," the bosun and his mates, along with sundry soldiers, ran back and forth on the ship's central catwalk, lashing out "when their divellish choller rose" at the oarsmen's naked backs with a tar-dipped rope's end or – their preferred whip for such work – a dried, stretched bull's penis: "a Bulls Pizzle."[39] The chase (or flight) was for many contemporary observers the greatest horror of all of galley slavery: those who witnessed (and, according to many, smelled) a corsair galley as it plowed its inexorable way across a flat sea, powered only by human suffering, never forgot the spectacle. Joseph Morgan called it

> That least-tolerable and most-to-be-dreaded Employment of a Man deprived of Liberty.... Those who have not seen a Galley at Sea ... cannot well conceive the Shock such a Spectacle must give to a Heart capable of the least Tincture of Commiseration. To behold Ranks and Files of half-naked, half-starved, half-tanned, meager Wretches, chained to a Plank, from whence they remove not for Months together ... urged on, even beyond human Strength, with cruel and repeated Blows, on the bare Flesh, to an incessant Continuation of the most violent of all *Exercises*[40]

The only labor on the galleys that some claimed was even worse than
the chase (evidently having experienced both first-hand) were the ceremonial displays that the*re'is* might periodically demand of their *gale -
otti* worse in the sense that the order to "row proudly" was occasioned
by no other necessity than the commander's desire for pomp and
display, to announce a capture or simply to celebrate coming home to
port:

> With a long stroake one in halfe a quarter of an hour; the action,
> their heads bowed to the Oares Geroone, their fall with a caper, a
> princely sport to the spectators, and most royall of navigations, but
> the most vile of all slaveries to the subjected.[41]

Not surprisingly, the galleys often proved fatal for their slave crews.
Marcello Costa, the Church's vicar in Tunis during the 1670s, made a
point of meeting the returning fleet well equipped with holy oil for
performing extreme unction, "since a number of the crews return here
gravely ill, and for their many sufferings and beatings, many of them
die." From Costa's point of view, those that made it back to port to die
were the lucky ones, since at least they could receive holy rites. Any
galeotto who died or fell seriously ill while out *al corso* was unceremoni-
ously and "immediately thrown into the sea, whether dead or alive," to
keep the ship's weight down.[42]

Fearing the possibility that they would die outside their religion, slaves
particularly dreaded being sent to sea: some made their wills before
setting off.[43] Owners knew they could exploit this fear to gain compliance
and threatened to sell to the galleys those who were disobedient or slow
in coming up with their ransom. If a master especially wanted to punish a
slave, he might sell (or threaten to sell) him to the Sultan's Imperial Fleet
operating in the Levant, a fate from which few ever returned or even
managed to get word back home.[44] In their use of such threats, slavers in
Barbary – and especially those operating out of Turkey's Balkan ports of
Dulcigno, Lepanto, and Santa Maura – were emotionally manipulating
their slaves in much the same fashion as did masters in the states of
Virginia or Maryland, who would threaten recalcitrant bondsmen with
sale to the frontier – which meant the "Deep South," to states like
Alabama or Georgia – where blacks feared they might disappear forever.[45]
In their letters home, Italian slaves still relatively close to home, in
Dulcigno or Santa Maura might themselves play on this theme, no doubt,
in the hope that it would resonate with their relatives. Typical was
Micozzo di Bastiano, from Città Nuova, who wrote home in 1677:

For the love of God, my Father, do not abandon me in this horrible captivity; for the Viscera of the Virgin Mary, that which you have to do, do it with all speed possible, since if my ransom does not arrive soon, my Master will send me to the Galleys, where others of my companions have [already] gone. For the Holy Souls of Purgatory, do not let me die in despair within the Galleys, but either with [public] Charity or with your help get me out of this Hell, where I remain, with irons and fetters and chains around my neck and shackles at my feet.[46]

Galley slavery was, in all, an unspeakably wretched existence, made worse (if possible) by the unhappy awareness that the main task of a slave oarsman was essentially to work himself to death to help his masters seize still more slaves like himself – an employment in which, as Mascarenhas lamented, "a man dies without acquiring any honor, in capturing Christians, his friends and relatives." Yet the galleys were not certain death for all who were sent to serve in them. Mascarenhas evidently was sent out a number of times during his five-year captivity ("for my sins," as he put it), as was Francis Knight. It is thanks to such "occular testator[s]," as Knight called himself, that we have as much knowledge as we do of the *galeotto*'s brutal life.[47] Others, though they may have not left such thorough accounts, endured the experience much longer. A list sent to the Venetian Senate in 1765, under the title "Slaves, subjects of the Serenissima Republic, who are Currently to be Found on the Galleys of the Grand Turk," gives the names of eleven Venetian *galeotti* who had grown old at the oar: their average age was 64, their average time in slavery had been 38 years. It is not clear if they were ever freed.[48]

Some modern-day scholars have explained this sort of tenacious survival among *galeotti* with the claim that the men went to sea only twice a year, usually for cruises of five to six weeks during the summer.[49] This seems to have been more or less the experience of Francis Knight, who observed that "[the corsairs'] custome to repose the winter ... [is] to the slaves advantage, for although they worke hard all day on land, yet they rest at night, and injoy their fills of water (which is precious in the Gallies)."[50] Not all the *re'is* practiced such a limited season for their piracy, however. Diego Haëdo, for one, praised the *re'is* of Algiers specifically because they were enterprising enough to go out *al corso* in the winter, when all the Christian galleys that might oppose them were home in port ("Trumpeting, Gaming and Banqueting," as Morgan put it). D'Aranda likewise noted in passing that in December "the *Turkish* Pirates cruze up and down along the Coasts of *Andalusia*,knowing that the wines and fruits are then transported in *English* and *Hamborough* Vessels."[51] What is certain is that the *galeotti* unfortunate enough to have been sent to the Sultan's Imperial Fleet had it much worse than those based in Barbary, since they were not only kept at sea for months at a time, but might also be denied any sort of shore leave for years at a stretch, even when their vessel was in port. Marcello Costa had to deal with these wretches first-hand, when he went to confess the men who had just arrived in Biserte on the Levantine galleys:

> I confessed them all in fifteen days, but what confessions they were! Some of them I found of thirty years [since the last confession] and the greater part of six, eight and ten years; oh, God! I asked them the cause of such neglect, and the poor dears responded to me that in the Levant they do not keep *bagni*, and being always on the galley, with no priest ever going to confess them, and not having anything to pay to the guards, they would never let them set foot on shore.[52]

Like slaves throughout history, galley slaves in Barbary tried to improve their situation and their chances of survival in whatever ways circumstances would permit. They appear to have arranged themselves in a hierarchical fashion while at sea, which offered some advantages, at least to those at the top of the pyramid and to those they may have chosen to favor with their protection. Heading this unhappy community were the dozen or so to be found on any given galley who did not have to row, or at least not very often. Most of these were the slave sailors, who operated the big lanteen sails and managed the other rigging. There were also one or more *scrivani*, or slave secretaries, on every galley, men whose literacy made them too useful for their *re'is* to waste rowing. As slaves themselves, the *scrivani* were primarily responsible for keeping track of the *galeotti*, allocating them their small rations, and, not infrequently, recording their deaths while at sea. At the same time, the *scrivani* were also expected to log in whatever prizes their galley may have taken while it was out *al corso*. They, along with whatever renegades happened to be on hand, also gathered information from new captives, to discover whether the merchandise on board and indeed the passengers themselves were protected by any treaties currently in force, or whether they could be safely impounded or enslaved. Once such a determination was made (and it could take several days), the *scrivani* had to tally up the loot seized, though by that time much of it might have disappeared into the pockets of the corsairs themselves.[53]

In addition to these privileged few, the *galeotti* themselves were organized so that every bank of oars had its own leader, called the *vogavan* – a corruption, in the *lingua franca* spoken between masters and slaves in Barbary, of the term *vogue-avant*, or pacesetter.[54] From what can be gleaned about them, the *vogavani* were the strongest and most experienced among the galley slaves, with the task not only of establishing and coordinating the rhythm of their oar with those throughout the ship, but also of acting in effect as squad leaders of their own bench. In this respect they resembled those known in America as "drivers" – the head slaves who were responsible for organizing and coercing their fellows to work on the plantations of the Old South. Like the drivers, the *vogavani* also spent their working days under the lash of the overseer – in this case the bosun – balancing the privileges to be earned by carrying out the master's orders with the dangers of arousing too much hostility from the other *galeotti*; also like the drivers, *vogavani* could easily enough desert the *re'is* and join those they helped to oppress, if the moment looked good for a mutiny.[55]

To an extent, then, the *scrivani* and the *vogavani* may well have served as a sort of slave leadership on the galleys.[56] As slaves themselves, of course, neither could provide much protection for their charges against the bosun's whip or the ire of any other Muslim. After all, as Knight wrote of the lot of the *galeotti*, "they are beaten to put on their clothes and beaten to take them off, they are beaten, to [make them] eate, drinke, sleepe, and wash, and are beaten for doing any of these."[57] Perhaps, however, the *scrivani* and *vogavani* could at least have promoted in some small way the welfare of a few favorites: extra rations, for example, or a different position, to "a more restful one" – relatively speaking, of course.[58] As with so much of the slave hierarchy in Barbary, even this wretched society of the galleys revolved for the most part around money. Slaves with money could at least hope to buy the goodwill of these unofficial leaders, getting for themselves those few, degraded pleasures and privileges that the life of the *galeotti* had to offer.

That slaves such as these were able to buy themselves a few wretched comforts is one of many indicators that money did circulate even among those who had been stripped of every possession at the moment of their capture and whose very being, with all its earning capacity, was meant to belong to their masters.[59] It was, indeed, the custom among many of the *re'is* to allow even the *galeotti*, who were about as far down in the slave world as it was possible to be, some share of the prizes and loot, along with everyone else who had a share of the galley, from the *armadores* and the *re'is* himself, to the sailors, passengers, and cabin boys. Of the seven-sixteenths allotted to the crew, Morgan claimed, the slave sailors, *scrivani*, *vogavani*, and *galeotti* could claim shares ranging from that given to "the meanest Swabber" to as high as some of the ship's officers. The masters of these slaves had a right to take whatever they wanted of these earnings, but, as Salvago put it, "according to the goodness of their nature, they make some recompense [*cortesia*] to the slave." According to Morgan, this might amount to upwards of half of the slaves' share of the prize money, though de La Motte claimed that those belonging to the ruling pasha or the *divan* were lucky if they got a third.[60]

When the corsair galleys were back in port, as Francis Knight observed, the *galeotti* "worke hard all day on land." Locked down for the night in the public (or semi-private) bagnos, they were lined up at dawn, six days a week, and assigned their day's work by the prison secretary, the *scrivan bagno*. As in the galleys, these slaves seem, when ashore, to have had little respite from their often extremely hard

Slaves digging lime or salt (from Pierre Dan, *Historie van Barbaryen en des zelfs Zee-Roovers,* Amersterdam, 1684)

labors, which, according to John Foss, ran, without a pause for lunch, "from day break in the morning, until a certain hour in the afternoon, which they call *Laza*, which is just half an hour before sunset, summer and winter."[61] Though the work they did varied according to the season or the special needs of their masters, these galley slaves – who could number into the thousands – were most typically put to quarrying and transporting stone. Thomas Saunders left a picture that was both bleak and succinct of this work:

> I was put to be in stones and other[s] to carrie stones and some to draw the Carte with earth, and some to make morter, & some to draw [cut] stones ... and thus we were put to al kind of slaverie that was to bee done.[62]

As a rule, the roughest aspects of construction were assigned to slaves such as these: "mostly dividing the tasks," as some claimed, "not according to just reason ... but giving the weakest the gravest labors, if they could not furnish some sort of gift." In the regency capitals and the port cities of Morocco, building projects on a pharaonic scale depended on a steady supply of cut stone, and slaves were driven hard to furnish it. In Algiers this meant enormous stones "for the maintaining and for the building of the Mole" – the large breakwater that turned Algiers into an especially protected (and well-fortified) harbor.[64] Quarried and blasted from the hills about 2 miles outside of the city and weighing anything between 20 and 40 tons, these blocks had to be dragged on a form of sled with upwards of "six or seven hundred men to each sled ... haul[ing] it with ropes about seven inches in circumference." The daily quota for each sled was set by the pasha and enforced by his overseers, who were held responsible for making the quota and in consequence drove on the workers

> with additional rigor and severity ... continually beating the slaves with their sticks, & goading them with its end, in which is a small spear, not unlike an ox-goad, among our farmers.[65]

It was, indeed, a common complaint among slaves that the overseers "treat [us] like beasts," such that the response to those who collapsed from exhaustion was simply "to beat them until they are able to rise again."[66] Still worse, if possible, was knowing the apparent futility of much of their labors. Foss noted, for example, that the breakwater on which he was working was so poorly constructed – really no more than a long line of rough-cut boulders, dumped on top of one another in the sea – that

> every gale that comes washes them into deep water. After a gale they have as much need of them as they had the first hour after the mole was built. So we may conclude that this work will never be finished.[67]

Somewhat less imposing stones had to be cut and hauled for ordinary building projects: Thomas Saunders wrote of being put to such work in Tripoli, while the English translation of Philemon de la Motte's account of his redemption voyage of 1719 prominently features a panorama of the Moroccan city of Mequinez with Christian slaves in the foreground engaged in all the rough construction work.[68] The description of the labors supposedly demanded a generation later from two Neapolitan slaves in Barbary could serve as a caption for this illustration:

> [T]heir labour [is] very hard, and their usage very cruel.... [They were] often employed in digging stone for lime, and carrying it to a great distance from the quarries, building houses, &c. They are also employed in cleansing the harbours of mud, breaking up rocks at the entrance of harbours, and other laborious, filthy, and dangerous undertaking.[69]

Slaves typically had to drag or haul these materials into the city, if that was where they were to be used: it was often even necessary for them to carry the smaller stones on their backs, since, as Dan observed,

> Those of the City do not serve themselves at all with horses for this purpose, because the streets are so narrow, such that those [stone] wagons are better pulled by these poor captives.[70]

In Barbary, as in the port towns of New Orleans, Havana, and Rio, slaves were fundamental for the transport and hauling of all sorts of goods, especially heavy and bulky ones. Foss observed how, in the docks, "some part of the slaves are constantly carrying hogsheads of sugar, pipes of wine, casks of nails, cannon, etc." Foss also echoed Dan in noting how "every article that is to be transported from one part of the [city] to another ... must be carried by the slaves, with poles upon their shoulders," since "the streets are so narrow, that no kind of carriage is used here, not even a wheelbarrow. In many of the streets it is difficult for one man to pass another." The need for human muscle and dexterity in house construction was especially strong in Algiers, where the wealthy liked to have their villas built on the scenic outskirts of town, high above the harbor. As d'Aranda observed,

> In the mean time we were at work about a house our Patron [Ali Pegelin] had built in the upper part of the city; for it is to be noted that the City of *Algiers* is built on the ascent of a high mountain, and the place where the house was built, was so steepy to get up to that a Mule could not go up it with any load. So that all the materials were to be carried up on men's backs, or in their arms.[71]

Other heavy tasks – chopping and hauling firewood from the nearby hills; mining salt; digging, mixing, and carrying mortar – were also imposed on these slaves. Men were moreover regularly sent into the hills behind Algiers and Tunis to cut heavy timber for building new galleys and for repairing ships that had been damaged or captured while on raids. Lacking any significant rivers on which they might raft the logs down to the coast, these slaves had to drag the trees overland – sometimes they were given oxen or horses for the job, but just as often they would apparently have to rely on their own brute strength.[72]

Unskilled slaves were also likely, at some time or other, to find themselves sent out to work on their master's farm, orchard, or vineyard – the usually small plots of land (perhaps a few hectares) that the slaves referred to as *masseries* or *giardini*. For peasants taken in coastal shore raids, such work would have seemed very much like what they were used to back home, although many complained about "the violent [summer] heats of those countries" where they were forced to labor. Dan listed four sorts of work they might be put to – herding, working the soil, cultivating, and harvesting – but there was also a host of other menial tasks to be done, such as gathering and pressing olives, hauling flour or produce, cutting reeds and ditch-digging, building mud walls, or harvesting grain of various sorts and grinding the wheat (either in a mill or by pounding it in a mortar).[73] Dan, along with other polemicists, also claimed that these slaves were "sometimes made to work the earth attached to a yoke, along with an ass or a horse, according to the pleasure or caprice of their Patrons or Masters." Such a sadistic (and obviously highly symbolic) task may have been just a literary trope – it was often used by writers who, like Dan, were clerics; or perhaps it represented a form of punishment. One wonders in any case how effective humans could ever be at such a task.[74] One thing, at least, that is fairly certain was that many slaves from comfortable backgrounds were not up to such demands, at least not by themselves: as one contemporary commented, even the rather basic demand that they "dig in the *giardino* of the master seems to them hard and very fatiguing."[75]

Visitors to Algiers in the seventeenth and eighteenth centuries claimed that there were thousands of these country slaves, each working somewhere in the wide agricultural belt that encircled the city, under the eye of an overseer who was usually a renegade but who might also be a hired Moor. As we have seen, the extent to which slaves were engaged in farm work is almost impossible to calculate and their numbers remain considerably more uncertain than, for example, those of the *galeotti.* Several observers reported that the *masseries* themselves amounted to somewhere around 15,000 plots, but their average size, the workforce they required, and the way they were organized are still largely open to conjecture. Those who wrote of being sent to toil in the country portray the work as fairly solitary – nothing like the gang labor in the towns or what is commonly held to have been imposed on African slaves in the Americas. Chastelet des Boys, for instance, said he was sent out of town to dig furrows in his master's "great garden" with just three other *camarades de labourage* (although there may have been others already there); d'Aranda likewise seems to have worked in his owner's vineyard as part of a group of a dozen or so slaves.[76] It certainly appears that these slaves were engaged in producing wheat, fruits, and vegetables for their owner's consumption or for local sale. Though one observer claimed that around Tunis "they grow orange trees in such great quantities that the trees are used for making charcoal," there is no indication that any crops were produced on a large enough scale for commercial export – at least not on the scale of the cotton, sugar, indigo, rice or tobacco grown by slaves on the big plantations in the Americas.[77]

It is also fairly certain that many of these "country slaves" spent their nights in the city, either in their master's house or in one of the bagnos. Rising at dawn, they made the trek out to the farm every day – not too difficult for Chastelet, whose master's *masseria* was less than a mile from his house, but rather more daunting for William Okeley, who had to travel 12 miles to reach his owner's "fair Farm."[78] Slaves whose master's land was still further away from town usually spent a week or more at a time there, often sleeping in the open or in a shed if they were more fortunate. Either way, many who had to spend weeks at a time in the country seem to have suffered in morale, both from being cut off from the company of their fellow Europeans and from the despair that came from having no chance to earn money to buy extra food or to save towards an eventual ransom. Okeley reckoned that, once relocated to the country, "I should lose ... *all means, all helps,* and therefore, *all hopes,* to rid myself out of this Slavery;" Father Francesco di S. Lorenzo moreover lamented that such unfortunates not only "stay naked in every sort of weather, [but] as to spiritual matters, they live like animals," denied the chance to hear mass or speak with a priest.[79]

Still more unsettling for these country slaves was the real possibility that they might be snatched up in – of all things – a slave raid. Neighboring mountain peoples, the Berbers and Tuaregs, appear to have occasionally attacked outlying farms and were happy to enslave anyone they found there, whether Moors, renegades, or slaves.[80] As bad as a slave's life might have been under a Turkish or Moorish master, things could turn much worse with these nomads, who often took their captives far into the interior, "feeding them as little as possible, taking from them the greatest amount of work they could give," and leaving them virtually no hope of eventual escape or contact with fellow Europeans.[81] A white slave in Barbary not surprisingly tended to dread the possibility (or even the threat) of being sent "up into the country, where he should never see Christendom again, and endure the extremity of a miserable banishment," much as European slaves still held in the Balkans feared being sold off to Barbary itself, and, as we have seen, black slaves in the American coastal states felt the danger of being sold off to Mississippi or Texas, to end their lives far from their families or friends.[82]

When the pasha, the *divan*, or the great slave owners had no immediate jobs that needed doing, they might rent their workers out to one or another entrepreneur in town. Some of these ran workshops, or proto-industrial factories, set up on the basis of cheap, readily available slave labor, enterprises that apparently resembled the slave factories that operated in New Orleans and Baltimore, where rented slaves were an essential part of the workforce.[83] William Okeley, for example, told how he had been "commanded ... to go work in the Looms with two other English-men that were Slaves, and Linen-cloth Weavers;" Father Dan wrote of brickyards "where [slaves] are employed in imitation of the Israelites held captive in Babylon;" d'Aranda was sent to a rope walk in Algiers, where the work, he noted, "laid me down extremely wearied" every evening. The slaves of Tripoli, on the other hand, complained of "the exhaustion of pounding gunpowder in this [city's] Powder mill."[84]

Not all slaves had to endure all these travails, however. In a world where everything could be had for a price, some of the "public slaves" were lucky or well-connected enough that they managed to buy themselves out of the galleys and indeed out of work altogether. This was by no means cheap, and it was obviously difficult for many of these men, who were generally the worst off of all slaves, to find the necessary cash. Some might have rowed with an especially successful (and generous) *re'is* and done well with prize money; others, less fortunate, might try to convince the local money-lenders that they had wealthy relatives who could repay a loan that typically carried interest of 4 or 5 percent per month.[85] To get out of galley service, slaves paid what was known as the *gileffo* (or *geliffo,* or *gelif* – supposedly a corruption of the Arab word *khalifa*) directly to the galley captain, money that was meant to allow him to rent or hire a replacement *galeotto.* Black Africans, either free or slave, were preferred for this.[86] The *gileffo* in Tunis in the mid-seventeenth century was typically around 20 Spanish pieces of eight. If a slave sought to buy his way out of the two voyages a year that might be expected of him, he would consequently need 40 pieces, or something like a sixth of what his master might demand for his ransom – not counting the interest he had to pay if he got the money on loan. Of course, paying such sums brought a slave no closer to freedom, and the fact that a good many chose to do so would seem to be evidence of either a general short-sightedness on their part or a genuine desperation to avoid the galleys at all costs.[87]

Nor did paying the *gileffo* get a slave out of the requirement to work while ashore. It was also possible to buy oneself out of these labor obligations, however, and the *gileffo* that allowed a slave to be left alone "to freely attend to his own business," was, according to Salvago, the not inconsiderable sum of 48 Venetian *zecchini* a year in the 1620s – more than double what it cost to get out of the galleys, and often as much as half the typical ransom of the time.[88] Such a sum represented, at the time when Salvago was writing, the equivalent of what a skilled worker could have expected to earn in Venice in a year. Paid to his master, it freed a slave from his obligations "of his daily labor;" but he still had to feed and clothe himself.[89]

A particular sub-group of slaves for whom this regular payment was especially important were slave priests. Throughout the sixteenth and most of the seventeenth centuries, there always seemed to have been a dozen or more such individuals scattered through the bagnos, men who usually had been picked up by the corsairs while traveling as passengers aboard a hostile ship. During the 1500s especially, the slave priests were essential in keeping up morale in the bagnos, in particular in preventing mass abjurings among slaves. It would appear that the original chapels in most bagnos were started by these men, who conducted religious services as regularly as possible, encouraged the dispirited, heard confessions, and (most important for many slaves) gave extreme unction to the dying. To guarantee that a priest would be available to perform these services, however, the slaves themselves had to chip in to buy their cleric off from the labor that would otherwise be demanded of him – generally something on the order of a thaler or scudo per week. They also were expected to pay their priests, captive or free, a small sum for services performed and masses said.[90] Such efforts cannot have been easy, as the average slave had to work hard just to keep himself alive, but if the slaves failed to come through, they would quite likely see their bagno priest sent off to a labor that might well be beyond his strength. Such was the lot of friar Agostino da Messina, a slave in Tripoli who wrote how he had "suffered as much as any other slave had experienced, being repeatedly mistreated with beatings, sent with 22 lengths of chain ... to Gargasso to cut stone." Friar Niccolò da Scio too wrote of priests who were sent to the Tripolitan quarries, "all four chained together to cut stone eight miles away [from town]."[91] The widespread belief among slaves that Muslim slave owners in Barbary generally – and the *Tagarin*, or Moorish refugee class in particular – bore a grudge against captive priests and liked to set them to hard labor was to an extent borne out in anecdotes told by the slaves and widely spread by missionaries and the priests themselves.

The services of a preacher were obviously highly regarded among slaves, worth the cost for the comfort such a man could bring and made all the more affordable the more slaves there were to contribute a share. Such efforts among Catholics were replicated to an extent among the many Protestant slaves in Barbary. William Okeley noted that in the 1640s the Protestant English slaves in Algiers contracted "a Person of very Sober, Grave, and Religious Deportment," named Devereux Spratt, to preach to them three times a week, in a hall that the slaves themselves rented. To do so the slaves "engaged to allow him a *Competency* to maintain himself, and satisfie the expectations of his Patron." Although Spratt was a junior minister, freshly ordained, Okeley reported that "to our Meetings resorted many, sometimes three or fourscore ... [and] we found our burdens much lighter." Such services were necessarily dependent not only on the slaves' willingness to pay a portion of their often very meager savings, but also on their masters' agreeing to let them (and, of course, the preacher) take part: Okeley went on to lament how

> It is true, that such were the circumstances of the Slavery of many poor Christians, that they *could not* attend [these prayer meetings]; and such the wretched carelessness of others, that they *would not* attend.[92]

Yet despite an often heroic commitment to the spiritual well-being of their fellow captives, the slave priests were evidently an uneven lot. Many who had been captured at sea seem to have felt no particular calling for this difficult work, and not a few of them complained vociferously and frequently to Rome of their wretchedness and sense of abandonment.[93] Those who were not quickly ransomed appear to have been especially prone to abjuring and converting to Islam. It was in fact a commonplace in Barbary that, when the corsairs took a prize, they (and renegades in particular) sought out any priest among the passengers, "not for the profit of the ransom but only to disillusion and convert him."[94] Even those who held to their religion could represent a problem for the missionaries that Rome began to send to the regency capitals after 1620. Freed from hard labor, yet often demoralized by their squalid condition, such men might refuse to heed the authority of the missionaries, who, in turn, wrote to Rome, denouncing them for drunkenness, womanizing, or other lapses. On the other hand, cooped up as these slave priests were with the other "public" slaves in the bagnos, they better understood the hardships of this life and might consequently be better placed to win their loyalty. As a result, bitter antagonisms could break out between the bagno slaves led by the slave priests and the missionaries, who not only lived outside the bagnos, but might consider it quite degrading even to spend one night in such a prison – and who therefore could lose touch with their bagno slave parishioners.[95] Their disputes not only produced a constant flow of letters of complaint to Rome from both sides – filled with gossip and invective about neglect, whoring, gaming, and financial scandals – but could also sometimes drag in the local Turks, who appear to have been annoyed and amused in equal degrees by such signs of Christian friction.[96]

The tariff, or *gileffo*, collected from slaves in lieu of work should be seen not as a privilege granted to a few captives but as a special case, or extension, of what was a defining element of slavery in Barbary. Essentially, all bondsmen there, whether publicly or privately held (the situation of women is not so clear), were seen by the slave owners as "obliged to pay their master a certain sum every month" – money they had to earn through work, if they could not come by it in other ways.[97] The notion was that a slave had to pay for his own slender maintenance allowance for food, clothing, and shelter; if he had funds left over after this, he could begin to think about buying himself off work altogether, by paying the *gileffo*. It was up to the slave to find ways to raise the sum demanded during whatever free time he could find, either on Friday (which was usually, though not always, a day of rest) or in the hour or two between the time when his assigned work stopped and the bagno was locked for the night.[98] This meant that when galley slaves were ashore, even though they were routinely set to work at various tasks about the city, they still had to pay the guardian *basha* of their bagno for their lodging, miserable as this was. In the 1650s, according to Francesco di San Lorenzo, this amounted to one Spanish piece of eight, to be paid every month in exchange for a place in one of the covered cubicles. Anyone who could not pay it slept on the stone floor in the open courtyard, without benefit of cover.[99]

Demands for maintenance payments were also typically imposed on the slaves of private individuals. William Okeley noted that, for a slave, "'tis very common, having a Monethly Tax imposed upon him by his Patron, which he must scrape up where he could, and besides maintain himself." Since few masters gave their slaves anything in the way of support, beyond the barest essentials of black bread and water, this tariff conflated the twin notions of the slave paying for the cost of his upkeep and also providing his owner with a steady return on the initial outlay that had been needed for his purchase price. Piecing together what little information is available on slaves' sale prices in the *badestan* and what is known of the "tax" that slaves said they were forced to pay gives the impression that masters were looking for something of the order of an annual return of around 20 percent on their initial investment.[100] Once again, however, the slaves of private owners still had to work, even after they had paid this monthly fee – unless, of course, they could come up with the *gileffo*.

The requirement that slaves pay their masters for the dubious privilege of being chattel may seem strange, and certainly it struck some contemporaries that way. As Okeley put it,

> My Patron ... told me, I must allow him *two Dollars per moneth*, and Live ashore where I would, and get it where I could. This was a *hard*

chapter. That he that could not *maintain himself,* should be compelled to contribute to the maintenance of *a n o t h e r,* it was difficult *t o
raise increase* out of *no stock,* and to *pay Interest* out of no *Principal*;
but there was no contending.[101]

Many, if not most, slaves found themselves at some point in the same
bind as Okeley, and it was not an idle problem. Chattel of private
owners who failed to come up with their monthly (or weekly, or daily)
payment could expect a beating to encourage them to show more spirit
in the future. Chastelet des Boys described how his first, not very
successful day trying to earn money for his master ended:

> The master, finding ... a shortage of what he had demanded, got
> himself ready to carry out his threats and commanded two of his
> English slaves to turn me over with my head down, and passed my
> feet inside a gadget or clamp of wood, which two others kept ele-
> vated while the Turks beat on the soles of my feet thus inserted and
> attached.[102]

Having no knowledge of either the customs or the language of the city
where they found themselves, most newly purchased slaves soon realized that to get started they had little choice but to turn for help to the
very master who was demanding this payment. Some masters, it seems,
did indeed already have their own ideas about how such slaves could
earn their keep. One of their favorite techniques was to send out these
otherwise unskilled newcomers to sell water around town. Dan claimed
that this was work "for those whose old age has taken away their
strength," but he also insisted that it was by no means an easy job, for
all of that. Chastelet des Boys, although certainly not old, would no
doubt have agreed. Soon after he arrived at the house of his new
master, a Moor named Oge Ali, he was

> ordered ... to carry water from the public fountains around the
> town to the house of individuals, selling enough of it that I should
> bring him twenty aspers (eighty deniers of our money) every
> evening, on pain of [getting] a hundred blows [with] a stick. The
> next day he did not fail to give me two great bronze jugs, which I
> could barely carry empty; but fear gives strength and wings to those
> who run, however loaded they may be. Like the others, I therefore
> displayed [myself] along the streets, crying at the top of my voice,
> *Ab el ma* (which is to say, who wants some water?).[103]

Despite the seeming difficulties in this trade, a few slaves apparently made a success of it; Chastelet compared himself unfavorably with "the old timers, who have their customers and know the short-cuts." No doubt they, like Chastelet himself, were encouraged in their efforts to bring home the necessary aspers by their awareness of the beating that would reward their failure to do so. Slaves were also sent out to hawk tobacco and spirits in the streets: Chastelet described a friend of his, a fellow French slave, who had to walk around town, loaded up "with his bottles of eau-de-vie and his little packets of tobacco." One gets the impression that such slave vendors operated in a gray zone between providing a necessary public service and simple begging. Certainly they seem to have been aggressive enough in seeking their customers, but vendors could also be competitive with one another, fighting for rights over the best territories, much like beggars did in Europe. They also treated new arrivals with the sort of contempt and mockery often heaped on the uninitiated in such situations – something that Chastelet had to undergo at the hands of the more experienced water-sellers in Oge Ali's household.

Such were the tasks and demands typically imposed on those slaves who could offer their masters little or nothing in the way of readily exploitable skills. This was, in fact, the way most slaves tried to present themselves, keeping quiet about any valuable abilities they might have had and generally following what George Elliot called "that Piece of Policy which the Christians frequently make use of in concealing their Qualities, and disguising their Conditions," since those with well-to-do relations or useful skills could then expect to see their sale price, and thus their possible ransom, shoot up accordingly. Training, as much as birth, was what most slave buyers in the *badestan* were looking for, with the result that every dealer there cried up the talents and skills of every captive they had for sale. Such boasts were often evidently pure noise, since it appears that buyers made their purchases more in the hope than the certainty that they were picking up a knowledgeable craftsman for the price of unskilled chattel. When they got their slave home, new masters had to set about trying to uncover what their purchase was usually trying so hard to conceal – the exact extent and nature of his marketable and exploitable skills. It was a process fraught with suspicion on the one side and fear on the other, made all the more difficult by the customary lack of a common language – though such opacity did not always prevent master and slave from exchanging religious insults that each found fully comprehensible.[104]

Slaves who turned out to be less than their masters had hoped for, who really had no special skills or any rich relatives to pay a high ransom – or who at least stuck with such a story – could get severely beaten just for the disappointment they had caused. Though both contemporaries and later scholars have often assumed that masters were generally too sensible (or simply too covetous) to harm their valuable property with such a show of pique, the slaves themselves often argued otherwise, especially when it came to these initial encounters, when tensions and suspicions were clearly high. George Elliot wrote that his new owner took a stick and "broke my Head in several places, and never ceast till he made me all in a Gore blood [and] I was not able to stir," simply out of rage at discovering that Elliot was neither as rich nor as well connected as the slave dealers had made him out to be. Beaten almost insensible, Elliot still recognized the bind he had inadvertently been put into:

> I found myself under much worse circumstances than other Christian Captives, by how much I sustained greater Expectations, and was least able to Answer them; but what was the greatest Aggravation of my Misfortunes was, that I should very much contribute to the calling into Question [my master's] Prudence and Judgement, because all the Town would admire when they shall see the Event, that the wise *Hamed Lucas* was imposed upon in giving 600 Pieces of Eight for a poor Slave, who was not worth a *Maravidi*.[105]

A master's pride, then, and his fear of facing public humiliation might cause a slave owner to forget his self-interest and beat a disappointing slave until the man was crippled or even killed. At least a dead slave could be quietly disposed of, without causing his master further embarrassment, and some masters would apparently have preferred simply to kill an unsatisfactory slave on some flimsy excuse; they were certainly within their rights to do so. Elliot reported that a friend of his master, with whom he was able to converse (in Latin), warned him that "if my Patron [were] ... to find himself Bilkt in all his great Expectations, he would certainly convert his Hopes into an extravagant Rage, and then put me to some cruel Death."[106] How common such abuse was is difficult to say, but it would be unwise to dismiss it altogether in a world where only a master's cupidity could protect his slaves from his possibly much stronger emotions of rage, contempt, and the fear of dishonor.

Nevertheless, not all slave owners were as volatile as Elliot's Hamed Lucas or Okeley's *Tagarine* master, whose father (and then the master himself) beat their new slave "with *severe blows*" for his (correctly) perceived insults to Islam.[107] Some were willing patiently to interrogate their recently purchased slave for hours, using whatever language or interpreter would function and hoping to persuade or trick him into revealing what abilities he had. Chastelet des Boys, for example, had claimed to be a poor soldier of fortune, captured on his way to serve the Portuguese Crown. It was one of the classic claims of Europeans taken at sea, since it implied neither wealth nor skills beyond the strictly military. But Chastelet's new owner made short work of such assertions, when "he fetched for me a great flintlock musket ... that he himself had loaded and presented it, smiling, with the order to shoot." To his embarrassment, Chastelet suddenly no longer seemed like much of a soldier, since he was unable even to support the weight of a large military musket, and his master was prompted to ask him, "with a mocking smile ... if many soldiers made like me had gone into the service of the Portuguese Crown."[108] Thédenat recorded another such exchange, this time of the mounting frustration of his own first master, "a Jew who spoke a bit of French," and who had picked him up in the *badestan* for 70 zecchini, having little or no idea what to do with him:

> This was money wasted on me, he told me, but, provided that I was well-behaved and that I worked well, he would not be at all sorry to have bought me.... As soon as we arrived at his house, he asked me what I knew how to do. "Nothing," I told him. "What? You do not have a trade?" "No." "You do not even know how to work in the garden?" "No, I only know how to write; indeed, that has always been my occupation." What good was writing to him? He had preferred that I would be a gardener, or any other occupation. "Well, then," he told me, "You are not worth anything to me: I will have to resell you, and I am afraid that if it gets out that you do not have a trade, then I will not get my money back."[109]

The hopes of Thédenat's master had not been unreasonable, for many slaves had practiced a trade before their capture, and new masters were always on the lookout for those who were accomplished tailors or weavers, knew bookkeeping or carpentry, or were able to organize and outfit a galley.[110] The most desirable skill seems to have been that of shipwright. This was especially so in the seventeenth century, when the rapid evolution of ship design – including the epochal shift from galleys to rigged sails – meant that the *re'is* had constantly to improve the quality of their corsairing ships if they were to remain competitive. Joseph Morgan, among others, claimed that the Barbary states were completely dependent on Christian foreigners for such knowledge, so much so that according to a 1633 report to the Venetian Senate, that when the Algerian *re'is* captured a vessel they looked more eagerly for shipbuilders than for loot. Given the fame of Venice's own ship-builders, the report went on, as far as the corsairs were concerned, sometimes "even though [their captives] were not master [shipwrights] it was enough just that they were Venetians."[111]

At a given time there might have been anywhere between a few dozen and several hundred shipbuilders at work in Algiers and in Porto Farina, the port town of Tunis.[112] A skilled shipwright might be given villas and mistresses of his choice; "many important Turks," it was said, "would fight among themselves to offer him silken garments, scarlet cloth, and money," if he would build their ships or train others to do so. Except for their lack of freedom, such men almost certainly led more comfortable lives in Barbary than they could ever have expected in Venice, Livorno, or Naples.[113] On the other hand, even as these and other skilled craftsmen commanded higher sale prices in the *badestan*, so their owners also demanded higher ransoms for them – sometimes very much higher than was customary for ordinary, unskilled laboring slaves, or even some gentlemen. Giovanni Battista Salvago estimated that for the especially prized master shipbuilder Giacomo Colombin, the Algerians would not settle for less than 1,000 Venetian *zecchini* – perhaps 10–20 times the going rate for a common seaman or unskilled worker.[114] Despite an intense desire to have Colombin back in the Venetian Arsenal (and out of the employ of its enemies), and despite the fact that patrician slaves regularly had to come up with similar sums to ransom themselves, the Venetian government apparently blenched at the idea of a single worker costing so much. In the end, Colombin obtained his freedom by escaping – after 31 years in slavery.[115]

Slavery was not always so alluring for more ordinary shipbuilders, however, and it would indeed seem that many of those who worked under coveted master craftsmen like Colombin were treated as badly as any captives in Barbary. In Porto Farina in particular, about 30 miles north of Tunis, the 300 or so slaves who were set to work building galleys or warships in the 1670s were, for want of a proper bagno to house them, herded every evening into the local *mattamoro*. This was a chamber constructed especially for slaves, a pit in the ground that was roofed over, with just a single, barred opening in the ceiling. As Father Marcello Costa described it, the *mattamoro* was

> dug underground 20 or 25 steps, a dark and gloomy place, full of the worst smells and every sort of filth ... those poor [slaves] being one on top of the other, and the place is so constricted and lacking sufficient air to breathe, that it happens that, leaving in the morning from that grave and feeling the [outside] air, [some] fall to the earth dead.[116]

These, then, were the working conditions and the sorts of tasks to which Christian slaves were assigned in Barbary. Some slaves, however, were apparently given no specific work at all, but simply told they were to come up with the necessary 20 or so aspers every evening, by any means they wished. It was a system that might be called chattel *laisser faire*, and if nothing else it must have contributed to the especially lively social and economic atmosphere that pertained in the North African ports. D'Aranda, for one, noted some of these activities, which might be as ingenious as they often were pathetic. Some slaves, he said, made toys out of scraps of wood or cloth and sold them to local children as Ramadan gifts; others who lacked any skills as toymakers might offer themselves as toys to neighborhood children, playing the horse to draw miniature chariots: the children piled in and, as d'Aranda recalled, "know what it is to give them their pains," beating them with sticks as adults might with an old donkey or nag. Another, somewhat more enterprising slave borrowed the equivalent of a few *livres* from a fellow slave and

> bought with it a pair of Nine Pins, and Pidgeon-holes. He went out of the City, neer the Gate, hir'd out his pins, and the Holes, to the children who were playing there, and so made a shift to live pretty well.[117]

William Okeley, who was in Algiers at about the same time as d'Aranda, seems to have been more entrepreneurial – or at least more fortunate – than those who tried to survive by catering to the local children. Faced with the usual demands from his owner for regular cash payments – two dollars a month in his case – he borrowed "a small modicum" from that same master to go into a partnership with another English slave in a shop that sold "Lead,

Iron, Shot, Strong-waters, Tabacco, and many other things." By combining their slender profits with what other credit they could get, Okeley was soon not only paying off his monthly tithe, but also making such major purchases as "no less than a *whole But of Wine*" which he and his partner were eventually able to resell.[118]

Despite his efforts (or perhaps because his partner drank the profits), Okeley seems to have only scraped by as a shopkeeper in Algiers, "[wearing] out three or four irksome Years in this way of Trading." He would have done much better if instead of selling wine retail he had managed to get a license to run one of the taverns that flourished in the bagnos. These dank and smoke-filled holes seem to have been the only place in the Barbary port cities where one could openly buy alcohol: Islamic law forbade believers from owning or running such establishments, but local Turks, Moors, and renegades were more than willing to spend their time getting drunk in them if they were run by Christians. Slaves were thus ideal for providing this neat loophole for those Muslims who wished to drink out of public view, while the tavern keepers themselves were able to do quite well for themselves in the process. That running a tavern could be so lucrative inevitably meant that there was considerable competition among slaves for permission to operate one, with the result that the taverners ended up having to pay not only the rent for their space and furnishings, but also a variety of bribes and fees to the guardian *basha*, the owner of the bagno, and sometimes to the pasha himself. It became a commonplace among those who, like Philemon de la Motte, believed that the slaves in Barbary "are not indeed so unhappy," to single out these tavern keepers in support of such claims, asserting that

> Some of them have, with three or four Years good Management, picked up as much Money as sufficed to defray all these Expenses [to set themselves up], to pay off the Debts they had contracted, which may amount to seven or eight hundred Pieces of Eight, and moreover to repurchase their Freedom, which amounts still higher.[119]

Since there was little viticulture in the vicinity of Algiers or Tunis (and none at all at Tripoli), the wine sold in the taverns, along with the stronger spirits, largely had to be imported from Europe or the Levant.[120] Sometimes this was legally purchased, but it would seem more likely that a fair amount of this tavern wine arrived in the form of loot, seized by the corsairs along with the prizes they took and sold in bulk to the tavern operators.[121] D'Aranda wrote of going to "the Tavern of our Bath, where there was good Sack brought in from the last prize which the *Turks* had taken, whence it came that our Bath was every day full of drunken *Turks* and *Christian* slaves who were Renegadoes." For those with the right connections it was possible to realize a 400 percent mark-up on captured wine: enough of a profit that some taverners at least provided those who ordered drinks with free food.[122]

Anyone who could purchase this sort of operation or who could buy a position as a gang boss or as *scrivan* – either of a galley or of one of the bagnos (or even as the *Scrivan grande* of all the slaves, although this would cost him a good 1,000 *zecchini*) – could "in a few years earn the price of his ransom." Having done so, one might presume, these few fortunate slaves would go back home, none the poorer for their experience. Yet the hold that the freewheeling world of the Barbary cities had on these men often turned out to be surprisingly strong. Slaves who had mastered the rules of this society to the extent that they could make a good living at it might prove unwilling to leave even when they could. Legends grew up around some of them who, having paid off all but the last ducat of their ransom, preferred to remain in slavery, in order to hold on to such jobs that were the preserve of slaves alone. D'Aranda wrote of one such entrepreneurial slave named Alferez of Majorca, who eventually reached the point where he ran three taverns and enjoyed great respect and status with his fellow Majorcans for his generosity.

Just how common these self-made taverners were among the slaves of Barbary is hard to say, but certainly not all those who got a hold of such a concession managed to make a go of it. The local guardian *basha* and the pasha were quick to claim as great a share of the profits for themselves as they could, but in any case, as the French diplomat Venture de Paradis cautioned, "the larger part of [the taverners] dissipate everything on gambling, high living, and debauches, and there are very few who conceive of procuring their own liberty with a wise economy."[123]

As meeting places for all the various ethnicities in Barbary, the bagno taverns were also the usual rendez-vous for selling or reselling stolen goods. Theft, according to d'Aranda, was "the profession most us'd" among slaves, in part, he claimed, because many a master, like his own Ali Pegelin,

does not allow his slaves any thing towards their sustenance, [so] the greatest part of them live upon what they can steal, and every night the booty of the precedent day comes to be sold.[124]

At the same time, it would appear that more than a few slaves were adroit thieves, either because they knew the craft before capture or were quick learners once arrived in Barbary. Ali Pegelin once supposedly said that "his *Christians* wore Hooks on their Fingers," and d'Aranda famously wrote of one Italian *galeotto*, whose *nom de guerre* was Fontimamma, who was so adept at thieving that he once managed to steal the anchor right off Pegelin's own galley and sell it to some passing Moorish iron merchants for five pataques (roughly five Venetian *zecchini*).[125] Slaves who trafficked in more run-of-the-mill goods typically brought in "Woollen and Linnen cloaths, Shirts, Brasspots, and other pieces of household-stuff," evidently filched from unguarded kitchens, clothes-lines, or market stalls and brought to the bagno at closing time. This kind of work took a good deal of nerve, however, and those who, like d'Aranda, lacked the "confidence and subtilty enough to steal" soon learned that "that profession requires practice, especially in a place where there are so many thieves, and consequently people are more distrustful."[126]

Seen through the eyes of d'Aranda and some other (mostly later) admirers, such light-fingered slaves appear as thoroughly picaresque characters, rebels who remained resiliently unbowed by their sufferings in captivity. (D'Aranda at one point wrote of a Spanish slave, "one much respected among the slaves, and who might well be a Graduate in the University of Thieves," who not only stole a sheep on his way back from work in the countryside, but then managed to smuggle it in a sack past the guards at the town gate.)[127] It was no doubt also true, however, that dozens or even hundreds of thieves let loose on a city like Algiers had a corrosive effect on local society. D'Arvieux, in fact, claimed it was the slaves of private individuals, those who were not locked down every evening in the bagnos, who did the most damage, since

> Having the convenience of going out at night, they form a gang and go to break through the walls of the storehouses and shops, and in a couple of hours they can empty the best filled warehouse.[128]

In the Americas, slave theft has largely been considered in the context of slaves stealing from their own masters, and thus as an act of more or less veiled resistance, carried out against both the owner and an entire system based on what might be termed the primordial crime in which the slaves had themselves been originally stolen from their African homes.[129] Some of this revenge and resistance against a society that had stolen their freedom can certainly be detected in Barbary Coast slaves, who, for example, preyed so insistently on the shops of the *souk* in Algiers that the whole area had to be locked down, barricaded, and patroled every night.[130] On the other hand, slave theft in Barbary, unlike most of that in the Americas, tended to be directed away from the master, in particular towards the middling class of Moorish or Jewish traders and craftsmen. It is difficult, in such cases, to decide, as Sherry Ortner has asked: "When a poor man steals from a rich man, is this resistance or simply a survival strategy?"[131] As long as locals such as these were the target, the great slave holders seem to have cared little about restraining their thieving chattel. Morgan quoted Ali Pegelin as saying that "'his Slaves were all pilfering Rascals; that he could not help it, but advised [those who complained] to be more careful of such Rogues in the future.'"[132] Since large-scale slavers like Ali Pegelin required his slaves "to work every day, yet not have a piece of bread from the Patron," he was in effect displacing the cost of maintaining his slaves onto the public at large, as a sort of indirect tax levied through their thieving. Indeed, Morgan reported that Ali Pegelin "had the Honour of having trained up the cleanest Set of Thieves that were anywhere to be met with," adding,

> Nothing was commoner than for People to repair to his *Bagnio* in order to buy or rather redeem their own Goods, where they were publicly put up for Auction. Indeed, none would acknowledge himself the person who stole them; only the Auctioneer would tell those who laid Claim to any things, 'That the Slaves who *owned* the Goods in Question had left with him the lowest Price.'[133]

Those slaves who were especially talented thieves, like those who ran the bagno taverns or certain shops, might, after some years, set aside enough cash to buy their freedom. Their ability to do so has persuaded many modern scholars that enslavement in Barbary was more like a business arrangement between master and captive than outright American-style slavery. This has led some to conclude that the desire to make money from the captives – through a regular payoff or an eventual ransom – would have persuaded masters to work their bondsmen less vigorously than did plantation owners in the Americas.[134] Still, one should recognize, as contemporary observers did, that many, if not most, Christian slaves came from such impoverished backgrounds that no one in Barbary seriously thought of holding them for ransom, much less lending them money to start a shop or open a tavern. Only when charitable ransoming expeditions became regular events in the later 1600s would there be much hope among masters of selling slaves as poor as these. Until then, these unfortunates – who, according to surviving ransom lists, would seem to make up at least three-quarters of all slaves through the sixteenth century and well into the seventeenth – were necessarily the "slaves of work," men whose masters, since they were enjoying a glut of captives, had little reason not to work as hard and care for as little as possible. Modern scholars who have assumed that the investment alone was sufficiently important to a slave owner in Barbary to guarantee a minimum of good treatment for his chattel should keep in mind that into the mid-1600s working slaves there were both cheap (often costing much less than a horse) and easily replaced. It has already been shown that sugar planters in the Caribbean found it easier to work their slaves to death and replace them than care for them as an investment: why should slave owners in Barbary have done things any differently?[135]

4
Slaves' Life

> All this while there was no dawning of Deliverance from our Bondage: As one Year left us, another found us, and delivered us over Captives to the next: Our condition was bad, and in danger every day of being worse, as the mutable Humours of our Patrons determin'd upon us.... The truth is, in time we were *so habituated to Bondage*, that we almost *forgot Liberty*, and grew stupid, and senseless of our Slavery.[1]

William Okeley, who wrote this, was just one of the tens of thousands of Europeans who passed years – or the rest of their lives – as slaves in one of the Barbary regencies during the early modern centuries. Okeley and his fellow slaves made up perhaps a quarter of the population of Algiers, a city whose very existence was predicated on corsair piracy and slave running. The proportion of European slaves in Tunis and Tripoli in these years was generally somewhat smaller than in Algiers – around 10–20 percent – but in all three of the regencies, white slaves were both a significant and highly visible presence.[2]

Slaves had their place, albeit a humble one, in the Maghreb's social hierarchy. At the top was a dominant stratum of Turks and renegade Christians, who amounted to around 12 and 8 percent respectively of the population in seventeenth-century Algiers, for example. By law, by force, or by social example, these men ruled over the indigenous Moors and the Moriscos, who in turn enjoyed higher status than the often considerable Jewish population to be found in each of the regency capitals.[3] Slaves, as individuals without rights or personhood in law, theoretically made up the bottom layer, although some observers put the Jews (who had to pay for their right of residence) even lower. Slaves' very lack of legal personhood could, however, allow those who belonged to prestigious masters – to Turks or prominent renegades in particular – to take on some of their owner's rank, allowing them to swagger with some (though not total) impunity around town. These may have been slaves that d'Aranda had in mind, in noting that, when it came to taking water from the public fountains, "those who come to these Conduits for water, take it in their Turns, save onely the Jews, who are to give way to every Slave who comes after them, and to be serv'd last of all."[4]

As everywhere in the pre-modern world, social hierarchies in the cities of Barbary were clearly marked by personal appearance. For men, who were the more public and visible sex in North African culture, this meant such indicators as dress, hairstyle, or the right to carry weapons, though the significance these implied were more likely to evoke one's religion, race, or ethnicity than his class, occupation, or wealth, as was the rule in European cities of the time. The Turks and janissaries, who mostly came to Barbary as soldiers, though they might eventually become administrators, dressed in a manner that Laugier de Tassy called "very modest," their shirt and pantaloons cut in a very baggy fashion, their sleeveless waistcoat surmounted by a long vest that reached to the ankles, and all of it tied with a sash. Their turbans, which Tassy noted were formed from "a little thin red Cap, very curiously wrapt round with several Ells of Muslin," were, he thought, "of a very unbecoming size."[5] As much as renegades could afford to do so, they imitated these social leaders, and even more than the Turks, they went round town fairly bristling with weapons, sporting not only a scimitar and a musket, but also sundry daggers and pistols tucked into their wide sashes. Moors, on the other hand, typically clothed themselves much more soberly, in a long, hooded burnous, often of white cloth for the more wealthy. The Jews, as Mascarenhas observed, "wear a sort of black surplice of serge or flannel, a white burnous, and a black cap on the head, so that they can be distinguished from the Turks and be known as Jews." According to Laugier de Tassy, writing a century later, Jews were required by law to dress entirely in black, "as if it were to stigmatize them."[6]

In contrast to all those they had to share the cities with, Christian slaves had no designated costume as such, but since they had to make do with whatever they were allocated by their masters, their dress and overall appearance tended to fall into two general types, depending on those owners. House slaves, for example, who essentially filled the same role and lived much the same life as servants in the wealthy households of Europe, might well be fitted out with some form of livery: d'Arvieux wrote of dining at the villa of the wealthy Mehmed Chelebi, served by an entire "troop of slaves, very appropriately dressed," and presumably slaves who went into town on their master's business also wore an outfit that conveyed who their owner was.[7]

One thing that does seem clear is that slaves were in general extremely unwilling to dress like Turks: wearing livery was another matter altogether. This was not necessarily because they scorned their masters and their masters' ways, but rather because such clothing was also the outfit of the renegade. Many seemed to feel, by a process of association, that simply putting on such garments was tantamount to apostasy. "Taking the turban" was in fact one of the most common expressions of those times for converting to Islam, and slaves accusing their master of trying to force them to apostasy often traced a mimetic process that might include "circumcizing us by force and making us dress as Turks."[8] This conflation of clothing and creed could extend to female slaves as well: little girls, newly captured, could be shaved bald, "to make them Turks," this being the customary look of Turkish girls. Grown women might be forcibly dressed in Turkish outfits for the same reason; thus, according to a story related by d'Aranda,

> About five days after [her capture], the Bassa's wife took notice that [this] Christian slave was an excellent Needle-woman, good at embroidery and other things of that kind; so she was much in her Mistresse's favour, who promised her mountains of Gold, if she would renounce her faith, and embrace the *Turkish* religion. But all her temptations prov'd ineffectual ... [such that the Mistress], at a loss between astonishment and indignation ... order[ed] that the poor Slave should receive three hundred blows with a Cudgel. And perceiving that she still continu'd firm and constant as a Rock, they stripp'd her of all her cloathes, and gave her others after the Turkish mode; which she put on, but protested publickly in the presence of God, that she took them only to cover her nakedness, and not for any change of religion.[9]

Dressing a slave was certainly an issue fraught with issues of identity and status. As we have seen, when a ship was about to be boarded by corsairs, it was common for the passengers to change hastily into any outfit that might help them conceal their true station and thus confuse their captors about their ransom potential. Only a select few seem to have rejected this ploy, possibly because they disdained such theatrical stratagems or perhaps because the opportunity did not present itself.

Among the former were evidently those – high churchmen, nobles, military commanders – who were determined to keep their usual clothing out of pride in their high stature, as if to say they would not deny their status in Christendom only to save a few thousand *scudi* in ransom. Corsairs who captured or bought such high-ranking individuals were often quite willing to indulge them in their demand for respect, to the extent that they might also arrange to have them lodged at one of the local consulates, for their comfort, both social and physical. Such high-status slaves were left idle in their captivity – presumably they were charged a *gileffo* which they were readily able to pay – free to move round town "having just a small iron band at their feet to mark their condition [as slaves]." Elite female slaves might receive much the same treatment, though local custom demanded that they be kept indoors out of the public gaze; they too seem to have been allowed to keep at least some of their own clothes and sometimes their serving maids. For such individuals, European dress was a privilege that clearly distinguished them from run-of-the-mill working slaves, just as their lodgings privileged them with social connections among the town's free foreign community – its resident merchants, missionary priests, and cadre of consuls.[10]

Some slaves, on the other hand, apparently remained in European attire not because of any superior status, but simply because their masters could not afford or be bothered to give them any other clothing. Some, like Chastelet des Boys, lived in their master's house, but others were placed by their owner in the public bagnos, where they evidently made wretched figures, in their inappropriate and increasingly shabby clothing, caught between the two worlds of slave and free, maintaining their neophyte status in a fundamentally dangerous world. Turks and Moors called such newcomers "savages," according to d'Aranda, who described one such hapless novice

> who was then in his Christian habit, after the *Spanish mode*; and indeed that habit is inconvenient for a slave, in regard it is thence inferr'd that he is of no long standing there.[11]

For the large percentage of "public" slaves in Barbary, however, there was a distinctive slave garb, one that was assigned to them soon after they were sold. Like their rations and accommodations, the clothing issued to these slaves apparently improved somewhat over the centuries, though not by much. Salvago observed in the 1620s that "the Masters of the *bagnos* do not provide the Slaves with anything more than a burnous with a hood, once only at the beginning, and one pair of canvas drawers per year;" the friar Francesco di San Lorenzo reported much the same outfit half a century later: "a shirt and a pair of trousers of rough cloth."[12] Throughout the seventeenth century slaves do not seem to have been issued with shoes or boots of any sort, and those who had not managed to keep their own footwear when they were captured had to work barefoot.[13] It does not appear that slaves were given anything like a full wardrobe until the 1720s, when Venture de Paradis observed that

> When a slave is brought to Algiers, he is given a coarse shirt, a corset of coarse fabric, a culotte and a little caftan of the same material, that descends on him to the knees, a red cap, a pair of shoes and a little wool blanket that he must always conserve. As to his clothes, they are renewed for him every year.[14]

Slaves' clothing seems to have improved still further by the 1780s, as John Foss related in his own experience:

> [A]s we passed, the Turk gave each man a small bundle. On examining it, we found it contained a blanket, a *capot* (which is a sort of jacket with a head), a waistcoat, made something like a frock, to draw over the head, it not being open at the belly, a shirt, with neither collar or wristbands, a pair of trowsers, made something like a woman's petticoat, (with this difference), the bottom being sewed up, and two holes, to put the legs thro' and a pair of slippers. There was neither button, or button-hole on the whole suit.[15]

This outfit was renewed every year, traditionally on the Friday after Christmas, but even this modest bounty did not come free of charge: Foss reported that a week or so after they got their new clothes, the slaves would be sent out into the country on some especially noxious task, one that "they tell us (by way of derision) is to pay for our suit of cloathes which ... by this time is generally half worn out."[16] Even at its apparent best, in the 1790s, the slave clothing allocation in Barbary seems to have fallen short of what was typically given by planters in the American South to their slaves. As a sort of standard in this regard, Eugene Genovese has quoted one Robert Collins, a long-time slave owner from Georgia, allowing that "Collins's report was basically accurate" for plantation slaves through the South, from the 1820s to the 1850s:

The proper and usual quantity of clothes for plantation hands is two suits of cotton for spring and summer, and two suits of woolen for winter; four pairs of shoes and three hats, with which articles of dress the negro merits, and the owner chooses to give, make up the year's allowance.[17]

Collins' description was obviously appropriate for a cooler climate than Barbary's, where "suits of woolen" were presumably not needed. Even so, and taking into account Genovese's caution that "the usual distribution probably included only two or three pairs of shoes" (but also his addition that "many planters provided socks and under-clothes"), the disparity between the dress of early nineteenth-century black slaves in the American South and late eighteenth-century European slaves in the Maghreb is still striking. Genovese, as a matter of some reproach, moreover noted that in the American South "even the most generous [clothing] allotments ... left the slaves little oppor-tunity to wash and change their clothes more than once a week." Washing their clothes (much less themselves) every week seems to have been unimaginable for most of the bagno slaves in Barbary: what water they could get often had to be paid for, and few indeed seem to have been able or inclined to buy more than what was necessary for drinking.[18] As a result, it is not surprising that most of this class of slaves made a rather sorry spectacle: "Their hair and beards ... cut off with a dagger, their face ... bruised with blows and covered with mud and filth," these "public" slaves went about town looking not much different than the local beggars, "their clothes being all covered with vermin."[19] Unlike beggars, however, slaves in Tunis or Tripoli were typically hobbled with a manacle and chain weighing about 25 or 30 lb, or with a *gambetto* (as the Italians called a fixed sort of iron shackle), to make sure they would not stray too far afield. (In Algiers this was generally not the practice, unless a slave "had done some-thing stupid or a French ship were in the harbor.")[20] Even those who were without such impediments were still recognizable as slaves by the iron ring that was traditionally hammered around their ankle to mark them; Gramaye also claimed that "in detestation of the Christian name," galley slaves might also be branded with a cross on the soul of their foot.[21]

The living conditions of slaves could vary as widely as their clothing, again depending on whether they lodged with their master as servant-slaves, or whether they were "public" slaves, destined for heavy work on the galleys, in the quarries, or around the town. The best off of all

Slaves in chains (from Pierre Dan, *Historie van Barbaryen en des zelfs Zee-Roovers*, Amersterdam, 1684)

were no doubt those whose masters rented them out to the Christian missionaries and consuls in town: these had a life that in many ways must have been virtually indistinguishable from a servant's in Europe. Not only were they probably given only moderate work to do, but they also had the advantage of passing their days among others of their own culture and language, unintimidated by regular conflicts with an alien religion or (for the most part) by the threats of sale to another master. Still, those who stayed to work in a Muslim household might also enjoy comfortable living conditions, since their work requirements were generally light and their food for the most part sufficient, if not especially refined. These are the ones about whom Laugier de Tassy claimed:

> As all of the Servants at *Algiers* are Slaves, some wealthy Masters take a pride in keeping them well drest and fed, as an Honour to his Family. Several among them have no less Sway in the House than their Master, lie in the same Chamber, and are, in all Respects, treated with the Indulgence of Children.[22]

At the opposite end of the slave continuum were the "public" or bagno slaves, those unfortunates who were purchased by the local ruler or the *divan* and then sent to live in the dormitory/prisons that the slaves themselves called *bains, banhos, baños* or *bagni* – that is, baths. There is some indication that the first of these "gloomy mansion[s] of horror and despair" had, in fact, been one of the public baths – not in Barbary, however, but in Constantinople, where some of the old bath houses supposedly had to be converted hastily into slave pens when captives began to flood into the city during the early 1500s.[23] In Barbary, by contrast, most of the bagnos seem to have been built specifically to house the slaves of the ruler, the town, and the largest private owners. The first one was apparently already in operation in Algiers by 1531, during the time of Barbarossa: this was the *Bagno Beyliç*, or prison of the state slaves, which could hold upwards of 2,000 captives, "the rest being dispersed in the City, or at the Farm and Pleasure-houses." By the time Pierre Dan came to write about them a century later, the bagnos had obviously multiplied considerably: there were six in Algiers alone, with another nine in Tunis, although Tripoli still had just a single "Great Bagno."[24] In the 1660s, the number of bagnos had increased still further: eight in Algiers, as many as fifteen in Tunis, and five in Tripoli, but this represents their peak in all three cities.[25] By the end of the 1680s Algiers was down to four bagnos, and, though a fifth was evidently set up around 1698, the number had dropped to just three by the 1760s; Tunis was down to twelve in the 1680s, though Tripoli still had five; half a century later the numbers were down to just five and two respectively.[26]

Charting the proliferation and eventual decline of the bagnos is made more difficult by the fact that many of these prisons had two names, one used by the Turks and Moors and another by many of the slaves themselves. Resident corsairs, slave owners, and the like called each bagno in their town either by the name of its current owner-operator (and this could often change), by some aspect of its function, or, more rarely, by that of the original builder; then again, the Tunisian bagno of Sidi Hamouda, according to one visitor, was so named "because of a mohammedan saint who is buried nearby."[27] Pierre Dan, who used these local names, thus listed the six bagnos in Algiers as the Bagno of the Pasha (or of the *dey*) and the Bagno Beyliç, the bagnos of Ali Mami, of Sidi Hassan and of Ali Arabadji (later taken over by and known as the bagno of Ali Pegelin), and one called the bagno of the *cogolis* (that is, the *koul-oghlu* in Turkish: "the sons of slaves," meaning the sons of janissaries and local women).[28]

On the other hand, the Redemptive Fathers, missionaries, and many other visitors tended in their writings (whether in reports to Rome or in their published narratives) to refer to the various bagnos after the saint whose chapel was within them. Thus, in Algiers, the bagno belonging to d'Aranda's master, Ali Pegelin, was known as the bagno of St. Roche, and the Bagno Pasha and the Bagno Beyliç were called the bagnos of the Trinity and of St. Catherine respectively. In Tunis, by the 1720s, there were seven bagnos named in this way: Holy Cross, St. Leonard, Rosary, St. Francis, Holy Trinity, St. Sebastian, and St. Lucy. For Tripoli the two public bagnos (called simply the great bagno and the small bagno by the locals) were known to Catholics as the bagnos of St. Michael and St. Anthony, while a third prison, known locally as the *trinella* and located about 5 miles outside of town, was referred to as Santa Reschia.[29] Since most of those held in a given bagno were Catholic, these alternative names gained wide currency among slaves, the more so because the chapels were important institutions in their own right and in some instances were quite large, able to accommodate several hundred worshippers at a time.[30]

It may be tempting to conclude that this alternative naming system was an expression of calculated resistance, on the part of the slaves and of their Christian supporters, to the dominance and authority of the ruling Islamic culture: a refusal, that is, by Westerners, captive or otherwise, to recognize and accept the cultural norms of the Muslim alterity in which they found themselves.[31] This is certainly possible, though as ethnographers are well aware, resistance is often deeply, even inherently, ambiguous: seeking signs of it in a group as thoroughly diverse as the Christian slaves in Barbary can oversimplify relations not only between slaves and their masters, but also among the slaves themselves.[32] It does seem, for example, that both missionaries and slaves were unclear about both the nature and the meaning of the names that locals assigned to the bagnos. In the reports of the former and the letters of the latter, these names, when they were used, were often garbled or misspelled, and the Bagno Pasha, for one, is also referred to as the Bagno of the State, or of the King. Moreover, the Trinitarians and Mercedarians who were responsible for the chapels – and thus, presumably, for the "Christian" names of the bagnos – fought among themselves and with the missionaries from Propaganda Fide in Rome over who would have control and naming rights over these sanctuaries. To an extent such conflicts were merely reflections of much larger disputes between the orders' patrons in the Christian world. Such a squabble in the 1670s between the Spanish-backed Trinitarians and the French apostolic vicar, Jean Levacher, for example, broke out when Levacher decided to change the name of what had been the two chapel bagnos of the Trinity and of St. John of Matha (patron saint of the Trinitarians) to St. Louis and St. Roche respectively. To drive the point home, he also had the painted arms of the Spanish Crown scraped off the entrance door to the chapels.[33]

Such disputes within the bagno population – especially those involving the *papassi,* or priests – seem to have greatly amused the Turks. Up to a point, the masters were willing to foster discord among their slaves, simply to weaken slave resistance to their control.[34] It does not appear that the bagno slaves needed much encouragement to squabble, however, for bagno life was clearly based on the fundamental antagonisms defined by confession, nation, and language, where a slave's social position was as much defined by his enemies as by his compatriots. The primary point of fracture, at least in the sixteenth and seventeenth centuries, was evidently religion, though this point may have been exaggerated by the Catholic priests and missionaries whose writings are a major source on social life in the bagnos. In Algiers and Tunis, Catholics were generally in the majority among bagno slaves, while the cities of Morocco might have had more British and Dutch, and Tripoli was, at least occasionally, reportedly crowded with large numbers of Greek slaves. As we have seen, the apostolic vicars in Barbary tended to leave non-Catholics – the "heretics and schismatics," or Protestants and Orthodox – out of their slave counts. In their reports to Rome, they and the missionaries had little to say about non-Catholic Christians, except when they were trying to convert them. These priests indeed devoted considerable effort to converting other Christians, not least because they were forbidden by strict accords between Rome and the regencies (under genuine personal danger to themselves) from trying to convert native Muslims or renegades to Christianity.[35] Despite such forays into missionary endeavors – which might include attempts to sabotage the religious activities of the local Greek Orthodox priests or the Protestant consuls – these Catholics were not especially successful, if one can judge from the rather mediocre numbers they reported back to Rome.[36] This was just one indicator of the underlying gulf between Catholics and non-Catholics, and probably the least of them: d'Aranda provided a much more explicit scene, detailing a brawl between a contingent of Orthodox Russians and a group of Spaniards and Italians, one of whom

went to the little room of the *Russes* or *Muscovites* and saluted them with this speech: *Dogs, Hereticks, Savages, Enemies of God, the Bath is now lock'd, and the Guardian hath sent word, that if you have the courage to fight, you should come out of your hole, and we shall see who will have the better.* He had hardly finish'd his speech ere the sixteen *Russes and Muscovites* appeared in the Field, falling on immediately, and the *Spaniards* and *Italians* receiv'd an answer to their Embassy in good bangs with Cudgels, for they had no other Arms than their fists; but in an instant, as the saying has it, *Furor arma ministrat.* Some Forms and Tables that stood before the Taverns, and some Ladders which they also met withall, they converted into Arms, Swords, Pikes and Muskets, defending themselves generously.... They continued in that posture till darkness began to get the upper hand, and yet neither party seem'd willing to quit the field. At last a Priest of one of the Religious Orders, who liv'd in the Bath, and was a person generally well-lov'd, came to the place of engagement with a Wax Candle in his hand, endevouring all he could to appease and separate them, telling them they were all Christians, notwithstanding the difference of Religions.[37]

Secular divisions like language or politics served as points of contention among slaves at least as often as religion, however, and it would seem that those sub-groups that were the closest in background were those that tended to squabble the most. Often their brawls reflected antagonisms brought from the slaves' home countries, as in the priestly dispute noted above, or in another skirmish described at some length by d'Aranda. This fracas, which occurred in 1641, was between the Spanish and Portuguese and was superficially over some of the Spaniards' attempt to rip the Portuguese royal arms out of the chapel in the Bagno Beyliç. In reality, however, the two sides were playing out in miniature the Portuguese rebellion against Spain that was then underway in Iberia.[38]

The regular brawls between varying contingents of Spanish, Portuguese, French, or Italians are a good indication that these slaves could understand each other well enough to trade insults and provoke friction. Communication difficulties among slaves and between slaves and masters (or their overseers) were obviously a fundamental issue in Barbary, much as it was with first-generation African slaves in the Americas. Indeed, the problem must have been greater in the Maghreb, simply because slaves were prevented from raising families, and without succeeding, acculturated generations in captivity, there could be no conduit to pass along a common slave language to newcomers.[39] What there was instead was the *lingua franca*. This was the original and model of all lingua francas throughout the world, an artificial language construct whose origins were evidently among medieval sailors and merchants in the Levant, but whose primary function in Barbary was as a language of command for masters and their agents to give orders to slaves. Taking as its base a mix of non-inflected nouns and verbs from the slaves' own Romance languages – with more Spanish terms in the western Mediterranean (and much of the Maghreb) and more Italian in the east – *lingua franca* then filled gaps as needed with a variety of local words, primarily from Arabic, Turkish, and Greek. Its usage in Barbary, by masters communicating with their slaves, reversed the usual direction of flow characteristic of pidgins and other lingua francas spoken elsewhere in the colonial world – Portuguese-Malay, Cape Dutch, Chinese pidgin, or slave talk in the Americas – where masters and colonizers used simplified, disinflected versions of their own languages, with the addition of some local terms (and occasionally diction) to command their slaves and underlings.[40]

In this, the original lingua franca masters, by contrast, spoke to their chattels in a version of Romance European, rather than in a form of pidgin-Arabic or pidgin-Turkish. Why this was so is not clear, although it may be because many of the slave owners were renegades with a Romance language background. In addition, *lingua franca*, as a trade pidgin, had pre-dated the blossoming of corsair slaving after 1500. It does at least seem clear that the elites and slave-owners of Barbary Coast society considered *lingua franca* appropriate only for giving orders to slaves: it has been said of Dey Mohammed, pasha of Algiers in the late 1700s, that he "understood and spoke Lingua Franca, but he considered it beneath his dignity to use it with free Christians."[41] Yet, though masters may have treated *lingua franca* as fit for little more than the bare necessities of giving orders, there are good indications that slaves spoke it among themselves, at least when they otherwise had no language in common: d'Aranda, for instance, mentioned having a fairly involved discussion with an Icelander in it. Moreover, Marott asserted that slaves on the galleys were forbidden from speaking to one another in any language other than *lingua franca*, so that their overseers could understand what they were discussing or plotting.[42]

While many slaves may have spoken *lingua franca* among themselves and with their masters, it was still not an easy language for many to grasp, especially under the tense situations when they had to understand it to carry out orders. One master, in talking to them, might unexpectedly substitute Spanish for the more commonly used Italian terms, or vice versa; sometimes he could seek to strengthen an expression using both languages together – disparaging a slave as a "dog" twice over, as *perro cane*, or *cani perru*. Some terms evolved over time to take on different, or at least additional, meanings: the Italian *mangiar*, for example, while still signifying "to eat," or "I eat," also came to mean "eaten up," such that one said *todo mangiado* to mean "all gone," or "vanished."[43] Other words that appeared to be of Romance origin to a newcomer turned out in fact to be of Arabic or Turkish derivation and meant something quite different from what they might otherwise seem. The ubiquitous term *fantasia*, though cognate in Italian, Spanish, French, and English, was, when used in *lingua franca*, derived from the Arabic term *fantàziia,* meaning "ostentation or show." When a master reprimanded a slave as one who *pigliar fantasia*, far from meaning that the slave was daydreaming, the indication was that he was resistant, hardheaded, or stubborn – a clear warning that a beating was on its way. D'Aranda, to his cost, found himself in a state of confusion of this sort over another misunderstood term, when he was sent to work in a rope walk:

> My Companion *Renier Saldens* and I were appointed to turn the Wheel, which we did with all our strength, and all the diligence we could, because the Guardian still cry'd out to us, *Forti, Forti*, and we thought it signify'd that we should turn it as fast as we could. But it seems, in *Lingua Franca* (which is the common Language between the slaves and the *Turks* ...) the word *Forti* signifies *Gently,* and therefore having not obtain'd what he would have by crying out upon us, he came with a good cudgel, and taught us what was the signification of the word *Forti.*[44]

This kind of confusion seems to have been typical among newly arrived slaves, who were often bewildered not only about the work they were supposed to do, but also about how to get along within the bagno and its hierarchy. The cannier newcomers tried to keep a low profile until they could learn the routine and what was expected of them, struggling to cope with their overseer's orders as best they could. Both d'Aranda and Foss ended up having to pass their first nights sleeping on the stone floor, in the open courtyard of their bagno, covered only by a cloak or thin blanket. Only those who could pay a monthly tariff were allowed to sleep in the smaller rooms that lined the upper galleries of the bagnos, though these spaces could be extremely crowded, as paying slaves tried to find room for their hammock or for the "little Mattrass and Rug for their Bed" that each could buy or make.[45] Judging by the letters that slaves wrote home, however, about how they were "forced to sleep on the naked ground as if [they were] dogs," it would appear that even this modest luxury was beyond the means of many of them.[46]

What percentage of the overall slave population was kept in the bagnos is not altogether clear, not least because some bagno operators rented out their facilities to private slave owners as places to lodge their human chattel when they had no wish to keep them in the house. Such slaves, as we have seen, were typically expected to reimburse their masters for the cost of this lodging, usually by hawking water or simply by stealing.[47] For something of a benchmark, it is at least possible to estimate the bagno population in Algiers by calculating the number of galley slaves needed to operate the Algerian fleet at some points in time. According to Pierre Dan, in 1588 the city boasted 35 galleys, which between them had over 680 banks of oars, with each oar requiring three to five men to pull it. The fleet, then, would have needed upwards of 6,000 men at the oars, plus sundry slave sailors, longshoremen, and shipbuilders. Since this was just the time (1587) that Lanfreducci and Bosio placed the servile population of Algiers at 20,000, it would seem that at least one in three of the city's slaves were "public slaves," and thus probably housed in the local bagnos.[48] Although there are no comparable figures for Tunis for this period, a report from the mid-1600s indicates that the percentage of bagno slaves was somewhat higher there than in Algiers: perhaps as many as 4,000 out of a total of under 6,000. In seventeenth-century Tripoli, by contrast, virtually all slaves were kept in the bagnos, since they were said to have been "all of a single master" – that is, of the ruling pasha.[49]

With the decline of the rowed corsair galleys, the proportion of bagno to private slaves also fell. By 1696, Padre Lorance, the apostolic vicar in Algiers, could note that "the number of slaves of individuals [*particolari*], far exceeds those public [ones] locked up in the Bagnos;" at just about the same time, the Capuchin missionary to Tunis, friar Donato da Cantalupo, observed that "few Christians live in the Bagnos [of Tunis]," while the earlier predominance of the Tripoli bagnos also declined somewhat, from having once held nearly all the slaves there to about 60 percent in 1701.[50] The private bagnos seem to have been abandoned first, even the fairly large one operated by the wealthy Ali Pegelin – who in around 1640 had kept between 550 (according to d'Aranda) and 800 men (according to Knight) in his own establishment.[51] It would thus seem that during Barbary slavery's period of precipitous decline, between 1690 and 1720, a large majority of slaves may well have experienced their captivity in the comparative comfort of a private master's house. This might help explain why some visitors in this period, such as Laugier de Tassy and Philemon de La Motte, concluded that slavery in the Maghreb was a fairly benign system, the latter noting that

> As for the Slaves at *Algiers*, they are not indeed so unhappy: The Policy of those in Power, the Interest of particular Persons [i.e., private owners], and the somewhat more sociable Disposition of those who inhabit the Towns, occasion their Lot to be less rigorous, at least for the Generality of them.[52]

This predominance of privately held slaves would not last, however. Over the course of the eighteenth century the number of private slaves sharply declined, while those held by the state remained more steady. By the late 1700s, it appears that at least half of the remaining slaves in Algiers were kept in bagnos, which had in the meantime been so reduced in number that life there may have been as overcrowded and wretched as it had been two centuries earlier. There appears, in fact, to have been only the one Bagno Beyliç still functioning there in the 1790s, though Grammont reported three there when the system was shut down for good by the invading French in 1830.[53]

Of the physical buildings themselves, no bagnos currently remain, and, except for some verbal descriptions, only a single, rather schematic floor plan of the bagno of San Leonardo in Tunis has turned up to give some idea of what these places looked like. Despite their disappearance, it is still clear that the state bagnos in all the Barbary capitals were, as slave quarters go, fairly elaborate complexes, with their offices, antechambers, taverns, chapels, and often a hospital. The Bagno Beyliç, the largest in Algiers, measured about 90 × 35 meters; the bagno of San Leonardo (or Kara Ahmed) in Tunis appears to have been around 50 meters square.[54] These larger prisons bore some resemblance to traditional caravansaries or *fonduks,*with several stories of doorless cells opening on to one or more courtyards that were generally roofed over "flat, with a Terrace, after the Spanish mode."[55] All in all, these big bagnos seem to have been fairly similar: "edifices of a uniform manner that differ little between each other," as d'Arvieux put it.[56] The smaller, privately owned bagnos, by contrast, may have had their own idiosyncrasies, some of them simply cobbled together by knocking out the walls between a cluster of adjoining houses and blocking up extraneous windows and doors.

Although they were large and housed many men, the administration of the bagnos was really quite simple. Overall control was in the hands of a guardian *basha*, usually a Turk but sometimes a renegade Christian.[57] To help him in this task, he had a handful of under-guardians (five or six for d'Aranda and his 550 fellow slaves in the bagno of Ali Pegelin), who might be Turks or renegade Christians: "those who," as d'Aranda put it, "have the oversight of the Christians, and what they do." Every morning at dawn they would wake the slaves, crying "'Get up you Dogs, come down you scoundrels!'" – "this was the[ir] good morrow," d'Aranda observed. They would then muster those who were to work that day, open the gates of the bagno, and march them off to wherever their labors were needed. Every evening at sunset, just before the gates were closed, the guards called off the roll, "and every one must pass the *Guardian Bachi*, as his name is called," to make sure all the slaves were accounted for. The guardian *basha* would end the day by "[crying] out aloud, that the next morning such a number of slaves, were needed to go to work at the break of day," at which point the bagno would be locked down for the night.[58]

This policing staff was rounded out by a handful of "scribes" – *scrivani* or *escrivains,* as the slaves called them – who kept track of who was to work where, who was too sick for work, who owed the guardian *basha* money, and anything else that required numeracy and literacy.[59] This position, for reasons that are not clear, was the sole prerogative of Christian slaves – so much so that should a scribe convert to Islam, it was understood that he would have to give up his job, even though he remained a slave. One free Christian merchant in Tunis asserted that "It is a laughable proposition to say that the Scribes could be renegades."[60] The scribes, some of whom might hold this position for more than one bagno at a time (and perhaps work for the pasha or another local dignitary on the side), made up something of a slave middle class. They were able to wield a certain amount of power in their own right, not only over their fellow slaves, but also over private masters who sought to lodge their slaves in the state bagno.[61] A 1721 report on the bagno of San Leonardo in Tunis claimed that "It is the custom that the governing of the bagno should go to a Christian [scribe], [he] who is a Turk serving only as Guard," and it was not unknown for the scribes to act as the representatives or mouthpieces of the bagno slaves, not so much in any confrontations with the local authorities, but rather with other Christians, such as the local consuls or free merchants.[62] Slave petitions addressed to Rome that concerned religious matters or disputes were often signed by a clutch of scribes. These were, of course, the slaves most likely to be literate, but they were also writing on behalf of all the slaves in their keeping, often introducing their petitions as from "The Slaves [or "The Christians"] of Tunis," or "The Humble Slaves of the Bagno of San Leonardo."[63]

The guardian *basha* also had control over the finances of his bagno, something that could be turned to considerable profit if managed shrewdly. He could, among his other privileges, rent out any unused physical space within the bagno walls, as d'Arvieux noted.[64] In this sense, the bagnos were operated more like a caravansary than a prison, with the guardian *basha* charging private masters for lodging their slaves with him (though it was well understood by all concerned that these charges would have to be met by the slaves themselves), as well as renting out rooms within the confines of his bagno. These went not only to the better-off slaves themselves, but also to local shopkeepers and entrepreneurs. The surviving floor plan of the bagno of San Leonardo in Tunis, for example, indicates shop space was leased to a baker and a herbalist, as a place for distilling aqua vitae, and as separate lodgings for the use of Turkish and Moorish tenants.[65] Slaves who had access to cash – whether through loans, charity from home, or from their own labors – paid the guardian *basha* for a variety of goods and services available in the bagno. Since inmates were given virtually nothing beyond their sporadic clothing allotment, 10 ounces or so of black bread a day (and not even this in some of the bagnos), and a ration of drinking water, virtually everything else, however much it might seem to the modern observer as a necessity of life, was a luxury to be purchased or rented from the guardian *basha*. This included slaves' bedding-hammock, reed sleeping mats, or covers; any clothing beyond the normal allocation; and such consumables as wine, meat, or tobacco.[66]

Although simple enough in their basic operation, the bagnos in time became more complicated, thanks to the parallel hierarchy of control that grew up around Catholic efforts to establish a religious presence in each of the prisons. If the missionaries were up to full strength, there was to be one priest for every bagno's chapel, often assisted by one or more of the slave priests living there. These priests chose a governing board for their chapel, perhaps four slaves known as *mayordomos* [*mag- giodomini* in Italian], older men known "for their good morals, piety, and devotion," who evidently functioned in the capacity of vergers or deacons. They also seem to have shared some of the authority of the *scrivani* – at least in the sense that they might join the latter in signing their names to petitions or letters sent to the Christian world on behalf of the generality of a bagno's slaves.[67] The *mayordomos* seem to have played a useful role in supporting and running the chapels. In some bagnos at least, they directed the activities of those whom Gramaye referred to as *matricularii*, or church wardens – men who would regularly circulate among the slaves with a locked contribution box, a *cassetta*, cajoling what they could in the way of contributions to support the chapel. The *mayordomos* also acted as their priest's assistants when he said mass, a task for which they were paid a small amount. Regularly involved with religious activities, they may have been a bit too rough-natured for the taste of some missionaries; as friar Crisostomo da Genova put it:

> The greater part of them are sailors, very low and vile people who do not agree with matters of reason and, wanting to run things in their own way, are difficult to manage according to reason and equitable justice.[68]

The contributions of slaves were hardly enough to maintain a bagno's chapel, since, according to some accounts, these might amount to as little as one Spanish real, or half a Venetian zecchino, per month. As a result, the missionaries worked out agreements with the bagno tavern keepers, who in some of the prisons at least contributed a percentage of the retail value of each barrel of wine they sold.[69] Things improved for the chapels by the later seventeenth century, however, as the Barbary regencies began to open more to legitimate European trade. As the number of free resident merchants in these cities slowly expanded, so too did their willingness to contribute to the upkeep of the bagno chapels, even though the Catholics among them would generally not have dreamed of attending mass in the bagnos (they went instead to chapels run in one of the local, usually French, consulates). More important, the missionaries also arranged to collect a voluntary anchorage fee from all those Catholic merchant ships that docked in port. This income – reported to be two Spanish pieces of eight (about 1.5 Venetian zecchini) per ship in 1668 – was far from steady, since its payment, along with legitimate trade itself, could fluctuate wildly during the frequent hostilities between any given regency and the various Catholic states.[70] Still, when trade was good it seems to have been sufficient to allow each priest to keep his chapel supplied with candles and communion materials and offer his communicants additional services: devotional confraternities, for example, choruses, or even an annual Christmas crèche.[71]

When chapels were properly funded and staffed, masses were held at least three times a week, if not daily: on major feast days in an important bagno, the resident priest might even offer two masses, one of them with a chorus and processional. Ideally, the chapels were big enough to accommodate all the Catholic slaves in their bagno – d'Aranda noted that in the bagno of Ali Pegelin, the chapel was "spacious enough to contain 300 Persons, who might there conveniently hear Mass."[72] Besides providing communicants with the sacraments and counseling for those who might be tempted to apostatize, the priests were no doubt also an important factor in providing a sense of community for the otherwise disparate body of their parishioners. It was perhaps the ideological divisions then under way between High Church followers and Puritans in England that led d'Aranda to conclude that there was no such community feeling among the English slaves in Algiers. As he put it:

> In fine, all of the nations made some shift to live, save only the *English,*who it seems are not so shiftfull as others, and it seems also they have no great kindness one for another. The winter I was in the Bath, I observ'd there died above twenty of them out of pure want. Nor are they much esteem'd by the *Turks*; for an *English* man is sold at sixty or seventy Patacoons, when a *Spaniard or Italian* is valued at one hundred and fifty, or two hundred ... when the value is set accourding to the body, and not according to the ransom that may be gotten.[73]

Connected to many of the chapels were small hospitals for the bagno's slaves. The first of these was started in Algiers by a Trinitarian father in the Bagno Pascia in 1551. A small affair with just five beds, it fell into disuse before long and had to be reinitiated, again by Trinitarians, in 1612.[74] A few years later, João Mascarenhas described the new hospital as having "nine beds with very clean sheets," attended by a doctor, a barber, and an apothecary, "all of them very well paid." The rebuilt hospital benefited greatly from alms collected from wealthy Spaniards in Peru, but perhaps it was also doing well because it was running several stills on the side, with the administrators selling the *aquavit* they produced at a profit to the slave-run taverns in the bagnos.[75] Half a century later, this operation too appears to have become greatly run down and was saved only by some dedicated Trinitarian alms-collecting in Mexico.[76] In the late 1600s, there were also three hospitals in Tunis, located in the bagnos of the Holy Cross, St. Francis, and

St. Lucy, "although these last two do not serve for much," according to one observer. In Tunis, as in Algiers, such "second-level hospitals" tended to come and go, both with the changing local rulers – not all of whom were supportive of these facilities – and with the fluctuations in funding they received.[77] Neglected by their supposed patrons in Christendom, a number of these hospitals eventually became defunct: possibly many of them were never intended to be anything but small and fairly simple affairs, less places to cure sick slaves than as sanctuaries for their repose, where a priest could "provide them with the Holy Sacraments and, in case of death, help them to die well."[78] This sort of minimal commitment is reflected in a late seventeenth-century proposal for reinstituting the hospital in the Tunisian bagno of the Holy Cross. The planning for space and provisions was a modest one, consisting of just

> a ward where there would be at least sixteen beds, with an altar to say the mass, a kitchen, one room for [he] who would care for the sick, and another to keep some things necessary for the service of the hospital and the sick.[79]

It was not until the end of the seventeenth century that those bagno hospitals that remained (or had been refounded) managed to establish relatively stable sources of income for themselves and thus hope to grow into something more substantial.[80] Some of these sources were small but consistent: the relative pittance of two *aspers* (less than a Venetian *soldo*) a day that bagno patients were charged for a bed and services. Much larger payments were demanded from the slaves of outsiders and from free Christians, however: sailors of Christian merchant ships, for example, were charged 4 pataques (just over 4 Venetian ducats) for services in the hospital in Algiers; free Christians living in the city had to pay 20*aspers*, or 9 Venetian *soldi*.[81] By the eighteenth century, the charter for the "Spanish" (that is, Trinitarian) hospital in Algiers envisioned an operation that would feature 24 beds, a surgeon, pharmacist, nurse, dispensary operator, and various slave staff. In order to pay for all this, agreements were worked out, evidently through the European consuls increasingly present in the city, that each Christian ship docking at Algiers harbor would pay the hospital a sort of self-tax of 3 or 4 *piastres* – that is, Spanish dollars: worth about $4\frac{1}{2}$ Venetian ducats. For ships of Catholic countries, this was apparently in addition to the sum they were already paying to support the bagno chapels themselves.[82]

Despite these sources of income and the right to obtain certain religious articles duty free – wines and vestments in particular – the hospitals in Algiers and Tunis remained an enormous financial burden on the Trinitarian Order: de La Motte put the total income of the main hospital in Algiers at 2,000 pieces of eight, which "yet suffice not for all the necessary Expenses."[83] Besides their constant search for new sources of income, the Trinitarians also endlessly struggled with the local Muslim hierarchy to situate their hospitals outside the bagnos with which they were associated, so that they opened directly on to the street rather than only into the bagno interior. The Muslims, seeing the hospitals essentially as prison facilities, refused to hear of such a thing, on the grounds that bagno slaves receiving treatment might escape. As a result, even the biggest hospitals remained stuck in a "small, cramped room," as missionaries repeatedly complained. Their greater concern, however, was that as long as the hospitals remained within the bagnos they served, they would consequently have to close down when the bagnos did every evening and so could not serve the many slaves belonging to private masters,

> such that ... when [the slaves] get sick they are treated by their Masters, with whatever tactless charity only the timorous interest of losing them could suggest to the heart of a Barbarian, and if [the Masters] do not know an easy remedy for the disease, they just abandon them, [and] many do not want Missionaries in their house to help [the slaves], such that they die for the most part without the sacraments; if, on the contrary, there was a Hospital capable [of treating] all sick Slaves, there would not be a Master who, for the self-interest that he has about the life of these unhappy ones, would not quite willingly send them to the Hospital so that they could regain health; dying, [the slaves] would have the help of the sacraments, and living they would leave healthy in body and soul.[84]

Often located next to the bagno chapel and its hospital were the slave-run taverns, which might number half a dozen or more in each prison: in the Tunisian bagno of San Leonardo there were no fewer than eleven on the ground floor alone, the biggest of which filled a large, open courtyard (the original bagno, in fact) of about 15 × 20 meters. The rest were much smaller, however: smoky little warrens rarely more than 30 square meters apiece. According to d'Aranda, the Bagno Beyliç in Algiers "receiv'd its Light, such as it was, through a certain Grate that was above, but so little that at mid-day, in some Taverns of the

said Bath, there was a necessity of setting up Lamps."[85] Since the slaves
who lived in the bagnos were for the most part too poor to enjoy the
taverns, the most enthusiastic patrons were not bagno residents at all:
"Those who come thither to Drink are Pirats and Turkish Souldiers," as
d'Aranda put it: "who spend their time there in drinking, and committing abominations."[86] Safe from public view, in the socially dead realm
of the bagnos, the taverns provided a refuge for those less-than-
observant Muslims who were happy to drink as long as they could do
so privately. Those who followed Islamic law more strictly seem to
have been content to let them do so, with the result that the taverns
generally did a roaring trade, especially when renegade corsairs were in
town, flush with their prize money. As d'Arvieux noted:

> These are places of assembly, where the soldiers, sailors, and the
> *menu peuple* come to drink, to eat, and smoke, & where they pass
> entire days.... The courtyards are furnished with a quantity of tables
> all filled with soldiers and seamen and other people, unemployed or
> debauched, who want to drink wine, sing, smoke, or carry out their
> affairs; since Tunis is a free country, Religion is no embarrassment,
> one prays to God when one wants to, one fasts when one cannot do
> otherwise, one drinks wine when one has the money, one gets
> drunk when one drinks too much.[87]

Priests and missionaries, whose work in the chapels brought them
into close contact with the taverns, professed to be repelled by what
they saw, calling them "abominable places, where [men] commit horrible crimes of every sort." What crimes they committed, the priests
wrote, were for the most part "picked up from the Turks": "detestible
liberty of the senses," according to the fathers, which amounted primarily to "drunkenness, with the vices that accompany it – swearing
and gambling."[88] Moreover, tavern keepers were accused of allowing
their tables and chairs to sprawl too close to the chapels, so that their
often drunken clientele ended up interrupting religious functions,
calling out rude jokes, mocking the liturgy, and even "bring[ing] in
some brazen women," as one priest put it, "to observe and make fun
of the ceremonies of the Holy Mass and some of our other devotions
... with laughter and jests."[89] Even when the tavern customers were
not actively disrupting the religious services, the clerics said, their
very presence was a bad example of excess and licentiousness,
especially for the younger slaves. In this regard, the missionaries were
particularly troubled, for they believed that younger slaves were

especially susceptible to the blandishments of renegades seeking to persuade them to abjure their Christianity and convert to Islam.

Some of these youths certainly "took the turban," as the priests feared, but as we have already noted, most masters were fairly or even openly hostile to such conversions, which they assumed were insincere and undertaken just to avoid hard work. The slave owner Ali Pegelin, for one, was inclined to beat such a designing renegade until he was willing to reconvert, and thus "cudgell'd a Christian into his Christianity, which he would have renounc'd," as d'Aranda put it.[90]

It would also appear, although many were loathe to say it in plain words, that the missionaries were at least as nervous that such young men would allow themselves to be seduced sexually as well as religiously, to become catamites even as they became Muslims. Indeed, many clerics, insofar as they had any notions of Islam, acted as if the two forms of seduction were closely linked: the Trinitarian Alfonso Dominici, writing in 1647, asserted that, among slaves, these "*Giovanetti* are all lost," because

> They are purchased at great price by the Turks to serve them in their abominable sins, and no sooner do they have them in their power, [then] by dressing them up and caressing them, they persuade them to make themselves Turks. But if by chance someone does not consent to their uncontrolled desires, they treat him badly, using force to induce him into sin; they keep him locked up, so that he does not see nor frequent [other] Christians, and many others they circumcise by force.[91]

It was the conviction among many observers that the *badestan* was haunted by sodomites, "Persons [who] are so abominable that they only buy [slaves] with this idea ... of making them give in to their horrid desires;" these buyers kept their eyes open for "the more attractive young Men, [who] often serve [them] for things that it makes one tremble to tell about."[92] The extent to which such practices went on is not clear. Venture de Paradis called sodomy the *vice à la mode dans Alger*, and stories circulated about young male slaves who allowed themselves to become the "perpetual concubines" of local elite men. All the Barbary capitals – but especially Algiers – had open and flourishing homosexual cultures: male prostitutes were said by visitors to be widely available, and Laugier de Tassy claimed that many of

> the Deys, the Beys, and the great Men, have practiced [sodomy], especially since it has been discovered, that several of their

Predecessors were destroyed by their Mistresses, whose Place is, at present, supplied by young and handsome Slaves.[93]

D'Aranda, who among all those writing about the experience of slavery in Barbary was probably the most matter-of-fact, appears to have accepted the homosexuality itself and homosexual relations between Turks or renegades and slave boys without expressing any particular shock or disapproval. He told the story of a young slave who was "debauch'd by a *Portuguez* Renegado for the sum of forty*Aspers*," with more apparent interest in the difficulties the renegade encountered trying to convert the boy to Islam than in the sexual act itself. He also mentioned, almost in passing, that in the harem of his master, Ali Pegelin, there were "forty young Boys between nine years of age and fifteen, who also dared not go out of the house, for fear of being debauch'd by the *Turks*."[94] Mascarenhas, using language more typical of the priests, claimed that the Turks brought their Christian slaves with them into the local bathhouses – of which there were sixteen in Algiers alone – where "they commit without being punished the sins of the flesh [that are] the most abominable and the most shameful to imagine." He also blamed sodomy, along with "usury, theft, violence, [and] assassination," as the habitual crimes committed by the inhabitants of Algiers and the reason they were punished by God, so that "they could never enjoy a life [that is] tranquil and completely secure."[95]

Mascarenhas' narrative, as its translators remark, was originally published in 1627 as a pamphlet of around 100 pages, an example of the *littérature de colportage* that was so pervasive in early modern Europe. It was hawked in Portugal by itinerant booksellers and, along with other cheap pamphlets, went by the name of *literatura de cordel*, or "string books," because of the way the volumes were strung together to be touted from place to place.[96] Works such as Mascarenhas', which often provided their readers with lurid descriptions of homosexual practices in Barbary, may have done much to fix the popular European notion that the inhabitants of the Maghreb were in general "incorrigibly flagitious ... sayd to commit Sodomie with all creatures and tolerate all vices."[97] For the priests and other Christians who denounced sodomy in Barbary, this particular vice was presented as just one more facet of the general godlessness of the region.

That tales like Mascarenhas' were so widely diffused may well have had another, unintended purpose, however, since such stories must have also brought the sexual culture of the regencies to the attention of Europeans with homosexual interests. One soon notices, in fact, how often the stories that circulated about homosexual activities in Barbary involved renegades – d'Aranda's account of the Portuguese renegade who "debauch'd a Lad" being typical.[98] It may not be too far fetched to conclude that some who voluntarily left Christendom, with its harsh strictures against homosexual practices, abjured and came to the Maghreb as much for what they saw as the region's sexual liberality as for its economic or religious opportunities.[99]

Conditions in the bagnos certainly may have contributed to homosexuality among slaves, who were not only denied access to women, but were also made to sleep packed together. In the great bagnos of Tunis, according to d'Arvieux, the slaves who stayed in the cubicles had to string up their hammocks like tiered bunk-beds, accessing them by means of rope ladders and by simply crawling across each other. The problem of overcrowding often weighed heavily on the quality of life in the bagnos: de La Motte wrote of the Bagno Beyliç in Algiers, for example, as "being extremely incommodious, by reason of the Stench arising from such Numbers of Slaves as were there lodged, upwards of 2000, they were;" d'Arvieux, who like de La Motte was never himself a slave and who (perhaps for that reason) generally described slaves' conditions as not too bad, nevertheless denounced the bagnos of Algiers as

Frightful prisons where these poor people are more packed together one on top of the others than lodged. These are places of horror, where the smoke of the cooking that transpires on every side, the noise, the cries, the blows, and the tumult reign everywhere.[100]

Although the large bagnos could overwhelm a visitor by their sheer scale of misery, it was probably the smaller, more ad hoc prisons that were the most squalid. Father Marcello Costa, the head missionary in Tunis, described one of these in nearby Porto Farina: "a wretched stall [*stallaccio*]," where "a hundred and more Christian [slaves]" were cooped up every night in a space

about thirty paces square ... and for the misery of the place, they have to stay one on top of the other and only with difficulty can one breathe ... for there not being a window nor any breeze, and with the door closed, such is the fetor that it sometimes causes [men] to faint, and I do not speak of the quantity of every sort of animal waste ... [and] at the break of dawn the Christians are let out and carried by the Moors off to work, and every night it is the same story.[101]

Those who were condemned to spend years or even decades in the bagnos did their best to amuse themselves when they could. Judging by the frequency with which the priests denounced gambling – especially in the bagno taverns – it would seem that cards and dice were common enough. After saving up for years towards their eventual ransom, some slaves were said to have simply lost their resolve and frittered everything away on games and drink in short order. But considering how much a ransom cost compared to what one could hope to earn by scrounging or stealing, it seems that most had little to lose in the first place. Slaves were also permitted to leave their bagno and wander about the city on Muslim holidays and in the hour or two after their work ended and before the bagno was locked at sunset. Okeley reported that in Algiers the slaves (who were generally not shackled) could even go outside the city walls, up to a distance of "somewhat above a mile" along the coasts, to what he referred to as "the end of our Tedder." There one might "take the fresh air of a Liberty," or even play at ninepins or quoits: Okeley mentioned some Englishmen playing at the latter, "for with such *Recreations* and *Diversions*, they are willing now and then *to beguile the tedious minutes* of lingering thraldom." There was always the risk, however, that "one of the Spies appointed constantly to watch, lest any of the Slaves should Run away" might denounce such a stroller for going too far or acting suspiciously, in which case the slave would then be arrested and dragged back into town for punishment – which was indeed what happened to Okeley.[102]

The actual extent of the brutality and hardship that slaves suffered in Barbary remains an open question. All slaves who lived in the bagnos and survived to write of their experiences stressed the endemic cruelty and violence practiced there, the "inhuman scenes of diabolical barbarity, which," as Foss observed, "will never be effaced from my memory."[103] Some of this violence, as we have seen, was between the bagno slaves themselves, but the better part was directed at the slaves by the guardian *basha* and his minions, either to urge them on at work or to punish them. Such beatings were, according to those who experienced them, meted out quite freely: shirking, missing a roll call or any unexplained absence, and pilfering materials on the job seem to have been the most common offenses, and any of them could merit up to several hundred blows with a stick or cudgel "some what larger than an ox-goad." The guardian *basha* in the Bagno Beyliç "commonly orders 150, or 200 Bastinadoes" for such infractions, Foss noted, and the beatings were administered by the guards to the soles of the slave's bare feet (using a special sort of clamp to hold the feet together and up in the air), to his belly, or to both. After his beating, the victim was "obliged to go directly to work among the rest of his fellow-slaves."[104] There were other, more extreme punishments, and these could be, as Okeley put it, "Arbitrary, and unlimited." Discipline was especially harsh for slaves caught trying to escape: death was certainly a possibility, though it was apparently more typical to lop off one or both of a slave's ears, cut off his nose, or give him between 300 and 500 blows to his feet, which could easily cripple him for life. The decision to impose such a severe punishment was generally not up to the guardian *basha*, however, since disciplining a slave to the point where he (or she) might be maimed or killed had to be left to the slave owner; it was the master who would possibly be left with someone incapable of working and with little or no resale value.[105]

In Barbary, punishments of this sort were merely extreme instances of ferocity played out against a background of continual, systematic violence between master and slave. Such brutality formed a kind of connecting force between master and slave, especially in the galleys, where beatings were constant. Mascarenhas told of how at the beginning of one voyage his galley captain loaded the vessel with fifty "big sticks" for disciplining the *galeotti*, but after just fifteen days, "there remained only one of the sticks: all the rest had been broken on the backs of the captives. Thereafter, they whipped with a tarred rope." Even deprived of their sticks, the overseers were still capable of keeping up a constancy of pain, according to Mascarenhas:

> Under the least pretext, they would employ the *Escurribanda*, which consists of their rushing down the walkway [between the banks of rowers] and beating ten or twelve times the naked back of each [*galeotto*] with a tarred, knotted cord, and they deal with the two hundred and fifty Christians on a galley one after the other, without anyone escaping.[106]

Despite the insistence by those who had been enslaved and who wrote that such extreme punishments were frequent, capricious, and occasionally fatal, there has nevertheless grown up a long tradition, beginning with some contemporary commentators and continuing to the present, that has denied such claims. Some have maintained, by way of countering them, that Muslim slaves in Spain or Italy were treated at least as harshly as Christians were in Barbary, as if to imply that this sort of reciprocal brutality meant that European slaves in the regencies

Slave punishment (from Pierre Dan, *Histoire de la Barbarie et ses Corsaires*, Paris, 1649)

felt their own sufferings less.[107] The anonymous translator of P. Philemon de la Motte's redemption narrative of 1719 so disagreed with his author's account of the sufferings of the slaves in Barbary that he took to attacking him in his own footnotes, crying out

> O Fie, Father! Tho' it is Part of your Function to make a dismal Story of Slavery among the *Infidels* … yet you should, methinks, adhere only to the Truth. You come lately from *Marseilles,* where you must, or might have seen the *Turks, Moors, &c,* in much worse Condition than the most unhappy *Beylic* Slave in *Algiers*…You likewise must needs have seen or heard, how Slaves are treated in *Spain, Malta, Genova, &c.*[108]

Others have asserted that conditions were not especially harsh in Barbary, that much of what has been written about the travails of

Beating slaves (from Pierre Dan, *Histoire de la Barbarie et ses Corsaires*, Paris, 1649)

slavery there was the invention of pandering priests of the redemptionist orders, or that in any case owners and overseers were far too covetous about their property and its possible resale value to risk harming
their slaves (thus playing one ethnic stereotype off against another).
Such a notion was common among eighteenth-century commentators,
as it is among scholars today. As one observer put it around 1730:

> It is well known that the *Algerines* set too high a Value on their
> Slaves (at least on the Money they cost them) ever to serve *Christian*
> Captives so, merely for Religion sake.[109]

It is easy to sympathize with many of those who have rejected the
more lurid claims about such *Barbarian Cruelty* – as some slaves called it
– that were put forth in the seventeenth and eighteenth centuries. One
cannot help being skeptical of the detailed descriptions of tortures and
executions offered by ex-slaves and especially by priests of the ransoming orders. Pierre Dan, for one, seems to have positively reveled in all
the various sufferings imposed on Christian slaves in Barbary, and he
presented his readers with a lengthy catalogue of the torments that
their Muslim oppressors favored. Dan's editors, no doubt mindful of
the sales value of such visceral attractions, thoughtfully accompanied
his prose with a set of grisly illustrations showing various slave-martyrs
undergoing their passions – some crushed alive, some impaled, some
burned, some crucified; different versions appeared in the French and
the Dutch editions.[110] Such litanies of suffering were especially dear to
Catholic commentators, but they also turn up in the slave narrations
of Protestants: John Foss, for one, devoted an entire chapter to "The
punishments which are common for Christian Captives, for different
offenses."[111]

Such accounts were denied or downplayed even at the time they were
being written. Joseph Morgan, for example, asserted in the 1730s that
"These terrible Executions are not very frequent in *Barbary*," though he
promptly undermined this claim somewhat by asserting that "all of my
time being there, I never heard of above three Persons impaled, all
which I saw."[112] Yet those, like Morgan, who have downplayed the brutality of slavery on the Barbary Coast have generally overlooked several
important points. One of these we have already noted: when a master
thought he was confronting a slave who appeared to challenge either
his honor or his religious sensibilities, his rage might easily overwhelm
all commonsensical notions of the slave's property value. Moreover, at
times when slaves were especially plentiful – and, as we have seen, they

could supposedly be traded for an onion in mid-sixteenth century Algiers – masters had no more incentive to spare the lash or hold back with their work demands than did Caribbean planters 200 years later, when replacements also seemed to always be available and at highly affordable prices.[113]

It is also true, however, that such punishments – often brutal and sometimes seemingly random – made a certain good sense in securing discipline among slaves generally. Even if the victim himself were beaten to the point of mutilation, and consequently lost most of his value as a worker, his punishment was probably intended to remove a potentially dangerous influence from the work gangs, by taking out someone given to *pigliar troppo fantasia.* Such beatings also served to *encourager les autres,* as a warning to all the other slaves who might witness or hear of it to be on their best behavior. Though for the private slave owner with only a dozen or so bondsmen this might seem an expensive lesson, for large-scale slavers, like Ali Pegelin and the state itself, the possibility of disciplining by example must have been worth ruining or even killing a handful of slaves. Such purposeful violence was well known among slave owners and overseers in the Americas as well. As one planter in the American South put it: "The fear of punishment is the principle to which we must and do appeal, to keep [slaves] in awe and order."[114] These manifestations of a master's total control over his property were seen, in Barbary as in the Americas, as fundamental for establishing the subsequent relationship of dominance between the two, a relationship that might eventually allow for less brutal forms of coercion or even possible rewards. But this was always based on the option of terror.

The systematic violence practiced in the galleys and bagnos was evidently effective in molding many slaves into passive obedience, demoralizing, if not dehumanizing them into subservience. Masters who damaged a few of their chattel with this rationale could supersede mere short-term cupidity for the sake of greater disciplinary ends. In describing his seasoning as a slave, d'Aranda showed how a new slave could be bent to the system through the experience and the sight of constant and often arbitrary violence. Over the course of his first six months, d'Aranda wrote how "I came by little and little to brook this kind of life." In these months he was also, as he noted, beaten with a cudgel a number of times, punched in the face hard enough to draw blood, and witnessed several examples of much more severe punishment meted out to individuals and groups. As a result d'Aranda seems to have become a thoroughly obedient slave: as he once recalled in passing, when two companions invited him to join them in shirking work, as they "hid themselves in some corner of the Bath, where they passed away the time at Cards," he declined, because, as he put it, they were "not fearing blows as much as I did."[115]

Stephen Clissold, writing about slavery in Barbary, concluded that slaves there described a life in the bagnos that was "a cross between a Nazi concentration camp, an English debtors' prison, and a Soviet labour camp."[116] It is indeed worthwhile to consider the bagnos as a concentration camp or Gulag, though different by being situated in the center of a densely settled urban area rather than out of public view, in a remote province or wasteland.[117] Indeed, the bagno was very much integrated into that urban life, for as Joseph Morgan noted at the time, the bagno "is open, for all to enter, till the Evening": with its taverns, hospital, and occasional shops, it was partly a public market providing essential services and partly a prison, at least during the daylight hours.[118] In this regard, then, the bagno was indeed a bit like a debtors' prison, with outsiders passing in and out freely during the day, sharing the space with inmates during the two hours or so between the end of work and lock-down, and perhaps dealing with them for one thing or another.

Nevertheless, the endemic violence, the contempt with which slaves were treated by their guards and masters, and in particular the harsh working conditions all made the bagnos more nearly resemble a concentration camp, especially because these men were condemned and punished simply for their membership of a social group – not for any crime they had committed, but for who they were born as and what they believed in. This is, of course, the definitive function of the concentration camp, which throughout the twentieth century was designed as much for isolating members of categories deemed inferior or dangerous as for supplying the state with a cheap source of labor.[119] The experience seems especially similar for those low-skilled, poorly connected men who were bought up as state slaves and placed in the bagno of the pasha or of the *beyliç*, left as they were with minimal (or non-existent) rations, regular and often random beatings, wretched accommodations, nightly lock-downs, degrading clothing, and enforced celibacy. Certainly there was something of the Gulag in their lives, though it must be admitted that at least those in the Soviet prison system were sent there as the result of some judicial process, however farcical, and that at the end of some term of years many would be set free – if not to leave Siberia, at least to leave the camps themselves. State slaves in Barbary were by contrast mostly condemned for life, not by any judicial pro cess but rather as a simple result of their status: those who were owned by the state essentially belonged to no one and had no individual master who could set them free or ransom them. As Mascarenhas noted, these were men who "never go out, since they are never freed."[120]

As we have seen, none of these once-infamous prison-barracks has been preserved, neither as a relic converted to other uses nor as a monument to the sufferings of tens of thousands of bagno slaves held there over three centuries. Indeed, just fifty years after the French had seized Algiers in 1830, it was already becoming difficult to locate where some of the bagnos had been in that city: in 1884, when Henri-David de Grammont came to write about Algiers' history of slavery, he found that the occupying French had so little interest in preserving the remaining bagnos there (much less turning them into memorials) that all the structures themselves had apparently vanished and even the very location of some of them was open to question.[121] In the century and a quarter that has passed since Grammont's time, the collapse of colonialism, various civil wars, and a demographic boom in the old regency capitals would seem to have obliterated even the final traces of these once-massive structures. In this sense, at least, the bagnos have scant resemblance to the concentration camp, that is as sites of memory. There has apparently been no interest in, effort to, or perhaps even the possibility of rebuilding these vanished locales as monuments to human suffering and perseverance, of the sort that have been created and resurrected in some of the Nazi camps or in certain slave-holding baracoons of the West African coast. In a very real sense, the places themselves, as well as much of what went on within them, have been buried by the passing of history.

Part III
Italy

5
The Home Front

> I had barely arrived here in Rimini than I saw all around me a great mob of poor Women, whose husbands were held as slaves in Dulcigno.... Your Lords could not imagine how great is the affliction and the damage that so many families [here] feel for the above mentioned slavery, and how much one is moved to compassion by so many poor wretches, with children nursing at the breast and with distress for the modesty of their daughters at their sides.[1]

Thus Cardinal Corsi found himself surrounded, almost besieged, when he first arrived in Rimini to take up his duties as Papal legate in 1696, though such a scene might have taken place in any town up and down the Adriatic and Tyrrhenian coasts of Italy during these years. The Italian peninsula had by then been prey to the Barbary corsairs for two centuries or more, and its coastal populations had largely withdrawn into walled, hilltop villages or the larger towns like Rimini, abandoning miles of once populous shoreline to vagabonds and freebooters. All along the Adriatic coast, a zone said to be "continually infested by Turks," populations were for the most part crowded into similar fortified centers – cities like Pesaro, Ancona, Civitanova, San Benedetto, Pescara, and Vasto.[2] Along the western coast the safest places were on a few defendable promontories: only towns like Civitavecchia, Anzio, Terracina, and Gaeta offered much protection to local farmers and fishermen, as the inhabitants of Sperlonga and San Felicità found to their cost, when they were kidnapped en masse in 1623 and 1727 respectively. Yet as Cardinal Corsi's letter makes clear, even a well-defended town like Rimini could offer little by way of protection for the local fishermen and coastal farmers, who continued to be hauled off to the slave pens of Dulcigno (modern-day Ulcinj, in southern Montenegro), Santa Maura, and Tunis, even as corsair slaving itself was going into decline.

How these innocents were taken varied only slightly from town to town and over the centuries. What happened to them along the Papal Marches was much the same as what happened to those who were snatched up along the extensive and poorly watched coasts of the Neapolitan territories, the Genoese littoral, the great islands, and all along Mediterranean Spain. In the three-centuries-long Christian–Muslim *jihad* that began around 1500, piracy and slaving became the policy instruments of state for both sides: enslaving ordinary civilians not only deprived the enemy of thousands of useful, productive citizens, but also provided serviceable labor and a significant source of income through ransoming. By the end of the sixteenth century, slave-hunting corsair galleys, both Christian and Muslim, roamed throughout the Mediterranean, seeking their human booty from Catalonia to Egypt – men and women, Turks and Moors, Jews and Catholics, Protestants and Orthodox: all were potential victims, to be seized and eventually herded into the slave pens of Constantinople, Algiers, Tunis, Tripoli, Malta, Naples, or Livorno and resold as galley oarsmen, agricultural laborers, or house slaves.

However widely such slaving activities may have spread, it is probably safe to say that Italy was among the most thoroughly ravaged areas in the Mediterranean basin. Lying as it did on the frontline of the two battling empires, Italy was known as "the Eye of Christendom," and it is the effects of corsair slaving on Italy and the Italians that we shall turn to henceforth.[3] After 1559, with the Peace of Cateau-Cambrésis, well over half of the peninsula's extensive coastline was under the direct or indirect rule – and often rather desultory protection – of Hapsburg Spain, making all these lands fair game for both Ottoman armadas and the Barbary corsairs. The region was politically fragmented, the coasts for the most part poorly guarded and without sufficient fortifications, their territorial defense forces weak and dispersed. Especially in areas close to some of the main corsair bases (western Sicily is just 200 kilometers from Tunis) slave taking rapidly burgeoned into a full-scale industry, with a disastrous impact that was apparent at the time and for centuries to come. Those who worked on coastal farms, even 10 or 20 miles from the sea, were unsafe from the raiders – harvesters, vine tenders, and olive growers were all regularly surprised while at their labors and carried off.[4] Workers in the salt pans

were often at risk, as were woodcutters and any others of the unpro-
tected poor who traveled or worked along the coasts: indigents like
Rosa Antonia Monte, who called herself "the poorest of the poor in the
city of Barletta [in Puglia]," and who was surprised together with 42
others, including her two daughters, while out gleaning after the
harvest, 4 miles outside of town.[5] Monasteries close to the shore also
made easy targets for the corsairs, who prized the monks they could
take for possible ransom and the lay workers for use as slave laborers
back in Barbary. The more enterprising raiders were just as willing to
attack the coastal watchtowers, in the hope of making off with the
guards themselves as booty.[6]

If those who made a living on the coastal lands found life a matter of
constant risk, those who worked offshore were in even more danger.
Fishermen were especially at peril. Fear of falling into corsair hands led
many to form convoys, going out in fleets of a dozen or more fishing
boats, in the hopes that some could act as lookouts while the others
cast their nets. The nature of their work still demanded that to be effective fishermen had to spread themselves across the sea, however, with
the result that, always hampered by their nets and gear, they could still
end up surprised and easily taken by the fast-moving corsair galleys –
even when "within sight of the harbor" before the eyes of their relatives and townsfolk.[7] Things could go just as badly for small merchant
ships that tried to sneak along unobserved, coasting from city to city,
only to find themselves snapped up by corsairs lurking behind the
many islands just off the southern Italian mainland. Indeed, for some
time in the sixteenth and seventeenth centuries the Barbary pirates set
up semi-permanent bases for themselves on Ischia and Procida, islands
that lay virtually within the mouth of the Bay of Naples and that gave
them ready access to the hundreds of small ships that sailed these
waters. Ambushing their prey – from behind an island or promontory,
from out of a fogbank, or at first light – was a favorite corsair tactic, but
the pirates could also run down fishing boats or merchant cogs when
they had to. Merchants who saw them coming could rarely hope to
outsail the corsairs' oared galleys or swift feluccas and had only the
choice of driving their ship onto land and making a run for safety or, if
the shore was too distant, simply jumping overboard and trying to
swim for it. Sometimes the pirates would content themselves with the
abandoned boat, but as often they would also try to pick up the fleeing
crew in the water or chase them along the shore, for it was the men,
more than the small ships or their poor cargoes, that were the corsairs'
real quarry.[8]

Once they had taken their human booty, the raiders might, as we have seen, come back the following day and offer up their victims for immediate ransom. Not infrequently they seem to have sailed away with their captives, however, leaving no word as to what had happened. For those who were left behind this must have been the most unnerving aspect of the corsair raids, that the victims, who were their relatives and neighbors, had sailed off to work one morning simply to disappear: "He left this city of Ascoli," as his neighbors said about a local sailor named Antonio Mezzaparte, "and from that time on, no one ever had any news about him."[9] The sea was always a hazardous place to make a living, and those who failed to come home in the evening could easily have gone down in a shipwreck, perhaps victims of a sudden storm. Unless a capture took place within sight of land or close to other Christian ships – as not infrequently happened – there was no news beyond perhaps the fishing boat itself, which might be found abandoned, adrift on the sea. Such a story was told by a pair of witnesses about a heist in 1697, although with its own, unusual twist:

> [The fishermen] were enslaved on the Roman beach [near Gaeta]. I know it because I was in the village when they found the tartana without people [on board] ... [but] in the tartana they found a little boy who had hidden himself and he said that everyone had been taken by the Turks ... and then also a letter came from Tunis.[10]

Only with such a letter, sometimes arriving months or even years later from Albania or Barbary, did the situation make itself clear. Until then, the wives, friends, and relatives of these men could only torment themselves over whether their kin had died at sea, were laboring as slaves somewhere far away, or had simply deserted them. When merchants or workers sailed beyond local waters, weeks might pass before a letter reached home, even in the best of circumstance: as Isabella Cafiero of Sorrento told her interviewer,

> It was about six months ago that [my] husband, Marco Antonio Mastellone, left for Malta so he could with his labors earn something to sustain his poor family, and not having had any news for a long time began to give [me] reason to suspect some sinister event. By now that has been verified, by a letter written by said Marco Antonio, with the news that he finds himself enslaved in Tunis.[11]

Mail was never fast in the early modern world and traveled even more slowly between the shores of the Mediterranean, two sides that were essentially at constant war. Even between regions at peace, it could still take weeks for a letter to travel a few hundred kilometers.[12] In their surviving messages home, slaves constantly ask why no one was writing to them, a sure sign that a high proportion of the letters they sent never got through. "I wrote you two or three times," lamented Filipo di Salvatore from Algiers, to his mother back in Palermo, "and I never had any reply; I don't know what happened – either you never got the letters or you have forgotten about me."[13] As with prisoners in any age, letters from home for the slaves in Barbary could be a tremendous boost to morale, just for news of family and neighbors to provide a sense of some remaining connection. Slaves wrote home repeatedly to their families, "don't abandon me in my slavery," but getting mail even from Sicily to Barbary could be difficult. Gio'Angiolo dall'Alicata tried to explain to his mother in Palermo how to get through to him in Algiers:

> You should know that when you write me you should send your letter by way of Trapani, or some other place, that is, in Sicily, that never lacks traffic [to Barbary], and send it to me by way of Biserta [near Tunis] to Algiers, [and] that I will receive letters more quickly when they are sent to the bagno of the slave owner Murat Re'is.[14]

Of course, the slaves had their own problems in getting word home, starting with the cost of the letter itself. Simply buying the paper and ink for their message might be beyond the means of many: one priest in 1735 complained that he was stuck with seven messages from slaves that he could not send because "to put them on a half sheet [of paper] costs five aspers each and the same for the envelopes." Francesco Antonio Ascentij, who had been a slave in Dulcigno for three years before he could write, underscored this point when he wrote to his mother by using the reverse of the letter she had sent to him, saying that he did "not hav[e] the least penny to buy a sheet of paper;" Ascentij drove home his forlorn condition with the closing claim that he had written "with the blood of my arm" – presumably for want of ink.[15] Moreover, poor slaves of this sort were for the most part illiterate and had to hire someone to write on their behalf. For those who labored as "public" slaves in the galleys or in the mines, with the slender opportunities such work provided for making money, it could take weeks to save up enough to hire a slave scribe to do the writing.[16]

On top of all this, slaves still had to find someone who could carry the message. This was not such a problem for obviously monied captives like d'Aranda, who not only had connections, but who also got some help from a master who was eager to see him ransomed. Peasants and fishermen, on the other hand, had to hope for a free sailor, a newly liberated slave, or a sympathetic merchant who might be both willing to take the trouble and was also planning to go somewhere near the town or at least the district where the slave had lived.[17] Finally, it is evident – perhaps more than has generally been realized – that slaves, and especially galley slaves, were moved around a great deal, making it hard for them to send a letter or give an address where they might receive one. As Giuseppe di Girardo wrote to his sister from Tunis, "I have written you from Constantinople and also from Alexandria, and from anywhere else I happened to find myself." Somewhat surprisingly, judging by his letter from Tunis, he had in fact managed to get through to her in Palermo at least once.[18]

Of course, Naples and Sicily were Barbary's nearest neighbors, and the problems in trying to get a letter through to northern Italy, for example, or to Britain or Holland were correspondingly greater. Though it should be taken as an extreme example, the experience of the Venetian shipbuilder Piero di Dimitri gives some idea of the difficulties that slaves and their kin could face:

> Among the sorrows of severe slavery I have dwelt for the course of 26 years, while never being able to get word through about the news of my disaster to my only sister (who believed I was dead).[19]

Left in the dark as to the fate of their relatives, those at home sought whatever help they could to ease their anxiety. Their tension is reflected in the variety of orations specially penned for them to sing in church on behalf of those lost at sea or enslaved; it is also shown in the frequency with which such unfortunates seem to have approached divinators for help in coping with their loss.[20] For such occasions there was always available a shadowy crowd of spell casters and charm chanters who were prepared to answer what must have been a constant litany of the same three questions about a relative lost at sea: Was he alive? Was he free or a slave? Had he turned Turk (i.e. converted)?[21] In 1627, for example, a pair of self-declared friars showed up in San Giovanni in Bragora district of Venice, claiming that "they knew what people far away were doing." This they did with the help of a certain Catte, a newly baptized Turkish girl, a *turchetta*, who by looking into mirrors could see an image of the lost relative, sometimes in consider-able detail:

> The child [*puta*], having looked in the mirror, said that Master Alessandro was alive, that he was a slave, that he had not turned Turk, and that he had two chains on his feet. And because the girl spoke in Slavic, the younger friar served to translate. And the child said also that she saw in the mirror said Master Alessandro with a red cap and a scarf on his head.[22]

For this little show, locals were willing to pay upwards of 20 ducats: a month's wage for the master craftsmen at Venice's Arsenal, and a good sign of how desperate the wives and mothers of these men could get.[23] For most others, possibly the majority of all those captured, 20 ducats was an enormous sum, for it is evident that many of those who eked out a living up and down the Italian coasts had no savings or property to sell at all. Instead, they got by like the fishing laborers of Fermo, who, according to one observer in the 1670s,

> having no other allowance to live on beyond that which they earn with their own efforts in fishing, [consider themselves] to have earned well if at the end of the year they do not remain in debt for the money that the Owner of their fishing boats [*tartane*] pays them a bit at a time to stay alive and maintain their poor families.[24]

Yet even such wretched working men and women, when suddenly snatched away, could be sorely missed by their families. It appears that, marginal though they seem to the economic world of their times, these fishermen, sailors, peasants, and gleaners still managed to support families of their own, often quite large ones. Their loss to slavery almost guaranteed not just greater penury for their wives, aged parents, and minor children, but also, without the social protection of a breadwinner, still greater marginalization. Without her husband Vincenzo as a "shield to defend [us]," Maria de Magio wrote from Procida in 1785, she and her two daughters had become village outcasts, such that "nowadays [we] are mocked and scorned with the opprobrium of insolent people."[25] It was women like Maria who were evidently behind the popular agitation that Cardinal Corsi encountered; or what the Augustinian Alberto Bianchini experienced, when coming to preach the Lenten sermons at Fermo in 1666, he found "many poor women coming to weep before me [about] the slavery of their sons and husbands in Turkey."[26] Such destitution became one of the recurring tropes in the letters received by the ransoming agencies, a standardized plea for pity and charity, though probably not the less real or experienced for all of that:

> [His parents] are not only old, decrepit, and infirm, [but] they are in the extreme need of poverty, one for [his] age and long illness [is] unable to work any more, and the other is not only feeble but also blind, nailed to the bed.... He has left behind a very poor Father, who lives by [his] sweat.... Dama Giulia, the wife of said Ottavio, is [so] very poor that she lives only by spinning.... He has left a young wife with two daughters, one of 17 and the other of 11 years; the poor woman is quite impoverished and remains in extreme need.... Since he has been a slave, we are always in extreme need of food and clothing, often with danger of dying of hunger for not having anyone to take care of our needs, and moreover of losing the honor of one of our daughters already grown at the age of 24, but so poor that she cannot find a way to get herself a dowry, having placed all her hopes in her wretched slave brother ...[27]

When a slave's letter finally arrived, months or even years after he had disappeared, it might be read aloud before the house of his wife or family. Such readings, in the street in front of the neighbors, were evidently dramatic occasions, and more than one witness would later testify that he "had seen [the slave's] wife cry and it [his capture] was the common rumor of our quarter."[28] The loud and public expressions of grief that kin might give on finally hearing that their relative was enslaved also provide a good sign that such concrete news was not always as welcomed as one might have expected. True, this meant that a father, son, or brother was still alive, but it also meant that the whole wrenching process of trying to get him out of slavery would now have to begin. Worse, the woman whose husband had disappeared months or perhaps years earlier and most likely declared dead suddenly had to come to grips with the realization, both personal and legal, that she was a "once widowed Wife."[29] No longer and never having been widows, such women were in an unnerving social limbo, especially those who had remarried and now found themselves potentially stuck between two husbands. Any kin, moreover, who had been declared legal heirs of a presumed deceased man's property now found themselves not only dispossessed, but also morally required to spend the very resources they had come to accept as their own for obtaining the release of their relative.[30]

The burden of raising a ransom obviously fell on well-to-do slaves as much as poor ones, but at least captives from comfortable backgrounds usually had a broad network of both relatives and financial institutions on which they could draw in this situation. Though their ransom price was often many times higher than that of a mere fisherman, such titled or wealthy slaves also enjoyed the attendant status that made them worthy objects of a slave exchange. In this regard, Emanuel d'Aranda was probably typical, traded as he was, along with his two Flemish companions (and a good many thousand *livres*), for five Turks held in Bruges.[31] Such exchanges were part of a long tradition of Mediterranean slave redemption, in Italy as throughout much of the Christian world, that dated back to the Crusades. They were especially pronounced during the decades of all-out imperial warfare in the sixteenth century, when great battles between the Turks and the Hapsburgs could produce huge lots of captives for exchange. For the most part such swaps were confined to the military sector and involved the larger European powers, like France and the Hapsburg Empire. As the Ottomans withdrew from engagement in the central and western Mediterranean, however, their successors in Barbary – the regents and *ra'is* who dominated there in the 1600s and 1700s – showed much less interest in slave exchanges, preferring either to hold on to their Christian prisoners as working slaves or to ransom those who could come up with the cash. As for their Muslim subjects, if these were ever captured and enslaved, the pashas who ruled in Barbary were generally willing to let them rot out their lives in the Christian galleys or bagnos; only a lucky few – the relatives of important *re'is*, perhaps – were considered worth a trade. D'Aranda's Ali Pegelin put it quite succinctly: "I have bought my Slaves to make some advantage by them, and not to exchange them for *Turks*."[32] On those occasions when a trade was offered – and this became increasingly infrequent in the seventeenth and eighteenth centuries – it was usually at such an unfavorable rate of exchange that few Christian powers would agree to do business: Barbary slaveholders might demand as many as ten Muslims for every Christian, while still insisting on getting their original purchase price back as well.[33]

As for ordinary peasants and fishermen, they might seek cash by writing to their wealthier relations, if they had any, in the hope of arranging a loan: their letters survive, though these give no sign of their success. When a poor man was captured, everyone in his family faced the problem of where to find the ransom money, which was probably much more cash than they had to hand, or had perhaps ever seen. For this reason, many slaves tried to cast their net across as wide a family network as possible: the Calabrese father and son, Vincenzo and Matteo Palamari, writing to their wife/mother in 1752, asked that she give their greetings (and remind of their need) to no fewer than twelve godfathers (presumably some of Matteo's and some of Vincenzo's), a godmother, two brothers-in-law, Vincenzo's various brothers, sons, and "all those in all their houses." They also asked that she make a special appeal to the prince and princess of Calabria.[34] Some families, or at least some individuals, seemed to have shirked the responsibilities of kinship, if one can judge by letters like that of a sailor named Nicola of Capri, who denounced his "Dearest Brother" with the following:

> For around a year and a half I have been a slave in Tunis, and I haven't had a single letter from you.... Oh, if only my mother and father lived and could hear my sorrows that this letter makes plain, they would try to cover me with their tears, but I already see that you do worse than a stranger: with all that you are my brother, you don't have [any] feelings of pity; I pray you, finally, for the love of God, to at least do it for charity as a neighbor [would], because to this you are obliged, since God commands it, seeing how you have forgotten you are my brother.[35]

Some slaves and their families did manage to raise enough money for ransom on their own, cashing in such possessions as the "oxen and some shacks" that might well have been their only possessions. The female kin of a slave might also be encouraged, or perhaps coerced, to sell off or pawn their dowries, though this was a decision that filled young girls and their mothers with dread, for it might well put an end to any hope of a decent marriage or honorable life.[36] As we have seen, the shifting of property that resulted must have represented a significant redistribution not only of wealth but also of the social hier- archy in these coastal regions, as entrepreneurs with ready cash moved in to buy the animals and property at discount rates, reducing some families from their one-time status as petty landholders – or at least privileged vassals – to that of impoverished rural laborers. Yet even this option was not open for the many captives whose personal resources, even after selling all they had, still fell short of the 200 or 300 *scudi*, *zecchini*, or pieces-of-eight demanded. So it was, for example, with the Tuscan Antonio Pasquale Mamberti, whose relatives reported that they had "sold his Maternal inheritance there [in Tuscany], and that not being enough for his payment, we had to add on that of the Father, and ... still we were around 150 *scudi* short." Likewise, in trying to free his only son Lucio d'Huomo, of Porto di Fermo, managed to sell "his little House, his sole Patrimony," but still came up with only 30 *scudi* of the *70zecchini* demanded.[37]

It was in an attempt to help captives as poor as these "wretched impoverished laborers [*faticatori*], [who] survive day-by-day," and whose plight had become so glaring by the latter half of the sixteenth century, that European nations, religious orders, and concerned individuals began to mobilize for the great redemptive efforts that would become one of the major social movements of the early modern Mediterranean world.[38] Slave ransoming as an act of charity and piety had deep roots in the region, following a pattern established centuries before by the two main redemptive orders: the Order of the Most Holy Trinity, or the Trinitarians, founded in France by Jean of Matha and Felix of Valois in 1193; and Our Lady of Mercy, known as the Mercedarians and begun by Pedro Nolasco in Barcelona in 1203. Both had been initiated primarily for freeing Christian slaves or captives – in particular, crusaders – in the hands of Muslims or other unbelievers. Both orders had flourished throughout the Middle Ages, mostly though not exclusively in the nations in which they were founded. Always closely associated with the Kingdom of Aragon, the Mercedarians were converted to a military order by King Jaime I in 1218; as such they would remain heavily involved with both the Spanish Crown and its ensuing crusading activities in the *Riconquista*. The Trinitarians, by contrast, focused on their network of monastic houses, which by the mid-1200s already numbered around 50; by the fifteenth century there were over 800 houses. The order claimed for itself the special distinction that it was founded as committing itself to giving the *tertia pars*, a third of all its income and donations, exclusively to the ransoming of slaves.[39] It was also a matter of particular pride among the Trinitarians that their order would dedicate itself completely to the business of redemption, such that "its fellows have agreed, with a solemn vow, not to accept Ecclesiastic offices, so as not to ever be distracted or displaced from the redemption of Slaves."[40]

As with many other religious orders, however, the Trinitarians and Mercedarians had both gone into decline by the first decades of the sixteenth century and therefore found it all the more difficult to cope with the sudden and massive upsurge of slave taking by both Christians and Muslims that occurred after 1500. One by one, the various Italian mini-states began to realize that the problem would not go away on its own, and that some sort of state-sponsored redemptive work would be necessary as a response to the large-scale slaving raids that were being conducted, first by the Turks and then by Barbary corsairs, on the coasts and in the shipping lanes of Italy.

The first to respond was Naples, whose territories were not coincidentally also the most directly threatened by the corsair raids: in 1548, the Emperor Charles V chartered the Real Casa Santa della Redentione de' Cattivi there.[41] The Neapolitan organization provided the model for many of the other Italian states when they came to form their own redemption societies, and, indeed, when the Vatican decided to commission its own ransoming confraternity in 1581–82, to handle the redemption of subjects of the Papal States, a request was made to examine the charter of the Santa Casa of Naples, specifically to see how these things were done.[42] After Rome, other principal cities and ports in Italy soon followed suit, including Bologna (1584), Lucca (1585), Venice (1586), Palermo (1596), Genoa (1597), and Malta (1607); many of these organizations, when first formed, imitated Rome and sent letters to their predecessors for advice about structure and procedure.[43]

Typically, each Italian state operated its slave ransoming through a confraternity, often one that had pre-existed this particular need and whose governing body consented to have the extra burden of slave ransoming grafted on to its existing obligations and activities. Naples' Santa Casa, for example, was grounded in the confraternity of Santa Maria del Gesù della Redenzione dei Cattivi; after instituting his Opera Pia del Riscatto in 1581, Pope Gregory XIII entrusted the organization's management to one of Rome's most prestigious confraternities, that of Santa Maria del Gonfalone.[44] The Gonfalone, as it was commonly known, had for centuries dedicated itself to such pious works as preaching and staging Passion plays (often highly anti-Semitic) during Holy Week and to welcoming pilgrims to Rome.[45] As an arch-confraternity (*arciconfraternita*), the Gonfalone was aggregated with other existing confraternities throughout the papal territories to take the lead, first in these earlier pious tasks and then in forming a web of redemptive centers in the towns and villages of central Italy. Wont to boast that it had been chosen by Gregory XIII from among its rival Roman confraternities, "as principal, ancient and Noble, and numerous of Men [ready] to embrace and accept this undertaking," the Gonfalone was prepared to share some of the prestige and honor connected to slave redemption with its aggregated affiliates, even those that were small brotherhoods out in some country backwater.[46] In return, it was hoped that local elites, in towns and villages, would eagerly sign on for this good work, adding both their names and cash contributions to a state-wide effort. Much the same had been done with the Neapolitan Real Santa Casa, where the governing body had been selected from among the leading nobles of that city, each of whom had given generously to set up operations.

Although levying a flat contribution from incoming board members might be enough to get a ransoming organization started, to keep it running required more permanent income, at least if things were not to end up like they did with Genoa's Magistratura degli schiavi, which, "not being sustained by massive contributions, only partially accomplished the objectives for which it was founded."[47] Charles V thus chartered Naples' Santa Casa with 4,000 ducats annually, while Palermo's Santa Maria la Nova had exclusive rights over certain classes of charitable bequests in wills. To fund the Gonfalone beyond the rather limited resources given it by Gregory XIII, Sixtus V assigned the confraternity 3,000 scudi annually from the fees levied on Rome's money-changers and another 3,000 from half the proceeds of the papal tax on playing cards, all of which had previously gone to the Hospital of San Sisto.[48] Such guaranteed income may well have represented a necessary inducement, especially for confraternities, to take up the burden of ransoming in the first place, and the funds had to be granted in clear distinction from whatever endowments, *rentes*, privileges, or other monopolies the organizations already enjoyed and needed to carry out their other work. This was something that the governors of the Gonfalone, for example, sought continually to stress: "that the Company's ordinary income should not go for or be converted to any other purpose [i.e. slave redemption] than for the traditional use[s] for which it was employed in the past."[49] In the tangled bureaucracies of these *ancien régime* states, monopolies granted by one authority could also be opposed or subverted by another, however, in legal wranglings that might take centuries to work themselves out. Thus, the Gonfalone's half of the playing-card tax was constantly contested by the Hospital of San Sisto, which, by the 1690s, had managed to reduce the confraternity's share to two-fifths of the take (often leaving even this in arrears) before taking it away altogether by the 1720s.[50]

Venice, as was so often the case, pursued a somewhat different course. Although the *Serenissima* and its mainland territories were fairly remote from the Maghreb, the Republic's extensive trading connections, its overseas empire, and its near-constant wars with the Ottoman Turks assured that its sailors and merchants were always targeted by corsairs based on the Barbary Coast, the Dalmatian islands, and around the mouth of the Adriatic.[51] When the time came to set up its

ransoming activities, the Venetian Senate did not turn to a confraternity or a religious order but rather to one of its own many pre-existing
administrative boards. In 1586, the Senate thus promised 50 ducats
every Christmas and Easter from the state's "ordinary charities" to the
Provveditori sopra Ospedali e Luoghi Pii to carry out this "most pious
task."[52] As its name indicates, this board, which had been originally set
up in the 1560s, was intended to manage the *Serenissima*'s many hospitals, hospices, and holy shrines. Such a choice may make it appear that
the Venetians were underscoring the charitable, and indeed religious,
nature of this sort of work, but there were also good, practical reasons
to entrust the state's ransoming effort to this particular board. Since
the Provveditori had control over bequests, both general and specific,
to all of Venice's charitable institutions, they could help themselves to
any unspecified funds in their care, whenever the demand for ransom
money was especially acute. There was also the matter of turf protection, with which a state board, rather than a religious confraternity,
was probably better able to deal. By entrusting the collection and disbursement of ransoming funds to the Provveditori sopra Luoghi Pii,
the Senate apparently hoped to have a state power strong enough to
stand up to the Republic's own *rettori*, or provincial governors, who
had a known tendency to take funds of this sort and "convert them to
other uses." Though only recently formed, the Provveditori moreover
had a reputation for defending Venice's charitable interests against
outside interlopers: at one point the Senate had particularly praised
them for regaining title to hospitals that had been "usurped ... with
false entreaties by the Holy See."[53]

Such safeguards against outsiders soliciting alms were commonplace
throughout the Italian states. Palermo's Santa Maria la Nova, for one, had
this right written into its original charter; likewise, the Gonfalone
accepted its ransoming charter with the clear understanding that it would
enjoy an absolute monopoly over alms collection throughout the Papal
States, meaning in particular that the Trinitarians were to keep well clear
of this territory.[54] This was a ban that the confraternity had to fight to
maintain throughout the seventeenth and into the eighteenth centuries,
before finally losing out not only to the more politically astute Trinitarian
fathers, but also to the Mercedarians.[55] Such proprietorial squabbles serve
to underscore an important anomaly about the financing of redemptive
efforts in Italy: the collection – as opposed to the disbursement – of funds,
regardless of who actually ran it, was still seen as fundamentally, if not
exclusively, a charitable enterprise, one based on voluntary alms-giving
rather than on any form of compulsory, direct or indirect taxation.

Why the various Italian states left slave redemption in this rather gray area, somewhere between a religiously driven charity and a matter for the public fisc, is not completely clear. Only the Sicilians among the large redemptive organizations relied on public taxation to fund their work at Santa Maria la Nova, asking each town and village on the island to levy a hearth tax on itself. Perhaps the authorities in Palermo were able to do so because the corsair threat was more acutely felt in Sicily than anywhere else in Italy; in the beginning, at least, the Sicilians came through with generous funding, and some villages were still contributing into the eighteenth century.[56] Nevertheless, it is evident that in these societies of rather limited social services an individual's enslavement was generally treated as his or her personal/family problem and not something for which government would accept much responsibility. It was for this reason, as much as for group solidarity, that many of those working men who were most exposed to the corsair depredations – the coral fishers of Genoa, for example, or the fishermen of Venice – had special confraternal groups in which all the members were expected to contribute to a slave redemption fund.[57]

Moreover, the problem was for the most part a distant one – at least from the perspective of capital cities like Rome, Milan, Venice, Genoa, or Naples, where the corsair threat seemed far removed and where the cash in Baroque Italy was generally concentrated. As a result, central governments tended to ignore the threat for long periods: public funds that had been earmarked for redemptive purposes would leak away into other projects and not get paid to designated ransoming boards – as happened with the Venetians, whose initial commitment of state funding every Christmas and Easter rapidly went decades in arrears.[58] Genoa's Magistratura degli schiavi likewise went moribund for years at a time due to lack of capital, while the Neapolitan Santa Casa, though supposedly funded from the largesse of the Spanish Crown, saw its income dwindle away until by 1667, unable to pay thousands of ducats it had promised for ransoming funds, it was forced to declare itself bankrupt.[59]

Faced with such inaction and uncertainty, slaves and their kin, as we have seen, might lament at having been "completely abandoned by their government." Yet one has to acknowledge that, even beyond their perennial funding difficulties, these government-based ransoming organizations did not always have the strongest incentives to ransom their subjects as quickly as possible. Such a policy could be counterproductive, claimed the more hard-hearted among administrators: after all, if sailors knew that they would soon be freed, they would be less likely to defend their ship-owner's property against corsair attack, "and so give away Merchants' estates."[60] At the very least, such willingness to pay might simply encourage slaveholders to increase their asking prices. When, by the late seventeenth century, more money did indeed become available and more slaves could be ransomed through charitable activity, this is precisely what happened, and by 1700 there is the clear beginning of an inflation spiral that would lead to ransoms more than doubling by the 1760s.[61] Moreover, nations that let it be known that they were disposed to buy back their enslaved citizens more or less promptly ran the further risk of making prime targets out of their own ships and citizens – as the United States would find to its immense cost in the 1790s.[62]

Rather than taxing their citizens, then, virtually every Italian state relied instead on a sort of "piety tax" to finance its ransoming activities. This levy tended to focus on two major areas: bequests in wills for the wealthier and direct alms-collecting from the general public. As a rule, the state agents seem to have been more comfortable in soliciting donations from those who were drawing up their wills, since these bequests could be quite generous, and, in any case, the state's licensed notaries could simply be ordered to remind testators of this option. The Venetian Provveditori in particular leaned heavily on local notaries, forever instructing them to remind their clients to "remember the poor slaves" when writing their bequests. This policy, first included in the Senate's enabling legislation of 1588, was tightened over the years, until by 1675 notaries in Venice and throughout Venetian territories were obliged to write into the texts of wills and codicils that they had specifically made mention of this charitable "duty" to their clients.[63] The Provveditori moreover required that each notary, immediately after a testator died and his or her will was opened, was to bring them "a copy of those legacies that were left for the aforesaid pious work," lest some ambiguous bequest might slip away to another charity or to a relative.[64]

Although the civil authorities also had a role in soliciting alms from the public at large, much of this task fell almost inevitably to priests and friars, men who were practiced in preaching for contributions and could exploit existing Catholic structures and customs to help them in their work. In Venice, which kept a tight secular hold of religious activities (especially fundraising activities), the Provveditori sopra Luoghi Pii were instructed by the Senate to work with the Patriarch to seek alms "in the usual ways," which meant having him order the city's preachers to include a special plea for contributions on at least three of

the six Sundays in which they customarily gave special sermons for the
Lenten cycle. The Provveditori also arranged to have lockable collection boxes made and placed in each of Venice's parish churches, with a
sign attached that read: *For the Recovery of the Poor Slaves.*[65] Such use of
the penitential weeks of Lent as a time to solicit alms was customary
among redemptive confraternities elsewhere: those affiliated with the
Gonfalone, for instance, made special Lenten efforts in their own
towns and villages throughout the Papal States, carrying out "the holy
work of alms gathering for the ransom of those wretches who weep
among the chains of Barbary [for] their lost liberty."[66]

The involvement of the Catholic hierarchy in alms collection was
made easier by the obviously charitable nature of the effort itself. It is
hard to imagine any social group that could have appealed more
directly or strongly to the charitable instincts of the times: without
question the most deserving of the deserving poor, these slaves were
innocent in their indigence and victimized for nothing more than
being Christians. By their very nature, they had been abandoned, by
their countries, by fortune, even by God – since slaves with the good
connections, positions, or wealth could get themselves out of Barbary,
often in just a few years.[67] These were all themes to which preachers
returned repeatedly, reminding their congregations that this would
"certainly be the means to acquire great merit with God."[68]

In making their appeals, priests always reminded their congregations
that there was a real urgency about this charitable work that made it
obligatory for those safe at home to give as much and as often as they
could. Abandoned slaves might at any time succumb to their miserable
diets and rough treatment and die away from their community and
religion. It was especially recommended to "redeem as soon as possible
the oldest ones, who are bad off for not being able to eat that bread
that is usually given out by the Turks; otherwise they will die within a
short time."[69] Haste was also necessary because of the possibility that a
slave would be sold and resold, until he was completely lost in the
vastness of the Islamic world. Corsairs operating out of the port of
Dulcigno, a sort of way-station in the Mediterranean slave trade, would
often warn their Italian captives "that they would sell them in Barbary
if the ransom does not arrive quickly."[70] This carried a double threat:
not only might the slave then effectively disappear "in the vastness of
the place and the multitudes of people" of the Levant, but also, once
sold to owners in Barbary or Asia, his ransoming price could rise considerably – perhaps by 100 percent or more.[71] The threat was by
no means an idle one, moreover: the lists gathered by the ransoming

organizations are full of references to slaves taken to Dulcigno and then "immediately sold and sent to Barbary."[72] Such threats could put close relatives "in continual pain and torment," but some slaves were not above passing them along, in the evident hope that this might speed up their redemption. Thus, Leone Catteno wrote from Tunis to his mother, on 12 January 1735, that

> My Master says that he wants to send me with the tartana to the Aegean Sea ... with the fear that they want to send me to Constantinople. I don't know if I will see you again, because if I go to Constantinople I go to die; at least here I take care of what work I do and [though] the lice eat me alive, I still have the hope to see you sooner or later, with the help of God.[73]

Another reason for speed was the fear that captives might give in to their despair, their hardship, and the blandishments of their masters and convert to Islam, thus "saving the body while also losing the soul."[74] The Barbary ports were full of such renegades: in Algiers, d'Aranda claimed that "There are Renegadoes of all Christian Nations and in my time [in the 1640s] I found above three thousand *French* ... and the 12,000 soldiers, which are the regular forces ... are most of them Renegadoes, dissolute persons, without Religion or Conscience."[75] It was widely believed in Europe that Muslim masters worked tirelessly to turn their slaves away from the Christian faith, and even if this is doubtful, as we have already noted, owners do seem to have tried to convert slaves they especially esteemed or who were considered "good looking and cheerful."[76] In any case, there still existed a pervasive anxiety throughout Christendom about the subversive attractions of Islam, a collective horror that expressed itself through many different strands of conscious and unconscious dread. Once converted, renegades became not only traitors to their religion but also traitors to Christianity's other fundamental social elements – the family and the state. Those who embraced Islam were seen as weakened yet also intrinsically corrupt, choosing a creed tailor-made to free them of the strictures of Christianity in order to "wallow in depravity," in a Faustian bargain that the renegade sealed by undergoing his public and sexually highly charged ritual of adult circumcision.[77] As with their threats that they might die far from home, slaves also knew how to use this possibility of spiritual suicide, probably the cruelest threat of all, to urge on those at home; as the young Nicola Sarcinelli wrote to his father from Dulcigno in 1739:

Don't leave me desperate [to] lose myself, because if you do nothing to procure the alms for my ransom, and I see that you are doing nothing, I will not be able to suffer any more and I too will turn Turk, since I am a youth of but 12 years old and I can't stand the beatings that they give me every day.[78]

Of course, merely appealing to the public for donations was not enough in itself: someone also had to collect the cash. Passive collection, through locked *caselle* placed in churches, though it was the custom throughout the peninsula, does not seem to have been markedly successful. The Provveditori in Venice noted with some displeasure that these iron-bound boxes were repeatedly vandalized or were carried off altogether. In any case, parishioners tended to fill them with clipped, counterfeit, or foreign coins that the mint refused to accept: in all of Venice, the pittance that was left was rarely enough to ransom more than a slave or two a year. Preachers generally did better when their exhortations were followed by more aggressive collection rounds, carried out during the masses and in the parish. This work was usually done by the beadle, who was armed with his own *cassella* and a printed license from the Senate, and who could bring in far more alms than a fixed box. On the other hand, to accomplish such aggressive fundraising it was also necessary that the beadle be paid for his efforts, at the rate of six *soldi* for each *lira* he collected – which is to say 30 percent.[79]

This policy of commissioning collectors to solicit donations soon became the norm in most Italian states, especially as a means of stimulating alms in outlying villages, where the purpose and indeed the very existence of a *cassella* in the parish church might soon be forgotten. Since there was a living to be made, the ecclesiastical alms seekers were joined before long by secular counterparts, licensed by the state and responsible to the local diocese. In the Venetian territories these men were known as *succolettori*, and by the 1760s there were some 35 of them operating in Venice's mainland provinces, with another twelve at work in Dalmatia. Each was meant to hold his commission and license for a decade, giving him the rather open-ended power "to act, promote and cooperate as much as necessary for the purpose [of collecting funds]."[80] Similar officials were authorized for ten-year stretches by the Santa Casa in Naples, and they were charged with "looking for alms with the *cassetta* and insignia;" furnished with a license that commanded "all ecclesiastical persons and each and every official, whether royal or baronial, to support and aid them in all that needs to be done."[81] The Gonfalone also had its agents, called "commissioners," and they too kept a third of what they took, along with recompense for their travel expenses.[82] Whatever they were called, all such agents seem to have followed a similar pattern when they came to a new town in their district, first registering to show their licenses and permissions with the local ecclesiastical authorities, then "going from house to house, seeking [and] collecting every sort of alms." They also posted a pre-printed edict on the door of the village church, to announce to the parishioners their arrival and intentions:

FOR THE REDEMPTION OF SLAVES, TO BE DONE ON ****, 16** BY THE
ARCH-CONFRATERNITY OF THE GONFALONE

Let notice be given that the Lord Guardians of the Venerable Arch-confraternity of the Gonfalone are sending some Rev. Capuchin Fathers to Algiers to ransom a goodly quantity of Christian slaves.

Therefore all faithful Christians are exhorted to help and to offer aid to subsidize this most pious ransom, remembering that to rescue so many poor slaves requires a great deal of alms.

Let all those who have Fathers, Brothers, Children, or other Relatives or Friends in the hands of the Turks know that they should give notice of this to the Rev. Sacristan of ***, by giving him their names and surnames, of whom they are slaves, with [which] other captives; and also make note who will have the means and the willingness to pay, if not everything, at least a part of their ransom, such that so many more poor and needy might be helped; [and] that of all this said Sacristan will give notice to the Lord Guardians, so that they can put [the names] on the list that will be created for this.

And those that want to give monetary aid should go and tell that to the Lord Guardians.

One comes away with the impression that by the seventeenth century the business of alms solicitation had become a significant part of the Italian social landscape. In a city like Venice the beadles were supposed to be out searching for alms "with fervor around the parish," every Sunday and eventually every day; in the Papal States the commissioners came so often to some villages that the inhabitants began to complain that "we cannot undertake such a solicitation, [the last one] being too fresh;" notaries throughout the peninsula, meanwhile, were forever reminding and wheedling their clients to "remember the poor slaves" when drawing up wills and bequests.[83] It would be surprising if some Italians had not suffered donor fatigue from all these appeals to their consciences, and this may explain why agencies like the Gonfalone worked so diligently at having its collectors present a trustworthy public image, requiring them to "dress in their ordinary clothes, and with the most moderation, discretion, and modesty possible [for] carrying out said holy work," and not come to town ringing a bell or making similar displays of showmanship.[84] All the ransoming agencies feared that "villainous people pretending to be [alms] Collectors might, with stolen and false permits, go about committing frauds [and] plundering Our State of the donations intended for such pious work."[85] On the occasion of the Holy Year of 1725, it came to the attention of the Gonfalone that "some alms seekers who went under the name of Our Lady of Ransoming [that is, Mercedarians], [were] soliciting with a white sack" right outside the Porte delle Basiliche in Rome. Protesting to the Cardinal Protettore who was their patron in the Curia, the Gonfalone decided to take no chances and to send "from our brotherhood four Alms Seekers, consigning to each one a *cassetta*, so that they can request donations," in the same area.[86]

Even when such poachers were successfully suppressed, it could still prove difficult to squeeze significant amounts of cash out of the Italian countryside. The Provveditori reported that over the course of a decade their *succolettori* on the *terraferma* had sent in an average of around 1,600 ducats a year – perhaps enough at the time to ransom five or six slaves. Many villages and even some mid-sized towns could barely generate two or three ducats a year: only in cities like Bergamo, Brescia, or Padua, where there were large churches with active congregations, were the collectors likely to gather 100 ducats or more annually.[87] The Gonfalone had similar problems in rallying its affiliated confraternities in the Papal States. The circular letters it sent out to get the confreres to start collecting mostly provoked what reads today like a mixture of sham enthusiasm and prevarication. The confreres of the village of Giove, for example, possibly with unintended irony, assured the Gonfalone that "having made all diligence and effort we have come up with one scudo for this purpose;" they wished to know what to do with it. The brothers in Sanseverino, on the other hand, admitted that their town had a confraternity of the Gonfalone, but "we never knew until now what Pious work it was supposed to carry out;" those of Congoli swore that "of the Confreres of this Venerable Confraternity there is not one who remembers being affiliated [with the Gonfalone]."[88] As with the Venetians, so the respondents to the

Gonfalone tended to blame the lack of funds on the "scarcity of money" and on the poverty of their district – due to failed harvests, excessive taxation, the depredations of passing German troops, or too many previous collections.[89] Faced with such excuses, collectors were sometimes ordered to make their rounds at harvest time, rather than during the traditional Lenten period, in the hopes that they could at least coerce landlords and peasants into making donations in "flax, hemp, linen, oil, wine, grain, bread, and anything else, all of which must be sold."[90]

The evasions and excuses offered by villagers and petty confreres may in any case have represented nothing more than an attempt to maintain local control over charitable fundraising – for ransoming or any other purpose. Understandably enough, villagers were none too keen to turn over their hard-won cash to outsiders to carry off to the capital, in the name of a general fund that may or may not have benefited anyone local. In the hamlet of San Giusto they put it quite simply: "thanks to the Most Blessed Virgin, we do not have any Slave Countrymen in those Barbarous regions," and would not therefore be contributing that year.[91] On the other hand, towns that did have a number of their own that needed ransoming seem to have seen no reason not to do as the confreres of Fermo did, when they appealed to the "heroic charity" of the Gonfalone for a speedy infusion of cash, to run their own redemption voyage to Dulcigno.[92] Such expressions of localist instincts can be found in Friuli, the Marches, and Puglia, but there were only a few towns lucky enough to go it alone. Bologna, for one, had a confraternity – Santa Maria della Neve – that was rich and important enough to harvest alms both in town and in their own surrounding district. On the other hand, the citizens of Ravello (near Amalfi) and those of Torre di Greco did not have such worries about funding, because of bequests left for them by their own elites, specifically and only to ransom locals.[93]

Most other towns, along with the individuals who lived in them, had to turn sooner or later to their state ransoming agencies, yet these were far from insensitive to local sensibilities about money, and indeed many had a policy requiring that "the alms that are taken from a certain place go to help those of that [same] place, according to the quantity of the donations [available]."[94] The Genoese followed a similar course, assuring those who put coins in the *cassetta* of a particular church that their money would go first to slaves from that place.[95] In a sense, this dictum was merely a parochial way of rendering what was for many agencies a state policy: that each state accepted responsibility for ransoming only its own citizens. As the Gonfalone (repeatedly) put it: "the money of our Arch-confraternity is destined solely for the Ransoming of Slaves ... [who are] subjects of the Papal States." No one who was not a citizen – or at least had not been in the service – of that country could expect ransoming funds from the state agency, a procedure that effectively punished anyone who moved around the peninsula in search of a new home or living. Thus it happened to Giuseppe Mazzocati, who had lived in Rimini for 26 years, had taken a wife and had fathered several children there, but had been born and baptized in Chioggia, in Venetian territory. When he was taken by pirates from Dulcigno in 1687, Mazzocati was stuck: the Venetians no longer felt a responsibility for him and the Gonfalone was forbidden by its charter from helping anyone not born in the Papal States.[96]

In keeping with this approach, the priests and collectors who traversed the backwoods and coastal reaches of Italy were instructed not only to collect the contributions of donors, but also the names of those from each area that were suspected to be slaves in Muslim hands. Along with the names, each agent was ordered to collect all relevant details that might help identify the individual slaves: that is, "their age, stature, skin [color], occupation, [and] every other clear indicator of [who they are], along with the time and the place where their capture took place."[97] In an era when many of the poorest workers were without even a patronymic and most slaves lacked any written form of identifications, such descriptions could get quite detailed. In consequence, these slaves sometimes emerge from their historical and class anonymity in little verbal sketches of startling clarity:

> Marco [di Severo] would be around sixty and not very tall; [he is] round-faced [with] curly and grizzled hair, his eyes [are] neither white nor black; [he is] bald on the top of the head, with big, brown eyebrows; large and full in the body.
> Nicolò di Pasquale is about 26, with brown, straight hair; [he has] a big nose, stubby at the tip; he has brown eyebrows but does not have a beard; he cannot easily stretch out the fingers of his hands.
> Cristofano di Pasquali ... is of middling stature, spare[?] of body, [with a] wretched face, black and straight hair, black eyes [and] eyebrows, thin nose, about 30 years old.[98]

Always cautious about possible frauds, the ransoming agencies were rarely content with physical descriptions alone for establishing identity, at least if these were provided by kinsfolk. Most central authorities also demanded a signed testimonial, or *fede*, to guarantee that the slave was indeed of that place, having been baptized there, was known to have been enslaved, and was poor enough to merit charity: for this latter, there may sometimes have been a separate chit, referred to as a "*fede* of poverty."[99] As to the sort of person best qualified to produce *fedi*, this depended both on what was being testified to and who was requiring it. The Venetian Provveditori declared themselves content with what they called "the ancient system, founded on a deposition of at least two sworn witnesses, who attest to the said Enslavement," although on occasion they might ask a half dozen neighbors and co-workers if they knew the person and his fate.[100] On the sometimes thornier issue of establishing citizenship, the parish priest, who controlled the baptismal records, was ideal, but sometimes the local lord, the mayor, or the village syndics – known in Neapolitan territories as the *eletti*, in the Papal States as *massari* – were called in to provide verification as well. Originally these *fedi* were just scraps of paper, on which writers put down what they knew of a slave, but by the late seventeenth century, ransoming authorities had begun to produce standardized forms – printed blanks that could be distributed to the appropriate authorities, filled out, and returned.[101] These secular elites seem to have been useful not only for identifying that a slave was personally poor, but also that (for example), "he has no one, except a poor mother, who almost has to beg [to survive], and he has no other hope except these [state] alms."[102] Sometimes, especially before the forms became standardized, they could even reflect on what would drive someone to risk slavery, as the mayor and *eletti* of Belvedere (near Salerno) wrote of one Domenico Rizzo, alias Minico:

> [he] is a native citizen [*cittadino originario*] of said City and he is very poor, not possessing anything, nor any property; indeed, just because of his great poverty, in past years he was reduced to [having to] go to sea to be able to live, although he was old; such that, continuing to go to sea, he was taken by Turks [in Tripoli], where presently he is found.[103]

Such *fedi* from home could be put to use only if corresponding testimonials could be procured from the other side: that is, from a missionary priest in the city in Barbary where the slave was held.[104] The slave himself apparently had to procure – that is, pay for – this scrap of paper, which some referred to as their "*fede* of enslavement."[105] As with the *fede* from home, these served to identify a slave, though in Africa this task was somewhat trickier than in Europe, since many slaves were clearly willing to fake their identity, to "rob the name" of another slave, or claim to be from any city in any Italy state, if that would get them out of Barbary.[106] For this reason those sent to do the ransoming were instructed to make special, careful, and descriptive, note of those captives who had died, so they could then be struck off the ransoming list – lest some other slave try to steal a deceased's identity, Martin Guerre style, and come back in his place, a free, if fraudulent man.[107] Most slaves of humble background presumably had no form of written identification and so had to demonstrate who they were by persuading fellow captives to vouch for them before the priest. Some included physical descriptions in their *fedi*, though these could also confuse the situation, since slaves might get so beaten over the course of their captivity that they no longer looked anything like they once had. This seems to have been the lot of one Simone of Cavi:

> Son of Romano and Catterina di Antonio of Cavi, around 24 years of age, [he is] with little beard, of fair skin, skinny of body, more tall than short in stature, with three marks on the body, that is: a cut on the thigh that was [from] birth, another cut on the temple from being hit by a rock, and another cut under the right eye that was [from] the point of a Moor's sword, from which eye he does not see, unless he holds it open like the other, but it is more white and bigger than the other, and [to keep it open] he had a string around his neck, where one can still see the mark. He has two brothers and a sister [and] he was captured in the Papal galleys near Monte Argentario in the year 1582.[108]

As with the *fedi* from the slaves' home towns, those from Barbary were needed to attest to more than identity alone. Also included in the document might be some mention as to how and when a slave had been captured, as well as the size of his ransom. The missionaries might also report on a slave's financial situation, noting whether he had put aside any savings during his captivity that might be used towards his ransom. Conversely, the priest had to find out if the slave in question had run up debts while in Barbary – surprisingly, some captives managed to borrow from local moneylenders – since these would have to be paid off before he was allowed to leave.[109] The men who were doling out the money in Naples or Rome also wanted reassurance that these slaves had remained deserving victims throughout their captivity: that they had not degenerated into drunken godlessness and in

particular that they had not been beaten or cajoled into making a conversion, even if a sham one, to Islam. Since there were rarely enough
funds available to free everyone from a given state at once, the priests
were apparently the ones who decided who should leave and who
would have to wait. Their choice seems to have been based on the wor-
thiness of the slaves themselves, both as good Christians and as
victims. By the mid-eighteenth century, these forms too were produced
as pre-printed blanks, with space made available for comments as to
whether the slave under review had been "living as a good Catholic
and true follower of what our Sacred Law prescribes."[110] Not surprisingly, some slaves were quite bitter when they found that others were
getting preference. As one Calabrian sailor grumbled, "I see liberty
coming to so many others, slaves [who are] newcomers here of just two
or three years at the most, while [for] me have passed four years going
on five."[111]

Despite the stringent requirements they imposed on those who
wanted their charity, not all the ransoming organizations paid a slave's
full ransom. Some, like Venice's Provveditori sopra Luoghi Pii and the
Neapolitan Santa Casa, instead offered only a fixed base sum, in the
form of a promissory note known in Venice as a *Cristo* and in Naples as
an *albarano*; by around 1720 these too were turned out as pre-printed
forms.[112] In both realms these notes carried a value of 50 ducats in the
later seventeenth century, rising to double that by the 1730s. However
much it increased, the sum never represented more than a quarter or a
third of the going ransom for fishermen or sailors.[113] Both the
Provveditori and the Santa Casa made out their notes in the name of
the slave himself and indeed sometimes seem to have sent one to the
man or woman in Barbary. Still, since slaves might easily lose their
award, it was more typical to give the form to the slave's family or to
someone in the ransoming business, with the understanding that to
collect on them it was necessary to bring the person named on the
form, "freed and before us, or our Successors," within the space of a
year.[114]

The idea, or at least the hope, behind these notes, as the Venetian
Provveditori once put it, was that "with the foundation of that
promise" the slave's kin would be able to come up with the rest, "from
the pledges of all the usual places": in other words, other charities.[115]
The intention seems to have been that the *albarano* or the *Cristo* might,
besides providing an eventual amount of cash, also smooth the bearer's
way with other charitable organizations, representing as they did the
state's certified knowledge about the slave's citizenship, economic

condition, civil status, and period of enslavement. As such, the business of collecting witnesses and *fedi* had to be done only once, which might have speeded up the process. An apparent drawback to this procedure, however, was that, having got one of these promissory notes, the relatives' task had only just begun. They still had to visit what other charitable societies were available, which often meant more trips from their home town out on the periphery to the capital, where the state and religious ransoming organizations – and with them, the money – were all to be found. Their search might well require interviews and pleas with both sacred and secular bodies, each of which might contribute something. In mid-seventeenth-century Naples, one might make the rounds between the ecclesiastics of Monte della Miseracordi, Santa Maria della Catena, Santa Maria di Porto Salvo, the Casa della Santissima Anna, and the Congregation of San Paolo.[116] In Rome, one also had to traipse all over the city, as one Elena Sargente sketched out in her petition to the Gonfalone:

> She has had promises from the Eminent Sig. Cardinal Barbarino, 50 scudi; from the Trinitarian Fathers of Santa Francesca Romana, another 80 scudi; from the Discalced Religious Fathers of the Spanish Congregation, 15 scudi; and from you Venerable Signori, another 50 scudi. And since despite the diligence undertaken she has not found other charity to make up the sum of 300 pieces [of eight] demanded for her said ransom, she humbly petitions for other alms.[117]

As Elena's experience shows, such piecemeal collection of funds, despite all the work involved, could still fall well short of the ransoms demanded in Barbary. Indeed, as the Provveditori sopra Luoghi Pii once admitted, "rarely do [the slaves] find a quantity that is sufficient for their liberation, which causes many of them to end their days in those miseries [of slavery]."[118] Moreover, with so many possible sources, each giving only a little, there were plenty of chances for delay and sometimes things went completely awry. As the mother of a slave from the town of Gaeta wrote to the Santa Casa in 1739:

> having obtained from the charity of the *Sacro Monte* [the Santa Casa] the usual *albarano* of 100 ducats ... in the month of March or May of the past year 1738, [she] gave it to a woman of this City [Naples?] so that she could [use it to] get other charities for the ransom of her son, and, passing on to a better life said woman, the aforementioned *albarano* [expired and] was lost.[119]

This already convoluted solicitation process was often further complicated by the slave owners themselves, especially those who held captives in Dulcigno or other Turkish ports near Italy.[120] Attempting to get
things moving, masters who held a group of slaves who had been
taken together, or who were at least from the same town in Italy,
might send one of their number back home with a safe conduct to
plead the group's collective case.[121] The advantages of dispatching such
a messenger were obvious: not only could he bring all the personal
letters and required enslavement *fedi* to the relatives and bureaucrats
who needed them, but he might also provide graphic, supporting testimony that the miseries his fellow slaves described in their letters were
actually true and going on even at the time. He could also explain in
detail what would happen to his companions if he did not return with
their collective ransom before the six or eight months of grace stated
in his *laissez passer* expired: as the slaves themselves put it, on one
occasion,

> We will receive all the damage if this man does not come back
> within the said deadline, and we are liable to pay the said [ransom]
> money, and we will be immediately sold to Barbary, where we will
> suffer a thousand torments.[122]

The slave messenger could be an effective instrument in driving home
such threats on behalf of his owner. Sometimes he could act as a personal shopper for those in Turkish lands who had a taste for European
products. On the back of the letter quoted above, the three *agas* who co-
owned the slaves, along with several other authorities in Dulcigno, put
in their own special orders to their freed agent, noting that "you should
pick up these goods with the money that will be given to you and
against the account of the ransom [funds]." The *Dulcignotti* requested,
among other things, "a load of majolica, a chest of drinking mugs and a
chest of plates;" "five *braccie* of green Velvet;" "ten *braccie* of fine silk of
dark blue color;" "a portable bar the size of ten decanters, eight big
decanters and two small [ones], and the bar should be of walnut."[123]
On the other hand, some owners who were evidently particularly
eager to do business might not send the slave messenger alone but
actually accompany him. Several times in the 1720s, Venice's
Provveditori sopra Luoghi Pii denounced Dulcigno slavers for bringing
Italian – and even Venetian – slaves right into Venice itself: one could
see them "going with chains on their neck begging around the City,
always escorted by the Turkish *Dulcignotto* owner, making a scandalous

show." Such, apparently, was the Venetian respect for private property that no one attempted to seize the slaves; instead, the Provveditori worried that it would be impossible to come up with the ransom, to make sure "that [the slave] is not taken back to Turkey" with their owners' imminent departure.[124]

Unlike Naples or Venice, Rome's arch-confraternity of the Gonfalone was set up from the beginning with the intention of paying off the entire ransom of papal slaves. The process was initially conceived in the style of the Trinitarians and Mercedarians, where a substantial collection drive throughout the national territory would culminate in a big ransom expedition to Barbary, based on the lists of names compiled during the drive. Between 1585 and 1589, the Gonfalone staged four of these grand events, and the Capuchins that they sent as their agents managed to ransom something like 1,000 slaves from Algiers and Tunis. Such events were promoted as a Christian Triumph, providing some much needed propaganda of the power of Christian faith (and money) at a time when slave raids from Barbary were depressingly frequent and effective.

Despite these apparent initial successes, the Gonfalone soon abandoned the big redemptions and went about negotiating and ransoming slaves on a piecemeal basis, more or less as their names were sent in from their homes out on the periphery. It appears that some of the crusading spark went out of the organization after a generation, but the confreres continued as much as possible to provide the entire ransom for the slaves on their lists, though even this put a tremendous drain on their resources, producing cycles of boom and bust that characterized Gonfalone operations thereafter. Indeed, it appears that the organization essentially went out of business at various times during the seventeenth century, only to be resurrected when it was put under the control of more energetic administrators. Even when it was functioning, the Gonfalone often managed to ransom only two or three slaves a year, leaving an ever-growing backlog of captives who felt, not surprisingly, that they had been forgotten and abandoned. It was at times such as these that slaves from the Papal States began to grumble "that the Pope, by not eating for a single day, could [have enough money] to amply ransom everyone."[125]

More than just the financing problems tended to argue against big redemptions. When the slave owners got wind that one of these expeditions was being planned, they tended, not altogether surprisingly, to "raise their prices, blocking the ransoming of [their slaves] and causing much toil for the Redeemers and obstacles for the Redemption."[126]

Everyone on the Christian side agreed that the greed of the slave owners was not easily put off, especially because masters generally understood that the ransomers were under considerable pressure to free a "conspicuous quantity" of slaves, and that to do so in a timely fashion they necessarily had to come to Barbary laden with cash.[127] Big redemptions required massive amounts of money to pull off: sometimes 50,000 or even 100,000 scudi, zecchini, or pieces of eight, all in coins that had to be physically transported to Barbary.[128] It was a mindset that gave considerable leverage to the slave owners, who were more than willing to use it to their profit. More than one ransoming expedition was frustrated and outmaneuvered, as the ruling pasha, the big slave-holding *ra'is*, and sometimes even petty masters with only two or three slaves raised their ransom demands, hid (or sometimes forcibly adopted) high priority slaves, or left the redeemers to cool their heels for weeks at a time.

The ransoming organizations compounded this problem, especially when they were first getting started, by sending agents to Barbary without any clear notion about what most of the slave masters intended to ask for their captives. Instead, the idea was to come up with a set price for each slave, in the expectation that owners would be happy to take what was offered. The Gonfalone decided on 150 scudi, for example, and the Sicilians only 100, though both left their agents some leeway if there were holdouts.[129] The policy was not especially successful: Santa Maria la Nova ended up spending an average of 142 scudi per slave, mostly just because the Tunisians they dealt with were shrewder negotiators. Those who tried to bargain with slave owners could find things going very badly indeed: Knight, among others, recounted a tale of how every time a French emissary tried to lower the asking price he found instead that the ruling pasha would raise it; when negotiations finally broke down completely, the Algerians seized his sails and made him pay for the privilege of leaving (without the slaves).[130]

In particular, however, those in Barbary took the general redemption as an opportunity to unload slaves who were not on the ransomers' lists – for the most part men who were past their prime, no longer fit for work, and hence without much value in the *badestan.*The term for such old or worn-out slaves was *aguaitas,* or *agaitas* – a word perhaps from the *lingua franca* – and those in Barbary realized that the redeemers, in their eagerness and determination to carry out a successful *redenzione generale*, could be coerced into paying for a certain number of these *aguaitas*, who were often not even from the country sponsoring the redemption.[131] One trick, used against the Sicilian redeemers on their second trip to Tunis in 1600, was to drag in one or more *aguaitas* and claim that ransomers on a previous trip had pledged that their successors would redeem these slaves on the next voyage.[132] If no such candidates were readily at hand, according to some ransomers, the authorities could try another trick that might work just as well:

> These individuals [the pasha and janissaries of Algiers] have sought to buy Christians throughout all of Algiers, both blind and crippled, of every quality, both old and useless, [and] although they had bought them for 15 or 20 scudi, they have forced the Redeemers to buy them back for 100 scudi each.[133]

Snarled in such ploys, the big redemptions often turned out more exercises in frustration and humiliation than the triumphs of piety hoped for back home. When the Gonfalone was making its first forays into ransoming in the 1580s, it found that nearly a third of those it had paid for and brought home were not papal citizens, but were from Venice to Calabria and from all over Christendom as well – including France, Germany, Hungary, Spain, and Malta. As their agents put it: "We have been forced to take those who are not from the Papal States in order to be able to have those who are."[134] Things evidently were going even worse for the Gonfalone a century later: in 1701, the diarist Francesco Valesio described Rome's welcome for "128 ransomed slaves … most beautiful men and of various nations," but went on to note that "of them only two were Romans." Likewise, the Venetians would complain in the 1760s that "we have been forced to ransom 35 Slaves, 30 of whom are not Venetian, and [for] these they would have us pay an exorbitant price."[135]

If, as indeed appears the case, these redemptions large and small – along with the alms collecting, the sermonizing, and of course the corsair slaving that necessitated them – were significant features of the baroque Italian social landscape, it is worth asking just how successful this vast communal and religious effort actually was. The numbers of slaves freed cannot, in themselves, really speak to this question, without keeping in mind the much larger numbers that were regularly taken. In any given year through much of the sixteenth and seventeenth centuries, as we have seen, probably not more than 3 or 4 percent of the white slaves in Barbary could hope to be ransomed. What is perhaps more telling, when considering the actual success or less of the whole ransoming enterprise, however, is to ask what chances a poor slave might have actually had, once taken and sold at the *badestan*, to regain his or her freedom and return home.

Few studies have been carried out on how long Christians were likely to remain in captivity, despite the fact that a good many ransoming lists – especially from the Trinitarians and Mercedarians – contain this information. In one such survey, conducted on three Mercedarian redemptions of the 1660s that brought back 757 predominantly Spanish slaves from Algiers and Morocco, Claude Larquié concluded that "In fact, the length of captivity was not considerable ... after five years, 75 percent of the captives had been redeemed."[136] These figures are nearly identical to those for a very similar ransom of 281 Spanish and Spanish-Italian slaves, also carried out in Algiers in the 1660s, by the Trinitarians: three-quarters of these captives were also bought out within just about five years after enslavement. The latter list makes it clear that slavery time could vary significantly for different subgroups, however. Children, for instance, but especially clerics were ransomed out rather more quickly than the average: 88 and 92 percent respectively got out within five years; indeed, 92 percent of the clergy were out in three years. For non-clergymen in general (who were the great majority of these particular slaves: 204, or 73 percent of the total), only two-thirds had been ransomed within five years; for the small number (20) of adult female slaves, just 61 percent were out within that time.[137]

Setting aside the rather pained question of whether five years' slave labor should be dismissed as a "not considerable" piece of one's life, the question still remains how typical such a stint was over the long haul of the sixteenth to eighteenth centuries and for countries other than Spain. It is indeed clear that when it came to ransoming, the Spanish and perhaps the French slaves were especially privileged groups. With the Trinitarian and Mercedarian orders actively competing to collect for and ransom the former and the French state regularly intervening for the latter, it would seem (despite the story recounted by Francis Knight, above) that men and women from these two countries probably spent less time than other nationalities enslaved in Barbary. Others were not so fortunate: a group of Venetians ransomed from Constantinople and Tripoli in 1730, for example, had an average slavery time of 12.8 years; only 46 percent managed to get out within Larquié's threshold of five years.[138] Even the Spanish and their allies did not always do very well: in a Trinitarian redemption to Algiers in 1720 that brought home 162 men (mostly soldiers), the average time in slavery had been just over 12.5 years and only 13 percent were ransomed, not in five, but in ten years or less.[139]

One soon begins to detect certain patterns in the redemptions of slave types and thus the time captives spent in slavery. Those whose perils resonated best with the charitable and sentimental instincts of the era tended to get out much faster than the norm – young virgins and children in particular, but obviously priests and friars got special consideration from the ransoming fathers. Adult men and women, as we have seen, might have to wait much longer. But it also must be remembered that these lists are of those who got ransomed, a point that may seem obvious to the point of redundancy, but it is significant that those who were not ransomed necessarily ended up in Barbary much longer. Indeed, when one examines lists prepared by various cities or agencies, not of ransomed slaves, but rather of those reportedly held in slavery, the numbers increase: such an inventory for 17 citizens of Ancona held in various ports in Barbary or the Balkans around 1670 indicated an average time in slavery of nearly seven years, with fewer than half the captives held for less than five.

Clearly, slaves who lacked the connections, nationality, or religion to get on the redemption lists – and they often begged those who ran the agencies back home to "put me on the list" – could easily be left to languish in captivity.[140] D'Arvieux noted in the 1660s that redemptions for Italian slaves were "a good deal rarer" than those for the French or Spaniards, probably because almost all the Italian redemptive organizations had gone torpid by the mid-seventeenth century. The problem for English, Dutch, and German slaves was apparently even worse.[141] But the time someone languished in slavery was not only a matter of his home country's alacrity or indifference to his plight. Those Italians who were taken to Dulcigno or Santa Maura tended to get out faster than those who were sold to Barbary, who in turn fared somewhat better than those who ended up in Constantinople, for example, in Aleppo, Tartary, or – worst of all, it seems – stuck "for the long course of 27 years living a pitiful servitude in the Port of Suez, [a] small and ignoble place on the Red Sea."[142]

At the same time, the purpose for which one was purchased could also make a big difference. Those who had the great misfortune to end up not just as galley slaves in Barbary, but as *galeotti* on the galleys of the sultan, did in fact disappear into that living death that so many neophyte captives seemed to fear so greatly. Since, as one missionary noted, "in the Levant there are no *bagni*, and [the *galeotti*] always stay on the galleys," it was virtually impossible for a slave to get word out as to where and who he was.[143] When, later in the eighteenth century and well past the twilight of the Turkish fleet, it became possible to ransom some of these unfortunates, they were found to have spent horrendous spells in slavery: of 103 *galeotti* rescued "from the Galleys of Constantinople" in 1729–30, fewer than 10 per cent had served less than five years, and their average time at the oar was around 19 years; likewise, as we have seen, the eleven Venetian *galeotti* ransomed in 1765 had spent an average of no fewer than 38 years in slavery.[144] On the other hand, women figured very little on the redemption lists in part at least because many of them evidently ended up as concubine slaves, who then converted to Islam in order to remain with their children, who were themselves brought up in the faith of their master. Indeed, few of the many renegade Christians in Barbary, female or male, ever figured into the redemption lists, for the simple reason that attempting to abjure one's abjuration and re-embrace Christianity was punishable by death in the regencies – not just for the slave himself, but also for any priests suspected of assisting him. Those renegades who did make it safely back to Christendom to reconvert almost inevitably did so by escaping or with the capture of their galley.[145]

With the calculations earlier in this book, we concluded that nearly a sixth of all slaves died every year. For the times this was hardly a horrific figure and considerably less, for example, than the percentage of sailors that might perish on a long sea voyage.[146] As we have seen, however, it was the newcomers, the *schiavi novelli*, who died in the greatest numbers in Barbary: the seasoning process for new captives could take several years and might exact a heavy toll. This makes it likely, therefore, that even if three-quarters of the Barbary slaves were ransomed within five years – a still somewhat debatable proposition – half or fewer of all those captured in the first place were likely to have survived those first five years. Moreover, though slaves who got through their first years of seasoning were clearly tougher than the newcomers, some of them continued to die – especially during the periodic outbreaks of plague – every year that they remained in Barbary. It may indeed have been just for this reason that such a high percentage of slaves was rescued within the space of Larquié's "not considerable" five years: only a small part of the total had managed to survive long enough to be ransomed at some point after that – 10, 15, or 20 years after their capture. Looking at the slave lists this way, we would have to conclude that anyone – or at least any of the poor Italian workers we have been talking about here – who was captured by Muslim corsairs and taken off to Barbary stood a less than 50/50 chance of returning home. They left their bones in unmarked plots in "Christian" cemeteries established just outside the city walls, often in shallow graves along the shoreline where dogs or waves could easily disinter them. John Foss claimed that "according to the records of the nation, upwards of 98,000 Christians have already been buried" in the cemetery of Algiers alone, which had only been set up "half a mile westward of the city" in the early 1600s – in the years before that, dead Christian slaves were said to have been simply thrown into the sea.[147]

The fate of these unfortunates – and of the wives, kin, and neighbors they left behind – would seem to have been not so different from that of the black Africans taken to the Americas in these same years. They could expect, in other words, to spend the rest of their lives laboring in slavery, dying far from their homeland in a brutalized community of fellow slaves, cut off from the life to which they had been born. If for many of them, unlike for African slaves, there existed some forms of communication and ransom, these functioned only fitfully, at least through the sixteenth and most of the seventeenth centuries: often only tenuous connections at best with home and the hope of return.

The long-term effects of this slaving traffic can only be described as a social and psychological disaster, for coastal dwellers from Dalmatia to Spain. "This lasted for more than two centuries," Henri-David Grammont pointed out in 1879, "and one wonders how these miserable people could withstand it and continue to live."[148] Indeed, other scholars have noted a pervasive "fear of the horizon" that gripped Italian coastal settlements through much of the sixteenth and seventeenth centuries. It was a trauma that, oddly enough, is rather less well comprehended today than that faced by the villagers and states of West Africa in those same centuries, and, although it is beginning to attract scholarly attention, its true extent and its impact on the coastal cultures of these regions are still largely matters of conjecture.

Unquestionably several centuries of the psychological trauma of enslavement or its threat left a mark on the culture of the Christian Mediterranean. Giuseppe Bonaffini has somewhat melodramatically dubbed the Mediterranean of this era "The Sea of Fear," but it is indeed quite likely that, for those who had to make their living there, the constant fear of corsair capture produced a genuine stress that could only be leavened with piety and fatalism: "I'm forced to do this work," as one Venetian sailor lamented, freshly returned from slavery and about to set off and risk his freedom again, "I don't know any other;" as another, freshly ransomed, put it,"we boarded a ship back to Venice, where we arrived stripped and naked, and I especially, if I hadn't gone out on another voyage, I would have had nothing to live on."[149] Surrounded by hostile seas on all sides, Italians in particular turned inland, away from such constant threats, and baroque Italy of the seventeenth and eighteenth centuries became a curiously self-absorbed society. "We retired to the countryside. We lost [our] freedom and [our] love of the sea," complained one Italian essayist recently, lamenting that, in the face of continuous corsair piracy, the people who had in such short order once produced Columbus, John Cabot, and Amerigo Vespucci were no longer "a nation of navigators, although we did become a nation of bathers."[150]

Societies under continuing trauma reorganize themselves, find solutions, or disappear. Mediterranean states obviously survived, though one could certainly say that, at least for Iberia and Italy, the seventeenth century represented a dark period out of which Spanish and Italian societies emerged as mere shadows of what they had been in their earlier, golden ages. For individuals themselves, we can see that the psychological traces of this trauma lasted beyond the time that the larger societies had rebuilt themselves as modern states, long after "even the idea ha[d] been lost of these dogs that had brought so much terror." It continued just below the surface of the coastal culture of the European Mediterranean even into the first years of the twentieth century, when, as one Sicilian woman put it,

The oldest [still] tell of a time in which the Turks arrived in Sicily every day. They came down in the thousands from their galleys and you can imagine what happened! They seized unmarried girls and children, grabbed things and money and in an instant they were [back] aboard their galleys, set sail and disappeared.... The next day it was the same thing, and there was always the bitter song, as you could not hear other than the lamentations and invocations of the mothers and the tears that ran like rivers through all the houses.[151]

6
Celebrating Slavery

> Consider for a while ... [the way] in which our fortune has reduced us to such a miserable state of slavery. But all our slavery derives from the love of our sins that makes us slaves in the hands of the Barbarians, [and] from this bodily slavery we will have faith in God and the Blessed Virgin to be freed.... God, who thus permits these misfortunes for the profit of our souls, so that gladly we resort to Him and we recognize that this world is full of woes and no one is ever content with his lot. May God know that which will help me and may [He] give me strength to resist the torments, and hold me in His grace, and I can make penitence for my sins with perfect resignation.[1]

The two slaves whose letters make up this composite meditation on the role of sin and redemption in slavery may not have written the actual words: the first was a rural laborer from Camini (a village on the central Calabrian coast) and the second was a Neapolitan sailor; both of them were quite possibly illiterate. As we have seen, scribes were available for hire in the Barbary regencies to compose such messages, and though they no doubt took down a slave's words as dictated, they also had a lexicon of set words and phrases to enhance any client's message of pathos and suffering to those back home. Nevertheless, these themes of sin, piety, retribution, and salvation are all-pervasive in the writings from white slaves in Barbary, and there is every indication that the slaves themselves, as much as their scribes and their clerics, embraced such concepts as a way of making sense of the "purpose" God must have had in inflicting this scourge on His believers. "What is the crime for which these poor Slaves are subjected to such a heavy punishment?" the Piedmontese abbot Pietro Caissotti once rhetorically asked; and he answered straightaway: "Their fault, their crime, is [that of] recognizing Jesus Christ as the most divine Savior ... and of professing Him as the True Faith."[2] On the one hand, this could be taken to mean that these slaves were being singled out for no other crime than simply that of being Christians, but the captives themselves seem to have seen things differently, holding that they had been enslaved because, as Christians, they were also sinners, deserving of punishment. "For my sins I was captured in a place called Ascea," began one slave's account in 1678, and these men and women often did present themselves as subjected to God's divine wrath in an inferno specially created for this purpose. "Now," as a slave put it in 1735, "I seem to be in another world, of sufferings and of the torments of Hell;" another described himself "like a soul in Purgatory awaiting some relief;" while yet another wrote of "my great pain, the pain of Purgatory and of the flames of Hell;" and confessed that "I have no hope, only that the help of God and of good Christians might raise me from this Inferno."[3] This retribution, "under the cruel yoke of slavery," meant for most slaves that they would be "beaten, cursed, and called faithless dogs" by their tormentors, "nourished on the vilest of food, [and] always exposed to the greatest dangers."[4] Even those who enjoyed a life of relative ease, however, perhaps as a favored house slave or a semi-independent slave merchant, still found that "Long Bondage breaks the Spirits, it scatters *Hope off*, and discourages *all attempts for Freedom.*"[5]

At the same time, enslavement, for all its torments, could be cast in somewhat more affirmative terms, as a way in which God tested the faithful, proving the strength of their devotion in the hard forge of bondage: "Trying me," as one Venetian sailor put it, "with all the greatest cruelties and torments that those Barbarians could devise."[6] Slaves who failed this test were plain to see: they had abandoned their faith and ended up "living no better than the beasts," in drunkenness and degradation; others, still worse off, succumbed to the blandishments of their masters and embraced Islam, thereby giving up their souls as surely as if they had made a pact with Satan himself.[7] Slavery could be seen as testing the religious mettle not only of the slaves themselves, however, but also of their kin and countrymen back home. Though safe from enslavement's direct brutality, relations were still expected – by both slaves and the ransoming agencies – "to sell [everything] including their own beds and mattresses," to raise the necessary redemption funds; in other words, "to contribute with their own destitution," to alleviate the suffering of their kin in Barbary.[8] At the very least, relatives were expected to keep in contact with a slave in the hope that their letters would help him maintain his morale and withstand the corrosive effects that bondage could have on his faith.[9] Judging by the frequent complaints in slave letters, not all kin managed to pass even this modest test, evidently preferring instead to give up their enslaved kinsman for dead rather than shoulder the moral or financial burden of his support, despite the fact that, as one captive put it, "God commands it."[10] Others at home appear to have failed the challenge of slavery in another, more personal way: many of these women, children, and elderly had lost to slavery the very men who were their primary breadwinners, and now, facing starvation, they demeaned themselves and their faith by resorting to beggary, crime, or prostitution in order to survive.[11]

Such at least were the accusations and laments that slaves often made in their letters. They could go further, however, occasionally leveling such indictments at their home communities and indeed at their native state, for having failed to respond to

> [t]hose of us, poor and abandoned, who do not have anyone who is moved to compassion [for us], since, with that hope ... we could go on living and being constant, not abjuring due to the many blows that we have to endure from the hands of these Barbarians.[12]

The problems of state-run redemptive agencies were, as we have seen, many and mostly got worse as time went on: they lacked dependable funding, reliable information about who was enslaved, and negotiating skills for dealing with slave owners in Barbary. On top of all this, the uneven quality of often dilatory administrators meant that ransoming efforts in many of the Italian states might be suspended for years at a time. Towards the end of the seventeenth century, however, things began to change, in part because the Trinitarians and the Mercedarians became more involved in this sorry situation. So great was their success – not only in returning slaves home, but also in responding to the moral and religious challenges posed by slavery itself – that by the mid-1700s these two orders had come to dominate ransoming activities throughout Italy.

In part, the redemptive fathers gained such dominance in this business because of the changing economic landscape of the times. By the early 1700s, Muslims in Barbary who invested in slaves increasingly did so with the intention of making a quick profit through ransoming rather than exploiting them for labor. Such dealers soon came to rely on the

Trinitarians and Mercedarians as the best way to unload their chattel, since in the Maghreb these orders had long since proven themselves as reliable trading partners in the large-scale redemptions they mounted every year or two throughout most of the seventeenth century. It was largely due to their efforts on behalf of the Spanish Crown that, as d'Arvieux noted, Spaniards became the most readily bought and quickly redeemed among all the Christian slaves.[13]

The stabilizing political situation in the Mediterranean after 1700 also favored the ransoming orders, transnational organizations that enjoyed greater flexibility in freeing slaves of various backgrounds who had been captured in the service of, for example, the Austrian Hapsburgs or the Spanish Empire. At a time when most states had established consulates at one or more of the Barbary regencies, the Trinitarians and Mercedarians ran permanent hospitals in the principal cities that could, in effect, serve them as consular centers.[14] Finally, these redeemers had, over the centuries, simply acquired superior skills as traders in slaves.[15] With agents on the spot, or with the help of friendly consuls, the Trinitarians and Mercedarians were generally well informed about conditions in the local slave market and knew better than most state agents who was enslaved. They had also picked up the tricks of the trade, having acquired the sort of insider knowledge that protected them from the bullying tactics of the Muslim rulers and slave owners.

The Trinitarians made some of these slave dealing talents clear in 1762 when they pitched their services to the Venetians. Although the order had long been banned from collecting alms in Venetian territories, the fathers nevertheless offered to serve as Venice's ransoming agents, perhaps as a first step towards broadening their presence both in the Veneto and in Italy more generally.[16] The Trinitarians had tried such a move a generation earlier, but had run into jurisdictional conflicts with the Venetian state and ended up being expelled from the Republic. Their timing was better in the 1760s, however: dozens of Venetian subjects had been enslaved for years in Barbary, and Venice, which had never had a consulate in the Regency states and whose success at ransoming had never been great, was growing desperate. To make their case, the Trinitarians provided the Venetian Senate with a remarkable collection of persuasive materials. These included a number of printed lists, or *cataloghi*, that enumerated all the slaves they had recently redeemed on behalf of other client states. They also drew up a price comparison between the ransoms they typically paid and those charged by the "heretics and Jews" who had hitherto served Venice as ransoming agents. To drive home the point that in their expeditions they were freeing slaves for barely a third what the Venetians had been paying, the Trinitarians not only offered various examples of captives brought back for Milan, Germany, and Turin, but also compared the prices of various categories of higher- and lower-class slaves.[17] Their successes, they claimed, were due to their being on the spot for the negotiations and enjoying the protection of local rulers. As a result, the Trinitarians could keep control of their ransoming funds and avoid paying (or charging the Venetians) the hefty 14 percent exchange rates, the *cambio marittimo* exacted by "those who make a living out of this." Having dealt for years in the slaves from many nations, the Trinitarians (like the Mercedarians) were "practiced in managing this ransoming with dexterity," wise to all the tricks that slave owners used to increase ransoms, while knowing a few of their own:

> It is our custom ... to take sick slaves into our hospital, [and] with such opportunity we take in also those who are not sick, [but] who have, with some small coins that they have paid to the Guardian of the Bagno, entrusted themselves to our care; it being necessary [for] this that they should have some sort of illness, we call the physician of the King and, by showing him a certain sum of money, have him recognize the slave [as] sick, and he speaks to the King his master, making him believe of the danger of his [slave's] death, such that one arranges with advantage [the slave's] ransom, and it is contrived with a small sum [of money].[18]

Beyond offering slaves at a tidy savings to their Italian clients, the Trinitarians also sought to imbue the whole ransoming enterprise with a religious symbolism and significance that seems to have eluded the state agencies, with their legions of notaries, beadles, and miscellaneous pitchmen. Heirs to the crusading vision under which they had originally been founded, the redemptive fathers brought a passionate dedication, not just to fundraising, but also to preaching, to the transactions of ransoming, and to the processions that closed most redemptive cycles. Having honed their skills as preachers and fundraisers in Spain and France, they brought to the Italian states a combination of piety and showmanship that resonated strongly with the religious sentiments of the peninsula. Like the Mercedarians elsewhere, the Trinitarians were especially well known for their grand processions of ex-slaves, events that father Camillo di Maria once called "A Triumph of peace, of liberty, and of jubilation, without the mourning or the sadness of even one [person] to interrupt the joy."[19] Extraordinarily popular with the public of all classes, these processions were among the most characteristic of urban spectacles in eighteenth-century Italy. When freed slaves were presented to the Romans in 1701, "the road was jammed by a great number of carriages and by the assembled people, from the church of Santa Susanna up to the Pontifical Palace [the Quirinal]." Those in Milan who lived along the processional route showed their enthusiasm by "beautifying the walls [of their houses] with tapestries and flags of various colors, and with many other embellishments." The 1771 procession in Palermo was hailed with

> particular admiration [by] a numerous Citizenry that turned out everywhere the Procession passed, both from the balconies and from the windows of the Palaces, such as has rarely been seen in other observances and public celebrations of the City of Palermo; and enormous was the jubilation that was aroused in the souls of onlookers of every status, in [seeing] pass such a tender and edifying display.[20]

It has often been assumed, perhaps a bit glibly, that what one scholar has termed "all this hoopla" was ultimately no more than a means of generating contributions, a spectacle that aimed at little more than stimulating the emotions and thus the donations of the pious.[21] Well

Procession of Freed Slaves (from Pierre Dan, *Historie van Barbaryen en des zelfs Zee-Roovers* Amersterdam, 1684)

aware of how popular the slave processions were in particular, many Italian states collaborated with the Trinitarians to stage them, and sometimes for just a handful of returned slaves. Such was the Venetian enthusiasm for these events that at one point in the mid-1700s the Trinitarians had to caution the Provveditori not to put on too many, lest both the state and the order exhaust their cash reserves in the process.[22] According to the magistrates' own expense accounts, the fathers seem to have been right: when all the labor and the outlay for wax, paint, canvas, flowers, music, gunpowder, fireworks, and so forth were added up, an extravaganza like the big procession of January 1764, where 91 ex-slaves were paraded through the city of Venice, cost more than 2,500 ducats.[23] Since this figure is around 5–10 times what was typically collected through donations on such occasions, it does indeed appear that these big slave processions, far from being money-making schemes, were more likely to represent a serious financial drain – on the state, on the local church hierarchy and confraternal system, and on the ransoming orders themselves.[24]

Nevertheless, the Italian states virtually competed with one another for putting on the most extravagant and expensive productions, right up to the close of the eighteenth century and the collapse of most of these *ancien régime* societies. Unlike the redemptive processions staged in France or Spain, where weeks might be needed for the returning fathers and ex-slaves to stop by the various cities of the realm, in the smaller city states of Italy the focus was generally on the capital.[25] First it was necessary for the whole contingent – the ex-slaves, their accompanying priests, and aides – to pass through quarantine: by the seventeenth century such a period of forced isolation was mandatory for anyone arriving in Italy from plague-ridden North Africa and the Levant.[26] Upon their emergence from the lazaret, which may have been as near to the capital as the original *lazaretto* was to Venice, or as far as Ancona is from Rome, these freed men and women were not, as a rule, actually free to go home. Instead they were formed into a group and headed off to the capital; if necessary, their priest-guides might also supply them with shoes or even horses for the journey. It was not too difficult to persuade slaves from the Papal States to make the trip to Rome: many apparently had already made a vow to go there or to Loreto if they were ever freed.[27] By the later seventeenth century, however, the priests seem to have begun making each slave's agreement to take the trip as a condition of his or her ransoming, perhaps because they had gone too often through the disheartening experience of one lay ransomer, who found that, as soon as he landed in Ancona with 47 freed slaves, "no one hesitated, but, wanting to enjoy their liberty in their own homes, all [the slaves] left him abandoned, no one remaining at all to accompany him to Rome."[28]

Although the processions might differ in detail from one place to another, most of their main features were similar. As a rule, after completing their quarantine, the ex-slaves were mustered at a church connected with the redemptive order: Santa Susanna in Rome, for example, San Michele in Turin, Santa Maria la Nova in Palermo, or San Ferdinando in Livorno. The processions usually set out in the late morning, often led by soldiers, but sometimes by "trumpeters [and] drummers, with a chorus" (who sang such appropriate psalms as "In exitu Israel de Ægypto" or "Super flumine Babylonis"). Behind these state agents and representatives followed one or more large banners – ambulant placards, really – depicting the sufferings of the slaves in Barbary, the redemptive act itself, the sign of the redemptive order involved, or (at least if the redeemers were Trinitarians) the vision of the order's founder.[29] Such devices were evidently 3 or 4 meters square – so big that they often had to be mounted on wooden frames – though light enough that they could still be carried, or at least guided, by "many children dressed in the manner in which the Angels are depicted." These *angioletti* were followed by members of the local ransoming agency or confraternities, the heads of charitable organizations, and the city's various religious orders. These latter could be quite numerous: Palermo, on one occasion, mustered no fewer than eight groups of regular clergy, plus the cathedral canons, with each cadre carrying its own insignia and images, in the form of crucifixes and banners, and accompanied by its own musicians and choruses.[30] After the local religious there came the three or four redemptive fathers who had gone on the ransoming expedition, and finally the slaves themselves, accompanied and followed by local elites and then townspeople marching behind them. Closing the procession was often another military contingent: in Palermo this meant a company of Swiss grenadiers; in Milan, in 1764, a corps of such grenadiers "proceeded, flanked, and closed the procession," but they were also joined by a "large Symphonic Band [playing] *alla Turca*, from the famous Baden-Baden Regiment."[31]

However much the local religious and townsfolk may have strutted in these affairs, the ex-slaves were necessarily the focus, enjoying an importance reflected by their centrality in the processional line. It was the custom of the Mercedarians, in the processions they staged in France and Spain, to clothe freed slaves in the rags they had worn in

Barbary, also furnishing them with chains (broken, however) to carry along the processional route. In Italy, where the Trinitarians predominated, chains could also make their appearance, but the slaves seem to have been more typically tied together by rose and turquoise ribbons – the colors of the Trinitarian order – or they might carry olive branches.[32] Rather than their old rags, ex-slaves in Italy tended to have special costumes made for the occasion: "a white soutane with the [Trinitarian] Cross of the Redemption on the breast and a red beret on the head;" in many processions, they were paired with local notables – in Venice, the patriarch and the "noble protectors of the *scuole pii*" had this role, with any extra slaves beyond their number accompanied by Senators of the Republic.[33]

Processions typically made their way from the church of the redeemers to one that was especially associated with the redemptive act – the Salvatore in Venice, for instance. There the entire company was treated to a mass and *Te Deum*, followed by a sermon on the meaning of slavery and redemption.[34] Then, at least in the principalities, it was customary to proceed to the local palace (or the Quirinale in Rome), for a blessing and reception by the prince – though in Palermo the viceroy received the slaves from his special enclosure (*gabbia*) in the cathedral.[35] Usually the prince (or pope) distributed a gold coin to each ex-slave, and with this act, the procession was often concluded. In some instances, however, the redeemed slaves might be taken back to the convent of the ransoming fathers or to another of the city's cloisters, where a meal was served to them in the refectory by those who at any other time would have been their immeasurable social superiors – the local bishop (the patriarch in Venice), various aristocrats, and the leadership of the state ransoming agency.[36] With this, and with various alms safe in their pockets, the slaves were finally sent back to their homes, often far away in the hinterland.

Except for the occasional cautionary note about overdoing these processions, there is little indication that anyone – not even the notoriously frugal Venetians – complained about this expensive "hoopla" as money wasted.[37] Quite possibly this was because the states and clerical organizations that paid for them, as well as the public that so enthusiastically supported them, saw the significant psycho-civic role that these processions could play, not only for the ex-slaves, but also for the larger society to which all participants belonged. The structuring of these events – with their layered elements of church and state, angelic *putti,* and ex-slaves marching in company with their social betters – all speak of a ritual of reintegration, where those who had been stripped of their personhood and had been subjected to the social death of enslavement were visibly returned to their original status as free Christians.

The reintegration of the procession can be seen as only the last act of an entire process of purification – deprogramming, one might say – that had begun for the slaves with their ransoming in Africa. This repurchasing itself had interesting overtones: after all, in an obvious sense the redemptive priests bought humans, like any other slave dealer. So thought many of those who lived in Barbary, well aware that not only did both missionaries and consuls regularly "rent" Christian slaves as servants, but also that the redemptive priests willingly went to the *badestan* and competed in the bidding with the Turkish and Moorish slave traders there for any new captives they thought desirable – especially those boys and girls who were considered at risk for sexual or religious seduction by Muslim masters.[38] Just as newly arrived slaves when first brought ashore in Barbary went through a time of liminality as they passed from the group ownership of the *ra'is,* galley shareholders, and local pasha to that of their buyer in the *badestan,* so these now ransomed slaves, while no longer belonging to a master, still remained in some ways the possession of the priests who had bought their freedom – as symbolized by the ribbons that they bore in place of chains during the processions. Such tacit bondage was especially true for those who had had to rely on charity for their ransoms; by contrast, slaves who had contributed at least some of their asking price had more freedom of action, whether it came to returning directly to their homes without traveling to the capital first, or even deciding (as a few did) to remain in Barbary as free men or women.[39] Poor slaves purchased outright by the priests, on the other hand, were generally well aware of the debt they owed not only to the fathers, but also to those in their homeland who had contributed towards their freedom.

As such, these men and women passed from being the chattel of a Muslim master to being a ward of priests and the state. In the various legs of their trip home, they remained in the more or less stringent custody of the ransoming fathers. Once arrived in Livorno, Civitavecchia, Ancona, or Palermo, they were handed over to state authority, locked up in quarantine for a month or so to be sure they were plague-free. Yet here too the ex-slaves were still in wardship to their redeemers, in particular to special clerics (often Jesuits) who worked to recatechize them, cleansing their souls of the corrupting influence of Islam, even as the quarantine purged them of the miasma of Barbary.[40] Once the ex-slaves had been brought into the capital city, dressed in white and cleansed of their moral and physical contamination, they could be symbolically re-entered into their society, their moment of liminality – several months, more likely – finally closed. For such closure it was necessary, not just to present them to their fellow citizens – though this was certainly a central function of the slave procession – but also to recognize their transference from the wardship of the redeemers, who had guided them through their liminality, back to their normal status as subjects in a civil society. By participating in the mass that was the climax of the procession, the ex-slaves were symbolically freed from the religious tutelage of the redemptive fathers and given over, in turn, to the quotidian care of the secular clergy. Presented to their prince (or to the pope), where obeisance on their part was recognized and repaid by their lord's handing them a gold scudo or zecchino (carrying his image), they likewise returned to their old lives as "free" men or women – once again subjects of the state and no longer slaves of a master. At the culmination of the great Palermo procession of 1771, the Rev. Camillo di Maria was thrilled to see them thus transformed and returned among their brethren:

> so many generous Christians, who ... having conserved the liberty of the Evangelist among the chains of the Barbarians ... lined up now here in good order, [making] a beautiful show of themselves, and with their faces, with their acts, with their gestures do they not seem to want to give back to the viewing Public the History of their past sufferings and of [their] present adventurous doings?[41]

Certainly many hoped that such "a joyful spectacle" would stimulate donations and bring out the faithful, until the "roofs, windows, and terraces [were] stuffed with watching People."[42] To the participants and onlookers of the Milanese procession of 1739, Father Giovanni Ricolui encouraged such giving by praising charity aimed at freeing slaves as above all other forms of philanthropy:

> As the Holy Father Pius V said to you, "This holy work is about every other work of mercy, and in it all the others work together almost in compendium." Yes, certainly: to loosen one from the chains of slavery is to feed the starving, give drink to the thirsty, dress the naked, cure the sick, console the afflicted, aid one in danger, and is finally to return the Citizen to the Fatherland, the Subject to the Prince, the Father to his Sons, the son to the Parents, the Faithful to the Church.[43]

186 Christian Slaves, Muslim Masters

Through the avenue of charity, advocates of the great slave processions also saw these events as occasions to make manifest what the priest Camillo di Maria referred to as the "double Redemption" inherent to the whole process. In this sense, these costly affairs not only aimed at celebrating the redemption of the slaves themselves, but also of those at home who had willingly provided the necessary "labors, industry, expense, and the discomforts of dangerous voyages ... to serve to the profit of the Citizens, to the good of the Fatherland, to the advantage of the State, to the advantage of the Prince, [and] to the dignity of Religion."[44] Preachers presented the apparent scourge of enslavement as an opportunity, a chance for free Christians to redeem themselves. They invited participants and onlookers to

> follow the example left to them by Our Lord Jesus Christ, who with the effusion of all his most Precious Blood redeemed Humanity from the Infernal Enemy; [so] we with part of our wealth, we will undertake to free our Brothers from the barbarous slavery of the Infidels, and show ourselves in a certain way as true examples of the *Salvatore*[45]

From the many sermons given at the culmination of these great processions, one can detect the hope that through the enterprise of self-sacrifice there might emerge a true realization of brotherhood, a single, holy, and fraternal community, following the principle of *imitatio Christi*. Such was the lesson offered by Giovanni Ricolui, who explained to his listeners that out of the tribulations, disruptions, and expenses of the slave ransoming process a greater good could emerge, redemptive for the entire society:

> With us, everyone shares in the blood of the same Parents, our souls with that of the Divine Redeemer.... You celebrate today, indeed, as the Israelites celebrated when, in returning to Jerusalem, they restored the temple and lit again the sacred fire. Just as many Temples of God are these Ransomed ones.... Since in ransoming your brothers, the slaves, you have in a certain way rendered to the Savior the exchange for the infinite benefit of the redemption.... In ransoming them from the hands of the Barbarous Mohammedans... you have been given to see the Slaves as limbs of a single body and as children of a single Family, you love them all as yourselves, and you believe the chains of others to be yours, and you give first place in your souls to the tender feeling of compassion.[46]

Yet simply paying ransoms and bringing the slaves home were not, in themselves, the end. Those who had undergone years of degradation and abuse could not always readily return as functioning members of their society, and it is possible to detect a sense of depression and defeat that haunted many returned slaves, especially those whose poverty and work experience left them little choice but to return to sea and risk enslavement again. Interviews conducted with ex-slaves reveal something that today we might term post-traumatic stress or shell shock, their comments not unlike those of soldiers returning from combat and unable to re-engage with their past lives:

> In the meantime I have remained in a rented bed at [San] Tomé, living miserably [and] not having anything of my own.... Here I don't have anything: I'm living off charity....
> Meanwhile, I am in the house of my wife, living in complete misery....
> I live badly, in the house of my aforementioned sister in Castello, making a living when the chance comes to me to earn something....
> I stay at Santa Margarita, in the house of my mother, who takes care of me, since I have been stripped of everything, and if the opportunity presented itself, I would do the same work [as a sailor]....
> I would wish to do, or rather I am forced to do the same trade [as a sailor], not knowing any others, and in the meantime I live with my mother and my two sisters, not knowing how to obtain any solution for myself.[47]

It may have been to offset the profoundly alienating trauma of enslavement that some processions were structurally set up to help reintegrate these freedmen into the fabric of their home societies, re-bonding them to the local power structure. In Venetian processions, for example, each ex-slave's pairing with a noble escort was intended (or at least hoped) to form a bond that would last beyond the event itself, as "Every slave found in his Gentleman an individual Protector [*Protettore*], who, with alms, with jobs, [and] with advice facilitated his future condition." Others who were not so well favored could at least hope to receive a job from the state: "appropriate to their various abilities, some among the soldiers, some in the navy, and some in the [state] Arsenal;" judging by the many petitions it granted for such sinecures, it would seem that the *Serenissima* took its responsibility in this regard seriously.[48]

One might ask whether such pairings – and the many other acts of obeisance to authority that were expected of them – really seemed all that liberating to the ex-slaves. It would appear that the regimes that had brought them back wanted there to be no mistake that they had returned to the heavy embrace of a home-grown hierarchy and patronage network that could demand as much subservience as the system of bondage they had just escaped. Certainly most of the peasants, seafarers, and fisherfolk who walked in the processions knew the interplay of servility and deference that was required of them in the baroque Christian world. They probably saw nothing paradoxical, when still slaves, in seeking aid from the elites back home with such promises as "if Your Excellency will do me the charity to free me from said Turk, I will commit myself to be your slave for life."[49] It may have been the additional measure of oppression that many had experienced in Barbary – the seemingly random beatings and the continual violation of their physical integrity – that opened their eyes to even that little freedom they had lost as slaves and could enjoy once returned to Christendom.[50] Though there were slaves who admitted they had been "apt to put on the Temper and Spirit of Slaves with the [Slave's] Habit," for others, their ownership by a Muslim master underscored the virtues of personhood and thus the value of individual liberty in ways that they had never much thought about until these had been lost. Thus Erasmo Antonio Russo, a new slave in Algiers, lamented to his mother in 1735 that

> Right now I am not suffering, but consider that I am a slave, deprived of my such dear liberty, because I never knew freedom to be so dear, until now that I see myself a slave and always mistreated with continuous toils without being able to [say] a word in reply.[51]

Many asserted that the only genuine liberty – Christian liberty – came from God, and that only by surrendering to the Divine Will could a slave discover true freedom, even though he might still be enslaved: "God by Himself without human help," as Constanzo Gazzoli wrote to his son, Antonio, enslaved in Tunis, "will give you your freedom with every other contentment."[52] For those at home, however, freeing slaves, and fellow citizens in particular, was not only a matter of personal redemption, but also of national honor. Father Enrico Capra could point with pride at the broken chains that the ex-slaves carried in a Venetian slave procession of 1727: "The pleasing sign of this triumph," as he put it, "are the manacles of the subjects, shattered by the compassion of their Prince."[53] Whatever the quality and extent of personal liberty at home, freedom from enslavement was increasingly something that observers came to believe should be guaranteed by the state, both through the redemptive process itself and through diplomatic and military efforts abroad. The notion that citizens might deserve such protection was a vast improvement over prevailing conditions at the beginning of the early modern era, when slaves without the personal wealth or connections to gain their freedom on their own had usually found themselves abandoned and permanently forgotten by those back home.

By the eighteenth century, when even clerics were speaking out about these slaves' "natural instinct to reacquire liberty," observers could single out this white slavery as living proof of humanity's "innate love of freedom," the existence of "a natural dominion over oneself," that survived in these ordinary men and women despite the brutality they had to endure while in bondage.[54] Such Enlightened benevolence was not directed solely at the Barbary slaves, however: more than a few Europeans and Americans, both then and later, presented the pernicious existence of white slavery as an argument against those who would legitimize any enslavement, in racial or any other terms. As early as 1680, the Oxford don Morgan Godwyn was rebutting the notion that the capacity for enslavement was in some way linked to origins or race by raising what might be termed the Barbary Analogy:

> [If] some one of this island going for *England* should chance to be snapt up by an *Algerine*, or *Corsaire* of *Barbary*, and there to be set on Shore and Sold; Doth he thereupon become a Brute? If not, why should an *African*, (suppose of that or any other remote part) suffer a greater alteration than one of us?[55]

Knowingly or not, Godwyn was tapping into a redemptionist approach to enslavement as a demonstration of God's plan of retribution and redemption that was, as we have seen, being worked out at the same time by Jesuit and Trinitarian preachers.[56] Many divines and abolitionists would follow this path, to provide empathic proof that the capacity for enslavement was no less innate than was the desire for freedom, a misfortune to be blamed on circumstance rather than on the destiny of birth or race. It was not only clerics, moreover, who sought to draw attention to the close similarities between these two forms of slavery, white and black, urging the notion that abolishing the one certainly meant doing away with the other. As Joseph Morgan once mused,

> I have often heard say, that our *American* Planters, tho' they have no Gallies, are passable good *Algerines:* "But their Slaves are *Negro* Dogs, they say, what are such no-souled Animals good for?" – Smart and *Christian*-like! – Those who have not seen a Galley at Sea, especially in chacing, or being chaced, cannot well conceive the Shock such a Spectacle must give to a Heart capable of the least Tincture of Commiseration.[57]

This wide-ranging concern about Barbary Coast slavery that both religious and secular observers expressed in the early modern era was rooted in a very real problem: fellow citizens – and sometimes they themselves – constantly risked capture, violence, and exploitation at the hands of an alien and generally hostile culture. At the same time, these concerns served as the basis for addressing and examining such basic human values as community, liberty, the social contract, and the search for salvation. It is a good indication of just how central white slavery was to the European self-conception of the time, but it also presents modern scholars with the crucial need to confront what this self-conception, and indeed the whole notion of slavery, actually meant to early modern Europeans. It has become almost a given in modern scholarship that slavery in these centuries was comprehended and justified on strictly racial grounds: the so-called Curse of Noah, or Children of Ham argument that sought (and still seeks) to explain the enslavement of blacks by whites as biblically ordained. Such an approach to the question, which finds its sources primarily in the writings of Atlantic slave runners and American plantation owners (and with whom it was widely popular), sets out to prove what it already assumes, however: that slaves in the early modern world were by definition black Africans by origin. So dominant is the assumption in the literature that slaves must have been black, that several recent studies proposing to deal with the era's "other slavery" make no mention at all of the Barbary Coast, but instead treat the enslavement of sub-Saharan blacks by Arabs.[58] How the white slaves of the Barbary Coast might be made to fit into our current notions of pre-modern slavery remains for the moment as uncertain as does how they might have fit into the world view of their contemporaries.

Given the number of whites who fell into slavery in Barbary and how aware their contemporaries were of their plight, it is difficult to accept that Europeans unanimously believed that, since "slaves were almost without exception Africans ... the fact that Africans were black made it possible to explain their condition in racial terms," as one student of the period recently put it.[59] The experience of so many tens of thousands of white slaves, natives of every country between the United States and Russia, and the stories told by those lucky enough to be ransomed or to escape made sure that slavery in early modern Europe was not conceived just in such color-conscious terms as many modern observers would have it. Thus, Samuel Pepys wrote in his *Diary* of meeting British slaves just returned from Algiers and of hearing their stories; at about the same time, the Icelanders were composing sagas about their people's sufferings as slaves in Algiers during the 1630s. What was arguably the first American novel, *The Algerine Slave*, was about a New Englander who both ran black slaves from West Africa and was himself enslaved by the corsairs of Algiers, a story that followed an already established tradition of Barbary enslavement tales stretching back to Cervantes or earlier.[60] A glance through the scores of fundraising sermons and the hundreds of letters from slaves themselves makes it plain that Europeans of all classes and creeds spent considerable time wrestling with the religious and psychological implications of what it meant to fall into this particular form of social death:

> At sea, on land, everywhere they are miserable Slaves, deprived of sweet liberty, far from their homeland, relatives, friends and Christian customs, under the command of someone who for nothing can beat them and with [those] beatings make them die wretchedly.[61]

Lacking the comfortable rationalization of the American slave runners and planters that their enslavement could be justified by race, by "some fundamental difference between master and slave" – the chances were that their master was a renegade, as white and European as themselves – these slaves in Barbary could find little solace in racial explanations for their condition. If anything, they might have to confront a strikingly inverted form of racial oppression, as Francis Brooks detailed in his rather lurid (and best-selling) tale of his enslavement in Morocco, a story that fairly crawls with the picture of black task-masters lording it up over white slaves at hard labor, as

> [t]he poor Christians were grievously hurried and punished by those Hellish Negroes ... and had scarce any time to take any nourish-

ment, or eat any of their bad Bread that was allowed them, but with a great many Threats, Stripes and Blows by the Negroes, bidding them turn *Moors*.[62]

The questions of liberty and race, which would loom so large in the nineteenth and twentieth centuries, were already gaining form and urgency in the seventeenth and eighteenth, at least in part through the discursive possibilities offered by Barbary Coast slavery. If these issues were later subsumed by other, more immediate and universal social movements, and above all by the pressing issue of chattel slavery in the Americas, this is hardly surprising: the decimation inflicted on sub-Saharan Africa and on black Africans in the Americas hugely outweighed, in its scope if not in all its specific horrors, that which was imposed on white slaves in Barbary. The Abolitionist movement that black slavery spawned would, over the course of nearly a century, bring a halt to perhaps the greatest, most efficient, and most ruthless system for the exploitation of humans by other humans devised up to that time. It also gave a new sense and content to the notion of human rights, protection under law, and universal equality. Nothing so grand can be claimed for the attempts, rather haphazard and quite often self-serving, that were undertaken to eliminate slavery in Barbary, and this may explain the comparative disinterest that it has provoked in recent years. As we have seen here, early modern discourse on white slavery tended towards the mystical, with an enthusiasm for pious communitarianism and a praise for absolutist Christianity enveloped in a spirit of personal and group identity. The celebration of slavery, as it was promulgated in the pulpits and processions of the time, flirted with notions of liberty and citizenship, but ultimately felt more comfortable with those of retribution and redemption.

In the end, the purging of white slavery from the Maghreb was caught up in the great power politics and colonial adventures of the eighteenth and nineteenth centuries. Napoleon's buccaneering raid into Egypt in 1798 showed how clearly the balance of power between the northern and southern shores of the Mediterranean had changed in favor of the former. The final battle for control of this corner of Africa would not be between Muslims and Christians but between two Christian states – the British and French fighting for dominance over the region. When the French returned to the Maghreb in 1830, they came not only to destroy white slavery and the system that tolerated it, but also to annex Algeria itself. The French intrusion into Barbary has induced many scholars to assume a rather condescending teleology towards European activity in Maghreb even during earlier centuries, tending to see almost every move there by the Christian states in the preceding 300 years as somehow inculcating (or trying to deny) this "movement toward a destiny" of eventual colonial rule and white dominance.[63]

In the course of the study, it has been difficult to square the experience of individual slaves in Barbary, whether rich or poor, well connected or abandoned, with the overarching themes of European world conquest that have become so central to scholarship on the early modern era. Slaves were still slaves, whether they were black or white, labored on a plantation or sweated on a galley. Trying to insert the story of Barbary Coast slavery into the master narrative of European imperialism risks losing not only this essence of bondage, but also the sense, once so prevalent, of just what a thorn the Barbary corsairs could be for Christendom, of how much suffering and expense they could cause. At the same time, we have also lost, it would seem, the sense of how large enslavement could loom for many of those who lived in and around the Mediterranean, and the long shadow this threat once cast over the lives of the great and the small. We started this study wondering why no one ever asked the extent of the Mediterranean white slave traffic, and now we come to realize that in good part it was because it never served anyone's purpose to know or even guess at the answer. In exploring both the pervasiveness and complexity of Barbary Coast slavery and also its power to shape societies and cultures in Christendom, we have tried to provide some cause to investigate this compelling phenomenon still further.

Notes

Introduction and Acknowledgments

1. Archivio Segreto Vaticano (hereafter ASVat), Gonfalone, bu. 1139, fol. 157.
2. Philemon de La Motte, *Voyage pour la redemption des captifs aux royaumes d' Alger et de Tunis* (Paris, 1721), English trans. (by Joseph Morgan?) as *Several Voyages to Barbary* (London, 1736), p. 42; Jacques Philippe Laugier de Tassy, *A Complete History of the piratical States of Barbary*, trans. Joseph Morgan (London, 1750), p. 222.
3. Francis Brooks, *Barbarian Cruelty* (London, 1693); and Thomas Troughton, *Barbarian Cruelty: Narrative of the sufferings of the British Captives Belonging to the "Inspector," privateer* (London, 1751).
4. As quoted in Joseph Morgan, *A Complete History of Algiers* (London, 1731; reprint, Westport, CT, 1970).
5. Which has, moreover, been indexed: see Federico Cresti, ed., *Documenti sul Maghreb dal XVII al XIX secolo: Archivio storico della Congregazione "De Propaganda Fide", "Scritture Riferite nei Congressi – Barbaria"* (Perugia, 1988).

Chapter 1

1. Francis Knight, *A Relation of Seaven Yeares Slaverie under the Turks of Argeire,* 2 bks. (London, 1640), bk. 1, pp. 1–2.
2. *Proceedings in the Opening Session of the Long Parliament, House of Commons*, vol. 1 (3 November to 19 December 1640), ed. Maija Jansson (New Haven, forthcoming), p. 560; *Calendar of State Papers, Domestic Series, of the Reign of Charles I*, vol. 16 (1640) (Liechtenstein, 1967), p. 588 (my thanks to David Cressy for bringing these sources to my attention); Paul Lovejoy, "The Volume of the Atlantic Slave Trade: a Synthesis," pp. 473–501 in *Journal of African History*, 23 (1982), pp. 478–82.
3. *Calendar of State Papers, Domestic*, vol. 16, p. 438; W. Laird Clowes, *The Royal Navy. A History from the Earliest Times to the Present*, 5 vols. (London, 1897–98), vol. 2, pp. 22–3 and 49; Joseph Morgan, *A Complete History of Algiers,* p. v. In 1617, a Salé raider was captured in the Thames; in 1631, the Algerians took 237 Irish from the town of Baltimore, in Munster; in 1640, 60 Algerian sail were sighted off the south coast of England; in 1645, a corsair raid hauled off 240 slaves from the coast of Cornwall; as late as 1654, their galleys were spotted in the Bristol Channel: see Salvatore Bono, *Corsari barbareschi* (Turin, 1964), p. 178, citing from the *Gazette de France*.
4. De La Motte, *Several Voyages to Barbary*, p. 99; also Morgan, *Complete History of Algiers*, p. v. Morgan claimed that between July 1677 and October 1680, 160 British ships were taken, with a loss equal to 600–1,000 slaves annually.

5. Philip Curtin, *The Atlantic Slave Trade: A Census* (Madison, WI, 1969), esp. pp. 95–126. For a recent survey of ongoing efforts to plot the course of the Atlantic trade, see Hugh Thomas, *The Slave Trade. The Story of the Atlantic Slave Trade: 1440–1870* (New York, 1997), pp. 861–2.
6. Fernand Braudel, *The Mediterranean and the Mediterranean World in the Age of Philip II* (New York, 1972), pp. 886–7. Systematic attempts to estimate slave populations have been few and of mostly limited scope: see, for example, Federico Cresti, "Quelques reflexions sur la population et la structure social d'Alger à la periode Turque (XVIe–XIXe siècles)," pp. 151–64 in *Les Cahiers de Tunisie*, 34 (1986); and J. Mathiex, "Trafic et prix de l'homme en Méditerranée aux XVIIᵉ et XVIIIᵉ siècles," pp. 157–64 in *Annales, Economies Societés Civilisation*, 9 (1954); and Lucette Valensi, "Esclaves chrétiens et esclaves noirs à Tunis au XVIIIᵉ siècle," pp. 1267–85 in *Annales, Economies Societés Civilisation*, 22 (1967).
7. Bartolomé Bennassar and Lucile Bennassar, *Les Chrétiens d'Allah. L'Histoire extraodinaire des renégats, XVIᵉ–XVIIᵉ siècles* (Paris, 1989); Leîla Blili, "Course et Captivité des Femmes dans la Régence de Tunis aux XVIe et XVIIe Siècles," pp. 259–73 in *Captius i esclaus a l'Antiguitat i al Món Modern* (Palma de Mallorca, 1996); Giuseppe Bonaffini, *La Sicilia e i Barbareschi. Incursioni corsare e riscatto degli schiavi (1570–1606)* (Palermo, 1983); Ellen Friedman, *Spanish Captives in North Africa in the Early Modern Age* (Madison, WI, 1983); Wipertus H. Rudt de Collenberg, *Esclavage et rançons des chrétiens en méditerranée (1570–1600), d'apres les Litterae Hortatoriae de l'Archivio Segreto Vaticano* (Paris, 1987).
8. Paul Baepler, ed., *White Slaves, African Masters: an Anthology of American Barbary Captivity Narratives* (Chicago, 1999), p. 3.
9. Braudel, *The Mediterranean*, pp. 885–7. Braudel completely wrote off Tunis and Tripoli as corsairing powers after 1620, despite a good deal of evidence to the contrary; he likewise dismissed corsair attacks on Britain, saying that "their appearance on the English coast in 1631 was remarkable for its novelty rather than for the actual danger they represented." See Salvatore Bono, *Corsari barbareschi* (Turin, 1964), 178, citing from the *Gazette de France, Calendar of State Papers, Domestic*, pp. 321, 328, 438, and 450; also W. Laird Clowes, *The Royal Navy. A History from the Earliest Times to the Present*, 5 vols. (London, 1897–98), ii, pp. 22–3 and 49; Paul Lovejoy, "The Volume of the Atlantic Slave Trade: a Synthesis," pp. 473–501 in *Journal of African History*, 23 (1982), pp. 478–82; Morgan, *Complete History*, p. v.
10. This notion of essential reciprocity was also advanced by Braudel, who also stressed the extent to which European corsairs (especially the English) were likely to attack their fellow Christians, though obviously more with the aim of simple piracy than slave taking: Braudel, *The Mediterranean*, pp. 867–8, 877–80, and 887.
11. Ellen Friedman, "Christian Captives at 'Hard Labor' in Algiers, 16th–18th Centuries," pp. 616–32 in *The International Journal of African Historical Studies*, 13 (1980); Claude Larquié, "La Méditerranée, l'Espagne et le Maghreb au XVIIe siècle: le rachet des chrétiens et le commerce des hommes," pp. 75–94 in *Les Cahiers de Tunisie*, 44 (1991).
12. Robert Ricard, "Ibero-Africana, Le Père Jérome Gratien dela Mère de Dieu et sa Captivité à Tunis (1593–1595)," pp. 190–200 in *Revue africaine* 89 (1945),

pp. 196–7; Dan, *Histoire de Barbarie*, p. 320; *Calendar of State Papers, Domestic*, vol. 16, p. 766; C. R. Pennell, ed., *Piracy and Diplomacy in Seventeenth-Century North Africa: The Journal of Thomas Baker, English Consul in Tripoli, 1677–1685* (London, 1989), p. 46, tab. 4.

13. Taoufik Bachrouch, "Rachet et libération des esclaves chrétiens à Tunis au XVIIe siècle," pp. 121–62 in *Revue Tunisienne de Sciences Sociales*, 11 (1975), p. 128.

14. Laird Clowes, *The Royal Navy*, vol. 2, p. 22; also, Henri-David Grammont, "Relations entre la France & la Régence d'Alger au XVIIe Siècle," in *Revue Africaine*,23(1879), pp. 137–8; Morgan, *Complete History*, p. v.

15. Robert Playfair, "Episodes de l'histoire des relations de la Grande-Bretagne avec les Etats Barbaresques avant la conquête française," pp. 305–19 and 401–33, in *Revue africaine*, 22 (1878); Bono, *Corsari barbareschi*, pp. 138–78; also A. Guglielmotti, *Storia della Marina pontificia*, 10 vols. (Rome, 1886–93), vol. 4, p. 125; Grammont, "Relations," in *Revue Africaine*, 28 (1879), pp. 426–7; 28 (1884), pp. 208–9; Braudel, *The Mediterranean*, pp. 881–2; *Calendar of State Papers, Domestic*, vol. 16, p. 450.

16. Archivio di Stato di Napoli, Santa Casa della Redenzione dei Cattivi (hereafter ASN, SCRC), busta 14, cases #581 and #582 (both of 7 January 1678/79); cases #1458–61 (all of 30 June 1697), for examples.

17. Pennell, *Piracy and Diplomacy*, pp. 120 and 124; Baker also referred to the corsairs as going "man-stealing" or setting out "to Fish for Dutchmen."

18. So said William Davies, *True Relation of the Travailes and most miserable Captivitie of William Davies, Barber-Surgion of London* (London, 1614), B2v.

19. Braudel, *The Mediterranean*, p. 871.

20. Thomas Hees, "Journal d'un voyage à Alger (1675–76)," G.-H. Bousquet and G. W. Bousquet-Mirandolle, eds. and trans., pp. 84–128 in *Revue Africaine*,101 (1957), pp. 104–24.

21. Bonaffini, *La Sicilia e i Barbareschi*, pp. 35–52, esp. p. 43, n. 15, for one of the larger raids, netting 80 slaves from Gela in 1582, noted in G. E. di Blasi, *Storia cronologica de' Vicerè, Luogotenenti e Presidenti del Regno di Sicilia*,2 vols. (Palermo, 1974), vol. 2, p. 227.

22. Bonaffini, *La Sicilia e i Barbareschi*, pp. 42–56. For similar allusions to unnamed companions, see Archivio di Stato di Venezia, Collegio, *risposte di dentro* (hereafter ASV, CRD), filza 27, 23 Jan 1636 (*more veneto*: the Venetian year began on 1 March); also ASN, SCRC, busta 14, cases #639, #640 (17 August 1678), and #646; also ibid., cases #575, 581, 582, and 617–19, for a slave referring to 37 others, all from the Pugliese city of Barletta, taken during a raid in July 1677.

23. Jean-Baptiste Gramaye, *Diarium rerum Argelae gestarum ab anno M.DC.XIX* (Cologne, 1623), trans. and republished as *Alger, XVIe–XVIIe siècle: Journal de Jean-Baptiste Gramaye, évêque d'Afrique*, ed. and trans. Abd El Hadi Den Mansour (Paris, 1998), p. 287.

24. Now more commonly spelled Kheir-ed-din Barbarossa (?–1546), Emanuel d'Aranda, *The History of Algiers and its Slavery* (London, 1666: English trans. of *Relation de la captivité du sieur E. d'A. mené esclave à Alger en l'an 1640 et mis en liberté l'an 1642*, Brussels, 1656), pp. 106–7.

25. Pierre Dan, *Histoire de la Barbarie et des ses Corsaires* (Paris, 1649), p. 317.

26. For a vivid description of the convict rowers in the galleys of Tuscany in the 1790s, see John Foss, *Journal of Captivity* (Newport, n.d.), pp. 151–2.

27. Salvatore Bono, *Corsari nel Mediterraneo. Cristiani e musulmani fra guerra, schi - avitù e commercio* (Turin, 1993), esp. pp. 191–201; idem, "Schiavi maghrebini in Italia e Cristiani nel Maghreb: Proteste e attestazioni per la reciprocità di trattamento," pp. 331–51 in *Africa,* 49 (1994); Michel Fontenay, "Le Maghreb barbaresque et l'esclavage méditerranéen aux XVIe–XVIIe siècles," in *Les Cahiers de Tunisie* 44 (1991), pp. 8–43; Ciro Manca, "Problemi aperti sul commercio e sul riscatto degli schiavi cristiani nel Mediterraneo dopo Lepanto," pp. 549–72 in *Africa,* 29 (1974); idem, *Il modello di sviluppo eco - nomico delle città maritime barbaresche dopo Lepanto* (Naples, 1982) esp. pp. 41–93; Vittorio Salvadorini, "Traffici con i paesi islamici e schiavi a Livorno nel XVII secolo: problemi e suggestioni," pp. 206–55 in *Atti del convegno, "Livorno e il Mediterraneo nel età medicea"* (Livorno, 1978), esp. pp. 218–21; J. Mathiex, "Trafic et prix de l'homme," pp. 157–64.

28. Blili, "Course et Captivité," p. 259; Federico Cresti, "Gli Schiavi cristiani ad Algeri in età ottomana: Considerazioni sulle fonti e questioni storiografiche," pp. 415–35 in *Quaderni storici,* 36 (2001), p. 417; also Bachrouch, "Rachet et libération des esclaves," p. 121, claiming that: "The archives of the *Dar du Bey* do not [for the seventeenth century] ... possess one single document relative to slaving society or to the conditions of servitude": for Algiers, see Friedman, *Spanish Captives in North Africa*, p. xviii.

29. Collegio di Propaganda Fide Scritture Riferite nei Congressi Generali (hereafter, CPF, SOCG), Barbaria, bu. 3, folio 23, 28 March 1691; ASV, Provveditori sopra Ospedali e Luoghi Pii (hereafter ASV, POLP), bu. 99, *Terminazioni,*13Sept. 1713; Archivio Segreto Vaticano (hereafter, AsVat), Gonfalone, bu. 8, filza 14 and filza 65, fol. 343.

30. Paul Deslandres, *L'Ordre des Trinitaires pour le rachet des Captifs,* 2 vols. (Toulouse, 1903), vol. 1, p. 391, citing H. De Grammont; see also Morgan, *Complete History of Algiers,* p. 305, who ascribed this saying to the aftermath of Charles V's disastrous attempted invasion of Algiers, after which "Multitudes [of Christians] were made Captives; mostly by the *Turks* and citizens of *Algiers.* And to reduce this Misfortune to a Proverb, some parted with their new-taken Slaves for an Onion *per* Head."

31. Cresti, "Gli Schiavi cristiani," p. 417, tends to dismiss such estimates as "a kind of bidding contest [*gara al rialzo*], in which each author seems to challenge his predecessor [by] magnifying the dimensions and the power of the city [of Algiers] through the number of its inhabitants – and also of the Christians held in slavery there." The estimates collected here for Algiers from 1580 to 1680 – which are double the number of those offered by Cresti – do not really reflect any such increase, however, but rather a continual fluctuation around a norm of 25,000 to 30,000 slaves. Also see Marcel Emerit, ed., "Un Mémoire sur Alger par Pétis de la Croix (1695)," pp. 5–24 in *Annales de l'Institut d'Études orientales,* 11 (1953), p. 21, n. 29.

32. CPF, SOCG, "Barbaria, bu. 1, fol. 503; Venice, Museo Correr (hereafter, VMC), *Carte Mocenigo,* bu. 515, fol. 77; Pétis de la Croix, "Un Mémoire sur

198   *Notes*

Alger," p. 21, n. 29; F. Bombard, "Les Vicaires Apostoliques de Tunis et d'Alger (1645–1827)," 6 parts in *Revue tunisienne*, vols. 1 and 2 (1894–95), vol. 2, p. 73.

33. Norman Bennett, "Christian and Negro Slavery in Eighteenth-Century North Africa," pp. 65–82 in *Journal of African History*, 1 (1960), p. 67.
34. Morgan, *Complete History*, p. iii.
35. Deslandres, *L'Ordre des Trinitaires*, vol. 1, pp. 436–7, felt that Trinitarians were especially prone to exaggerate – he said by a factor of ten – the total number of slaves they had ransomed; Valensi, "Esclaves chrétiens et esclaves noirs," 1276–8 and notes; Mirella Mafrici, *Mezzogiorno e pirateria nell'età moderna (secoli XVI–XVIII)* (Naples, 1995), pp. 95–100.
36. Henri-David Grammont, "Correspondance des Consuls D'Alger," in *Revue Africaine*, 31 (1887), pp. 164–212; idem, "Relations entre la France & la Régence d'Alger," *Revue Africaine*, 23 (1879), pp. 134–9; Giuseppe Bonaffini, *Sicilia e Tunisia nel secolo XVII* (Palermo, 1984); and idem, *La Sicilia e i Barbareschi*, pp. 21–34; Giorgio Cappovin, *Tripoli e Venezia nel Secolo XVIII* (Verbania, 1942); ASV, POLP, bu. 98, "Parti et ordini concernenti alla liberatione de' poveri schiavi;" Sergio Pagano, *L'Archivio dell'Arciconfraternita del Gonfalone* (Vatican City, 1990), esp. pp. 29–32.
37. François Lanfreducci and Jean Othon Bosio, "Costa e Discorsi di Barbaria (1 Settembre 1587)," pp. 421–80 in *Revue Africaine*, 66 (1925); Giovanni Battista Salvago, "*Africa overo Barbarìa*" *Relazione al doge di Venezia sulle Reggenze di Algeri e di Tunisi del Dragomanno Gio.Batta Salvago (1625)*, Alberto Sacerdoti, ed. (Padova, 1937); VMC, *Carte Mocenigo*, busta 515, folio 77.
38. Compare, for example, the estimates that Salvago made in 1625 – 25,000 slaves in Algiers and "fewer than 10,000" in Tunis – with those of Dan from ten years later – 25,000 slaves in Algiers, with 7,000 slaves in Tunis and the surrounding *masseries*: Salvago, "*Africa overo Barbarìa*" pp. 88–9; Dan, *Histoire de Barbarie*, pp. 318–19.
39. ASV, POLP, bu. 98, fol. 3.
40. Mansour, *Alger, XVIe–XVIIe siècle*, p. 138, and n. 6. A century later, Joseph Morgan, translator of de La Motte's *Several Voyages*, p. 13 and n., claimed that the number of these "Garden-houses ... upon Register, is said to be 18,000;" also Diego de Haëdo, *Topografia e Historia General de Argel* (Valladolid, 1612), French trans. by MM. le Dr Monnereau and A. Brubrugger as *Topographie et Histoire Générale d'Alger*, in *Revue Africaine*, 14 (1870), pp. 414–33; also, Dan, *Histoire de Barbarie*, pp. 318–19; CPF, SRC, Barbaria, bu. 3, folio 408, 7 Sept. 1701 ("10,000 *Giardini*"); and Knight, *A Relation*, p. 51 ("16,000 Gardens").
41. CPF, SOCG, "Barbaria," bu. 3, fol. 408, 7 September 1701; also, d'Aranda, *The History of Algiers*, pp. 15 and 18; R. Chastelet des Boys, *L'Odyssée. Ou Diversité d'Aventures, Rencontres et Voyages en Europe, Asie, et Afrique*, in *Revue Africaine* 12 (1868), pp. 27–8; Knight, *A Relation*, pp. 14–15; see also Francesco di S. Lorenzo, *Breve relatione, del calamitoso stato, crudeltà, e bestiali attioni, con le quali son trattati da' barbari li cristiani fatti schiavi, e tutto quello, ch'è passato nel viaggio della redentione de' fedeli di Christo nella città di Tunisi l'anno 1653* (Roma, 1654), pp. 15–16, for a glimpse of this sort of farm labor.

42. Fontenay, "Le Maghreb barbaresque," p. 15 and nn. 25 and 26; Knight, *A Relation of Seaven Yeares Slaverie*, p. 51.
43. Such lists are alluded to in the *Correspondance des Beys et des Consuls*, p. 251 (27 April 1670) and p. 317 (1683); see also J. M. Venture de Paradis, *Notes sur Alger*, republished as "Alger au XVIIIᵉ siècle," E. Fagnan, ed., pp. 265–314 in *Revue Africaine*, 40 (1896), pp. 33–4 and 37.
44. CPF, Scritture Originali riferite nelle Congregazioni Generali (hereafter CPF, SORCG), bu. 254, "Tunisi," fol. 64, 13 March 1664; CPF, SOCG, Barbaria bu. 3, fol. 305, 6 September 1696; de La Motte, *Several Voyages*, p. 59.
45. Grammont, "Relations," in *Revue Africaine*, 23 (1879), pp. 234 and 318; Eugene Plantet, ed., *Correspondance des Beys de Tunis et des Consuls de France avec la Cour, 1577–1830* (Paris, 1893), p. 251; CPF, SOCG, "Barbaria," bu. 1, fol. 455 (1682).
46. This tendency emerged in CPF, SOCG, "Barbaria," bu. 1, fol. 478, 25 August 1680; and fol. 502, 18 May 1681; ibid., bu. 2, fol. 455; and ibid, bu. 3, folio 305, 6 September 1696. On the resulting confusion, see Mafrici, *Mezzogiorno e pirateria*, pp. 97–8 and nn. 17–18.
47. Dan, *Histoire de Barbarie*, pp. 319–20; Ricard, "Ibero-Africana," pp. 190–200 in *Revue Africaine*, 89 (1945), 194; CPF, SOCG, "Barbaria," bu. 3, fol. 418, 20 November 1701.
48. CPF, SOCG, Barbaria, bu. 3, fols. 408 and 414, where fra. Giovanni di San Bonaventura, writing to Rome on 7 September 1701, reported "they say that there are more than 20,000 Christians" in Algiers. In fact, as Lorance, the apostolic vicar, noted the next day, there were only 3,000, thanks to a major redemption and the plague.
49. CPF, SOCG, Barbaria, bu. 1, folio 455, dated 1682; and ibid., busta 3, fol. 31, 9 May 1691, in which fra. Maurizio da Lucca observes that "of us Catholic Christians there are few slaves, for [reason of] the ships being in the Levant."
50. On the pasha of Tripoli sending slaves as a gift to the sultan in Constantinople, CPF, SOCG, Barbaria, bu. 1, fols. 259–60, "Breve relatione della ribellione successa in Tripoli di Barbaria," dated 30 November 1672; on the pasha of Algiers, see *Catalogo de' schiavi riscattati nel anno 1660 nella città d'Algieri dal sacro ... ordine della Madonna della Mercede* (Roma, 1661), p. 6; Dan, *Histoire de Barbarie*, p. 395; on corsairs swapping groups of slaves, see Louis Marott, *A Narrative of the Adventures of Lewis Marott, Pilot-Royal of the Galleys of France*, trans. unk. (English trans. London, 1677), p. 13.
51. A figure that is accepted by virtually all modern historians of Mediterranean slavery: see Bono, *Corsari nel Mediterraneo*, pp. 193–94; Lucien Golvin, "Alger a la Periode Ottomane (rythmes de vie)," pp. 165–74 in *Les Cahiers de Tunisie*, 34 (1986), p. 167.
52. Morgan, *Complete History*, pp. 516–17; John B. Wolf, *The Barbary Coast: Algiers under the Turks, 1500 to 1830* (New York, 1979), pp. 223–67; also Chastelet des Boys, *L'Odyssée*, p. 357.
53. Norman Bennett, "Christian and Negro Slavery," pp. 79–81; also Bachrouch, "Rachet et libération," esp. pp. 128–35.
54. In 1816, there were said to be 1,600 European slaves in the city: Cresti, "Quelques reflexions," pp. 158–60.

55. Braudel, *The Mediterranean*, p. 885.

56. Bonaffini, *La Sicilia e i Barbareschi*, pp. 35–52; also Jean Pignon, "L'Esclavage en Tunisie de 1590 a 1620," pp. 145–65 in *Les Cahiers de Tunisie*, 24 (1976), p. 145; on the need for slave labor in Algiers: Friedman, "Christian Captives," pp. 629–30.

57. Including Salé and Fez in Morocco. Although clearly of significance in the trade in European slaves, these centers have largely been left out of the present survey, both because they lay in the independent Kingdom of Morocco, which followed a different historical and political path than the Barbary regencies further east, and because their slaving activity was generally directed at Atlantic shipping alone: see Thomas Phelps, *A True Account of the Captivity of Thomas Phelps at Machaness in Barbary, and of his strange escape* ... (London, 1685); and Francis Brooks, *Barbarian Cruelty* (London, 1693).

58. Marcel Emerit, ed., "Les Aventures de Thédenat, Esclave et Ministre d'un Bey d'Afrique (XVIIIe Siècle)," 142–84 and 331–62 in *Revue Africaine*, 92 (1948), p. 184, n. 6; also CPF, SOCG, Barbaria, bu. 1, fols. 165–6, 12 June 1669; fol. 322, 20 August 1675; fol. 503, 18 May 1681; ibid., bu. 2, fol. 309, 22 August 1687 and fol. 346, 26 December 1687; also F. Bombard, ed., "Les Vicaires apostoliques de Tunis et d'Alger (1645–1827)," in *Revue Tunisienne*, vols. 1 and 2 (1894–95), vol. 1, p. 388.

59. Morgan, *Complete History*, p. 670.

60. Dan, *Histoire de Barbarie*, pp. 318–19; Dan's calculation also included 1,500 slaves in the Moroccan city of Salé.

61. On percentages of female slaves, see Blili, "Course et Captivité des Femmes," pp. 259–63; Bono, *Corsari barbareschi*, pp. 236–7. On the seclusion of women, see d'Arvieux, *Memoires*, p. 285; also Foss, *A Journal*, pp. 35–8.

62. Occasionally, when whole families were enslaved and allowed to remain together, children might be born in captivity: see, for example, "Relatione delli Schiavi Christiani riscattati, l'anno 1662 nella Città di Algieri" (Rome, 1663), pp. 3–5. Slaves could also be borrowed or bought from elsewhere in the Muslim world. This practice was certainly followed, though it never reached a level approaching that of new captures: see Valensi, "Esclaves chrétiens et esclaves noirs," p. 1277.

63. ASN, SCRC, bu. 7, letter from Aniello Russo, slave in Tunis, in the bagno of the Bey, dated 22 February 1651.

64. Francesco di S. Lorenzo, *Breve relatione*, p. 19; Friedman, "Christian Captives," pp. 624–5; Dan, *Histoire de Barbarie*, pp. 411–13. Some masters, as we will see, refused to give their slaves any provisions at all, expecting them to obtain the means to feed themselves during the few hours between the end of their assigned labors and the closing of the bagno: Morgan, *Complete History of Algiers*, p. 674.

65. Friedman, "Christian Captives," pp. 619–20; Louis Marott, *A Narrative*, p. 19; Knight, *A Relation*, p. 29.

66. De la Motte, *Several Voyages*, pp. 47–8; Fontenay, "La Maghreb barbaresque," pp. 21–3.

67. D'Aranda, *History of Algiers*, pp. 14, 18, 151, 158; Friedman, "Christian Captives," pp. 621–2; R. Chastelet des Boys, *L'Odyssée*, in *Revue Africaine*, 12 (1868), pp. 26–7.

68. Fontenay, "Le Maghreb barbaresque," pp. 22–3.
69. Dan, *Histoire de Barbarie*, p. 320.
70. Salvago, "*Africa overo Barbaria*," p. 96; ASV, POLP, busta 98, "Legge" Senato Mar, 8 March 1628. On the young and fleet escaping the raiders, see Guglielmotti, *Storia della Marina pontificia*, vol. 4, p. 220: quoted in Bono, *Corsari barbareschi*, p. 148.
71. Bornsteinn Helgason, "Historical Narrative as Collective Therapy: the Case of the Turkish Raid in Iceland," pp. 275–89 in the *Scandinavian Journal of History*, 22 (1997), pp. 275–6.
72. Examples of deaths due to shock are in Brooks, *Barbarian Cruelty*, pp. 31 and 48; Francis Brooks also noted how such "hard Usage" caused many new slaves in Morocco to fall sick: Brooks, *Barbarian Cruelty*, p. 31.
73. Valensi, "Esclaves chrétiens et esclaves noirs," pp. 1277 and 1282; Bono, *Corsari barbareschi*, p. 316; Bombard, "Les Vicaires apostoliques," *Revue Tunisienne*, 2, p. 429.
74. Although accounts are less complete for sixteenth- as opposed to seventeenth-century plague outbreaks, it is significant that as early as 1624 Salvago could say that the disease came to cities like Tunis "every third or fourth year": Salvago, "*Africa overo Barbaria*," p. 94.
75. CPF, SOCG, Barbaria, bu. 3, folio 377, 6 May 1698; and folio 541, report from Tunis dated 9 September 1707, with the complaints of fr. Basilio da Torino that "Again we have been in some fear ... for there having come here from Sciò three vessels of this Bey, infected because of some merchandise loaded on them; and along the way there died [aboard] more than thirty persons from the plague; none the less, having reached Porto Farina the passengers were allowed to quickly disembark and everyone was left to come and go where he pleased, without any caution."
76. Laugier de Tassy, *A Complete History*, p. 101, noted that "The Kingdom of *Algiers* has always valued itself on having omitted every Prevention to hinder the spreading of the Plague: for to have acted otherwise, would have argued an Opposition to the eternal Decrees of God, and to absolute Predestination, the Result of them." From his experience of a plague in Adrianople, however, John Covel deduced that the Turks were as likely to flee the plague as anyone: "for that same is a story that they are not afraid of the plague, because their fortunes are wrote in their forehead; for all fled, but those as were poor, or had offices about Court, and could not get away" (from *The Diary of John Covel, 1670–79* (Hakluyt Society, NY, 1893), p. 244).
77. "Relations entre La France et la Régence d'Alger," letter from M. Guillerny, 136; Bombard, "Les Vicaires apostoliques," *Revue tunisienne*, 2, p. 261.
78. CPF, SORCG, vol. 254, "Tunisi," 7 August 1663; CPF, SOCG, Barbaria, bu. 1, 6 April 1676; ibid, bu. 3, 29 April 1691.
79. Bombard, "Les Vicaires apostoliques," *Revue tunisienne*, 2(1895), 74; ASN, SCRC, busta 14, letter from Algiers dated 10 July 1663, from Antonio Piretta of Torre di Lauria, with the claim that "more than twenty thousand Christians" had died in the recent *Konia*. CPF, SORCG, vol. 254, "Tunisi," 15 March 1664; ibid., vol. 253, "Tripoli," fol. 95, 12 November

202 *Notes*

1665; L. Ch. Feraud, *Annales Tripolitaines* (Tunis-Paris, 1927), pp. 123–4 (cited in Bono, *Corsari barbareschi*, p. 220, n. 7); also Saunders, *A True Discription,*p. 16.

80. Foss, *A Journal*, pp. 125 and 160–1.

81. Salvago, "*Africa overo Barbarìa*," p. 93; J. M. Venture de Paradis, "Alger au XVIIIᵉ siècle," in *Revue Africaine*, 41 (1897), p. 105; de la Motte, *Several Voyages to Barbary*, pp. 41–2.

82. See Braudel, *The Mediterranean*, p. 889; thus, Saunders, *A True Di scription*, p. 18, wrote of eighteen Venetians who "ran awaie from Tripolie in a bote."

83. Bennett, "Christian and Negro Slavery," pp. 69–70; Friedman, "Christian Captives," p. 620.

84. For an extensive (though not complete) bibliography of the lists published by the redemptive orders, see Bono, *Corsari barbareschi*, pp. 470–1 and 473–4.

85. Deslandres, *L'Ordre des Trinitaires*, p. 437 and n. 1. Already by 1640, Okeley could say that "The *Spaniards* every Year return a considerable sum of money to *Algiers* to be employed in the Redemption of such of their own country as are there in Slavery," William Okeley, *Eben-Ezer: or, a Small Monument of Great Mercy* (London, 1675), p. 28; on redemptions by the Spanish Mercedarians, see Claude Larquié, "Le Rachet des Chrétiens en Terre d'Islam au XVIIᵉ Siècle (1660–1665)," pp. 297–351 in *Bibliothèque de la Revue d'Histoire Diplomatique*, 94 (1980); and Ellen Friedman, "Merchant Friars in North Africa: the Trade in Christian Captives," pp. 94–8, in *The Maghreb Review*, 12–13 (1987).

86. CPF, SOCG, Barbaria, bu. 3, fol. 377, 6 May 1698. Ivone Lorance observed that the "principal and primary cause" of this decline was that the corsairs were no longer taking as many prizes as previously. As secondary causes, he pointed to the plague and redemptions, mentioning four redemptions carried out by the Spanish, French and Portuguese in the previous two years, freeing a total of 930 slaves. Also, ibid., fol. 414, 8 September 1701, ascribing the declining slave numbers to the plague and "to a Collection [redemption] of Spain that has liberated a goodly number."

87. For two especially bungled ransoming expeditions that the Sicilians organized in 1599 and 1600, see Bonaffini, *La Sicilia e i Barbareschi*, pp. 79–104.

88. Bombard, "Les Vicaires apostoliques," *Revue tunisienne*, 2, p. 584, writes of "the silence and indifference of the Court of Turin." Also: "As to the English, French, Poles, Hungarians, Germans, and Belgians, not a single one of them has been, in the memory of man, taken out of captivity thanks to the charities [of redemption] … to the shame of their countries and to the princes who rule them," Gramaye, *Diarium rerum Argelae*, p. 291, said in 1619.

89. For the specific study of a Polish redemption, for example, see Bronislaw Bilinski, "220 schiavi Christiani liberati e portati a Roma nel 1628," pp. 77–91 in *Strenna dei Romanisti*, 1980; on redemption activities by the Italian town of Lucca, see Marco Lenci, *Lucca, il mare e i corsari barbareschi nel XVI secolo* (Lucca, 1987), esp. pp. 96–104.

90. Jean Dams, "Une 'Redemption' de captifs Chrétiens au XVIIe siècle," pp. 141–8 in *Mélanges de Science Religieuse*, 42 (1985).
91. Larquié, "Le Rachet des Chrétiens," p. 326; also Karray Kossentini, "Les Esclaves Espanols à Tunis au XVIIe Siècle," pp. 325–45 in *Captius i esclaus a l'Antiguitat i al Món Modern* (Palma de Mallorca, 1996), esp. pp. 335–8.
92. See, for example, the *Redenzione di Venezia* (Rome, 1731), which indicated that returning Venetians had spent an average of eleven years in slavery; or CPF, SOCG, "Barbaria," bu. 2, fol. 437, 16 November 1689, listing slaves from the Papal States in Tunis, who had apparently waited an average of nearly eighteen years for ransoming.
93. *Proceedings in … the Long Parliament, House of Commons*, p. 560.
94. Dan, *Histoire de Barbarie*, p. 341. This is a clear decline from half a century earlier: around 1580, fra. Diego de Haëdo estimated there were about eighty percent as many renegades as slaves in Algiers alone (20,000 vs. 25,000). In 1701, Fr. Giovanni di S. Bonaventura claimed a ratio of only thirty percent in Algiers – 6,000 renegades and 20,000 slaves: CPF, SOCG, "Barbaria," bu. 3, folio 408, 7 September 1701; in 1689, there were estimated to be 1,000 renegades in Tripoli and "barely 500" slaves: ibid., bu. 2, fols. 378 and 381.
95. *Proceedings*, p. 560.
96. Morgan, *Complete History*, p. 489; for such examples and excuses of renegades returned to Christendom, see ASV, Sant'Uffizio, bu. 87, filza 1, testimony of Andrea Rossi da Valcamonico; and bu. 90, filza 2, testimonies of Domenico Lucido da Orvieto and Gregorio de Minal.
97. Bartolomé Bennassar, "Les chrétiens convertis à l'Islam 'Renégats' et leur intégration aux XVI°–XVII° siècles," pp. 45–53 in *Les Cahiers de Tunisie*, 43 (1991).
98. See the *Catalogo di cinque cento venti Schiavi riscattati nel presente Anno del Giubileo 1675* (Rome, 1675), p. 6, asserting that, out of 200 Spanish soldiers who were captured on their way to Italy, no fewer than 50 abjured their Christianity "within a few days."
99. Gramaye, *Diarium rerum Argelae*, p. 140; Dan, *Histoire de Barbarie*, 320; Bombard, "Les Vicaires apostoliques," *Revue tunisienne*, 2, p. 73.
100. Padre Alfonso Dominici, *Trattato delle Miserie, che patiscono i Fedeli Christiani Schiavi de' Barbari, & dell'Indulgenze che i Sommi Pontefici han con-cesse per il Riscatto di quelli* (Rome, 1647), p. 27.
101. "For the Moors having them in their power, would not suffer them to change their Religion, because a Christian slave is worth much more than a Renegado; for the former are employ'd to row in the Gallies, and the latter are not," d'Aranda, *History of Algiers*, p. 128. Among slaves "favored" for conversion were virtually all women, most children, and men skilled in any craft that was in demand in Barbary – especially writers, accountants, soldiers and shipbuilders.
102. CPF, SOCG, Barbaria, bu. 2, fol. 298, 29 June 1687; folios 380r and 381v, 8 January 1689/90, that termed as "tolerable" the apostasy of eight Catholics out of around 500 Christians of all sects; see also ibid., fols. 298 (29 June 1689), 336 (n.d.); and ibid., bu. 1, fols. 165–6, letter dated 12 June 1669.

103. Dos Sanctos quoted in Margo Todd, "A Captive's Story: Puritans, Pirates, and the Drama of Reconciliation," pp. 37–56 in *The Seventeenth Century*, 12 (1997), p. 41.

104. On the idleness and ease of many renegades, see Knight, *A Relation*, p. 2; on the poverty of many of them, however, see Jean Du Mont, Baron de Carlscroon, *Nouveau voyage du Levant* (The Hague, 1694), English trans. as *A New Voyage to the Levant*, 2nd edn. (London, 1696), p. 337.

105. That is, around 1,700 new captives a year. Based on a century-long average of around 5,000 slaves in Algiers, around 1,500 in Tunis, and not more than 1,000 in Tripoli, Salé, Biserta and elsewhere, for a total of 7,500. If death rates may have diminished somewhat, redemptions evidently increased in compensation.

106. Braudel, *The Mediterranean*, pp. 880–6; Bono, *Corsari barbareschi*, p. 146.

107. Morgan, *Complete History*, p. 408.

108. Lovejoy, "Volume of the Atlantic Slave Trade," p. 474.

109. Lovejoy's estimates for the sixteenth century range from an annual average of 2,100 for the first quarter of the century, to 2,200 for 1526–50, 3,100 for 1551–75, and 5,600 for 1576–1600: Lovejoy, "The Volume of the Atlantic Slave Trade," p. 480, tab. 2.

110. Guglielmotti, *Storia della Marina pontificia*, vol. 3, p. 191, quoted in Bono, *Corsari barbareschi*, p. 140; ibid., p. 150; Marott also noted that the Algerians with whom he rowed in the 1660s were disappointed with their visit to Calabria, where "there were hardly any more persons upon that Coast": Marott, *A Narrative*, pp. 14–15; also Braudel, *The Mediterranean*, pp. 881–4.

111. On the depopulation of West Africa, see David Henige, "Measuring the Immeasurable: The Atlantic Slave Trade, West African Population and the Pyrrhonian Critic," pp. 295–313 in *Journal of African History*, 27 (1986); for fairly up-to-date a bibliography, see Paul Lovejoy, "The Impact of the Atlantic Slave Trade on Africa: A Review of the Literature," pp. 365–94 in ibid., 30 (1989).

112. Most important, when the time came – after 1680 – the major European naval powers, each in their turn, aggressively set out to punish the corsair states, free their slaves and gain protection for their merchant ships. The result, of course, was that the *ra'is* thereafter concentrated their efforts even more on the many Italian states (and later the Americans) that had no such treaties: Wolf, *The Barbary Coast*, pp. 223–67; Venture de Paradis, "Notes sur Alger," in *Revue Africaine*, 40 (1896), p. 35.

113. Dan, *Histoire de Barbarie*, pp. 317 and 320; Bombard, "Les Vicaires Apostoliques," *Revue tunisienne*, 2, p. 432.

114. Mafrici cites convincing evidence of coastal communities in the Kingdom of Naples that, once they were pillaged one or more times by corsairs, suffered permanent population declines, sometimes by as much as 80 percent: Mafrici, *Mezzogiorno e pirateria*, pp. 95–6.

115. Dan, *Histoire de Barbarie*, pp. 308–9; according to Morgan, *Complete History*, p. 626, three-fifths of the Algerian fleet in 1600 was captained by renegades; in 1679, nearly two-fifths of the *ra'is* in Tripoli were renegades: See Baker, *Piracy and Diplomacy*, p.106.

116. Anon. *Voyage dans les États Barbaresques de Maroc, Alger, Tunis et Tripoly. Ou lettres d'un des Captifs qui viennent d'être rachetés par MM. les Chanoines*

réguliers de la Sainte-Trinité (Paris, 1785), p. 101; also Braudel, *The Mediterranean*, p. 884; and Lucien Herault, "Les Troubles d'Alger et la Rédemption des Esclaves en 1645 (d'après manuscrit marseillais)," pp. 87–107 in *Mémoires de l'Institut historique de Provence* 10 (1933), J. Billioud, ed., pp. 87–8: "In the first half of the seventeenth century, the number of captives held itself around a fluctuating population figure of around 20,000, that, joined to the 20,000 renegades and to the numerous contingents of Albanians and Bulgarians serving in the militia, made of Algiers a white city, approaching closer [in terms of] blood and of race to the various European ports on the other bank [of the Mediterranean] than to all the other Moorish or Turkish cities."

117. See Morgan, *Complete History*, pp. 532–3, for the "Parties of *Renegadoes*, sitting publically on Mats, costly Carpets and Cushions, playing Cards and Dice, thrumming Guitars, and singing *a la Christianesca*, enebriating like Swine, till the very last Day of the Moon *Shaâban* [Ramadan], and, in their drunken Airs, ridiculing, and even reviling the *Mahometans* and their Religion." Also, Hugo Schuchardt, "On Lingua Franca," pp. 26–47 in T.L. Markey (ed. and trans.), *The Ethnography of Variation: Selected Writings on Pidgins and Creoles* (Ann Arbor, MI, 1979).

118. ASN, SCRC, bu. 18, letter of 10 October 1780.

Chapter 2

1. Baker, *Piracy and Diplomacy*, pp. 154–5.
2. Ibid., pp. 75–194; Baker noted the movements of quite small transport ships, down to the size of barks, ketches, and sloops; he apparently left out the smallest local vessels, feluccas and the like, that may well have also had a role in the corsairing trade.
3. Ibid., pp. 120, 124, 129 and 138. Baker often wrote of galleys setting off to go "a Christian stealing," or "a men-stealing;" once he even wryly noted that the corsairs had set off "Westward to Fish for Dutchmen, whom ... they hope to meet in Great Scooles."
4. Bono, *Corsari barbareschi*, pp. 140–50; Morgan, *Complete History of Algiers*, pp. 258–93 and 438–74.
5. This account from Morgan, *Complete History of Algiers*, pp. 576–8. In later years, with smaller fleets, the Algerians might accomplish much the same course, but in several successive sweeps: cf. Knight, *A Relation of Seaven Yeares under Slaverie*, pp. 9–10.
6. "The *Algerines* ... are out upon the Cruise Winter and Summer, the whole Year round," according to Morgan, quoting Haëdo, in *A Complete History of Algiers*, pp. 618–19.
7. Morgan, *Complete History*, pp. 670–1; Braudel, *The Mediterranean*, pp. 880–6: Braudel called 1560–70 Algiers' "first brilliant age," and 1580–1620 its second.
8. The closest most European slavers were willing to get to the actual sources of slaves was in "boating," when sailors from a slave ship were sent in launches and boats upriver in the Gold Coast or Biafra to pick up captives who had already been brought from further inland to villages along the

river banks: Michael Gomez, *Exchanging Our Country Marks: The Transformation of African Identities in the Colonial and Antebellum South* (Chapel Hill, 1998), p. 158.

9. Thornton, *Africans and Africa*, pp. 98ff. Thornton allows, however, that the extent to which Europeans instigated and nurtured slave taking in the African interior – by adroitly supplying contending rulers with guns, horses, or other war supplies – as opposed to their merely "tapping into existing slave markets" is still under debate.

10. Even if the Barbary slavers were the most extensive and sophisticated of the lot, virtually *everybody* in the sixteenth-century Mediterranean was trying to enslave someone else: Christians took Muslims in numbers that, on occasion, nearly equalled those achieved by their Muslim counterparts; moreover, Catholic and Protestant states regularly enslaved each other's sailors and merchants and were also willing to take Greeks, Jews, Nubians, Russians, or anyone else unlucky enough to present him or herself for capture: see Alberto Tenenti, *Piracy and the Decline of Venice, 1580–1615* (Berkeley, 1967); Edward Webbe, *His Trauailes* (London, 1590; reprint, 1868); William Davies, *True Relation of the Travailes and Most miserable Captivitie of William Davies* (London, 1614), parts 3–4 (no pagination).

11. Morgan, *Complete History of Algiers*, p. 616: "purchase" meaning prizes.

12. Ibid., p. 621, for this breakdown; also d'Arvieux, *Mémoires*, p. 270; and de La Motte, *Several Voyages to Barbary*, p. 45.

13. Morgan, *Complete History of Algiers*, pp. 438–9; Bono, *Corsari barbareschi*, pp. 19–23.

14. Morgan, *Complete History of Algiers*, p. 616; Okeley, *Eben-Ezer*, p. 39; as a result, Okeley's master had to sell all his slaves, including Okeley himself.

15. See Blackburn, *The Making of New World Slavery* on capital formation and modernity in the context of slaving.

16. Baker, *Piracy and Diplomacy*, pp. 166, 172–3, 191. A month later, Caddi came back empty-handed, "As I had foretold."

17. Quotes from Morgan, *Complete History of Algiers*, pp. 616–17.

18. On Christians shipwrecked in Barbary, see Thomas Troughton, *Barbarian Cruelty: Narrative of the sufferings of the British Captives Belonging to the "Inspector," privateer* (London, 1751), pp. 9–13; Viletta Laranda, *Neapolitan Captive. Interesting Narrative of the Captivity and Sufferings of Miss Viletta Laranda, a Native of Naples* (New York, 1830), pp. 6–7.

19. See, for example, Baker, *Piracy and Diplomacy*, p. 147, who noted on 16 September 1682: "Att Noone was sent in Prize a ship of Raguza Laden wth Salt. But the Christians thought fitt to save their Liberty by escaping ashore in the Boat on the coast of Calabria."

20. Thornton, *Africa and Africans*, p. 4.

21. Cf. Saunders, *A Most Lamentable Voiage*; Phelps, *A True Account*, esp. pp. 1–7; Foss, *A Journal*.

22. Bono, *Corsari barbareschi*, pp. 138–40.

23. Morgan, *Complete History of Algiers*, pp. 608–9; Knight, *A Relation of Seaven Yeares Slaverie*, p. 20.

24. Braudel, *The Mediterranean*, p. 882; Morgan, *Complete History of Algiers*, p. 618; on the general incompetence of the government of Naples in such

matters of self-defense, see Dino Pacaccio, "La Desolazione dell'estate 1566: Ortona invasa dai Turchi," pp. 55–75, in Elio Giannetti and Luciano Tosi, eds, *Turchi e barbareschi in Adriatico*, atti di convegno di studi, Ortona, 10–11 October 1992 (Ortona, 1998), esp. pp. 58–9.

25. Pacaccio, "La Desolazione dell'estate 1566," p. 58. Only the fortified cities of Ortona and Termoli, midway along this stretch of coast, seem to have been spared.

26. Haëdo, *De la Captivité*, vol. 39, p. 241.

27. Mafrici, *Mezzogiorno e pirateria*, pp. 95–6; also the observation of Marott that, although the corsairs with whom he rowed returned with their freshly captured slaves to the Calabrese coast to offer a possible redemption "according to custom," there was "no body coming, whether it were for the want of money, or charity, or else that there were hardly any more persons upon that Coast." Marott, *A Narrative*, pp. 14–15.

28. Blili, "Course et captivité des femmes," pp. 260–1; Claude Larquié, "Captifs Chrétiens et esclaves Maghrébins au XVIIIe siècle: une tentative de comparison," 347–64 in *Captius i esclaus a l'Antiguitat i al Mónd Modern* (Palma de Mallorca, 1996), pp. 354–56; ibid., "Le rachet des Chrétiens," p. 319. It must be remembered, however, that such estimates that are currently available represent only those women who were ransomed; whether the percentage was the same for those captured overall remains an open question, but it is highly likely that many women, once absorbed into the harems of North Africa, converted to Islam and were never offered for ransom at all.

29. Rudt de Collenberg, *Esclavage et rançons des chrétiens en méditerranée (1570–1600)*, pp. 303–4, 323–4.

30. As happened with the sack of Fondi, 6 miles inland from Terracina, in Lazio, in 1534, Rapallo in 1550, and Reggio Calabria in 1551: see Bono, *Corsari barbareschi*, pp. 141–8.

31. Biblioteca Nazionale di Roma, Mss F. Varia, n. 137/742 Curthio Mattei, "Il sacco e rovina di Sperlonga terra nella spiaggia di Gaeta, fatto dai Turchi alli 4 luglio 1623, in ottava rima composto da C.M., chirurgo da Lenola," fols. 53r-v.

32. Baker, *Piracy and Diplomacy*, p. 165, noted the time that the corsair man-of-war *Europa* returned to Tripoli "without any Purchase Except a poore French hermit, whom they took off from Lampadosa a small uninhabited Island."

33. Morgan, *Complete History of Algiers*, pp. 608–9, for corsairs under Morat Re'is setting up such a shore camp at Capo Passero, in southern Sicily in 1595; Knight, *A Relation of Seaven Yeares Slaverie*, p. 20; also Haëdo, *De la Captivité à Alger*, vol. 39, p. 241.

34. Braudel, *The Mediterranean*, p. 881, observed that by 1560 the corsairs began to have "the audacity ... to show themselves in broad daylight." By the end of the century, however, night attacks appear again to have become the norm; Knight, *A Relation of Seaven Yeares Slaverie*, p. 18; also, Mascarenhas, *Esclave à Alger*, pp. 153–4.

35. Mascarenhas, *Esclave à Alger*, p. 154; Mattei, "Il sacco e rovina di Sperlonga," fol. 46r.

36. Marco Lenci, "Riscatti di schiavi cristiani dal Maghreb. La Compagnia della SS. Pietà di Lucca (secoli XVII–XIX)," pp. 53–80 in *Società e storia*, 31 (1986), p. 56, n. 10.

37. On the effectiveness of the forces of the Marquis di Geraci, particularly active in policing the west coast of Sicily in the 1550s, see Bono, *Corsari barbareschi*, pp. 148–9. For Dallam, see J. Theodore Bent, ed., *Early Voyages and Travels in the Levant*, 2 vols., vol. 1, *The Diary of Master Thomas Dallam, 1599–1600* (London, 1893), p. 17.

38. Thus, much of the system in Calabria was said to be "nonexistent, either because it was in ruins, because it was abandoned immediately [after building] or for the lack of upkeep;" see Gustavo Valente, *Le torri costiere della Calabria* (Cosenza, 1960), p. 22, cited by Bono, *Corsari barbareschi*, p. 25. For an Algerian raiding party "taking many Towers upon ... [the] Ilands of *Sardena*, and *Corcica*," in 1637, see Knight, *A Relation of Seaven Yeares Slaverie*, p. 9.

39. Knight, *A Relation of Seaven Yeares Slaverie*, p. 18.

40. Mascarenhas, *Esclave à Alger*, p. 153.

41. This was supposedly the impulse behind the brilliant raid made by the Algerians on Iceland in 1627, although there is some disagreement as to whether the rovers were guided by an Icelandic renegade, as Morgan claimed, or by captured English fishermen: Morgan, *Complete History of Algiers*, p. 670; Helgason, "Historical Narrative," p. 276; d'Aranda, pp. 247–9.

42. Mascarenhas, *Esclave à Alger*, p. 154; V. Morelli, *I "barbareschi" contro il regno di Napoli* (Naples, 1920), p. 52, quoted in Bono, *Corsari barbareschi*, p. 151; Morgan, who provides the figure of ten ducats apiece for captives, does not make clear if this sum is in addition to each corsair's share of the loot overall, cf., Morgan, *A Complete History of Algiers*, p. 622.

43. In such works of dialect fiction by Andrea Camillieri as *Il ladro di merendine* (Palermo, 1999), pp. 13 and 218.

44. Mattei, "Il sacco e rovina," fols. 46v and 47r.

45. It was evidently too much (or too little), however, when some raiders came back from a recently abandoned Sardinian village in 1623 with nothing more than a blind boy: the *re'is* mocked them and ordered the boy left behind on the beach: Mascarenhas, *Esclave à Alger*, p. 153.

46. Lenci, "Riscatti di schiavi cristiani," p. 56 and n. 10.

47. ASN, SCRC, bu. 14, case #643; also Morgan, *Complete History of Algiers*, p. 576.

48. Guglielmotti, *Storia della Marina pontificia*, vol. 4, p. 125, cited in Bono, *Corsari barbareschi*, p. 145.

49. Bono, *Corsari barbareschi*, p. 141; and Davies, *True Relation of the Travailes*, part 2: insofar as bells could raise the alarm, it was also a good idea to silence them.

50. Knight, *A Relation of Seaven Yeares Slaverie*, p. 19.

51. Morgan, *History of Algiers*, p. 608.

52. As is evidenced by a number of ex-votos still extant. Even Icelanders sought supernatural protection from the corsairs, "casting spells on the raiders with their poems": Helgason, "Historical Narrative as Collective Therapy," p. 285.

53. Bono, *Corsari barbareschi*, p. 145, cites such a vendetta. Morgan, *Complete History of Algiers*, pp. 489–501, for the story of Ochali, who took the Muslim name Ali Basha Fartas.

54. Morgan, *Complete History of Algiers*, p. 505.

55. See Mafrici, *Mezzogiorno e pirateria*, pp. 165–78.

56. Fondo Salvatore Marino, Palermo, Carte sciolte, no. 204.

57. Bono, *Corsari barbareschi*, p. 146; Marott, *Narrative*, p. 14.

58. Du Chastelet des Boys described his own first moments after capture: "As to me, I noticed a great Moor approaching me, his sleeves rolled up to his shoulders, holding a saber in his large hand of four fingers; I was left without words. And the ugliness of this carbon [face], animated by two ivory [eye] balls, moving about hideously, with the pirouetting glimmer of a short, wide and shining blade, terrified me a good deal more than were [frightened] the first humans at the sight of the flaming sword at the door of Eden." Du Chastelet, *L'Odyssée*, p. 99.

59. Nilo Calvini, "Opere sanremasche per la redenzione degli schiavi e cenni sull'attività del Magistrato di Genova e dei Trinitari di Torino," pp. 31–5 in *Corsari "Turchi" e barbareschi: Prigionieri schiavi riscatti* (Ceriale, 1992); for the documentation recording the sale of such a house to free Domenico Francesco Moro, of Civitanuova in the Marche, see ASVat, Gonfalone, bu. 733, f.297, filza 43, 11 December 1722.

60. This held true of fishermen as well, many of whom were forced to pawn their catch ahead of time, to obtain the simple necessities of their trade: ASVat, Gonfalone, bu. 1139, fols. 159–61. Mafrici likewise notes that, even as the overall population of many coastal villages in the Kingdom of Naples was decreasing after 1550, the number of those classified as "beggars" was on the rise: Mafrici, *Mezzogiorno e pirateria*, p. 96.

61. A situation that Dan recounts in some detail: Dan, *Histoire de Barbarie*, pp. 409–10.

62. Pacaccio, "La Desolazione dell'estate 1566," p. 62.

63. Morgan, *Complete History of Algiers*, p. 625.

64. As recounted by Knight, *A Relation of Seaven Yeares Slaverie*, pp. 21–6.

65. Bono, *Corsari barbareschi*, pp. 173, 180–92. For an exhaustive account of the raid on San Felice Circeo, its effect on Rome, and the attempts to ransom the victims, see ASVat, Gonfalone, bu. 16, fols. 218–628.

66. Braudel, *The Mediterranean*, pp. 886–7.

67. Hees, "Journal d'un voyage à Alger," pp. 123–4; Baker, *Piracy and Diplomacy*, p. 142.

68. Morgan, *Complete History of Algiers*, p. 282; also Foss, *A Journal*, p. 9; Elliot, *A True Narrative*, p. 6.

69. See, for example, Phelps, *A True Account*, pp. 2–3; also ASV, POLP, bu. 102, case #9, 30 May 1765, letter from Tunis.

70. Gramaye, *Diarium rerum Argelae*, p. 321 and note 1.

71. Bono, *Corsari barbareschi*, pp. 171–9.

72. Citizens of states at peace with the Ottomans but who were traveling as merchants (and not passengers) on a Spanish ship could also be enslaved, as Thédenat found out to his cost in 1785: "Les Aventures de Thédenat," p. 159.

73. Gramaye, *Diarium rerum Argelae*, pp. 320–1.

74. Ibid., p. 321. Salé and the Moroccan corsairing ports were completely independent of both Ottoman control and any foreign observers until well into the seventeenth century, and were therefore well suited for unloading such clandestine slaves, except for the fact that the Moroccans themselves were quite often at war with the Algerians: Du Chastelet, *L'Odyssée,* vol. 10, p. 263.

75. See in Baker, *Piracy and Diplomacy*, introduction by Pennell, esp. pp. 45–50 and tables.

76. Baker, *Piracy and Diplomacy*, pp. 119–20, 123.

77. It also emerges from Baker's lists that the ships themselves were worth little: to "an empty Barque" he assigned the value of just $600, the equivalent of three slaves: Baker, *Piracy and Diplomacy*, p. 156, also p. 189.

78. Above all the Spanish. By the 1790s, among the most readily ransomed were the sailors of the United States: Baepler, *White Slaves, African Masters*, pp. 8–9.

79. Salvago, *"Africa overo Barbaria,"* p. 91. See also ASV, Senato Mar (hereafter, ASV, SM), filza 286, 20 September 1633; and ASV:CRD, filza 19, 20 Dec 1628, where the Venetian shipwright Annibal Ricciadei wrote in his petition to the Collegio:

   > Fate chose that I should be bought by the son of Usuman Dey, king of Tunisia, to whom I was revealed as being skilled in the craft of shipwright (which they hold great esteem), and it was my lot to be forced by barbarous tyranny to work and build diverse ships and galleys, to his satisfaction; with the result that I merited to be chosen as the head shipwright of his workforce, but this, by him reckoned as an honor, rendered me eternally his slave, such that I could never (for any amount of gold) hope for my liberation.

80. Du Chastelet, *L'Odyssée,* pp. 258–9.

81. See ibid.

82. Ibid., pp. 97–8. Seeing his ship inexorably pursued by corsairs, Jean Bonnet decided to throw his sea chest overboard even the day before capture, "so that they would not so easily know who I was, due to the very handsome and fashionable clothes with which it was filled," Antoine Galland, *Histoire de l'Esclavage d'un marchand de la ville de Cassis, à Tunis*, ed. Catherine Guénot and Nadia Vasquez (Paris, 1993), p. 27.

83. Du Chastelet, *L'Odyssée,* p. 260; also Grammont, "La Course," pp. 5–6. On the other hand, Bonnet asserted that everyone on board his ship sought to change his *chemise* before the final battle, so as "at least [be able] to fall with a white shirt," Galland, *Histoire de l'Esclavage*, p. 26; on adopting false names and the possible consequences once one was enslaved, see D'Aranda, *The History of Algiers*, pp. 21–4.

84. Du Chastelet, *L'Odyssée*, pp. 98 and 257; also Dan, *Histoire de Barbarie*, pp. 301–2.

85. "This [stratagem] succeeded so well to me," Marott claimed, "that I was in a manner the only person who was exempt from their cruel treatments," Marott, *A Narrative*, pp. 8–10.

86. Du Chastelet, *L'Odyssée,* p. 98.

87. Gramaye, *Diarium rerum Argelae*, p. 321; after a similar experience, Du Chastelet, *L'Odyssée*, vol. 12, p. 14, wrote of "*une terreur panique* by which I was surprised;" also Thomas Phelps, *A True Account of the Captivity of*

Thomas Phelps at Machaness in Barbary, and of his strange escape ... (London, 1685), p. 4; Gomez, *Exchanging Our Country Marks*, p. 159.
88. Richard Haselton, *Strange and Wonderful Things* (London, 1595), p. 5; Gramaye, *Diarium rerum Argelae*, p. 321; Morgan, *Complete History of Algiers*, p. 622.
89. Struys, *The Voyage and Travels*, vol. 2, p. 80.
90. Elliot, *A True Narrative*, p. 7; Gramaye, *Diarium rerum Argelae*, pp. 321–3, 325–7; also Gramaye in *Purchas and his Pilgrimes*, vol. 9, p. 279; Foss, *A Journal*, p. 15; also Marott, p. 10; d'Aranda, *History of Algiers*, p. 7. Some prisoners, however, especially women and those who made no attempt to conceal their wealth or status, could be treated much better on the voyage back: cf., Mascarenhas, *Esclave à Alger*, p. 52; Thédenat, "Les Aventures," p. 158.
91. Bono, *Corsari barbareschi*, p. 146; Elliot, *A True Narrative*, p. 8.
92. Okeley, whose ship was taken in the English Channel, took "five or six weeks" to arrive in Algiers; d'Aranda, by contrast, arrived there in just two weeks, and Thédenat in just four days: Okeley, *Eben-Ezer*, p. 5; d'Aranda, *History of Algiers*, pp. 6–7: Thédenat, *Mémoires* p. 158; Phelps, *A True Account*, pp. 4–7; also *Purchas and His Pilgrimes*, vol. 9, "Nicholas Roberts and the Pirates," pp. 311–22. Perhaps because he was taken with some extremely rich Portuguese travelers (one of whom was found to be carrying diamonds worth 12,000 cruzados), Mascarenhas asserted that "The treatment that the Turks reserved for [us] ... was very good, and not what one would have expected on the part of Barbary pirates": Mascarenhas, *Esclave à Alger*, p. 52; see also ASN, SCRC, bu. 15, letter of 20 January 1735, from Erasmo Antonio Russo, slave in Algiers.
93. ASN, SCRC, bu. 14, case #2901, letter of 20 January 1735, from Erasmo Antonio Russo, in Algiers; also Gomez, *Exchanging Our Country Marks*, p. 157.
94. Morgan, *Complete History of Algiers*, p. 625; Mascarenhas, *Esclave à Alger*, p. 54.
95. Du Chastelet wrote of how "our miserable party [of slaves] was conducted to the palace of the pasha to the racket of trumpets and drums [atabales]," Du Chastelet, *L'Odyssée*, vol. 12, p. 159.
96. Foss, *A Journal*, pp. 16–17.
97. Morgan, *Complete History of Algiers*, p. 625.
98. Morgan claimed that

> For this singularity is practiced by the *Algerines* (and I believe by all other *Barbary* Cruisers) that whoever happens to be on board at the taking [of] any Prize, whether *Christians* or *Jews* Passengers, and, if I mistake not very much, even Women and Children, they are absolutely intitled to each a single share.

Even the slaves on the corsairs' galleys received a share or more apiece; the pasha of Algiers took his share as representative of the *Beylic*, or public authority: Morgan, *Complete History of Algiers*, pp. 616, 621–2.
99. D'Aranda, *History of Algiers*, p. 8; Mascarenhas, *Esclave à Alger*, p. 55.
100. Gomez, *Exchanging Our Country Marks*, p. 170; Mascarenhas, *Esclave à Alger*, p. 55.

101.   Galland, *Historie de l'Esclavage*, p. 34.
102.   Thus, Jean Bonnet learned that he was expected to kiss the hem of the robe of authority figures once he had arrived in Tunis: Galland, *Histoire de l'Esclavage d'un marchand*, pp. 29 and 34.
103.   Laugier de Tassy, *History of Algiers*, p. 226; also Mascarenhas, *Esclave à Alger*, pp. 54–5, 58–62; d'Aranda, *History of Algiers*, pp. 135–8.
104.   After 1670, the pashas of Algiers also took the title of *dey*, or supreme magistrate: Emerit, "Un Mémoire sur Alger," p. 20.
105.   Mascarenhas, *Esclave à Algers*, p. 55; d'Aranda, *History of Algiers*, p. 7; Du Chastelet, *L'Odyssée*, pp. 160–1; de la Motte, *Several Voyages to Barbary*, p. 43; Okeley, *Eben-Ezer*, p. 8; Laugier de Tassy, *History of Algiers*, p. 221; Dan, *Histoire de Barbarie*, p. 390.
106.   Laugier de Tassy, *History.*
107.   Du Chastelet, *L'Odyssée*, pp. 160–1.
108.   Foss believed that this particular pasha, Hassan Basha, was angry at what he perceived as earlier disrespect from the United States: Foss, *A Journal*, p. 17.
109.   Du Chastelet, vol. 11, p. 161; vol. 12, p. 23; Galland, *Histoire de l'Esclavage*, p. 34.
110.   De la Motte, *Several Voyages to Barbary*, p. 44; Laugier de Tassy, *Complete History*, p. 223.
111.   Saunders, "A True Discription," p. 10; Elliot, *A True Narrative*, pp. 14–15; Laugier de Tassy, *A Complete History*, p. 230.
112.   According to Cervantes, it was also misfortune to be chosen by the city authorities, the *almacen*, "since belonging to everyone and not having a specific master, even if they are able to pay their ransom, they cannot find anyone with whom to deal, even if they are able to pay their ransom." Cervantes, *Don Quixote*, cited in Mafrici, *Mezzogiorno e pirateria*, p. 110. Dan described the *badestan* as "Right in the middle of the city ... a square plaza in the form of four galeries, all of which are uncovered," Dan, *Histoire de Barbarie*, p. 392; also Bachrouch, "Rachet et libération des Esclaves," p. 134; for mention of the *batistan* in Tripoli, see CPF, SOCG, Barbaria, bu. 3, fol. 66, petition of 16 May 1692, from slaves there.
113.   D'Aranda, *History of Algiers*, p. 7; d'Arvieux, *Mémoires*, p. 166; de La Motte, *Several Voyages*, p. 43.
114.   George Elliot, *A true narrative of the life of Mr. George Elliot, who was taken and sold for a slave; with his travels, captivity, and miraculous escape from Salle, in the Kingdom of Fez* (London, 1770?), p. 14; d'Aranda, *History of Algiers*, p. 9. Dan, *Histoire de Barbarie*, p. 392, claimed that the slaves were paraded about at this point all chained together.
115.   Du Chastelet, vol. 11, p. 161; d'Arvieux, *Mémoires*, pp. 266–7.
116.   D'Aranda, *History of Algiers*, p. 157.
117.   Dan, *Histoire de Barbarie*, pp. 392–3.
118.   D'Aranda, *History of Algiers*, p. 9; Dan, *Histoire de Barbarie*, p. 393; Davies, *True Relation of the Travailes*, p. 2Bv; Okeley, *Eben-Ezer*, pp. 9–10, commented that "a good, strong, entire set of Grinders will advance the Price considerably.... [For] they intend to keep them *at hard meat all the Year*, and it must *not be gums*, but *solid Teeth* (nay, if it were possible, *case-harden'd Teeth*) that must *chew it*; and when all is done, they had need of

the *Ostriches Stomach* to digest it." Du Chastelet found himself pronounced "weak in the body and stronger in the teeth than elsewhere;" not surprisingly he was soon sold to one of the *re'is*, for use as a galley slave: Du Chastelet, *Mémoires*, vol. 12, p. 356.

119. Salvago, *"Africa overo Barbaria,"* p. 94: "The women [who] are made slaves, if they are beautiful and virgin, for the most part [the Turks] transgress; the weathered and old stay in the houses of the master and serve the mistresses;" also Okeley, *Eben-Ezer,* p. 10.
120. Dan, *Histoire de Barbarie,* p. 379.
121. D'Arvieux, *Mémoires,* p. 267; Dan, *Histoire de Barbarie,* p. 392.
122. D'Arvieux, *Mémoires,* pp. 267–8; also Morgan, *Complete History of Algiers,* pp. 270–1. Presumably the Dutch and Flemish, who were much sought after as captives, could fetch the highest markups, although d'Aranda observed, somewhat wryly, that he had been sold for a "mere" 200 pataques, or 566 livres: d'Aranda, *History of Algiers,* p. 9. Young slaves in the American South might also boast and compete with each other over who was worth the most: Genovese, *Roll, Jordan, Roll,* p. 506.
123. Okeley, *Eben-Ezer,* p. 11; Davies, *True Relation,* p. B2v.
124. And sometimes to their great regret: Du Chastelet, *Mémoires,* vol. 12, pp. 24–32; Thédenat, *Mémoires,* pp. 159–60.
125. During the bargaining for his second resale, Du Chastelet reported that
> One [of the *maquignons*] said that he had seen me going with the *négrines* [slaves from Guinea or Angola] to the shops of Oge Ali [his first master]; another had seen me carry water [for him] languidly and without strength; some other knew that the said Oge Ali had gotten rid of me in the middle of the Badestan, at a loss, into the hands of the wife of a renegade, who could be the one who was presently offering me for sale. (Du Chastelet, *Mémoires,* vol. 12, p. 356.)
126. See de La Motte, *Several Voyages to Barbary,* p. 43; Okeley, *Eben-Ezer,* p. 11; Bennett, "Christian and Negro Slavery," p. 77.
127. De la Motte, *Several Voyages,* p. 43.
128. *The Famous and Wonderful Recovery of a Ship of Bristol,* p. 255.
129. Laugier de Tassy, *A Complete History,* p. 222.

Chapter 3

1. Mascarenhas, *Esclave à Alger,* pp. 57–8.
2. Grammont, "La Course," p. 11.
3. Okeley, *Eben-Ezer,* p. 33.
4. Grammont, "La Course," p. 11, cited in particular the verse "You should pardon him seventy times a day if you would want to merit divine clemency."
5. Slaves, that is: Okeley, *Eben-Ezer,* p. 9.
6. Grammont, "La Course," pp. 14–17.
7. Bachrouch, "Rachet et libération," p. 130; also Morgan, *Complete History of Algiers,* p. 487, who noted how "the Spanish Slaves greatly dread falling into the Hands of a *Tagarine* or *Morisco* Patron (who still remember the

Injuries done to their Fore-Fathers); they being, generally, the worst Masters they can have, on Account of those old Grudges."

8. Knight, *A Relation*, p. 9; also d'Aranda, *History of Algiers*, pp. 12–13, 33. With 500 or more slaves, Pegelin could use some for work and some for investment; it would appear that Knight fell into the former category and d'Aranda into the latter.

9. Although a great deal of information is available through the records of the redemptive orders on the prices paid for ransoming slaves, much less is known about initial sale (or resale) prices, and most of this is limited to personal accounts: see Rawlins, p. 256 (150 *doublets*); d'Aranda, p. 9 (200 *patacoons*) and p. 32 (250 *patacoons*); Thédenat, p. 159 (70 *zecchini*).

10. Venture de Paradis, "Alger au XVIIIe siécle," p. 314 in *Revue Africaine*, vol. 39.

11. Pignon, "L'Esclavage en Tunisie," pp. 151–6; Fontenay, "La Maghreb barbaresque," pp. 8–10.

12. D'Aranda, *History of Algiers*, pp. 11 and 121.

13. D'Arvieux, *Mémoires*, pp. 43–4.

14. William Okeley was sold by a bankrupt master: "My Patron had been *sincking in his Estate* a pretty while, the last Ship he had put to Sea *broke his back*; At last he was grown (insensibly) so low, that it could no longer *be daubed up with his Repute*, but he must be forced to sell all his Slaves to pay his Debts" (*Eben-Ezer,* p. 39).

15. Laugier de Tassy, *A Complete History*, p. 225.

16. CPF, SORCG, bu. 254, "Tunisi," fol. 213, letter (no date, but evidently the mid-1660s) from fra. Girolamo da Sassari in Tunis.

17. As to female slaves, Dan only added that "they are employed in house-keeping and at the service of the household," Dan, *Histoire de Barbarie*, pp. 406–7.

18. Chastelet des Boys, *L'Odyssée,* in *Revue Africaine*, 12(1868), p. 350.

19. Ibid., p. 25.

20. Mascarenhas, *Esclave à Alger*, p. 148; Dan, *Histoire de Barbarie*, pp. 407–10.

21. Grammont, "La Course," pp. 9–10.

22. One such gentlemanly talent that did occasionally prove marketable was that of reading and writing: see below and Thédenat, "Les Adentures".

23. The Venetians in particular kept a large contingent of free, paid oarsmen in their galleys throughout the sixteenth century up to the conversion of rowed to sailed ships around 1650: Frederic C. Lane, *Venice: a Maritime Republic* (Baltimore, 1973), pp. 364–9.

24. The number of oarsmen required varied with the size of the galley and number of oars: Mascarenhas, *Esclave à Alger*, p. 148; Knight, *A Relation of Seaven Yeares Slaverie*, p. 29, claimed "three hundred or more" per ship; see also Morgan, *Complete History of Algiers*, p. 626; Fontenay, "La Maghreb barbaresque," p.10.

25. Although the Christian use of galley slaves was of neither the extent nor duration of that of their Muslim rivals, by all accounts those nations that did enslave Muslims and Protestants for this purpose showed as little or less Christian spirit than did their Islamic rivals: see Haselton, *Strange and Wonderful Things*; also Grammont, "La Course," p. 12.

26. Dan, *Histoire de Barbarie*, pp. 308–9, citing Haëdo, gave the number of warships in Algiers in 1588 as 35; also d'Arvieux, *Mémoires*, p. 264, who estimated "around thirty Vessels of war" in the city in 1665.

27. Typical of these reduced crews might be that of *The Little Moor*, on which Chastelet des Boys shipped, with fifteen other "slave sailors ... for the most part Flemish and English, and me the only Frenchman," Chastelet des Boys, *L'Odysséė* p. 357. On the Algerian fleet, see also CPF, SRC, Barbaria, bu. 1, 18 May 1681, letter from P. Gatta in Tunis, indicating that Algiers boasted "46 corsairing vessels, in addition to two galleys and other small ships;" also in the early 1700s de La Motte, in *Several Voyages to Barbary*, p. 97, reported the Algerians as having "twenty-five [ships, ranging] from 18 to 60 Guns, exclusive of Caravels, Brigantines, &c.;" see also CPF, SRC, Barbaria, bu. 3, fol. 414, 8 September 1701, letter from Lorance in Algiers, for the observation that "[the Algerians] still have, between large and small, sixteen vessels, and two Galleys, but they do not have between the two of them enough oarsmen to equip one alone, and therefor this year they remain in Port, useless;" also ibid., fol. 444, 3 August 1703.

28. Mafrici, *Mezzogiorno e pirateria*, p. 112; Freidman, "Christian Captives," p. 118.

29. The larger galleys – especially those of the sultan's fleet – might have as many as six men chained to their very large and heavy oars: Morgan, *History of Algiers*, p. 616; also Friedman, "Christian Captives," p. 619.

30. The cause of much fear among *galeotti*, since "If [the galley] capsizes – as happens every day – none of them can thus get out alive," Mascarenhas, *Esclave à Alger*, p. 148.

31. Saunders, *Of a Most Lamentable Voiage*, p. 10; Marott, *A Narrative*, pp. 61–2, also noted that "it is for this purpose also that the Chain is as long as the Bench."

32. Mafrici, *Mezzogiorno e pirateria*, p. 113 and n. 51.

33. Haëdo, quoted and translated in Friedman, "Christian Captives at 'Hard Labor,'" p. 619; Mascarenhas, *Esclave à Alger*, p. 148; Knight, *A Relation of Seaven Yeares Slaverie*, p. 29; Morgan, in *History of Algiers*, pp. 617–18, defines *Burgol* as "Wheat boiled, dried and broke in a Mill."

34. Grammont, "La Course," p. 20.

35. Friedman, "Christian Captives at 'Hard Labor,'" pp. 619–20; Morgan, *History of Algiers*, p. 617, noted that free crewmen might bring aboard such extras as "*Burgol* ... some Rice, Potted Meat, Butter, Cheese, Oil, Olives, Figs, Dates, Raisens and the like, associating themselves into Messes, just as they please, and fare tolerably well."

36. Saunders, *Of a Most Lamentable Voiage*, p. 10; Knight, *A Relation of Seaven Yeares Slaverie*, p. 29; Mascarenhas, *Esclave à Alger*, p. 148.

37. Knight, *A Relation of Seaven Yeares Slaverie*, p. 29; Marott, *A Narrative*, p. 19, also wrote of the special suffering that he experienced, "never to lye in a bed."

38. Morgan, *History of Algiers*, p. 517; also Mascarenhas, *Esclave à Alger*, p. 149, described the results of such a chase: "I have seen some men who, after this, fell exhausted on the oar and others who died under the whip, without the Turks having the least pity for them."

39. Saunders, *Of a Most Lamentable Voiage*, p. 10.

40. Morgan, *History of Algiers*, p. 517.
41. Knight, *A Relation of Seaven Yeares Slaverie*, p. 17.
42. Grammont, "La Course," p. 20; CPF, SRC, Barbaria, bu.1. fols. 251–2, letter of 20 July 1672, from Marcello Costa in Tunis.
43. Pignon, "L'Esclavage en Tunisie," p. 152.
44. For complaints of the lack of any news from such slaves, see ASVat, Gonfalone, bu. 1139, fol. 57; fol. 169; also Pignon, "L'Esclavage en Tunisie," p. 151.
45. T. Stephen Whitman, *The Price of Freedom: Slavery and Manumission in Baltimore and Early National Maryland* (Lexington, 1997) pp. 75–6.
46. Micozzo, 24 years old, had been taken from a fishing boat off the coast of Ancona about sixteen months earlier: ASVat, Gonfalone, bu. 1144, fol. 331, 27 December 1677, letter from Micozzo di Bastiano, in Lepanto; see also ibid., bu. 1139, fol. 151, for a letter from Micozzo's father to the Gonfalone. For others who feared being sent to the galleys in Barbaria or the Levant: ibid., bu. 1144, fol. 526, 10 March 1686.
47. Mascarenhas, *Esclave à Alger*, p. 148; Knight, *A Relation of Seaven Yeares Slaverie,* pp. i-ii.
48. ASV, POLP, bu. 102, filza 11, 1 July 1765; the slaves ranged from 33 to 88 years in age, their time in slavery from 17 to 55 years. For petitions from Venetian ex-slaves that mention long periods at the oars, see ASV, SM, filza 221, 19 April 1619; and ASV, CSD, filza 43, 17 Sept 1652; and ibid., filza 64, 19 August 1665.
49. Fontenay, "Le Maghreb barbaresque," p. 23.
50. Knight, *A Relation of Seaven Yeares Slaverie*, p. 10.
51. Unlike some later observers, Haëdo claimed that the Algerians "are out upon the Cruise Winter and Summer, the whole Year round;" they were thus "able to make three or four Voyages in a Year, and even more if they are inclined to exert themselves": quoted in Morgan, *History of Algiers*, pp. 618–19; also d'Aranda, *History of Algiers*, p. 17.
52. CPF, SRC, Barbaria, bu. 1, fol. 325, letter dated 20 August 1675, from Marcello Costa in Tunis.
53. Gramaye, *De Miserijs*, p. 323; Mascarenhas, *Esclave à Alger*, pp. 50–3.
54. Mascarenhas, *Esclave à Alger*, p. 148; Marott, *A Narrative*, pp. 27 and 29; also d'Aranda, *History of Algiers*, p. 22, who called them "*Bogavands* that is the outermost men at an Oar."
55. Marott, *Narrative*, pp. 29–30; on drivers and the difficult position they held between master and slaves, Fogel, *Without Consent or Contract*, pp. 41–59; Genovese, *Roll, Jordan, Roll*, pp. 365–88.
56. Marott, *A Narrative*, pp. 17, 21, 27 and 29; Genovese, *Roll, Jordan, Roll*, pp. 383–5.
57. Knight, *A Relation of Seaven Yeares Slaverie*, p. 29.
58. Mascarenhas held, for example, that places along the side of the ship were "less painful positions" than those in the center; on the other hand, some side places required that the *galeotto* stand up to row, and for this reason were to be avoided; Mascarenhas, *Esclave à Alger*, p. 156.
59. Ibid, pp. 159–61.
60. Salvago, "*Africa overo Barbaria*," p. 92; Morgan, SOCG, *History of Algiers*, p. 621; de La Motte, *Several Voyages to Barbary*, p. 45.

61. Foss, *A Journal*, p. 26; see also CPF, Barbaria, bu. 1, fol. 407, for a letter from a slave who complained of "their forcing me to do great labors on the walls."
62. In fact, they were building a church on behalf of the pasha of Tripoli: Saunders, *Of a Most Lamentable Voiage*, p. 17.
63. Francesco di S. Lorenzo, *Breve relatione*, p. 11.
64. Dan, *Histoire de Barbarie*, p. 407.
65. Ibid.; Foss, *A Journal*, pp. 22–4.
66. ASVat, Gonfalone, bu. 1144, fol. 482, 5 November 1685; Foss, *A Journal*, p. 23.
67. Ibid., p. 23.
68. The view is titled "The East Prospect of the City of Mequinez, ye usual Residence of the Sherifs, present Emperors of Morocco (Wherein is represented ye Servile Laboir & manner of Work in wch ye Christian Captives are employed. Drawn by Henry Boyd, Master of y^e *Neptune* during his Captivity there," de la Motte, *Several Voyages to Barbary*, following p. 18; also Saunders, p. 15 (no pagination); for a slave who was put to work for seven years "in the hardest slavery at a lime-burning furnace in the country [outside Algiers]," see ASVat, Gonfalone, bu. 1157, filza 1, petition from Lorenzo Cassandra of Rimini.
69. John Kingdon, *Redeemed Slaves, being a Short Narrative of Two Neapolitans Redeemed from SLAVERY on the Coast of Barbary* (Bristol, 1780), p. 4.
70. Dan, *Histoire de Barbarie*, p. 407; Saunders, *Of a Most Lamentable Voiage*, p. 11; CPF,SRC, bu. 2, fol. 106, letter of 8 November 1684, from Agostino da Messina in Tripoli; ibid., bu. 3, fol. 434, letter of 20 February 1702, from Niccolò da Scio in Tripoli.
71. Foss, *A Journal*, pp. 23–4; d'Aranda, *History of Algiers*, p. 25.
72. ASV, POLP, bu. 101, file marked "1633," letter from Agostino Pinna; CPF, SRC, Barbaria, bu. 1, fol. 322, 20 August 1675, letter from P. Marcello Costa in Biserta.
73. Dan, *Histoire de Barbarie*, pp. 406–7; Galland, *Histoire de l'esclavage d'un marchand*, pp. 58–9.
74. Dan, *Histoire de Barbarie*, p. 406; also Dominici, *Trattato delle Miserie*, p. 17.
75. Dan, *Histoire de Barbarie*, p. 406; d'Aranda, *History of Algiers*, p. 15; Foss, *A Journal*, p. 30. CPF, SRC, Barbaria, bu. 4, fol. 465, letter of 30 May 1720, from fr. Francesco da Modena in Tunis.
76. Chastelet des Boys, *L'Odyssée*, pp. 26–7; d'Aranda, *History of Algiers*, p. 18.
77. Keeping in mind, of course, that, in the American South at least, large plantations with gang slave labor were in the distinct minority, with 75 percent of all farms holding fewer than 50 slaves and around half holding fewer than 20: Genovese, *Roll, Jordan, Roll*, pp. 7–8. Also, Anon., *Voyage dans les États barbaresques de Maroc, Alger, Tunis et Tripoly. Ou lettres d'un des Captifs qui viennent d'étre rachetés par MM. les Chanoines réguliers de la Sainte-Trinité* (Paris, 1785), p. 150.
78. Chastelet des Boys, *L'Odyssée*, vol. 12, p. 27; Okeley, *Eben-Ezer*, p. 41.
79. CPF, SOCG, Barbaria, bu. 1, fol. 4, letter of ca. 1713 from P. Emanuele da Cunha Suarez in Algiers; Okeley, *Eben-Ezer*, p. 42; Francesco di San Lorenzo, *Breve Relatione*, p. 16; de La Motte, *Several Voyages to Barbary*, p. 41; CPF, SRC, Barbaria, bu. 1, fol. 478, letter of 25 Aug 1680, from P. Francesco Gatta in Tunis.

80. De La Motte, *Several Voyages to Barbary*, p. 41.
81. Grammont, "La Course, l'Esclavage, et la Rédemption," pp. 13–14. For a graphic account of such an experience, see *The Narrative of Robert Adams*, reproduced in part in Baepler, *White Slaves, African Masters*, pp. 214–45.
82. Rawlings, *The Famous and Wonderful Recovery*, p. 256.
83. Whitman, *The Price of Freedom*, pp. 33–60.
84. Okeley, *Eben-Ezer,* p. 37; Dan, *Histoire de Barbarie*, p. 407; d'Aranda, *History of Algiers*, p. 14; CPF, SOCG, Barbaria, busta 4, fol. 406, 5 December 1716. Okeley went on to lament that "Alas, I was a very bungler, and understood nothing of the Craft and Mystery of Weaving more or less; but there I wrought till I had spoyled all that I laid my Hands on." After which his master demoted him to a *"filler of Quills* for the other two ... [and there] I continued about a Month."
85. De La Motte, *Several Voyages to Barbary*, p. 45; Grammont, in "La Course," p. 27, claimed the interest on such loans could be higher: 25 percent per trimester, or (presumably) 75 percent per year.
86. Pignon, "L'Esclavage en Tunisie," p. 153.
87. CPF, SRC, Barbaria, bu.1 fol. 153, letter from Fra Agostino de Roberto in Tunis, dated "ca 1649"; ASVat, Gonfalone, bu. 1144, fols. 208r & 208v; Salvago, *"Africa overo Barbaria,"* p. 92, set the sum at 10 *zecchini* (or 15 *talars*) per voyage, in the 1620s.
88. For sample ransoms demanded in Venetian *zecchini,* see ASVat, Gonfalone, bu. 8, fols. 250–3.
89. Salvago, *"Africa overo Barbaria,"* p. 92. Writing at about the same time, João Mascarenhas supports this price: "about two to three pataques [that is, four talers] a month," *Esclave à Alger*, p. 74; Francesco di San Lorenzo, *Breve Relatione*, p. 10, noted that in Tunis in 1654, the price was three pieces of eight a month.
90. On the order of a half a *piastra* for mass: see CPF, SRC, Barbaria, bu. 3, fol. 64, letter of 16 April 1692, from Donato da Cantalupo in Tunis; also, ibid., fol. 21,*relazione* of 28 March 1691, from fr. Francesco da Capranica in Tripoli.
91. CPF, SOCG, Barbaria, bu. 1, fol. 106, letter of 8 November 1684, from fr. Agostino da Messina in Tripoli; for the story of a slave priest in Algiers who, unable to pay off his master, "was therefore sent to work in the Country, where, for the labors given him and for the fatigue, he died," see ibid., fol. 4, letter (no date, but ca. 1713) from P. Emanuele da Cunha Suarez, in Algiers; also ibid., fol. 251, letter of 20 July 1672, from Marcello Costa in Tunis, for a slave priest sent to the galleys "with unbelievable contempt."
92. Okeley, *Eben-Ezer,* pp. 23–4.
93. CPF, SOCG, Barbaria, bu. 3, fol. 482, letter of 5 May 1706, from P. Pietro da Miraglia in Tripoli; ibid., bu. 4, fol. 151, letter of 24 July 1710, also from P. Pietro da Miraglia in Tripoli.
94. Chastelet des Boys, *Revue Africaine*, vol. 12, p. 17; also CPF, SOCG, Barbaria, bu. 5, fol. 606, 10 May 1738, letter from Mariano di Firenze, prefect in Tripoli, for a Cappuchin slave who abjured there.
95. See, for example, CPF, SOCG, Barbaria, bu. 1, fol. 478, letter of 25 August 1680, from P. Francesco Gatta in Tunis; ibid., bu. 3, fol. 123, letter of 30 May 1693, from Maurizio da Lucca in Tripoli.

96. CPF, SOCG, Barbaria, bu; 5, fols. 425–6: two declarations of 1733 from Carlo di Bernardi of Malta and Tomaso Bado of Genoa, both slaves of the Bagno Beliç in Algiers; CPF, SORCG, bu. 255, "Algeri," fol. 33, letter of 17 September 1650 from Algiers.
97. CPR:SRC, Barbaria, bu. 1, fol. 4, letter from P. Emanuele da Cunha Suarez, in Algiers, ca. 1713.
98. See Foss, *A Journal*, p. 26: "On Fridays they hoist a green flag, this being the favorite color of Mahomet. All the slaves at this hour are ordered to leave work, except when they are fitting the corsairs for sea in a hurry. Oftentimes when this is the case they are obliged to work all night."
99. Francesco di San Lorenzo, *Breve Relatione*, p. 10; also Foss, *A Journal*, pp. 28–9: "Many are obliged to sleep every night upon the cold stones, with nothing but the heavens to cover them, for want of money to pay this tribute." Woe to those who said they could pay and then failed to come up with the money at the end of the month, said Foss: "If any one who has slept in a room during the moon [month], has not procured the money, and cannot pay it down, his hands are put into irons behind him, and his legs chained to a pillar every night, until the money is paid. They are released in the morning to go to their work and are chained again at night. Those miserable objects are commonly relieved by the rest of their fellow-sufferers."
100. Rawlins, *The Famous and Wonderful Recovery*, p. 256; Salvago, "Africa overo Barbaria," p. 92; Okeley, *Eben-Ezer*, p. 18; d'Aranda, *History of Algiers*, pp. 9, 18, 32; Dan, *Histoire de Barbarie*, p. 438; Chastelet des Boys, *L'Odyssée*, in *Revue Africaine*, 12 (1868), p. 26; Thédenat, "Les Aventures," p. 159.
101. Okeley, *Eben-Ezer*, pp. 16–17.
102. Chastelet des Boys, *L'Odyssée*, p. 26.
103. Dan, *Histoire de Barbarie*, p. 405; Chastelet des Boys, *L'Odyssée*, pp. 26–7.
104. See, for example, the brawl Okeley got himself into (which "well nigh cost me my Life") when first arriving at his new master's house: Okeley, *Eben-Ezer*, pp. 12–14.
105. Elliot, *A True Narrative*, p. 16.
106. Ibid., p. 17.
107. Okeley, *Eben-Ezer*, pp. 33–4.
108. Chastelet des Boys, *L'Odyssée*, p. 26.
109. Thédenat, "Les Aventures," pp. 159–60.
110. Okeley, *Eben-Ezer*, pp. 14–15.
111. ASV, POLP, bu. 101, "Atti diversi: 1633," letter of Agostino Pinna; Morgan, *Complete History of Algiers*, p. 628.
112. CPF, SOCG, Barbaria, bu. 1, fol. 322, letter of 20 Aug 1675 from P. Marcello Costa in Tunis. Costa wrote that at the moment "there [in Bizerte] one finds around 300 Christians, and they will be there for some years, because they are at present building two vessels of sixty guns, and when they have finished with those, they are going to build some others."
113. Of Giacomo Colombin, who trained ten master shipwrights for the Algerians, it was said that "for each galley [that he built] he could receive as a gift 800 or more ducats, beyond which he was permitted to sell any sort of goods ... for which one can judge that he was a rich man": ASV,

SM, filza 286, 20 September 1633; also ASV, CSD, filza 19, 20 December 1628, petition of Annibal Ricciadei.

114. The Englishman John Rawlings was sold in Algiers in 1622 for around 32 *zecchini,* although he was lame; d'Aranda, nearly twenty years later, was sold for just over 200 *zecchini.* Dan, writing about the same time as d'Aranda, claimed that "the most wretched" slaves sold for 200 or 300 French livres, equal to 75–115 *zecchini:* Dan, *Histoire de Barbarie,* p. 438; also Mafrici, *Mezzogiorno e pirateria,* pp. 104–7.

115. Thus, when Giovanni Battista Barozzi, podestà of Cittanova, was captured by the corsairs of Dulcigno in 1687, along with his wife, daughter, and entourage, the Venetian government took only three months to pay the demanded 15,000 *zecchini;* VMC, Archivio Gradenigo, bu. 171, fol. 144. On Colombin's daring escape, see ASV, SM, filza 286, 20 September 1633.

116. CPF, SOCG, Barbaria, bu. 1, fol. 322, letter of 20 August 1675 from P. Marcello Costa in Tunis; George Elliot, *A True Narrative,* p. 13, described an apparently rather similar *mattamoro* in Salé, in Morocco: "At Evening we were conveyed to our Lodgings... a large Celler under the Street, Arched and supported with two Rows of Pillars; the Light it was furnished with, came through three Holes in the Street strongly Grated; through one of which, by a Ladder of Ropes we descended in this Room, called the King's *Masmoro,* capacious enough to hold 300 Persons ... besides a whole Leystal of Filth, in which, whosoever's lot it was to be there, he must wade up to the Ancles."

117. D'Aranda, *History of Algiers,* pp. 47–8, 156, 158; Okeley, *Eben-Ezer,* p. 20, for an English glover, who set himself up making "Canvas Cloaths for Sea-men that are Slaves;" and p. 35 for mention of when he "espyed some *English men* at Quoits."

118. Ibid., pp. 18–20.

119. De La Motte, *Several Voyages to Barbary,* p. 46; also Laugier de Tassy, *A Complete History,* p. 224.

120. D'Aranda, *History of Algiers,* p. 18: d'Aranda wrote that he was sent "to delve in a Vineyard" outside of Algiers, but this may have been for table rather than wine grapes.

121. D'Aranda, *History of Algiers,* p. 21.

122. Ibid., pp. 17, 21, 157.

123. Venture de Paradis, "Alger au XVIIIᵉ siècle," *Revue Africaine,* vol. 39, p. 314; vol. 40, p. 37.

124. D'Aranda, *History of Algiers,* pp. 13 and 157.

125. Morgan, *Complete History of Algiers,* p. 674; d'Aranda, *History of Algiers,* pp. 152–4. When the Moors came to take delivery of their new anchor, Ali Pegelin ordered his Turkish guards to drive them off "with good Bullspizzles." He then asked how the Italian could have dared to sell such a thing and "*Fontimamma* reply'd, that he thought the Galley would go better being discharg'd of that weight. All the Galley could not forbear laughing at that answer, and *Fontimamma* kept the five Patacoons."

126. Ibid., pp. 13 and 17.

127. Ibid., pp. 186–7.

128. D'Arvieux, *Mémoires,* p. 225.

129. Genovese, *Roll, Jordan, Roll*, pp. 599–609.
130. D'Arvieux, *Mémoires*, p. 225.
131. Sherry Ortner, "Resistance and the Problem of Ethnographic Refusal," pp. 173–93 in *Comparative Studies in History and Society*, 37 (1995), p. 175.
132. Morgan, *Complete History of Algiers*, p. 674; d'Aranda, *History of Algiers*, p. 17.
133. Morgan, *Complete History of Algiers*, p. 675.
134. Beginning with Grammont, "La Course, l'Esclavage, et la Rédemption," pp. 18–19; also, Mafrici, *Mezzogiorno e pirateria*, pp. 107–8.
135. Robert Forster, "Three Slaveholders in the Antilles: Saint-Dominque, Martinique, Jamaica," forthcoming in *The Journal of Caribbean History*.

Chapter 4

1. Okeley, *Eben-Ezer*, p. 21.
2. Knight, *A Relation*, pp. 50–1, claimed that Algiers held "28,000 Families, besides *Jews* uncounted, who cannot be less than 30,000 souls;" Knight, writing of the 1630s, put the number of Christian slaves, "by common probabilitie," at around 16,000, while others, as already noted, put the figure at over twice that. Lanfreducci and Bosio, "Costa e discorsi di Barbaria," pp. 461, 466–7, and 472. D'Arvieux put the ratio in Algiers somewhat lower, giving a total population of "more than 100,000," with 10,000–12,000 "Christian slaves," *Mémoires*, pp. 223 and 224.
3. D'Aranda, *History of Algiers*, p. 99.
4. Ibid.: possibly explained by the precedence given to those many slaves who were selling water on behalf of their masters. Jews' inferior status may have been due to the ambiguous nature of their residency: in cities like Algiers, according to Mascarenhas, they were required to pay 1,800 *doblas* annually for the right to remain; Mascarenhas supports d'Aranda's assessment of low Jewish status in Barbary: see Mascarenhas, *Esclave à Alger*, pp. 75–6.
5. Laugier de Tassy, *A Complete History*, pp. 67–8.
6. Mascarenhas, *Esclave à Alger*, p. 76; Laugier de Tassy, *A Complete History*, p. 61.
7. D'Arvieux, *Mémoires*, pp. 43–4.
8. CPF, SOCG, Barbaria, bu. 3, fol. 420, letter of 28 November 1701, from Fr. Niccolò da Scio in Tripoli; also ibid., bu. 5, fol. 555, letter of 20 October 1735, from slaves in Tunis. On "taking the turban," see Galland, *Histoire de l'Esclavage*, pp. 46–7.
9. D'Aranda, *History of Algiers*, p. 121; also ASVat, Gonfalone, bu. 16, fols. 227–36.
10. Peyssonnel, *Voyage dans les régences*, p. 57, writing of Tunis in the 1720s.
11. D'Aranda, *History of Algiers*, p. 17.
12. Salvago, "Africa overo Barbaria," p. 93; d'Aranda, *History of Algiers*, p. 11; also Francesco di S. Lorenzo, *Breve relatione*, p. 10.
13. Elliot, *A True Narrative*, p. 25. See ASVat, Gonfalone, bu. 1139, fol. 234 (1691); and ibid., bu. 1144, fols. 189–92, letter of expenditures from Cattaro, dated 4 October 1672, listing the cost of two *zecchini* to buy

shoes for around 40 ransomed slaves, "[they currently] being barefoot, so that they can make the journey from Ancona to Rome."

14. Venture de Paradis,"Alger au XVIIIe siècle," in *Revue Africaine*, vol. 39 (1895), p. 39.
15. Foss, *A Journal*, pp. 19–20.
16. Ibid., pp. 30–1. The job was to go to the swamps about 7 miles from town, to cut reeds for stringing up the pasha's runner beans.
17. Genovese, *Roll, Jordan, Roll*, pp. 551–3.
18. See, for example, CPF, SOCG, Barbaria, bu. 5, fols. 65–6 (1725): Letter from the Mission di Tripoli; ibid., fol. 555, 20 October 1735, from the slaves of Tunis; also Salvago, *"Africa overo Barbaria,"* p. 93.
19. Grammont, "La Course," p. 13; Galland, *Histoire de l'Esclavage*, p. 45.
20. Salvago, *"Africa overo Barbaria,"* p. 92; cf., CPF, SOCG, "Barbaria," bu. 1, letter of 12 January 1671, from Gratio Nechet in Tripoli; Foss, *A Journal*, p. 20; Venture de Paradis, "Alger au XVIIIe siècle," *Revue Africaine*, vol. 40, pp. 35–8.
21. Gramaye, *Purchas His Pilgrimes*, p. 280. Gramaye was the only observer to make this claim, however.
22. Laugier de Tassy, *A Complete History*, p. 224.
23. Foss, *A Journal*, p. 123; Grammont, "La Course," p. 21; Mascarenhas, *Esclave à Alger*, p. 171, n. 2.
24. Haëdo cited in Morgan, *Complete History of Algiers*, p. 275; Dan, *Historie de Barbarie,* p. 412. Mascarenhas stated there were just four bagnos in Algiers in the early 1620s, which traces the outline of a growth cycle in the city's "public" slave sector over the course of the century: Mascarenhas, *Esclave à Alger*, p. 71. See also Friedman, "Christian Captives," p. 624, citing Alonso Cano.
25. CPF, SOCG, "Barbaria," bu. 1, fols. 165–6, letter of 12 June 1669, from fra. Mansueto da Castrogiovanni in Tripoli; ibid., fols. 411–12, 4 July 1677, letter from fra. Crisostomo da Genova in Tunis.
26. CPF, SOCG, "Barbaria," bu. 2, fol. 157, letter of 14 July 1685 from Vincenzo da Frascati in Tunis; and fol. 159, letter of 28 June 1685, from Francesco da Monreale in Tripoli; also ibid., bu. 3, fol. 144, letter of 24 October 1693, and fol. 377, both from Lorance in Algiers; ibid., bu. 5, fol. 346, letter of 15 October 1731, from Giuseppe Carta in Tunis; and ibid., bu. 7, fol. 6, letter of 24 March 1761, from Tripoli; and fol. 122, letter of 10 December 1763, from Algiers.
27. Venture de Paradis, "Alger au XVIIIe siècle," in *Revue Africaine*, vol. 40, p. 33.
28. Dan, *Histoire de Barbarie*, p. 412, who went on to list the nine bagnos of Tunis: "the primary two are those of Issouf Dey; the others are the Bagno of Morat Bey; the Bagno of the Master; that of Soliman; that of Sydi Mamet; the Bagno of the Bascia; the Bagno of Mamy; & another recently made, which is that of Cigale." "Since at Tripoly in Barbary the number of slaves there is small," he noted, "they have but one great Bagno."
29. Grammont, "La Course," p. 22; Mascarenhas, *Esclave à Alger*, p. 74; Alberto Sacerdoti, "Le Plan du bagne de Tunis dit de Saint Léonard et de Kara Ahmed," 149–52 in *Revue Africaine*, 94 (1950), n. 4; CPF, SOCG, "Barbaria," bu. 5, fol. 9, letter of 6 December 1723, from Benedetto della

Casa, merchant in Tunis. For Tripoli, see ibid., bu. 1, fols. 115 and 116: no date, but evidently around 1680; and ibid., bu. 2, fols. 123–4, letter of 12 February 1685, from Francesco da Monreale in Tripoli.

30. So said d'Aranda, *History of Algiers*, p. 12, about the bagno of Ali Pegelin; CPF, SOCG, Barbaria, bu. 3, fol. 418, letter of 20 November 1701, from fr. Niccolò da Scio in Tripoli.

31. Thus, Baepler, *White Slaves, African Masters*, p. 37, refers to this sort of narrative strategy as a "rhetorical gesture of erasing local history."

32. Scott and Kerkvliet, *Journal of Peasant Studies*, vol. 13 (1985–6).

33. CPF, SOCG, Barbaria, ibid. bu. 3, fol. 163, 12 December 1693; ibid., bu. 7, fol. 122, 10 December 1763; ibid., bu. 1, fol. 54, no date (but around 1693–4) from the Trinitarians of Algiers.

34. On *papassi*, see Schuchardt, "On Lingua Franca," pp. 26–47, in T. L. Markey, ed., and trans., *The Ethnography of Variation: Selected Writings in Pidgins and Creoles* (Ann Arbor, 1979), pp. 32–3.

35. With the founding of its congregation *De Propaganda Fide* in 1622, Rome committed itself to providing missionaries to preach all over the world, which included Catholic slave populations in Barbary. In the decades that followed, priests arrived in all the major port cities of the Maghreb, generally taking over from slave priests the running of the chapels in each bagno. On successful conversion of Protestants, see, among many examples, CPF, SOCG, Barbaria, bu. 1, fols. 165–6, letter of 12 June 1669 from fra. Mansueto da Castrogiovanni, in Tripoli.

36. CPF, SOCG, Barbaria, bu. 1, fol. 4, undated (but ca. 1713), letter from P. Emanuele da Cunha Suarez, slave priest in Algiers.

37. D'Aranda, *History of Algiers*, p. 23.

38. Ibid., pp. 192–3, titled "A Scuffle between the Spanish and Portuguez Slaves."

39. If this role fell to anyone, it was to the renegades.

40. An excellent survey of this "language of necessity" can be found in Hugo Schuchardt, "On Lingua Franca," pp. 26–47. On "Black English" among North American slaves, see Genovese, *Roll, Jordan, Roll*, pp. 431–41.

41. Example cited in Schuchardt, "Lingua Franca," p. 39.

42. Marott, *A Narrative*, p. 22; d'Aranda, *History of Algiers*, pp. 247–9.

43. Clissold, *The Barbary Slaves*, p. 56.

44. D'Aranda, *History of Algiers*, p. 14; also Schuchardt, "Lingua Franca," pp. 30–1, 38.

45. Foss, *A Journal*, pp. 20 and 28; d'Aranda, *A History of Algiers*, p. 12; Laugier de Tassy, *A Complete History of the Piratical States*, p. 223; d'Arvieux, *Mémoires*, p. 6.

46. ASVat, Gonfalone, bu. 1144, fol. 576, letter of 15 June 1691, from Domenico di Pietro della Gomata, slave in Algiers.

47. Knight, *A Relation*, p. 16; Mascarenhas, *Esclave à Alger*, p. 74; Hees, "Journal d'un voyage," p. 103.

48. Dan, *Histoire de Barbarie*, pp. 309–10; Lanfreducci and Bosio, "Costa e discorsi," p. 473.

49. CPF, SORCG, bu. 254, "Tunisi," fol. 65, letter of 13 March 1664, from le Vacher in Tunis; CPF, SOCG, Barbaria, bu. 1, fols. 165–6, letter of 12 June 1669, from fra. Mansueto da Castrogiovanni in Tripoli.

50. CPF, SOCG, Barbaria, bu. 3, fol. 64, letter of 16 April 1692, from Donato da Cantalupo in Tunis; ibid., fol. 305, letter of 6 September 1696, from Lorance in Algiers; ibid., fol. 418, 20 November 1701, letter of fr. Niccolò da Scio in Tripoli, noting that "If the mass is said in their Chapels, up to 500 from the Bagni come, as well as 300 or more [belonging to] Individuals."

51. D'Aranda, *History of Algiers*, p. 12; Knight, *A Relation*, p. 16; Grammont, "La Course," p. 32.

52. De La Motte, *Several Voyages to Barbary*, p. 42; Laugier de Tassy, *Complete History of the Piratical States of Barbary*, pp. 226–7.

53. Foss, *A Journal*, p. 18; Venture de Paradis, "Alger au xVIIIe siecle," in *Revue Africaine*, vol. 39 (1895), p. 314; ibid., vol. 40 (1896), pp. 33–4; Grammont, "La Course," p. 32.

54. Sacerdoti, "Le Plan du bagne de Tunis," n. 9.

55. Grammont, "La Course," pp. 22–3.

56. D'Arvieux, *Mémoires*, bk. 4, p. 3.

57. CPF, SOCG, Barbaria, bu. 4, letter of 1722, from Tunis; d'Arvieux, *Mémoires*, p. 6.

58. D'Aranda, *A History of Algiers*, pp. 13 and 18; Foss, *A Journal*, p. 24.

59. Francesco di S. Lorenzo, *Breve relatione*, pp. 10–11.

60. CPF, SOCG, Barbaria, bu. 5, fol. 9, letter of 6 December 1723, from Benedetto della Casa in Tunis.

61. On slaves who were scribes at more than one bagno, see CPF, SORCG, "Tunis," bu. 254, "Tunisi," fol. 221; on a scribe throwing the slaves of a private owner out of "his" bagno, see CPF, SOCG, Barbaria, bu. 4, fol. 485, letter of 1722, from the Trinitarians in Tunis.

62. CPF, SOCG, Barbaria, bu. 4, fol. 485, letter of 1721, from Tunis.

63. The petitions might also be signed by the *mayordomo* of the bagno chapel, on whom see below. For such petitions, see, for example, CPF, SOCG, Barbaria, bu. 5, fol. 383, letter of 8 October 1733, from "The Slaves of Tunis;" and CPF, SORCG, bu. 254, "Tunis," fol. 221, letter of November 1668, from "The Christians of the Town and Kingdom of Tunis."

64. D'Arvieux, *Mémoires*, p. 3.

65. Sacerdoti, "Le Plan du bagne," p. 152.

66. Foss, *A Journal*, p. 28; d'Arvieux, *Mémoires*, p. 228.

67. See, for example, the very long dispute between Duchesne, the apostolic vicar, and one Carlo di Bernardi Maltesta, priest slave and *mayordomo* in the Bagno de Sidi Amuda, in Algiers: CPF, SOCG, Barbaria, bu. 5, fols. 397–476, letters dated 1733–34; also CPF, SORCG, "Tunis," bu. 254, fol. 221, November 1668.

68. CPF, SOCG, Barbaria, bu. 1, fols. 411–12, letter of 4 July 1677, from fr. Crisostomo da Genova in Tunis; on the role of the *mayordomos* as alms collectors, see ibid., bu. 4, fol. 246, letter of 25 January 1712, from the slaves of Algiers.

69. Francesco di S. Lorenzo, *Breve relatione*, p. 14. The tavern keepers paid "every year a half piece-of-eight for every barrel [*botte*] of wine, an almost intolerable tribute," CPF, SOCG, "Barbaria," bu. 5, fol. 383, letter of 8 October 1733, from the slave tavern keepers of the bagnos of Tunis. On slave contributions to the chapels, see ibid., fol. 9, 6 December 1723, letter from Benedetto della Casa, in Tunis.

70. CPF, SOCG, Barbaria, bu. 1, fol. 155, letter of 28 August 1668, fr. Girolamo da Sassari in Tunis.
71. Ibid., bu. 6, fols. 207–16, 9 August 1749, letter of Arnoldo Bossu from Algiers; ibid., bu. 3, fol. 418, letter of 20 November 1701, from fr. Niccolò da Scio in Tripoli; and ibid., bu. 2, fols. 123–24, letter of 12 February 1685, from Francesco da Monreale in Tripoli.
72. D'Aranda, *History of Algiers*, p. 12; also Laugier de Tassy, *A Complete History*, pp. 234–5.
73. D'Aranda, *History of Algiers*, p. 157.
74. De la Motte, *Several Voyages*, pp. 66–7.
75. Mascarenhas, *Esclave à Alger*, pp. 62–3, wrote that the hospital in the Bagno of the Pasha in Algiers took in "thirty or forty *pataques* every month," from the product of its stills, about twice what could be collected from the alms of the slaves.
76. Mascarenhas, *Esclave à Alger*, p. 63; Deslandres, *L'Ordre des Trinitaires*, pp. 425–6.
77. Bono, *Corsari barbareschi*, pp. 246–7; Deslandres, *L'Ordre des Trinitaires*, p. 427.
78. It would also seem that slaves of ambiguous status might be lodged in a bagno hospital: for example, the Marionite bishop of Cyprus was put in the hospital of the Bagno Grande in Tripoli during his captivity: CPF, SOCG, Barbaria, bu. 1, fol. 99, letter without place or date (but after 1678), from P. Giovanni da Randazzo, prefect of Tripoli.
79. CPF, SOCG, Barbaria, bu. 1, fol. 87, letter with no date (but after 1693), from Algiers.
80. CPF, SOCG, Barbaria, bu. 3, fol. 349, letter of 30 November 1696, from fr. Benedetto da Fossano in Tunis. Only in 1723 was a substantial hospital opened in Tunis, in the bagno of San Leonardo: see CPF, SORCG, bu. 634, fols. 162–4, 19 June 1722.
81. CPF, SOCG, Barbaria, bu. 3, fol. 349, letter of 30 November 1696, from fr. Benedetto da Fossano, in Tunis; Deslandres, *L'Ordre des Trinitaires*, pp. 427–8.
82. Deslandres, *L'Ordre des Trinitaires*, pp. 427–8; also de La Motte, *Several Voyages*, p. 71.
83. Hospitals were expected to supply sick slaves with "victuals, drink, medicine, and attendance," according to Foss, *A Journal*, pp. 51–2.
84. CPF, SORCG, bu. 634, fols. 162–4.
85. Sacerdoti, "La Plan du bagne;" and d'Aranda, *A History of Algiers*, p. 12, who noted that, in his bagno, there were also taverns on the upper floors.
86. On the poverty of slaves that restricted their drinking to water, see CPF, SOCG, Barbaria, bu. 2, fols. 378–82, letter of 8 January 1689, from P. Daniele in Tripoli.
87. D'Arvieux, *Mémoires*, p. 228.
88. CPF, SOCG, Barbaria, bu. 6, fols. 207–16, letter of 9 August 1749, from Arnoldo Bossu, apostolic vicar in Algiers; ibid., bu. 2, fols. 377–82, letter of 8 January 1689, from fra. Francesco da Capranica in Tripoli.
89. CPF, SOCG, "Barbaria," bu. 2, fols. 378–82, letter of 8 January 1689, from Father Daniele in Tripoli.
90. D'Aranda, *History of Algiers*, pp. 173–4.

91. Dominici, *Trattato*, pp. 27–8.
92. CPF, SOCG, Barbaria, bu. 6, fols. 207–16, letter of 9 August 1749, from P. Bossu in Algiers; also Laugier de Tassy, *A Compleat History*, p. 225.
93. Ibid., p. 65; Venture de Paradis, "Alger au XVIIIᵉ Siècle," in *Revue Africaine*, vol. 40 (1896), p. 37; Mascarenhas, *Esclave à Alger*, p. 75; CPF, SOCG, Barbaria, bu. 5, fol. 393, 23 October 1733, from Pietro di Giovanni, Francesco Merli, and Francesco Vanoso da Milano in Tunis.
94. D'Aranda, *History of Algiers*, 11, 126–7, and 132–3.
95. Mascarenhas, *Esclave à Alger*, pp. 76–7, 91.
96. Ibid., pp. 7–8, 11.
97. From Knight, *A Relation of Seaven Yeares Slaverie*, vol. 2, pp. 50–1; also Davies, *True Relation*, section 2.
98. See also Laugier de Tassy, *A Compleat History*, pp. 65–7.
99. D'Aranda, *History of Algiers*, p. 133; CPF, SOCG, Barbaria, bu. 1, fols. 323–5, letter of 20 August 1675, from P. Marcello Costa in Tunis; on those Europeans who fled Christendom because they "wanted to abandon the Religion and flee from ecclesiastical persecutions," see ibid., bu. 4, fols. 597–8, letter of 24 April 1723, from Cav. Laparelli in Tunis. See also, Lucia Rostagno, *Mi faccio turco* (Rome, 1983), pp. 73–85.
100. De La Motte, *Several Voyages to Barbary*, p. 59; d'Arvieux, *Mémoires*, p. 228.
101. CPF, SOCG, Barbaria, bu. 1, fols. 323–5, letter of 20 August 1675, from Marcello Costa in Tunis.
102. Okeley, *Eben-Ezer*, pp. 34–5; also Morgan, *Complete History of Algiers*, p. 275, on slaves celebrating Christmas by "making merry, and diverting themselves," some by playing at cards.
103. Foss, *A Journal*, p. 38.
104. Foss, *A Journal*, pp. 24–5; Okeley, *Eben-Ezer*, pp. 36–7.
105. For examples, see Knight, *A Relation of Seaven Yeares Slaverie*, p. 15; Okeley, *Eben-Ezer*, p. 37; Saunders, *Of a Most Lamentable Voiage*, p. 13.
106. Mascarenhas, *Esclave à Alger*, pp. 148 and 150.
107. For example, Claude Larquié, "Captifs Chrétiens et esclaves Maghrébins au XVIIIe siècle: une tentative de comparison," pp. 347–64 in *Captius i esclaus a l'Antiguitat i al Món Modern* (Palma de Mallorca, 1996); Friedman, "Christian Captives at 'Hard Labor,'" pp. 617, 622; Morgan, *Complete History of Algiers*, p. 621, for a similar treatment of galley slavery that ends with the comment that on the corsair galleys, "it all is no other than what is daily to be seen in every *Christian* Galley."
108. De La Motte, *Several Voyages to Barbary*, p. 44n; the translator may well have been Joseph Morgan. See also p. 52 and n., where de la Motte sketches out some of the possible punishments employed in Algiers, and the translator snaps back, "Pray, are any of them worse than your own Racks, Wheels, &c.?"
109. Ibid., p. 74, footnote comment by translator; also Friedman, "Christian Captives at 'Hard Labor,'" pp. 626–7.
110. That is, *Histoire de la Barbarie et ses Corsaires* (Paris, 1649), and *Historie van Barbaryen en des zelfs Zee-Roovers* (Amsterdam, 1684).
111. Foss, *A Journal*, pp. 31–44.
112. Morgan, *Complete History of Algiers*, p. 200.
113. Ibid., p. 305.

114. Quoted in Genovese, *Roll, Jordan, Roll,* p. 65.
115. D'Aranda, *History of Algiers,* pp. 14–15, 26–7.
116. Stephen Clissold, *The Barbary Slaves* (New York, 1977), p. 56; also Robin Blackburn, "Slave exploitation and the elementary structures of enslavement," pp. 158–80 in M. L. Bush, ed., *Serfdom and Slavery* (London, 1996), esp. pp. 158–62.
117. For a recent typology of "camps," in a variety of twentieth-century manifestations, see Joël Kotek and Pierre Rigoulot, *Le Siècle des camps* (Paris, 2000), esp. pp. 11–46.
118. Morgan, *Complete History of Algiers,* p. 275.
119. Kotek and Rigoulot, *Le Siècle des camps,* pp. 12–17.
120. Mascarenhas, *Esclave à Alger,* p. 74.
121. Grammont, "La Course," p. 22.

Chapter 5

1. ASVat, Gonfalone, bu. 1144, fol. 596, letter of 14 October 1691 from Cardinal Corsi in Rimini.
2. ASVat, Gonfalone, bu. 1139, fol. 196, baptismal *fede* of 1693.
3. Knight, *A Relation of Seaven Yeares Slaverie,* p. 19.
4. See ASN, SCRC, bu. 14, case #642, 17 August 1678, petition of Pompeo Casciaro del Casale di Maritima (Otranto), "taken with three other Christians in the vineyards of Otranto;" for a guardian of a vineyard, his wife and child, also all taken near Otranto that same year, see ibid., cases #633–5.
5. ASN, SCRC, bu. 14, petitions of Rosa Antonia Monte, and of Angela and Palma Grillo (#581 and #582), of 7 January 1678, and petition #617; also ibid., petition of Angela di Giovanni Tonto of Viesti (in Gargano: case #616), likewise taken "while gleaning grain and barley;" for a woodcutter taken on Monte Sant'Angelo (Gargano), see case #628, 27 May 1678.
6. See ASN, SCRC, bu. 14, petition of Antonio Romanello of Rossano, taken near Strongoli (in Calabria, case #584), of 2 November 1677; ibid. (case #643), 31 Aug 1678: petition of Carlo Mellis of Tursi (Basilicata), captured on a Jesuit plantation near Policoro; for an entire garrison of 23 soldiers – including the lieutenant, the sergeant, two corporals, the drummer, and 18 soldiers – taken from their post near San Ferdinando (Puglia), see ibid., bu. 18, dispatch of 29 January 1780.
7. Thus, ASN, SCRC, bu. 16, case #3264, for someone taken "while fishing within sight of Civitavecchia;" ibid., bu. 14, case #584, of 2 November 1677; also ASVat, Gonfalone, bu. 1139, fols. 57–9, no. 5, for a slave taken "a mile and a half from the port of Ancona;" and fols. 159–60, for 60 fishermen of Pesaro, "enslaved in the face of this city."
8. Baker, *Piracy and Diplomacy,* pp. 121, 142, 156, 174, and *passim.*
9. ASVat, Gonfalone, bu. 1144, fol. 267, *fede* of 29 April 1676.
10. ASN, SCRC, bu. 14, 30 June 1697, cases #1458–61; on Algerian corsairs taking the Christians and leaving the boat, see Baker, *Piracy and Diplomacy,* p. 157.
11. ASV, SCRC, bu. 14, case #630, 14 June 1678.

12. On the limitations on communications during this era, see Fernand Braudel, pp. 415–30 in *The Structures of Everyday Life*, vol. 1 of *Civilization and Capitalism, 15th–18th Centuries*, Siân Reynolds trans. (New York, 1981); also ASN, SCRC, bu. 17, cases #3911–12 dated 18 November 1752.

13. Palermo, Fondo Redenzione dei cattivi (hereafter PFRC), Riveli di cattivati di Palermo (hereafter RP), fol. 102, 24 April 1595: reproduced in Bonaffini, *La Sicilia e i Barbareschi*, pp. 148–9.

14. PFRC, RP, fols. 160–1, 10 September 1595: reproduced in Bonaffini, pp. 153–4.

15. Ascentij also included a lock of his own hair: ASVat, Gonfalone, bu. 1144, fol. 118, letter of 9 August 1667, from Francesco Antonio Ascentij (of Torre di Palma) in Dulcigno. On the cost of paper and envelopes, see ASN, SCRC, bu. 15, cases #2892 and 2893.

16. D'Aranda, however, mentioned such a scribe, called Francis the Student, who "writ Letters for the Slaves of *Dunkirk*," but "without any other reward, save that he would accept of a dish of drink." D'Aranda, *History of Algiers*, pp. 26 and 154–5.

17. See, for example, ASN, SCRC, bu. 14, case #2762, of 12 May 1730, which begins: "Dearest Mother, Already I have sent you a letter by means of a slave who was set free" (but which evidently never arrived); also d'Aranda, *History of Algiers*, p. 24.

18. PFRC, RP, fol. 121, 5 September 1595: reproduced in Bonaffini, pp. 151–2.

19. ASV, CRD, filza 93, 17 September 1680.

20. A good example of such an oration can be found in ASVat, Gonfalone, bu. 8, fols. 319–25, "Litaniæ et Preces Pro Capyiuis recidandæ" dated 1586, including a version of Psalm 136, "Super flumine Babylonis ..."

21. Such questions turn up repeatedly in Holy Office inquests on diviners and magicians: see, for example, ASV, Sant'Uffizio, *processi,* bu. 85 *contra* Zanetta, *meretrice*; bu. 103 *contra* Magdalena da Molin; bu. 105 *contra* Marula Magnata.

22. ASV, Sant'Uffizio, *processi,* bu. 85 *contra* Maddalena, part 6.

23. Providing news about lost relatives was only one of the services provided by Catte and her two *frati santi*: she also was prepared to tell inquirers who had stolen their property, wished them ill, bewitched them, or wanted to marry them: ASV, Sant'Uffizio, *processi,* bu. 85 *contra* Maddalena, parts 1–4 and 7.

24. ASVat, Gonfalone, bu. 1144, fol. 157, anonymous letter of 20 March 1671, from Porto di Fermo.

25. ASN, SCRC, bu. 18, 19 February 1785.

26. ASVat, Gonfalone, bu. 1144, fol. 96, letter of 3 May 1666; also ibid., bu. 1139, fol. 51, no date, but 1670s, from families of 44 fishermen of Senigallia, whose return would "protect their families from the desperation of not having anyone to earn and provide them with sustenance."

27. ASVat, Gonfalone, bu. 1193, fols. 57–9 and 151; bu. 1144, fol. 547; ibid., fol. 619.

28. See, for example, the instance where "They say [Giovanni] is in the hands of the Turks in Tunis, and in the street of Santa Teresa of the Spaniards

they read the letter sent by said Giovanni to his wife": ASN, SCRC, bu. 14, case #577, of 8 January 1678; also ibid., bu. 17, cases #3907–10.

29. P. Camillo di Maria, "Orazione recitata il giorno 5 agosto 1771 nella Metropolitana Chiesa della Città di Palermo in occasione della solenne processione dei Schiavi Cristiani riscattati in Tunisi," concluding section of *Relazione del risatto eseguito l'anno 1771 dei schiavi siciliani esistenti in Tunisi* (Palermo, 1771), p. 54.

30. See, in Venice, ASV, CRD, bu. 47 (15 September 1656), petition of Todero Mauro; also ASV, SM, reg. 75, 19 August 1617, concerning Piero di Dimitri, a slave in Tripoli for 26 years, during which "I was never able to get the news through about my disaster to my only sister (who believed me dead)." For a son seeking to establish his hereditary rights, see ASVat, Gonfalone, bu. 1157, filza 16, petition of 1783, from Leonetto Simonpietri, of Centuri (Corsica).

31. D'Aranda, *History of Algiers*, pp. 27–33: there were still a great many complications, even in this relatively simple case, which stretched d'Aranda's ordeal out for nearly another six months.

32. D'Aranda, *History of Algiers*, p. 31.

33. For some attempted exchanges of slaves, and their attendant difficulties, see, for example, ASVat, Gonfalone, bu. 1157, filza 8, petition of 5 May 1748, from Pietro Miliani of Giglio (Tuscany), slave in Tunis; ASV, POLP, bu. 98, 22 February 1765 (mv); for a surcharge of 100 ducats, see ibid., filza 7, petition of 27 July 1747, from Giuseppe d'Antonio Grandi, in Tunis.

34. ASN, SCRC, bu. 17, cases #3911–12; also bu. 14, cases #2874–5, for a letter of 15 October 1734, from Lodovico di Cesare in Tunis, who asked to be remembered to his mother, brother, sister, sundry uncles and aunts, and "all the neighbors, friends and everybody," closing with the nudge that "you know that Francesco owes me 15 *carlini*, and Nicola de Garella owes me a ducat, and Gioseppo [son of] Aunt Frosina owes me 12 *grane*."

35. ASN, SCRC, bu. 15, cases #2897–2900, 19 April 1735.

36. ASN, SCRC, bu. 7, *fedi* for 1652; bu. 18, 15 March 1783; ASVat, Gonfalone, bu. 1139, fol. 151.

37. ASN, SCRC, bu. 16, cases #3250–4, from Monasterace (Calabria) in August 1738; ASVat, Gonfalone, bu. 1139, fol. 34, no date, possibly before 1710; also ibid., bu. 1157, filze 13 and 14, petitions of 12 March 1770, made on behalf of Antonio Pasquale Mamberti, slave in Tunis.

38. ASN, SCRC, bu. 14, letter of 25 November 1677.

39. The Mother House of the Trinitarians was established near the Sorbonne, in Paris, and known as St. Mathurin: "Mathurins" was also the name commonly given to priests of the order by the French; the daughter houses were founded primarily in France, but also in Spain, Portugal, Luxembourg, Scotland, England, and Ireland. For a history of the order, see Deslandres, *L'Ordre des Trinitaires*.

40. Booklet titled "La Redenzione degli Schiavi sudditi di SSRM, fatta in Algeri, Tunisi, Tripoli, e Costantinopoli da' PP Trinitari Scalzi detti di S. Michele, dedicata a S.A.R. Maria Antonia Ferdinanda, duchessa di Savoja, colla Orazione fatta in tale Occasione dall'Illmo e Rev.^{mo} Sig.^{re} Abate Pietro Giochino Caissotti di Chiusano" (Torino, 1761), p. 22.

41. On the foundation of the Neapolitan Santa Casa, see ASN, SCRC, bu. 1; also Bono, *I Corsari barbareschi*, pp. 283–5.

42. ASVat, Gonfalone, bu. 1140, "Decreta Redemptionis," fol. 8, 3 February 1582.

43. Thus, the Venetians contacted the Romans, while those in Palermo wrote to Rome, Venice, Genoa, and Naples for copies of their organizations' charters: ASVat, Gonfalone, bu. 1144, fol. 52; Bonaffini, *La Sicilia e i Barbareschi*, p. 89; also Bono, *I Corsari Barbareschi*, pp. 283, 286, 300, 308–9; Marco Lenci, *Lucca, il mare e i corsari barbareschi nel XVI secolo* (Lucca, 1987), pp. 103–4; ASVat, Gonfalone, bu. 8, fols. 579–82.

44. Mafrici, *Mezzogiorno e pirateria*, pp. 133–4; ASVat, Gonfalone, bu. 1140, "Decreta Redemptionis," fols. 3–6.

45. Sergio Pagano, *L'Archivio dell'Arciconfraternita del Gonfalone: Cenni storici e inventario* (Vatican City, 1990), pp. 11–33.

46. See ASN, SCRC, bu. 1, "Notizie sulla Fondazione della Santa Casa;" also Salvatore Bono, *Siciliani nel Maghreb* (Palermo, 1989), pp. 16–17, for the example in Palermo; ASVat, Gonfalone, bu. 1140, "Decreta redemptionis," fol. 3.

47. Antonio Borzacchiello, "Carità: Decumano massimo," pp. 7–30 in (various eds.) *Corsari "turchi" e barbareschi: prigionieri, schiavi, riscatti: atti del 2. convegno di studi: Ceriale, 3 giugno 1989* (Ceriale, 1992), pp. 20–1.

48. ASVat, Gonfalone, bu. 8, fol. 55; Bono, *Siciliani nel Maghreb*, p. 17.

49. ASVat, Gonfalone, bu. 1140, "Decreta redemptionis," fol. 3v.

50. ASVat, Gonfalone, bu. 1139, fols. 123 and 179 (no dates, but apparently 1670s and 1690s respectively); the whole story of the battle over the rights is spelled out in ibid., bu. 1144, fols. 385–479.

51. Braudel, *The Mediterranean*, pp. 886–7.

52. ASV, POLP, bu. 98, *Parti et ordini concernenti alla liberatione de' poveri schiavi*, 19 February 1586 m.v. (in the Venetian calendar; 1587 by modern calculations); 3 June 1588; Bono, *Siciliani nel Maghreb*, p. 17; ibid., *I Corsari barbareschi*, pp. 283–4.

53. ASV, Senato Terra, reg. 45, 20 October 1565; ASV, POLP, bu. 98, 19 February 1586 m.v.; ibid., *Parti et ordini concernenti alla liberatione de' poveri schiavi*, 15 February 1614 m.v.; also Davis, "Slave Redemption in Venice, 1585–1797," pp. 454–87 in J. Martin and D. Romano, eds, *Venice Reconsidered: The History and Civilization of an Italian City State 1297–1799* (Baltimore, 2000), pp. 456–67.

54. Bonaffini, *La Sicilia e i Barbareschi*, pp. 25–32; also ASVat, Gonfalone, bu. 1144, fols. 37–40.

55. See, in particular, ASVat, Gonfalone, bu. 8, fols. 266–316 (filza 65), dated 1702 and titled "Informazioni di lite nella causa vertente tra la Ven. Arciconfraternita del Confalone da una parte e li RR.PP. Trinitari della Redenzione de Schiavi e dell'Ordine di S. Maria della Mercede della Redenzione de Schiavi dall'altra sopra la communicazione dell'Indulgenze et il Riscatto de' Schiavi."

56. Bonaffini, *La Sicilia e i Barbareschi*, pp. 66–72.

57. On the Genoese coral fishers, see Borzacchiello, "Carità: Ducumano Massimo," p. 20; on Venetian fishermen, whose confraternity of San Niccolò gave 10 ducats toward freeing each enslaved member, see ASV,

POLP, bu. 98, *Senato parti*, 24 August 1724, 25 May 1725, and 4 May 1765; ibid., bu. 102, filza 185, 15 April 1765.

58. ASV, POLP, bu. 98, *Parti et ordini*, 15 February 1614 and 6 June 1630; 28 May 1722; bu. 99, Senato Parte, 16 May 1671; ASV, Senato Terra, filza 1202, 4 February 1695 m.v.

59. ASN, SCRC, bu. 13, 31 October 1668, 5 August 1681.

60. Knight, *A Relation of Seaven Yeares Slaverie*, 2, pp. 51–2.

61. ASN, SCRC, bu. 5, 5 August 1703; CPF, SOCG, "Barbaria," bu. 7, fols. 129–50, report of 10 December 1763, from Teodoro Groiselle, apostolic vicar in Algiers.

62. According to Paul Baepler, to release just 87 sailors, the Americans paid "around a million dollars or roughly one-sixth of the federal budget": Baepler, *White Slaves*, p. 8.

63. ASV, POLP, bu. 98, *Parti et ordini*, 3 June 1588, 4 February 1695 m.v.; bu. 99, *Terminazioni*, 11 April 1608, 8 February 1622 m.v., 14 August 1669, 19 April and 15 January 1675 m.v. For further efforts on the part of the Provveditori, see Davis, "Slave Redemption in Venice," pp. 466–7.

64. For the benefit of the Gonfalone, Rome allowed ecclesiastics to leave up to 300 ducats to the arch-confraternity, out of fortunes that otherwise would have entirely reverted to the papacy: ASVat, Gonfalone, bu. 1144, fols. 37–44, item 7.

65. ASV, POLP, bu. 99, *Senato Parte*, 12 February 1585 m.v. ASV, SP, reg. 45, 20 October 1565.

66. ASVat, Gonfalone, bu. 8, fol. 426 (from Velletri), fol. 456 (Cingoli), fol. 474 (Fermo), fol. 507 (Torre Santa Maria), fol. 519 (Monte Nuovo).

67. D'Aranda, for example, had negotiations underway for his exchange in less than a year and was back in Christian territory just eighteen months after his capture; the papal proto-notary Jean-Baptiste Gramaye was held in Algiers for only six months. Most of the other slaves who wrote of their experiences during this period were held for at least five years, however, and got away by escaping.

68. Giovanni Paolo Ricolui, *Discorso in occasione della solenne Processione fatta da M.R.R.P.P. della Santissima Trinità del Riscatto degli Schiavi del Convento di S. Michele, li 18. Ottobre 1739* (Turin, 1740), p. 12; also ASVat, Gonfalone, bu. 1144, fol. 193, anonymous letter of 11 November 1672; also bu. 8, fols. 474, 507, and 519.

69. ASVat, Gonfalone, bu. 1144, f. 588.

70. See, for example, ASVat, Gonfalone, bu. 1139, fol. 169.

71. See, for example, the differential in ransom prices in the printed 1726 *Catalogo delli schiavi Christiani*, following fol. 582 in ASVat, Gonfalone, bu. 8; also bu. 1144, fol. 339, 6 May 1678, letter from Francesco Bucchia in Cattaro.

72. See, for example, the list (undated but evidently of the 1660s) of seventeen slaves from Ancona, fully twelve of whom in fairly short order ended up in Barbary.

73. ASN, SCRC, bu. 15, cases #2879–81; also ASVat, Gonfalone, bu. 1139, fol. 124.

74. ASVat, Gonfalone, bu. 1139, fol. 124.

75. D'Aranda, *History of Algiers*, pp. 102–4.
76. ASVat, Gonfalone, bu. 1139, fol. 143; also Dominici, *Trattato*, pp. 27–9.
77. D'Aranda, *History of Algiers*, pp. 102–3; Dan, *Histoire de la Barbarie*, pp. 370–85. On Christian attitudes towards "polluted" renegades, see Scaraffia, *Rinnegati*, pp. 51–3 and 86–9; and Rostagno, *Mi faccio turco*, pp. 5–23.
78. ASN, SCRC, bu. 16, case #3247; also bu. 14, case #2762, where Giuseppe Corso wrote to his mother from Tunis in 1729, threatening that "should I see that you have abandoned me, certainly I will commit some error and it will be on your soul;" also bu. 17, case #3914, from Giacomino del Vechio in Algiers.
79. The beadles were required to make the rounds at mass every Sunday and on the day of their church's patron saint, bringing in their take every two months; they were liable to a fine of 25 *lire* if they fell short at the collecting or the consigning: see ASV, POLP, bu. 99, 21 August 1721; bu. 101, 8 February 1775 (m.v.); bu. 114, 8 July 1735.
80. On the duties of the *succolettori* see ASV, POLP, bu. 101, *terminazioni* of 11 September 1762 and 17 August 1769.
81. ASN, SCRC, bu. 13, 27 November 1669 and 1 June 1679.
82. Two *giuli* if they traveled on foot and 3 if they went on horseback: ASVat, Gonfalone, bu. 8, files 4, 5, and 9.
83. ASV, POLP, bu. 101, 8 February 1775 m.v.; ASVat, Gonfalone, bu. 8, fol. 456.
84. ASVat, Gonfalone, bu. 8, filza 5, note 22.
85. Two *giuli* if they traveled on foot and $3\frac{1}{2}$ if they went on horseback: ASVat, Gonfalone, bu. 8, filze 4, 5, and 9.
86. ASVat, Gonfalone, bu. 63, fol. 154, 19 February 1725.
87. ASV, POLP, bu. 101, loose sheet titled, "Foglio Dimostrativo l'Elemosine pervenute al Prov.ᵒʳ Ori et Argenti in Zecca per conto Riscato Poveri Schiavi nel Decenio 1 March 1780–28 February 1789 ..."
88. ASVat, Gonfalone, bu. 8, fols. 456, 470, 512.
89. ASVat, Gonfalone, bu. 8, fols. 416, 442, 451, 456, 465, 472, 482, 501, 514.
90. ASVat, Gonfalone, bu. 1144, fols. 37–40; also ASV, POLP, bu. 101, *termi - nazione* of 29 July 1630.
91. ASVat, Gonfalone, bu. 8, fol. 451; also fols. 435 and 463.
92. ASVat, Gonfalone, bu. 8, fol. 474; also fol. 522, from Ancona.
93. ASVat, Gonfalone, bu. 8, fols. 336–45, 517, and 526; ASN, SCRC, bu. 7, will of D. Sebastiano Fenice, dated 18 July 1656; and ibid., bu. 13, will of Cesare Balsamo, dated 31 October 1668; also ASVat, Gonfalone, bu. 730, (*Istrumenti*), fol. 77. On the other hand, those Venetian slaves who were lucky enough to be from the specific parish of Santa Marina, benefited from the 1544 will of their parish priest: ASV, POLP, bu. 101, *testamenti*, 24 December 1544.
94. ASVat, Gonfalone, bu. 1144, fols. 37–44.
95. Calvini, "Opera sanremasche per la redenzione degli schiavi," p. 34.
96. ASVat, Gonfalone, bu. 1144, fol. 539. Eventually Mazzocati received funds from the Gonfalone.
97. ASVat, Gonfalone, bu. 8, filza 4, part 1.

98. ASVat, Gonfalone, bu. 1139, fol. 55.
99. ASVat, Gonfalone, bu. 1144, fols. 121, 549, 570, and 574.
100. See, for example, ASV, SM, filza 323, 24 March 1639; also ASV, POLP, bu. 114, para. 9.
101. In Naples, these printed forms turn up as early as the 1690s. See, for example, ASN, SCRC, bu. 14, cases #1458–61; also bu. 16, #3250–4, which include printed baptismal *fedi, fedi* to be filled out by the mayor, and a hand-written *fede* from Algiers. Also ASVat, Gonfalone, bu. 1139, fols. 196, 198, and 208.
102. ASN, SCRC, bu. 7, *fedi* from Massa Lubrense (near Sorrento), dated 1658; also ibid., bu. 14, #628, 27 May 1678.
103. ASN, SCRC, bu. 7, *fedi* dated 18 April and 12 May 1662.
104. An example, written by Gabriele da Montecuolo, the Capuchin apostolic vicar in Tunis on 16 February 1715, can be found in ASVat, Gonfalone, bu. 1139, fol. 27. On the requirement of having such a *fede* to be ransomed, see ASV, POLP, bu. 99, *terminazioni,*11December 1713 and 1 May 1736.
105. ASN, SCRC, bu. 15, cases #2882–8, 10 November 1734, and case #2901, 30 January 1735; ibid., bu. 16. case #3267, 16 May 1739; also ASVat, Gonfalone, bu. 1139, fols. 25–6.
106. "Catalogo di cinque cento venti schiavi riscattati nel presente Anno del Giubileo 1675" (Rome, 1675), p. 8.
107. ASN, SCRC, bu. 9, note 20; also ASV, POLP, bu. 98, 2 March 1762. It would also, of course, provide important news to the dead slaves' "poor wives and relatives" about their civil and economic status.
108. ASVat, Gonfalone, bu. 8, filza 14.
109. ASV, POLP, bu. 99, *terminazione* of December 1668; ibid., bu. 114, para. 10; ASN, SCRC, bu. 7, 12 May 1662, 3 November 1662; ASVat, Gonfalone, bu. 729, fol. 30, 14 September 1749.
110. ASV, POLP, bu. 101, loose paper, dated 27 March 1762.
111. ASN, SCRC, bu. 17, cases #3907–10, from 1751.
112. The *Cristo* was apparently so named from the image of Christ that it bore: ASV, POLP, bu. 98, *Senato Parte* of 16 April 1726; and ibid., bu. 99, *terminazione* of 18 January 1712, m.v. According to Mafrici, *Mezzogiorno e pirateria,*p. 138, the term*albarano* derived from the Spanish*albarán,*for a slip or chit; also see ASN, SCRC, bu. 7, for a pre-printed*albarano* of 4 February 1719.
113. Though with the near-collapse of the Santa Casa in the 1660s, this had to be reduced to 25 ducats; later the payout was returned to 50 and then increased to 75 and then 100 ducats by the 1730s: see ASN, SCRC, bu. 13, 5 August 1703; bu. 16, case #3277, of 1738; also Mafrici, *Mezzogiorno e pirateria*, pp. 136–7; for the Venetian notes of 1595–1625, see ASV, POLP, bu. 103, *Zornal Primo.*
114. At least this was the policy of the Santa Casa. For eleven slaves who were physically "presented freed in our said Royal House of Redemption," see ASN, SCRC, bu. 13, 13 July 1689. For one Rocco Rorsi of Burano, who was issued a *Cristo* in 1697, had lost it, and was still enslaved in 1712, see ASV, POLP, bu. 99, *terminazione* of 18 January 1712, m.v.

115. ASV, POLP, bu. 98, *Senato Parti* of 8 March 1628, 16 May 1671, 23 August 1724, and 5 May 1765; also ASV, CRD, filza 34, 19 October 1643.

116. ASN, SCRC, bu. 9, redemptive list with alternative sources of funds for some slaves, fols. 3–7; for the various sources of funds sought by Venetians, see ASV, CRD, filza 34, 19 October 1643; and filza 93, 16 January 1680 m.v.

117. The 190 scudi Elena had been promised were worth just over 230 pieces of eight. ASVat, Gonfalone, bu. 1139, fol. 102, no date, but 1670s.

118. ASV, POLP, bu. 98, Senate file from 16 May 1671.

119. ASN, SCRC, bu. 16, case #3267.

120. In Dulcigno there were said to be around 400 slaves, "the greater part of these from Puglia [and] from Sicily": ASVat, Gonfalone, bu. 1144, fol. 588, letter dated 16 August 1691.

121. Thus, ASVat, Gonfalone, bu. 1139, fol. 169; also ibid., bu. 1144, fol. 195, *fede* of 14 December 1672; ibid., fol. 201, for such a safe conduct pass, dated 1 August 1672, in Italian and Turkish.

122. ASVat, Gonfalone, bu. 1144, fol. 552, letter dated 20 June 1691, from Dulcigno.

123. Such requests from slave owners, at least those in Dulcigno, were not uncommon: see ASVat, Gonfalone, bu. 8, fols. 250–3 and ibid., bu. 1139, fols. 57–9.

124. Such instances, though termed "rare and extraordinary cases," still demonstrate remarkable *laissez-faire* on the part of the Venetian state: see ASV, POLP, bu. 99, *terminazioni*, 7 June 1721 and 2 August 1723.

125. ASVat, Gonfalone, bu. 16, fol. 227, of the travel diary of fra Paolo Maria da Matelica, titled "Giornale de l'affare del Riscatto," beginning on 11 February 1729; also Bombard, "Les Vicaires apostoliques," *Revue tunisi-enne*, 2, p. 584. For the income and outlay of the Gonfalone in the seventeenth century, see ASVat, Gonfalone, bu. 1139, "Ristretto delle Somme de denari depositati nel Sacro Monte della Pietà di Roma," running from 1648 to 1702, which indicates especially low payments in the 1650s and early 1680s.

126. "Catalogo di cinque cento venti schiavi," p. 8.

127. ASVat, Gonfalone, bu. 1144, fols. 207–10, dated 16 January 1672, and fol. 484, letter of 1 December 1685, from Giovanni Bolizza in Cattaro; also CPF, SOCG, "Barbaria," bu. 3, fol. 414, letter of 8 September 1701, from Lorance in Algiers; ibid., bu. 4, fol. 585, letter of 10 February 1723, from Cardinal Pico in Sinigaglia.

128. See *Catalogus captivorum per patres Johannem à Virgine, Michaelem à S. Raphaele, & Benedictum à S. Josepho Ordinis Excalceatorum Sanctissimae Trinitatis Redemptionis Captivorum Alumnos Juliae Caesarae, vulgò Algieri anno proximè elapso* (Rome, 1756), p. 37.

129. The Gonfalone allowed "10 or 15 more [scudi]" if absolutely necessary, the Sicilians up to 150 scudi: ASVat, Gonfalone, bu. 1139, fol. 306; Bonaffini, *La Sicilia e i Barbareschi*, p. 81.

130. Knight, *A Relation of Seaven Yeares Slaverie*, p. 8. The Bey of Tunis played a similar negotiating trick on a pair of Jesuit redeemers in the 1720s: see ASVat, Gonfalone, bu. 16, fols. 227–36, entry for 2 March 1729.

131. ASV, POLP, bu. 98, letter of 21 August 1764, from fra. Ignazio di San Giuseppe in Algiers; also ibid., bu. 99, 10 January 1764, m.v.
132. Bonaffini, *La Sicilia e i Barbareschi*, pp. 98–9.
133. ASVat, Gonfalone, bu. 1139, fols. 355–6, titled "Imputations and Duress done by the Pasha and the Janissaries of Algiers to the Redemptive Fathers of Spain and Portugal."
134. ASVat, Gonfalone, bu. 1139, fols. 369–74 and 379–83; also Bono, "La Missione dei Cappuccini," p. 154.
135. Francesco Valesio, *Diario di Roma*, 6 vols., edited by Gaetana Scano (Milano, 1977), vol. 1, entry for 12 August 1701; also ASV, POLP, bu. 98, letter of 21 August 1764, from fra. Ambrogio di S. Agostino in Algiers.
136. Larquié, "Le Rachet des Chrétiens," p. 326.
137. Based on *Relatione delli schiavi christiani riscattati l'anno 1662* (Rome, 1663).
138. *Redemptiones Captivorum. Constantinopoli, & Tripoli liberatorum per Familiam Redmptricem Discalceatorum SSme Trinitas, Provinciarum Germaniæ, & Status Veneti* (Rome, 1730?).
139. *Relazione de gli Schiavi riscattati in Algeri per li RR, PP. Trinitari Scalzi del Riscatto della Congregazione di Spagna l'anno 1720* (Rome, 1721).
140. Or even "at the head of the list": ASVat, Gonfalone, bu. 1139, fols. 173, 175, 177, 270, 293, and 295.
141. D'Arvieux, *Mémoires*, p. 267.
142. ASVat, Gonfalone, bu. 1139, fol. 157, letter from Padre Biaggio di Turena (no date, but 1670s).
143. CPF, SOCG, Barbaria, bu. 1, fol. 325, letter of 20 August 1675, from Marcello Costa in Tunis.
144. ASV, POLP, bu. 102, filza 11, 1 July 1765.
145. See, for example, ASV, Sant'Uffizio, bu. 87/1, 9 April 1630; bu. 98/1, 23 April 1643; bu. 98/2.
146. Captain Cook, on his maiden voyage to the Pacific in 1768, lost about two-fifths of his original crew.
147. Foss, *A Journal*, pp. 54–6.
148. Grammont, "Relations," pp. 408–48 in *Revue Africaine* 23 (1879), p. 427.
149. ASV, POLP, busta 103, file titled "1792, carte pel riscatto di 50 schiavi liberati in Tunisi," folio no. 44; cf., Marott, *A Narrative*, pp. 67–8; Giuseppe Bonaffini, *Un mare di paura: il Mediterraneo in età moderna* (Caltanissetta, 1997); ASV, CRD, filza 24, petition of 18 April 1633, from Marco de Francesco Piccolo da Chioza.
150. Piero Ottoni, "Gli Italiani e il Mare," *La Repubblica*, 7 August 1997.
151. Fondo Salvatore Marino, Palermo, Carte sciolte, no. 204. My thanks to Annì Governale for bringing this to my attention and providing a translation from the original Sicilian.

Chapter 6

1. ASN, SCRC, bu. 16, cases #3262–3, letter of 8 December 1738, by Nicolò Comodari in Tripoli; and case #3267, letter of 16 May 1739, by Giuseppe Lecciuga in Tunis.

2. Caissotti, "La Redenzione degli Schiavi," p. 14.
3. ASVat, Gonfalone, bu. 1139, fol. 118, no date; ASN, SCRC, bu. 14, case #624: Ascea is in the territory of Salerno; also ibid., bu. 16, case #3281, letter of 8 August 1739, from Giuseppe Tricarico in Tunis; and cases #2901-7, letter of 20 January 1735, from Erasmo Antonio Russo in Algiers.
4. Ibid., bu. 7, from Aniello Russo in Tunis, dated 22 February 1651; also bu. 18, group letter from Algiers, dated 10 October 1780.
5. Okeley, *Eben-Ezer,* p. 21.
6. ASV, CRD, filza 29, 1 September 1638, petition from Iseppo di Antonio Tesser; also ibid., filza 44, 12 August 1653, petition from Gasparo di Piero.
7. CPF, SOCG, "Barbaria," bu. 1, fols. 107 and 175.
8. ASVat, Gonfalone, bu. 1139, fol. 259, no date.
9. See, for example, ASN, SCRC, bu. 15, case #2901; and bu. 16, case #3281.
10. Ibid., bu. 14, cases #2897-2900.
11. Or at least threatened to do so: ASVat, Gonfalone, bu. 1139, fol. 255; and ibid., bu. 1144, fol. 205.
12. ASV, POLP, bu. 103, no. 47; Bombard, "Les Vicaires apostoliques," in *Revue Tunisienne,* 2(1895), p. 584.
13. D'Arvieux, *Mémoires,* pp. 167-8.
14. On the Trinitarian hospital in Algiers, see de La Motte, *Several Voyages to Barbary,* pp. 66-71.
15. As indeed they have been called by some scholars: Ellen G. Friedman, "Merchant Friars in North Africa: the Trade in Christian Captives," pp. 94-8 in *The Maghreb Review,* 12 (1987).
16. On the position of the Trinitarians in Italy, see Bono, *I Corsari barbareschi,* pp. 318-19; and Davis, "Slave Redemption in Venice," pp. 468-70.
17. For all the lists and explanatory comments, see ASV, POLP, bu. 98, Senato Rettori, filza 308, 13 May 1762.
18. ASV, POLP, bu. 98, Senato Parte, 2 March 1762; VMC, Provinenze diverse, bu. 515, fol. 77; ibid., bu. 516/III, fol. 11.
19. Camillo di Maria, "Orazione," p. 45.
20. *Relazione ... dei schiavi siciliani,* p. 32; Valesio, *Diario,* entry of 12 August 1701; *Catalogo ... del riscatto degli schiavi, del Real Convento di S. Maria di Caravaggio in Monforte,* p. 6; also ASV, POLP, bu. 103, "Processione schiavi."
21. Friedman, "Merchant Friars," p. 95.
22. The Venetians put on no fewer than eight processions between 1740 and 1761, for anywhere from 40 down to just four ex-slaves: VMC, Ms. Gradenigo, bu. 171, fols. 147-69.
23. Which went to pay for the military escort: ASV, POLP, bu. 98, *Summario de' Decreti,* Senato Parte, 17 December 1792; bu. 100, *Terminazioni,* 15 January and 1 February 1764 m.v.; bu. 103, *1792, Carte pel Riscatto,* fols. 21-3.
24. As an indication of the discrepancies between the cost of staging processions and what they might bring in through alms, the *scuola* of the SS^{ma} Trinità spent 260 ducats between 1748 to 1762 on seven "processioni per schiavi riscatti," and took in on those same seven occasions only 64 ducats in contributions: ASV, POLP, bu. 14, *1762, Bilanzo, Scoso e Spese.*
25. See, for example, "Catalogo di cinque cento venti schiavi," pp. 11-12.

26. For a good description of quarantine in Venice at the end of the 1600s, see Du Mont, *A New Voyage to the Levant*, pp. 387–97.
27. CPF, SOCG, Barbaria, bu. 5, fol. 441, letter from Duchesne in Algiers, 23 October 1733. On procuring shoes for the slaves, see ASVat, Gonfalone, bu. 1144, fol. 191.
28. ASVat, Gonfalone, bu. 1144, fols. 531–2, letter of 4 September 1686, from Cav. Boliza in Ancona.
29. See ASV, POLP, bu. 103, "Processioni schiavi." In Venice's 1764 procession there were

    Two great placards [*soleri*], one of which showed the Apparition of the Angel – to Saint Giovanni di Malta, founder of the Order of the Most Holy Trinity and to Pope Innocent III – who approved [the order] with his hands crossed over two Slaves, one Christian, the other Moor. Above the Angel one saw displayed the Symbol of the Most Holy Trinity for which the Order is named, and at [his] feet the two Companion Saints, Giovanni di Malta and Felice di Valois. The other [placard] represented a prison in Barbary with two Trinitarian Fathers, who, next to those Deys and Great [ones] are contracting for the Ransom of some Slaves.

30. Whereas, the Venetians might have as many as four participating confraternities: ASV, POLP, bu. 100, 11 January 1764 m.v.; *Relazione ... dei schiavi siciliani*, p. 29.
31. See, *Discorso di Giovanni Paolo Riccolui ... in occasione della solenne Processione fatta da' M.R.R.P. della Santissima Trinità del riscatto degli Schiavi ... li 18 ottobre 1739* (Turin, 1740), pp. 4–5; *Relazione ... dei schiavi siciliani*, pp. 31–2; ASV, POLP, bu. 103, "Processione schiavi," and fol. 92, "Modo con cui sarà formata la Processione;" also *Catalogo degli schiavi redenti dall'anno 1750, fino al corrente 1764 in Costantinopoli, Algeri, Tunis, e Tripoli, &c., da' PP. Trinitarj Scalzi del riscatto degli schiavi, del Real Convento di S. Maria di Caravaggio in Monforte* (Milan, 1764). For the musical arrangements and ordering of the Roman procession of 1701, see "Relacion verdadera del SOLEMNISSIMO TRIUNFO con que entrò en la Corte Romana la Redempcion, que execution en Tunez los Reverendos Padres Trinitarios Descalços" (Madrid, 1701).
32. Ricolui, *Discorso*, p. 5; *Relazione ... dei schiavi siciliani*, pp. 30–1; also Bonaffini, *La Sicilia e i Barbareschi*, p. 88.
33. *Relazione ... dei schiavi siciliani*, pp. 30–1; ASV, POLP, bu. 103, "Processione schiavi."
34. For greater specifics on the Venetian redemptive procession, see Davis, "Slave Redemption in Venice," pp. 471–6.
35. *Relazione ... dei schiavi siciliani*, pp. 33–4.
36. ASV, POLP, bu. 103, "Processione schiavi;" also *Relazione ... dei schiavi siciliani*, p. 35. In Rome, in 1661, at the convent of the Mercedarians, "all the ransomed ones were given a sumptuous and splendid lunch, served at table [by] many devoted lords and knights, with the Most Reverend Father Provincial, and all the other most important Fathers of the Order," from "Catalogo de' schiavi riscattati," p. 8.
37. By way of comparison to the 2,500 ducats for Venice's procession of 1764, it cost three Trinitarian fathers less than 500 ducats to travel to Algiers and

Tunis, bring the slaves back, and feed them while aboard ship and in quarantine.

38. Especially young women and boys: ASVat, Gonfalone, bu. 1144, fols. 208–9; also CPF, SORCG, bu. 254, "Tunisi," fol. 213.
39. Naturally, those who, like d'Aranda, arranged for their own release, had little or nothing to do with either the ransoming orders or their attendant rituals.
40. ASV, POLP, bu. 103, "Processione schiavi."
41. Camillo di Maria, "Orazione," p. 46.
42. ASV, POLP, bu. 103, "Processione schiavi."
43. Ricolui, "Discorso," p. 12.
44. Camillo di Maria, "Orazione," pp. 47 and 67.
45. Also, VMC, Mss Gradenigo, bu. 171, f. 168.
46. Ricolui, "Discorso," pp. 21–3.
47. ASV, POLP, bu. 103, "1792, Carte pel riscatto di 50 schiavi liberati in Tunisi," cases 18, 39, 41, 42, 44, 47, and 49.
48. ASV, POLP, bu. 103, "Processione schiavi." For such petitions and the *parte* with which the Venetian Senate granted them, see, for example, ASV, SM, filza 221, 19 April 1619; filza 313, 2 September 1637; filza 347, 9 July 1642; filza 398, 12 November 1647.
49. ASVat, Gonfalone, bu. 1144, fol. 577; also ASN, SCRC, bu. 16, case #3247.
50. My thanks to Els van Buren for pointing this out.
51. ASN, SCRC, bu. 14, cases #2901–10; also Okeley, *Eben-Ezer,* p. 22.
52. ASVat, Gonfalone, bu. 1144, fol. 118, letter from Torre di Palme, dated 15 June 1667.
53. Capra, "Discorso," p. 8.
54. Both quotes from Caissotti, "La Redenzione degli Schiavi," pp. 12 and 19.
55. Morgan Godwyn, *The Negro's & Indians Advocate, Suing for the Admission into the Church* (London, 1680), p. 28.
56. See Francesco di S. Lorenzo, *Breve relatione;* also *Discorso d'Enrico Capra della Compagnia di Gesù in occasione degli Schiavi Liberati e condotti da Costantinopoli a Venezia ... la Vigilia di Pentecoste 1727* (Venice, 1727); also Riccolui, *Discorso,* see also Carolyn Prager, "'Turkish' and Turkish Slavery: English Renaissance Perceptions of Levantine Bondage," pp. 57–64 in *Centerpoint,* 2 (1976); Morgan, *Complete History,* pp. 516–17.
57. Morgan, *Complete History,* p. 517.
58. In particular, Humphrey Fisher, *Slavery in the History of Muslim Black Africa* (New York, 2001); and Ronald Segal, *Islam's Black Slaves* (New York, 2001).
59. Robin Blackburn, *The Making of New World Slavery: From the Baroque to the Modern, 1492–1800* (London, 1996), pp. 12–20, 79–82; quote from Anthony Pagden, "The Children of Ham," review of Blackburn in *Times Literary Supplement,* 2 May 1997.
60. *The Diary of Samuel Pepys,* Robert Latham and William Matthews, eds., 10 vols. (Berkeley, 1970–83), vol. 3 (1661), pp. 33–4; Borsteinn Helgason, in "Historical Narrative as Collective Therapy," pp. 277–90, identifies no fewer than three sagas dealing with the Moroccan-Algerian raids on the Icelandic coast in 1627, collected and edited by Jón Borkelsson in a volume titled *Tyrkjaránid á Íslandi* (Reykjavik, 1906–1909); the novel and pastiche enslavement narrative, by Royall Tyler, is titled *The Algerine Captive: or, the Life and Adventures of Doctor Updike Underhill [pseudo.], six years a prisoner among the*

Algerines and was originally published in 1797 (Hartford, 1810; reprint: Gainesville, FL, 1967, Jack B. Moore, ed.).

61. Salvago, pp. 93–4. On slavery as a form of social annihilation, see Orlando Patterson, *Slavery and Social Death: a Comparative Study* (Harvard University Press, 1982), esp. pp. 105–208.

62. Brooks, *Barbarian Cruelty*, p. 12. See also Cotton Mather's "The Glory of Goodness;" see Baepler, *White Slaves, African Masters*, pp. 59–69, and 13–14; Charles Sumner, *White Slavery in the Barbary States* (Boston, 1847); Lotfi Ben Rejeb, "America's Captive Freemen in North Africa: the Comparative Method in Abolitionist Persuasion," pp. 57–71 in *Slavery and Abolition*, 9 (1988). This theme of inversion was also exploited in Tyler, *The Algerian Captive*.

63. David Spurr, *The Rhetoric of Empire: Colonial Discourse in Journalism, Travel Writing, and Imperial Administration* (Durham, NC, 1993), pp. 98–9, quoted in Baepler, *White Slaves*, p. 37.

Index

abjuring, among slaves, 156, 164, 176
Acqua dei Corsari (near Palermo), 44
aguaitas (old slaves), 168–9
Algiers, 47, 48, 57, 73, 85, 86, 89, 98,
    108, 125–6, 128
  bagnos in, 110–12, 117, 121–3, 127,
    135
  Berbers and, 87
  capture of, in 1830, 14, 135, 192–3
  Christian cemetery in, 173
  demographics of, 9–10, 103
  fleet of, 3, 28–9, 75
  free foreign community in, 106, 109
  harbor of, 16, 83
  plague in, 17–18
  racial makeup of, 25, 26
  shipyards, 50, 96
  slave populations in, xvii–xviii, 6,
    10–15, 19, 21–3, 116–17
  thieves in, 100
  wine making in, 98
Ali Pegelin (slave owner), 70, 71, 85,
    99–101, 111, 116, 118, 125, 126,
    133, 147
Ancona, 182, 183
Ascoli (Marche), 142
Atlantic slave traffic, 24, 30, 53, 57

Bachrouch, Taoufik, 70
badestan (slave market of Algiers), 43,
    59–64, *65*, 125, 185
  selling techniques in, *60, 61*, 62–3
  slave prices in, 91, 96, 132
  Souq el Berka (Tunis), 59
bagno hierarchy, 115, 118, 119
  bagno slaves, 110, 116
  guardian *basha*, 12, 91, 118, 119,
    128, 129, 180
  mayordomos, 119, 120
  scrivan bagno, 82, 99
Bagno of San Leonardo (Tunis), 118,
    119
  floorplan of, 117

bagnos (slave pens), 12, 86
  alternative names for, 110–12
  Bagno Beyliç (Algiers), 12, 110, 113,
    117, 123, 127, 128, 134
  chapels in, 12, 120–1, 124
  conditions in, 110
  hospitals in, 117, 121–3, 134, 178,
    179
  number of, in Algiers, 12
    in Tripoli, 12
    in Tunis, 12
  mattamoro, 96, 97
  of Ali Pegelin (Algiers), 110, 121
  origins of, 110
  taverns in, 98, 99, 120, 123, 124, 128
Baker, Thomas (British consul in
    Tripoli), 7, 27, 28, 32, 33, 48, 49
Barbarino (Cardinal), 165
Barbary slavers and corsairs
  aga (military commander), 31
  armadores (corsair backers), 31, 39,
    64, 82
  economic organization of, 30–2
  extractive nature of, 30
  from Algiers, 28–9, 33
  from Tripoli, 28, 32, 48
  from Tunis, 75, 140
Barletta (Puglia), 141
beggars, in Barbary, 93, 108
Belvedere (Salerno), 162
Bennett, Norman, 10, 19
Bergamo, 159
Biaggio di Turena (missionary), xxiii,
    xxv, xxvi
Bianchini, Alberto (Augustinian
    canon), 145
Biserta (or Bisterte: Tunis), 14, 80, 143
Bonaffini, Giuseppe, 173
Braudel, Fernand, xxix, 4, 5, 7, 29, 45
Brescia, 159
Brooks, Francis (slave), 192

Caissotti, Pietro (abbot), 175

cambio marittimo, 180
Camillo di Maria (priest), 180, 186, 187
Camini (Calabria), 175
Capra, Enrico (priest), 189
Capuchins, 158, 167
cataloghi (lists of redeemed slaves), 178, *180*
Chastelet des Boys (slave), 50, 52, 73, 86, 92, 95, 106
Christian enslavement of Muslims, 8, 9, 34, 140
circumcision, adult, 156
Clissold, Stephen, 134
Collins, Robert (American slave owner), 107, 108
Columbus, Christopher, xxv
Congoli (Papal States), 159
Congregation De Propaganda Fide, xxviii
Constantinople, 171
  galleys of, 172
consuls, French, 12, 120
  in Algiers, 48
  on merchant shipping, 25
Corsair attacks
  Bari, 8
  Bay of Naples, 6, 141
  Christian defenses against, 29, 35, 36, 38, 51
  Cornish coast, near Penzance, 7
  extractive nature of, 30
  Granada, 6
  Iceland in 1627, 7, 17
  in the Adriatic, 35
  Ireland, 17
  Madeira, 7
  on American shipping, 154
  on Calabria, 7, 40
  on Corsica, 29
  on Genoa and Liguria, 29, 153
  on Merchant shipping, 46, 49, 154
  on Naples, 28
  on Sardinia, 29
  on Sicily, 38, 140, 153, 174
  on the Spanish coast, 29
  San Pietro Is., off southern Sardinia, 45
  seizing church bells, 40
  source problems with, 34

Tabarca, 17, 45
techniques, 34, 35, 37–42, 46
Vieste, 6
corsair ships
  fuste and xebecs, 46
Corsi (Cardinal), 139, 145
Costa, Marcello (apostolic vicar), 78, 80, 97
Crisostomo da Genova (missionary friar), 120
Curtin, Philip, 4, 9, 106

D'Aranda, Emanuel (slave), 8, 58, 60, 61, 71, 79, 85–7, 97–100, 104, 105, 112–16, 118, 121, 123–7, 133, 134, 144, 147, 156
D'Arvieux, Laurent (diplomat), 60, 62, 63, 71, 100, 105, 117, 119, 124, 127, 171
Dallam, Thomas (diplomat), 38
Dams, Jean, 20
Dan, Pierre (ransoming priest), 8, 13, 15, 21, 23, 25, 61, 73, 84, 85, 87, 92, 110, 116, 132
  on forms of slave labor, 72, 73
Davies, William (slave), 40
de La Motte, Philemon (ransoming priest), 31, 60, 64, 82, 84, 98, 117, 123, 127, 130
délats (slave auctioneers), 60, 64
Denyan, Jacques (ship master), 50
Dey Mohammed (pasha of Algiers), 114
diviners, for slaves, 144–5
Dominici, Alfonso (Trinitarian priest), 22, 125
Donato da Cantalupo (missionary friar), 116
Dragut Re'is (corsair), 10, 28, 31, 34, 35, 40
Dulcigno (Ulcinj, in Montenegro), 78, 140, 143, 155, 156, 161, 166, 171

Elliot, George (slave), 54, 60, 93, 94

fede (testimonial), 162–6
  Cristo and *albarano*, 165
  of enslavement, 162
  pre-printed, 162, 164

Ferdinand and Isabella (of Spain), xxv
Fermo (Abruzzi), 145, 160
fishermen, as corsair targets, 40, 141, 142, 188
Florence, 47
Fondi (in Lazio), 40
Fontenay, Michel, 12, 16, 17
Forìo (on Ischia), 40
Foss, John (slave), 54, 55, 58, 83, 84, 107, 115, 128, 132, 173
Fosso dei Saraceni (near Ortona), 44
Francavilla al Mare (Puglia), 35
Francesco di S. Lorenzo (Trinitarian priest), 87, 91, 107
Friedman, Ellen, 76

Gaeta (Lazio), 37, 54
galley crews(*galeotti*), 14, 53, 73–82, 171
    their lengthy terms in slavery, 80, 171–2
    rations of, 33, 76–7
    scrivani, 80, 82
    shares of the loot, 82
    vogavani, 81, 82
gambetto (leg shackles), 108
Genoa, 47
Genovese, Eugene, xxvi, 107, 108
gileffo, 88, 90–1, 106
Giovanni di S. Bonaventura (missionary), 12
Giove (Terni), 159
Girolamo da Sassari, friar, 72
Godwyn, Morgan (Oxford don), 190
Gracián, Jeronimo (slave friar), 13
Gramaye, Jean-Baptiste (slave), 11, 33, 48, 53, 108, 120
Grammont, Henri-David, 70, 117, 135, 173
Gregory XIII, 150

Haëdo, Diego de (slave friar), 12, 23, 35, 76, 79
Hamed Lucas (slave owner), 95
Hassan Pasha, 28–9
Hees, Thomas (diplomat), 7
homosexuality, in Barbary, 125–7
Hospital of San Sisto (Rome), 151

Ischia, 40
    and Procida, 141

Janissaries, 32, 71, 104, 169
Jaõno dos Sanctos (friar), 22
Jewish captives, 51, 53
Jews, in Barbary, 48, 51, 53, 55, 59, 101, 103, 104
    as slave owners, 95
    as slave ransomers, 178

Kheir-ed-din Barbarossa, 10, 23, 28, 34, 35, 40
Knight, Francis (slave), 3, 38, 40, 76, 77, 79, 81, 82, 116, 168
Koran, and slavery, 69

Larquié, Claude, 20, 170, 172
Laugier de Tassy, Jacques Philippe (diplomat), xxvi, 64, 72, 104, 109, 117, 125
lazaret (quarantine), 182, 185
Lepanto (Greece), 78
Lepanto, Battle of, 28, 75
Levacher, Jean (apostolic vicar), 111, 112
Licastelli (Calabria), 42
lingua franca, 25, 57, 81, 113–15
    compared with pidgins elsewhere, 114
Livorno, Church of San Ferdinando in, 183
Lippi, Fra Filippo, xxix
Lorance, Ivone (apostolic vicar), 116
Loreto, 182
Lovejoy, Paul, 4, 24

Mafrici, Mirella, 36
Malta, Knights of, 47, 53
    Francois Lanfreducci and Jean Othon Bosio, 11, 116
Manfredonia (Gargano), 36, 37
maquignons (slave traders), 61, 62, 64, 74
Marott, Louis (slave), 52, 74, 76, 114
Mascarenhas, João (slave), 54, 69, 73, 76, 77, 79, 121, 126 129, 135
    in Algiers, 104
massari and eletti, 162

masseries, 11, 16, 85–7
Mattei, Curthio (poet), 41
Mehmed Chelebi (aka Dom Philippe, slaver), 71, 105
Mequinez (Morocco), 84
Mercedarians, 19, 149, 152, 159, 167, 170, 177, 178, 183
slave counts provided by, 10
Milan, 180, 183
Mohammed Ali (*re'is*), 45
Monasteries, as corsair targets, 141
Monson, Sir William, xxviii
Montmasson, Michel (apostolic vicar), 22
Moors and the Moriscos, xxiv, 101, 103
in Algiers, 104
Morgan, Joseph, 21, 30, 32, 33, 41–3, 53, 55, 76, 77, 79, 82, 96, 101, 132, 134, 191
Murat Re'is (*re'is*), 29, 143
Mustafa Caddi (*re'is*), 32

Naples, 28, 35, 36, 47, 140, 144, 150, 153, 163, 165
Napoleon, Buonaparte, 193
Napoleonic Wars, 14
Nazi concentration camps, 134
Niccolò da Scio (missionary), 13, 89

Ochali (aka Ali Basha Fartas, *re'is*), 42
Oge Ali (slave owner), 92, 93
Okeley, William (slave), 32, 62, 63, 69, 70, 86, 87, 89–92, 97, 98, 103, 128, 129
Ortner, Sherry, 101

Padua, 159
Palermo, 8, 36, 44, 143, 144, 150, 153, 181, 183, 184, 186
Parliament, British, 4, 21
Peace of Cateau-Cambrésis, 140
penjic (pasha's cut of prize), 31, 57
Pepys, Samuel, 192
Perasto (in Dalmatia), 17
plague, 17–18, 172, 182, 185
in Algiers, 17, 18
in Tunis, 18
Konia, 18

supposed Muslim attitudes towards, 18
Port of Suez, 171
Porto Farina (Tunis), 50, 96, 127
processions of ex-slaves, 179–86, *180*
aspect of "double Redemption", 187
as rituals of reintegration, 184–6, 188
cost and equipment for, 182
in France and Spain, 181
in Milan, 181, 183, 186
in Palermo, 181, 183, 184
in Rome, 184
in Venice, 183, 184
processional makeup and line, 183, 184
processions of new slaves in Barbary, 55, *56*

Ramadan, 56, 97
ransom costs, 165, 168–9, 179
collecting, 146–8, 164–6
ransoming by Italian states, 150
by commissioners, 158
by *succolettori,* 159
Casa della Santissima Anna (Naples), 165
Congregation of San Paolo (Naples), 165
Discalced Religious Fathers of the Spanish Congregation (Rome), 165
Magistratura degli schiavi (Genoa), 151, 153
Monte della Misericordi (Naples), 165
Provveditori sopra Ospedali e Luoghi Pii (Venice), 152, 154, 157, 162, 164, 166, 167, 182
Santa Casa della Redentione de' Cattivi (Naples), 150–1, 153, 157, 164–5
Santa Francesca Romana (Rome), 165
Santa Maria del Gesù della Redenzione dei Cattivi (Naples), 150
Santa Maria del Gonfalone (Rome), 150–1, 155, 158–61, 165, 167–9

ransoming by Italian states   *continued*
    Santa Maria della Catena (Naples),
      165
    Santa Maria della Neve (Bologna),
      160
    Santa Maria di Porto Salvo (Naples),
      165
    Santa Maria la Nova (Palermo), 151,
      153, 168
    scarcity of specie, 160
    using lockable collection boxes,
      155, 157, 159, 160
ransoming by slaves themselves, 99,
    147, 155, 185
ransoming expeditions, 102, 168–70
ransoming of slaves, 49, 50, 167–70,
    177–9
    at point of capture, 43–4, 142
Ravello (Salerno), 160
re'is (corsair captains), 47, 49, 53, 64, 76
    of Algiers, 79
redenzioni generali, 167–70
renegades, 22, 42–43, 71, 77, 99, 104,
    126–7
    converting slaves to Islam, 125
    forced conversions, 105
    guiding raiders, 38, 43
    in Algiers, 21, 22
    priests, 90
Ricolui, Giovanni (priest), 186, 187
Rimini, 139–40
Rome, 28, 35, 36, 45, 159, 167, 181,
    182, 184
    Santa Susanna (Roman church),
      181, 183
Royal Navy, British, 6

Salé (Morocco), 60
Salvago, Gianbattista (dragoman), 11,
    50, 82, 88, 96, 106
San Felice Circeo (Lazio), 45
San Felicità (Lazio), 139
San Giusto (Vitterbo), 160
Sanseverino (Marche), 159
Santa Maria la Nova (Palermo), 183
Santa Maura (Greece), 78, 140, 171
Saunders, Thomas (slave), 75, 83, 84
Senate, Venetian, 79, 96, 152, 154,
    157

Serracapriola (Puglia), 35
Sixtus V, 151
slave amusements, 128
slave clothing, 104–8, *109*
    as disguises, 95, 105
    for galeotti, 76
slave escapes, 19, 96
slave kinsmen, 142–6, 176, 177
slave labor
    as galeotti, 73–82, 129
    "rowing proudly", 78
    construction work, 83–5
    female labor, 71, 105
    household slaves, 72, 73, 109
    in dockyards, 55, 84
    in proto-industrial factories, 87
    logging, 85
    on farms (*masseries*), 85–7
    quarrying, *82*, 8 3 – 4
    rented to free Christians, 109
    scribes, 99, 118, 175
    shipbuilders, 95–7
    shopkeepers, 97–8
    taverners, in *bagnos*, 98–9, 101
    tobacco and spirits vending, 93
    toy making, 97
    water vending, 92–3, 116
slave punishments, 128, 129, *130–1*,
    132
    beating with bull's penis, 77
    escurribanda 129
    foot beating, 92, 94, 95, *131*
slave rations, 16, 17, 58, 119, 134
    as galeotti, 53, 76
slave resistance, 100–1, 111–12
slave theft, 99–101,116
slaves, in Barbary
    antagonisms between slave
      nationalities, 112–13
    as investment, 70, 71, 91, 102,
      177–8
    chains and, 108, *109*
    Dutch, 49, 171
    English, 49, 89, 121, 128, 171
    female slaves, 36, 58, 105, 106, 172
    French, 49, 62, 63, 113
    household slaves, 104
    Icelandic, 114, 192
    in Algiers, 23, 107, 109, 117

in Tripoli, 87, 89, 108
in Tunis, 108, 144
Porto Farina, 96–7
in Turkish imperial fleet, 20, 78, 80, 170
Italian, 78, 113, 171
Calabrian, 148, 175
Neapolitan, 144, 175
Piedmontese, 20
Sicilian, 143, 144
Tuscan, 148–9
Venetian, 96, 144, 180, 187
liminal states of, 56, *65*, 185
newcomers (*schiavi novelli*), 172
Portuguese, 113
post-traumatic stress and, 187–8
"public slaves", 12, 13, 16, 58, 59, 88, 90, 106, 108, 110, 143
resistence by, 100–1, 111
Russian, 112–13
Spanish, 63, 113, 170–1, 178
slavery, in the Americas, xxv, xxvi, 15, 16, 24, 133
"curse of Noah" argument, 191
estimates of extent, 4, 23–4
slavery, Mediterranean
as a "form of Hell", 69, 75, 79, 176, 192
average time in slavery, 170–3
Christian defenses against, 29, 34–5, 37, 40, 42, 46, 140–1
compared to slavery in the Americas, 24, 53, 57, 71, 78, 86–87, 100–1, 107–8, 113, 133, 173, 191
extractive nature of, 30, 43
slaves, letters home, 78, 142–4, 146–8, 166, 175-7
slaves, miscellaneous individuals
Agostino da Messina (friar), 89
Alferez of Majorca, 99
Ascentij, Francesco Antonio, 143
Barbarella, Antonio Tedaldi, 11
Carlo de Mellis, 40
Catteno, Laone, 156
Colombin, Giacomo, 96
Filipo di Salvatore, 143
Fontimamma, 100
Gazzoli, Constanzo (slave's father), 189

Gio'Angiolo dall'Alicata, 143
Giuseppe di Girardo, 144
Lucio d'Huomo, 149
Mamberti, Antonio Pasquale, 148, 149
Maria de Magio (slave's wife), 145
Mastellone, Marc'Antonio, 142
Mazzocati, Giuseppe, 161
Mezzaparte, Antonio, 142
Micozzo di Bastiano, 78
Monte, Rose Antonia, 141
Palamari, Vincenzo and Matteo (father and son), 148
Piero di Dimitri, 144
Rizzo, Domenico, 162
Roberts, Nicholas, 54
Russo, Erasmo Antonio, 189
Sarcinelli, Nicola, 156
Sargente, Elena (slave's wife), 165
Simone da Cavi, 163
Sprat, Devereux (slave minister), 89, 90
Soviet gulags, 134
Sperlonga (Lazio), 37, 41, 139
St. John of Matha (Trinitarian founder), 112, 149
States of the Church, 47, 151, 159
Struys, Jan (slave), 53

Tagarins (Moroccans of Spanish origin), 29, 70, 89
The Algerine Slave, 192
Thédenat, P.P. (Slave), 95
Torre di Greco (Naples), 160
Trinitarian Order, 19, 111, 121, 123, 149, 152, 167, 170, 177, 178, 180, 182, 184, 190
redemptions by, 19, 25, 177–9
slave counts provided by, 10, 178
Tripoli, 27, 33, 48–9, 58, 59
corsairs of, 27, 32
death rates in, 16, 17
fleet of, 30, 75
slave populations in, xx–xxi, 14, 15
Tunis, 28, 45, 58, 59
fleet of, 75
slave populations, xx–xxi, 14, 15
Turin, Church of San Michele, 179,183
Turkish Imperial fleet, 28, 78, 80, 172

Turkish-Hapsburg conflict, 28, 38, 140, 147
Turks, in Algiers, 25, 104, 106

Valesio, Francesco (diarist), 169
Valone (Vlorë, Albania), 45
Venice, 47, 50, 144, 151, 152, 154, 155, 157, 158, 166, 170, 174

Arsenal of, 96, 145, 188
Church of the Salvatore, 184
Venture de Paradis, J. M. (diplomat), 71, 99, 107, 125
Vieste (Gargano), 36, 37

West Africa, effects of slave trade on, 24, 173

CPSIA information can be obtained at www.ICGtesting.com
Printed in the USA
LVOW082139301211

261868LV00004B/7/A